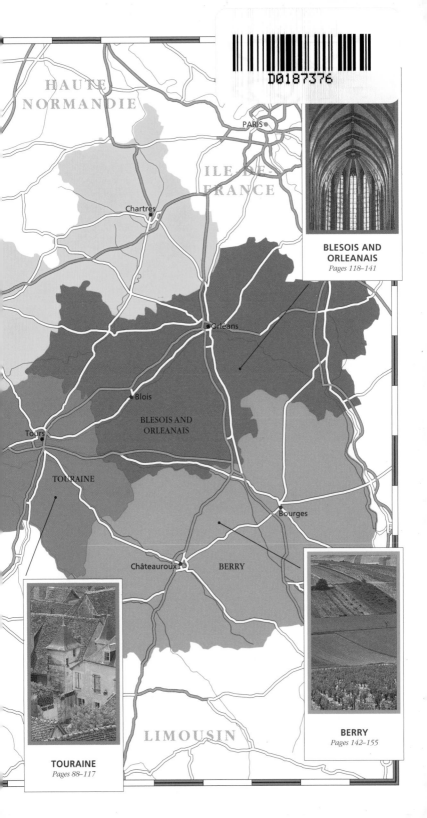

HAUTE NORMANDIE

PARIS

ILE-DE-FRANCE

Chartres

BLESOIS AND ORLEANAIS
Pages 118–141

Orleans

Blois

BLESOIS AND ORLEANAIS

Tours

TOURAINE

Bourges

Châteauroux

BERRY

BERRY
Pages 142–155

TOURAINE
Pages 88–117

LIMOUSIN

EYEWITNESS TRAVEL

LOIRE VALLEY

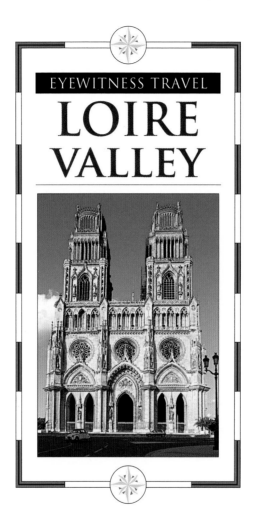

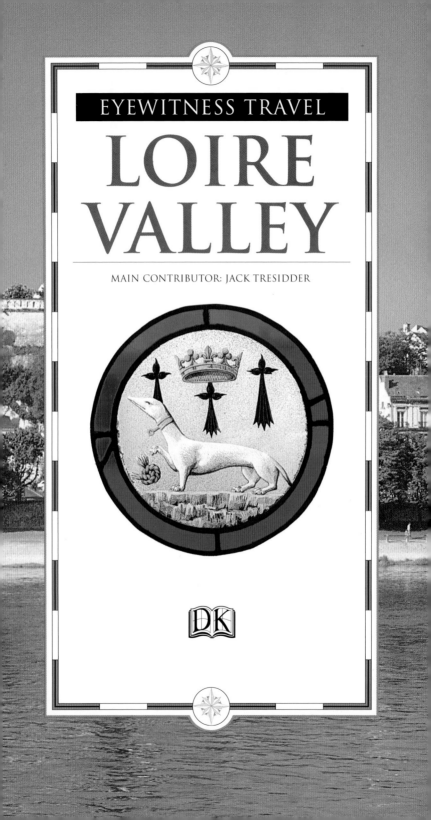

EYEWITNESS TRAVEL

LOIRE VALLEY

MAIN CONTRIBUTOR: JACK TRESIDDER

LONDON, NEW YORK,
MELBOURNE, MUNICH AND DELHI
www.dk.com

PRODUCED BY Duncan Baird Publishers
London, England

PROJECT EDITOR Stephanie Driver
EDITOR Slaney Begley
EDITORIAL ASSISTANT Joanne Levêque
DESIGNERS Paul Calver, Jill Mumford
DESIGN ASSISTANT Christine Keilty

PHOTOGRAPHERS
John Heseltine, Paul Kenward, Kim Sayer

ILLUSTRATORS
Joanna Cameron, Roger Hutchins, Robbie Polley,
Pat Thorne, John Woodcock

Reproduced by Colourscan (Singapore)
Printed and bound in China by Leo Paper Products Ltd

First American Edition, 1996
10 11 12 13 10 9 8 7 6 5 4 3 2 1

Published in the United States by DK Publishing,
375 Hudson Street, New York, New York 10014

Reprinted with revisions 1997 (twice), 1999, 2000, 2001, 2003,
2004, 2007, 2010

Published in Great Britain by Dorling Kindersley Limited.

A CATALOG RECORD FOR THIS BOOK IS AVAILABLE FROM
THE LIBRARY OF CONGRESS

ISSN 1542-1554
ISBN 978-0-75666-141-0

FLOORS ARE REFERRED TO THROUGHOUT IN ACCORDANCE
WITH EUROPEAN USAGE; IE THE "FIRST FLOOR"
IS THE FLOOR ABOVE GROUND LEVEL.

Front cover main image: Château de Chenonceau, Touraine

We're trying to be cleaner and greener:

- we recycle waste and switch things off
- we use paper from responsibly managed forests whenever possible
- we ask our printers to actively reduce water and energy consumption
- we check out our suppliers' working conditions – they never use child labour

Find out more about our values and best practices at www.dk.com

---

The information in this DK Eyewitness Travel Guide is checked regularly.

Every effort has been made to ensure that this book is as up-to-date as possible at the time of going to press. Some details, however, such as telephone numbers, opening hours, prices, gallery hanging arrangements and travel information are liable to change. The publishers cannot accept responsibility for any consequences arising from the use of this book, nor for any material on third party websites, and cannot guarantee that any website address in this book will be a suitable source of travel information. We value the views and suggestions of our readers very highly. Please write to: Publisher, DK Eyewitness Travel Guides, Dorling Kindersley, 80 Strand, London, WC2R 0RL, Great Britain.

◁ **Château de Saumur, Anjou**

CONTENTS

Statue in La Lorie

INTRODUCING THE LOIRE VALLEY

King Louis XIV portrayed as Jupiter, conquering La Fronde

The town of Argenton-sur-Creuse

Manoir du Grand-Martigny

Stained-glass portrait of Agnès Sorel

Young boys fishing at Pornichet marina in Loire-Atlantique

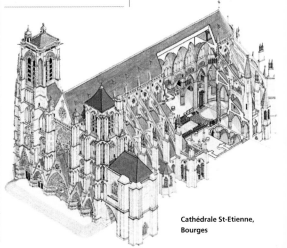
Cathédrale St-Etienne, Bourges

HOW TO USE THIS GUIDE

This guide will help you get the most from your stay in the Loire Valley. It provides both expert recommendations and detailed practical information. *Introducing the Loire Valley* maps the region and sets it in its historical and cultural context. *The Loire Valley Area by Area* describes the important sights, with maps, photographs and illustrations. Suggestions for food, drink, accommodation, shopping and activities are in *Travellers' Needs*, and the *Survival Guide* has tips on everything from the French telephone system to getting to the Loire and travelling around the region.

THE LOIRE VALLEY AREA BY AREA

In this guide, the Loire Valley has been divided into six regions, each of which has its own chapter. A map of these regions can be found inside the front cover of the book. The most interesting places to visit in each region have been numbered and plotted on a *Regional Map*.

Each area of the Loire Valley can be quickly identified by its colour coding.

1 Introduction
The landscape, history and character of each region is described here, showing how the area has developed over the centuries and what it has to offer the visitor today.

A locator map shows the region in relation to the whole of the Loire Valley.

2 Regional Map
This gives an illustrated overview of the whole region. All the sights are numbered, and there are also useful tips on getting around by car and public transport.

Features and story boxes highlight special or unique aspects of a particular sight.

3 Detailed information on each sight
All the important towns and other places to visit are described individually. They are listed in order, following the numbering on the Regional Map. Within each town or city, there is detailed information on important buildings and other major sights.

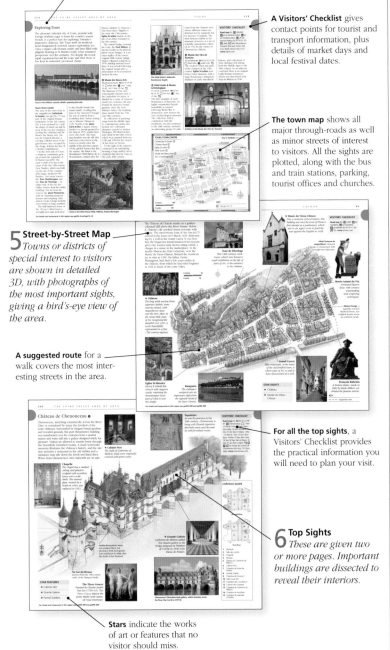

4 Major Towns
An introduction covers the history, character and geography of the town. The main sights are described individually and plotted on a Town Map.

A Visitors' Checklist gives contact points for tourist and transport information, plus details of market days and local festival dates.

The town map shows all major through-roads as well as minor streets of interest to visitors. All the sights are plotted, along with the bus and train stations, parking, tourist offices and churches.

5 Street-by-Street Map
Towns or districts of special interest to visitors are shown in detailed 3D, with photographs of the most important sights, giving a bird's-eye view of the area.

A suggested route for a walk covers the most interesting streets in the area.

For all the top sights, a Visitors' Checklist provides the practical information you will need to plan your visit.

Château de Chenonceau

6 Top Sights
These are given two or more pages. Important buildings are dissected to reveal their interiors.

Stars indicate the works of art or features that no visitor should miss.

INTRODUCING
THE
LOIRE VALLEY

DISCOVERING THE LOIRE VALLEY

This fertile land was once the playground of kings and their courts, who left behind a trail of magnificent châteaux ranging from exuberant Renaissance to Classical grandeur. But the Loire Valley offers more than just castles. Ancient cloistered abbeys, majestic cathedrals such as those at Chartres and Bourges, and prosperous modern

Statue of Joan of Arc

cities like Tours are all part of the rich heritage of this engaging area. Picturesque rural Loire, with its dense forests, misty marshes, windswept coastline and neat vineyards, tempts the visitor off the beaten track. These two pages give an at-a-glance flavour of each region, plus a quick guide to where to go and what to see and do.

Château d'Azay-le-Rideau on an island in the Indre River

ANJOU

- **Tales of the riverbank**
- **Striking Saumur and the Abbaye de Fontevraud**
- **Regal Angers**

The landscape of Anjou is threaded with sparkling tributary rivers creating ideal roaming and picnic territory. The **Corniche Angevine** *(see p68)* route curves lazily around the south side of the Loire and is dotted with unspoiled villages and vineyards, while the **Basses Vallées** *(see p70)* are a magnet for bird-watchers. Fascinating tufa caves, once troglodyte dwellings, are now chic homes and restaurants.

Amid lush countryside to the east lie two must-see sights: **Saumur** *(see pp80–83)* with its hilltop château and the vast **Abbaye de Fontevraud** *(see pp86–7)*, France's most complete abbey complex.

Angers *(see pp72–7)*, straddling the River Maine,

was once the capital of an enormous empire. Its forbidding château contrasts with today's modern city, bursting with culture and energy.

TOURAINE

- **Renaissance châteaux**
- **Prosperous Tours**
- **Delicious ruby red wines**

Breathtaking château architecture characterises Touraine. Be a king for a day and check out the fairytale turrets of Renaissance pleasure-palaces such as **Azay-le-Rideau** *(see pp96–7)* and **Chenonceau** *(see pp106–9)*, with its striking arched gallery spanning the River Cher. Head to **Villandry** *(see pp94–5)* for fine ornamental gardens and ponds.

Regional capital **Tours** *(see pp112–17)* is a great base for visiting the châteaux. Its lively old quarter is crammed with cafés and boutiques, yet still retains a medieval charm. In

contrast, the area's rolling pastoral terrain attracts lovers of outdoor persuits. Cycling among these fertile fields will work up a thirst for the fine Chinon and Bourgeuil wines.

BLESOIS AND ORLEANAIS

- **Chambord:** *folie de grandeur*
- **Grand medieval towns**
- **Lush landscapes**

Teeming with wild boar and deer, this area boasts some magnificent royal hunting lodges. **Château de Chambord** *(see pp132–5)*, the largest château in the Loire, is a truly exuberant, Disney-like example.

Blois *(see pp124–7)* and **Orléans** *(see pp138–9)* were once powerful medieval strongholds. Now busy commercial towns, their charming old quarters are full of interest to the visitor. A casualty of war, Orléans

A quiet street of the medieval town of Blois

has been reconstructed, but retains some delightful historic buildings. Blois has many steep cobbled streets and half-timbered houses.

For a more bucolic experience, the scenery of the **Sologne** *(see p141)*, is scattered with pretty woods and lakes, while architecture fans will adore the water gates, stone buildings and bridges of **Vendôme** *(see p122)*.

BERRY

- **Remote rural villages**
- **Gallo-Roman Bourges**
- **La Brenne's wooded beauty**
- **Sancerre wine estates**

The rolling vineyards around the town of Sancerre

This rural area is surprisingly overlooked by many tourists. **Bourges** *(see pp150–53)*, the region's capital, is an architectural gem with a majestic cathedral. Of the many fine old buildings in this medieval city, Palais Jacques Coeur is the finest.

The region boasts a lush landscape where remote villages punctuate undulating hills, ancient woodlands and lakes, and swathes of wheat fields. Berry is a haven for nature enthusiasts, and at the **Parc Naturel Régional de la Brenne** *(see p146)*, bird-watchers can find a wide variety of species.

In the eastern corner sits **Sancerre** *(see p154)*, where you can enjoy its celebrated wine from dry, zingy whites to soft, fruity reds made from vines that grow on chalky limestone slopes.

NORTH OF THE LOIRE

- **Great fishing and walking**
- **Cathedral city of Chartres**
- **Car racing in Le Mans**

Once the haunt of poets and painters, today this region is a paradise for anglers and walkers. The **Alpes Mancelles** *(see p161)*, with its heather-cloaked hills and stream-lined gorges, is best visited on foot. Cruising the rivers by boat is a fun way to discover pretty Loire tributaries. Fringed by trees, the Sarthe glides past the **Abbaye de Solesmes** *(see p162)*, while the Mayenne Valley offers views of hilltop villages and one of the area's main towns, **Laval** *(see p160)*.

Along the banks of the Loir, early churches mark the pilgrim trail. The magical Gothic spires of the cathedral of **Chartres** *(see pp171–5)* rising up from the surrounding wheat fields provide an unforgettable sightseeing experience. Racing enthusiasts should head for **Le Mans** *(see pp164–7)*, which also has a pretty historic centre.

LOIRE-ATLANTIQUE AND THE VENDEE

- **Vibrant Nantes**
- **Navigating the Marais Poitevin**
- **Wind-swept Atlantic coast**

Geographically this region faces out to the bracing Atlantic Ocean and turns its back on the châteaux. At the gateway to the ocean, **Nantes** *(see pp190–93)* was once the

The early Gothic cathedral of Notre-Dame in Chartres

busiest port in France, and its riches were gained from ship-building and a thriving slave trade. It is a fascinating place to explore, with many historic buildings, notably the castle and the Musée des Beaux Arts, both bursting with treasures. The elegant shopping streets also have a good choice of cafés and restaurants.

Battling constantly against a sea invasion, the low-lying landscape of the **Marais Poitevin** *(see pp182–5)* is strikingly diverse, with a vast range of wildlife. The wet marsh, known as "Venise Verte", is ideally explored by *barque*, the traditional flat-bottomed boat. Punt through the maze of waterways edged by willows and take a break at one of the pretty ports.

At the Vendée coast, wide sandy beaches and thundering waves act as a magnet for windsurfers.

The beach of La Baule, in the Loire-Atlantique

Putting the Loire on the Map

The Loire Valley lies in central France, bordered by the regions of Brittany, Normandy and the Ile de France to the north, the Massif Central and Poitou to the south, Burgundy to the east, and the Atlantic Ocean to the west. The river itself, the longest in France, flows for 1,020 km (634 miles) from its source in the Cévennes to the Atlantic Ocean just south of Nantes at St-Nazaire. The region covers an area of 71,228 sq km (27,500 sq miles) and has a population of about 5.7 million.

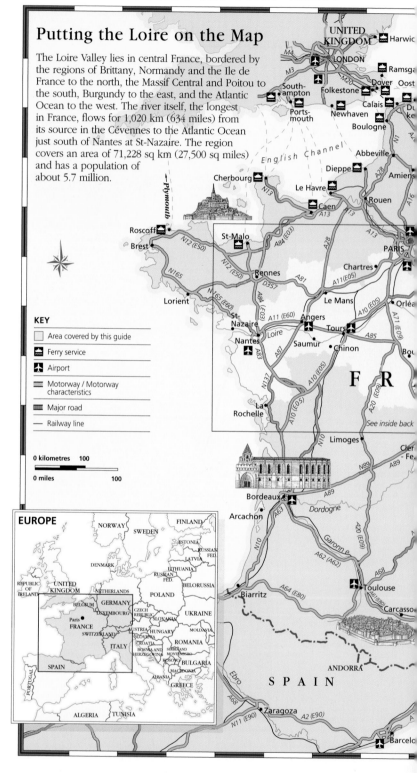

KEY

▨	Area covered by this guide
⛴	Ferry service
✈	Airport
▬	Motorway / Motorway characteristics
▬	Major road
—	Railway line

0 kilometres   100

0 miles   100

See inside back

EUROPE

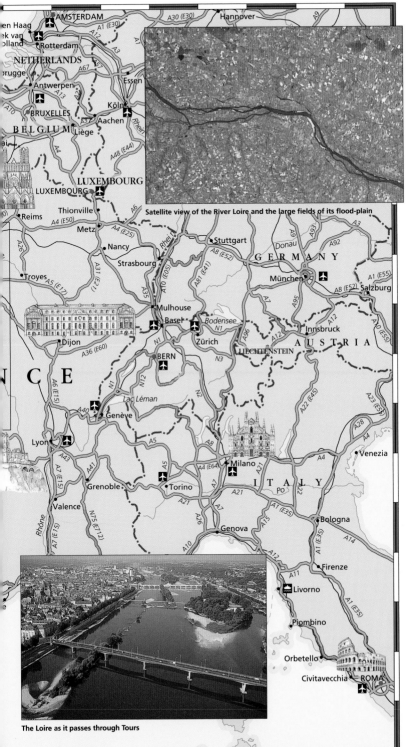

Satellite view of the River Loire and the large fields of its flood-plain

The Loire as it passes through Tours

A PORTRAIT OF THE LOIRE VALLEY

The Loire Valley, world-famous for its beautiful châteaux, has long been described as exemplifying la douceur de vivre: *it combines a leisurely pace of life, a mild climate, mellow wines and the gentle ways of its inhabitants. The overall impression conveyed by the region is one of an unostentatious taste for the good things in life.*

In this central region of France, the people have neither the brisk, sometimes brusque, demeanour of their northern counterparts, nor the excitable nature of the southern provinces. They get on peacefully with their lives, benefiting from the prosperity generated not only by the region's centuries old popularity with French and foreign visitors alike, but also by a fertile soil and a favourable climate, which rarely succumbs to extremes of heat or cold.

The Loire as a region is far from being a cultural and historical anachronism, although the wealth

Cyclist on the Île de Noirmoutier causeway

of well-preserved historical monuments harks back to the past. Many local people are surprisingly proud of the nuclear power stations at Avoine-Chinon and at St-Laurent-des-Eaux near Beaugency, both symbols of the region's role in the technological revolution. The well-publicized (and successful) campaign in the mid-1980s to have the high-speed TGV train rerouted was based not on any intrinsic dislike of new-fangled schemes, but on alarm at the potential damage to the bottles of wine stored in their underground cellars close to the planned track.

The bridge across the Loire at Blois, one of several historic bridges in the region

◁ **Berry village in the evening**

Folk dancers in costume at the Château de Blois

Yet the way of life in the Loire Valley remains largely anchored to the traditional values of *la France profonde*, the country's conservative heartland – seeking to perpetuate a way of life that has proved its worth over the centuries. This is particularly true of the Berry, the easternmost region of the Loire covered in this guide. It is the geographical centre of the country – several villages claim the honour of being situated at "the heart of France" – and it seems to the visitor charmingly off the beaten track. It comes as no surprise to discover that folk traditions and, some say, witchcraft are still part of everyday life in some of these timeless villages. In November 2000, UNESCO made the Loire Valley one of its protected areas of natural beauty.

LOCAL ATTRACTIONS

The opportunity to stay in a private château is one of the many treats for visitors to the Loire Valley, where hospitality is a serious business. Even in Orléans, whose proximity to Paris has led to its reputation as a dormitory town, a warm welcome in hotels and restaurants is assured. And in the towns and villages of Touraine and Anjou, conviviality is everywhere apparent. The many fairs, fêtes and festivals devoted to local wines and produce – garlic, apples, melons or even chitterling sausages – bear witness to the large part, even by French standards, that food and drink play in the social life of these old provinces.

They also play a major role in the region's economy: around 12 per cent of the local population is involved in agriculture or the food industry in some way. Many a *primeur* (early fruit or vegetable) in the markets and restaurants of Paris has been transported from the fertile fields and orchards beside the Loire, and the region's melons and asparagus are sold all over the country. So are the button mushrooms, known as *champignons de Paris* (Paris mushrooms), grown in tufa quarries near Saumur.

Colourful summer display

Although some local wines are reputed not to travel well, many of them do so very successfully, not only in France but also abroad, adding to the region's prosperity. In terms of the volume of production, the

The Loire at Amboise, dotted with sandbanks

A walk along a river bank at Rochefort-sur-Loire, one of many country pursuits to enjoy

region ranks third in France and, although production is on a smaller scale than the famous wine giants of Bordeaux and Burgundy, the quality and popularity of Loire wines are both increasing. Sancerre and Muscadet are probably the best known, but others, such as Vouvray and Bourgueil, are also much in demand.

The restaurants and hotel dining rooms of the Loire Valley take full advantage of the excellent produce available locally – no wonder so many Parisian families have been attracted to the area. Just as once the nobility of France established their châteaux and stately homes in the area, now wealthy Parisians are flocking to the Loire Valley to buy *résidences secondaires*. The influx has been swelled in recent years with the advent of the TGV, which takes less than an hour to reach the region from Paris.

RECENT DEVELOPMENTS

In the west of the region, Nantes has adapted to changing economic times. The closure of its once-flourishing shipyards has led to a new focus on advanced technology and international

Sign offering wine-tastings

business. In the mid-1980s a science park, the Technopole Atlantique, was built on the banks of the River Erdre, an electronic research institute opened and the city acquired a World Trade Centre (*Centre Atlantique du Commerce International*). Yet here, too, the broad streets and avenues (formerly water-courses) create a feeling of spaciousness that helps to perpetuate the mood of *douceur de vivre* beside the new economic dynamism. In the same way, Tours' chic conference centre in the heart of the city does not seem to have detracted from the bustle of streets often thronged with foreign students. They have come to learn to speak what is alleged to be the purest French in France. By "pure", the experts mean well-modulated speech devoid of any strong accent – a fine symbol for a populace admired for being pleasant and relaxed.

Locally grown asparagus

From Defence to Decoration

Over the centuries, châteaux in the Loire Valley gradually developed from feudal castles, designed purely as defensive fortresses, into graceful pleasure palaces. Once the introduction of firearms put an end to the sieges that medieval castles were built to withstand, comfort and elegance became key status symbols. Many defensive elements evolved into decorative features: watchtowers became fairy-tale turrets, moats served as reflecting pools and crenellations were transformed into ornamental friezes. During the Renaissance, Italian craftsmen added features such as galleries and formal gardens, and carved decoration became increasingly intricate.

Château d'Angers in 1550, before its towers were lowered

Slate and stone walls

Fortifications with pepper pot towers removed

Angers (see pp74–5) *was built between 1228 and 1240 as a mighty clifftop fortress, towering over the River Maine. Along its curtain wall were spaced 17 massive round towers. These would originally have been 30 m (98 ft) high before their pepper pot towers were removed in the 16th century.*

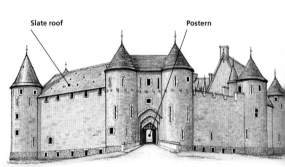

Slate roof

Postern

Ainay-le-Vieil (see p148), *dating from the 12th century, contrasts two styles. An octagonal walled fortress, with nine massive towers topped by pepper pot turrets and lit by arrow slits, was entered through a huge medieval postern gate across a drawbridge that crossed the moat. Inside, however, there is a charming, early 16th-century Renaissance home.*

Ainay-le-Vieil's delightful living quarters, hidden inside an octagonal fortress

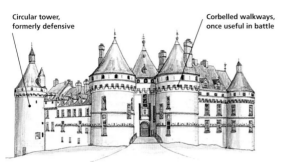

Circular tower, formerly defensive

Corbelled walkways, once useful in battle

Chaumont (see p128) *stands on the site of a 12th-century fortress, destroyed in 1465 by Louis XI to punish its owners for disloyalty. The château was rebuilt from 1498 to 1510 in the Renaissance style. Although it has a defensive appearance, with circular towers, corbelled walkways and a gatehouse, these features have been lightened with Renaissance decoration.*

Chaumont's walls *are carved with the crossed Cs of Charles II d'Amboise, whose family rebuilt the château.*

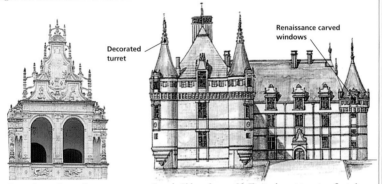

Decorated turret

Renaissance carved windows

Decoration on the north façade of Azay-le-Rideau

Azay-le-Rideau (see pp96–7), *its elegant turrets reflected in a peaceful lake, was built from 1518 to 1527 and is considered one of the best-designed Renaissance châteaux. Its interior staircase, behind an intricately decorated pediment with three storeys of twin bays, is very striking.*

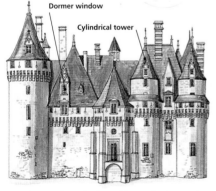

Dormer window

Cylindrical tower

Ussé (see p101) *was built in 1462 as a battlemented fortress. Later, the walls overlooking the main court-yard were modified during the Renaissance, with dormer windows and pilasters. In the 17th century the north wing was replaced by terraced gardens.*

Château d'Ussé, once a fortress, now an aristocratic château

Inside the Châteaux

Stone carving on staircase

The typical Loire Valley Château boasted several large, lavishly furnished reception rooms, adorned with luxurious tapestries and paintings and featuring decorative panelling and ceilings. The main rooms included the Grand Salon, often with an imposing fireplace, and an elegant dining room. The gallery was a focal point for host and guests to meet to discuss the events of the day, admire the views over the grounds or the paintings displayed on the gallery walls. The châtelain's private rooms, and those reserved for honoured (particularly royal) guests, were grouped in a separate wings, while servants were housed in the attics.

Apartments in one wing were for private use.

Grand Escalier (Grand Staircase)

Chairs *were often spindly – elegant but uncomfortable. The more comfortable models with armrests might be covered with precious tapestries, as with this one from Cheverny, upholstered in Aubusson.*

The Grand Salon, mostly used for entertaining, had a majestic marble fireplace carved with the owner's coat of arms, emblem or intertwined initials.

The Grand Escalier, *or Escalier d'Honneur (grand staircase), had richly carved balustrades and an elaborately decorated ceiling, such as this magnificent Renaissance staircase at Serrant (see p69). The staircase led to the owner's private suites, as well as to state guest bedrooms and rooms used on special occasions, such as the armoury.*

Main entrance

Galleries, *like this one at Beauregard (see pp130–31), were where owners and guests met to converse or to be entertained. They were often hung with family and other portraits.*

State dining rooms, *for receiving important visitors, were as sumptuously furnished and decorated as the other main reception rooms. This one in Chaumont (see p128) features Renaissance furniture.*

Château rooms *were filled with costly tapestries, paintings and fine furniture, and attention was paid to detail. Decorative features, such as this French Limoges enamel plaque, or intricately carved wooden panelling were common. Even the tiles on stoves that heated the huge rooms were often painted.*

The Salle d'Armes, or armoury, displayed suits of armour and weapons beside fine tapestries and furniture.

The east wing was reserved for important guests.

Dining Room

King's Bedroom

The King's Bedroom *was kept permanently ready for a royal visit. Under the droit de gîte (right of lodging), château owners were bound to provide accommodation to the king in return for a building permit. This room, at Cheverny (see p130), was used frequently.*

Gallery

Kitchen

CHEVERNY

A dignified Classical building in white tufa, Cheverny *(see p130)* has scarcely been altered since it was built between 1620 and 1634. The central section, containing the staircase, is flanked by two symmetrical wings, each consisting of a steep-roofed section and a much larger pavilion with a domed roof. The interior is decorated in 17th-century style.

Kitchens *were in the cellars, or separately housed. Huge spits for roasting whole carcasses were worked by elaborate mechanisms. Though often dark, the kitchens gleamed with an array of copper pots and pans, like these at Montgeoffroy (see p71).*

Churches and Abbeys

The Loire Valley is well-endowed with medieval ecclesiastical architecture, ranging from tiny Romanesque village churches to major Gothic cathedrals like Chartres and Tours. In the early Middle Ages, the Romanesque style predominated, characterized by straightforward ground plans, round arches and relatively little decoration. By the 13th century, the rib vaulting and flying buttresses of Gothic architecture had emerged, enabling builders to create taller, lighter churches and cathedrals. The Late Gothic style in France, often referred to as Flamboyant Gothic, features window tracery with flowing lines licking upwards like flames.

LOCATOR MAP

① Romanesque architecture

⑨ Gothic architecture

ROMANESQUE FEATURES

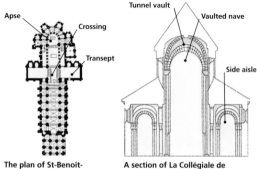

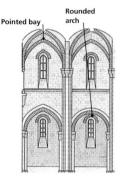

The plan of St-Benoît-sur-Loire *is typical of Romanesque architecture, with its cross shape and rounded apse.*

A section of La Collégiale de St-Aignan-sur-Cher *shows Romanesque tunnel vaulting. The vaulted side aisles provide added support for the high nave.*

The round arches of St-Aignan *are typically Romanesque, while the pointed nave bays predict the Gothic style.*

GOTHIC FEATURES

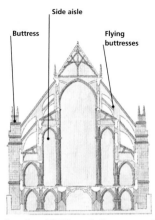

The plan of Chartres Cathedral *shows its very wide nave, and its apse ringed with chapels.*

A section of St-Etienne *in Bourges reveals its five divisions with two aisles on either side of the nave. The building also has five portals rather than the usual three.*

Pointed arches *withstand greater stress and allow large windows, as in the nave at Bourges.*

WHERE TO FIND ROMANESQUE ARCHITECTURE

① St-Maurice, Angers *pp72–3*
② L'Abbaye St-Vincent, Nieul-sur-l'Autise *pp182–3*
③ Notre-Dame, Cunault *p79*
④ L'Abbaye de Fontevraud *pp86–7*
⑤ St-Maurice, Chinon *pp98–9*
⑥ La Collégiale, St-Aignan-sur-Cher *p129*
⑦ St-Eusice, Selles-sur-Cher *pp24–5*
⑧ La Basilique de St-Benoît-sur-Loire *p140*

WHERE TO FIND GOTHIC ARCHITECTURE

⑨ St-Etienne, Bourges *pp152–3*
⑩ St-Louis, Blois *pp124–5*
⑪ St-Hubert, Amboise, *p110*
⑫ St-Gatien, Tours *pp116–17*
⑬ La Trinité, Vendôme *p123*
⑭ Notre-Dame, Chartres *pp172–5*
⑮ St-Julien, Le Mans *p166*
⑯ Asnières-sur-Vègre *p163*

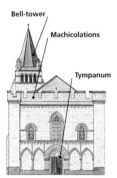

Bell-tower
Machicolations
Tympanum

The west façade of Notre-Dame *at Cunault is simply decorated. Its machicolations and lateral towers give it a fortified appearance.*

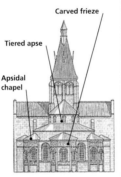

Carved frieze
Tiered apse
Apsidal chapel

The east end of St-Eusice *in Selles-sur-Cher, with its three apsidal chapels, is decorated with friezes of carved figures.*

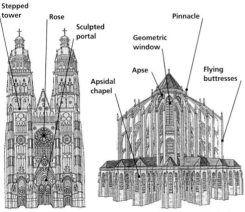

Stepped tower
Rose
Sculpted portal
Apsidal chapel

Pinnacle
Geometric window
Apse
Flying buttresses

The west façade of *St-Gatien in Tours has richly carved, Flamboyant Gothic portals.*

The east end *of St-Julien cathedral in Le Mans has a complex arrangement of paired flying buttresses, each topped by pinnacles.*

TERMS USED IN THIS GUIDE

Basilica: Early church with two aisles and nave lit from above by clerestory windows.

Clerestory: A row of windows illuminating the nave from above the aisle roof.

 Rose: Circular window, often stained glass.

Buttress: Mass of masonry built to support a wall.

 Flying buttress: An arched support transmitting thrust of the weight downwards.

Portal: Monumental entrance to a building, often decorated.

 Tympanum: Decorated space, often carved, over a door or window lintel.

Vault: Arched stone ceiling.

Transept: Two wings of a cruciform church at right angles to the nave.

Crossing: Centre of cruciform where transept crosses nave.

Lantern: Turret with windows to illuminate interior, often with cupola (domed ceiling).

Triforium: Middle storey between arcades and the clerestory.

Apse: Termination of the church, often rounded.

Ambulatory: Aisle running round east end, passing behind the sanctuary.

Arcade: Set of arches and supporting columns.

Rib vault: Vault supported by projecting ribs of stone.

 Gargoyle: Carved grotesque figure, often a water spout.

Tracery: Ornamental carved stone pattern within Gothic window.

Flamboyant Gothic: Carved stone tracery resembling flames.

 Capital: Top of a column, usually carved.

Writers and Artists of the Loire Valley

The valley of the River Loire is well known for its agricultural fertility, and it has also proved to be productive ground for literature, too. Over the centuries, internationally famous writers such as François Rabelais, the great lyrical poet Pierre de Ronsard and the novelists Honoré de Balzac and George Sand have lived close to the mighty river, often drawing inspiration from their native soil. Perhaps strangely, however, the pure light that so appeals to visitors to the region does not seem to have inspired as many of the country's greatest painters, although Claude Monet spent a fruitful period in the peaceful Creuse Valley.

Novelist Honoré de Balzac

Writer Marcel Proust, in a late 19th-century portrait by Jacques-Emile Blanche

WRITERS

One of the earliest authors to write in the "vulgar" French tongue was born in Meung-sur-Loire in the mid-13th century. Jean Chopinel, better known as Jean de Meung, produced the second part of the widely translated and influential *Roman de la Rose*, a long, allegorical poem about courtly love. While the first half of the poem focuses delicately on two young lovers and their affair, Jean de Meung's sequel undermines the idealistic conventions of courtly love, taking a more cynical view of the world.

During the Hundred Years' War, a century and a half later, aristocratic poet Charles, Duc d'Orléans was imprisoned by the English for 25 years. While in prison he was able to develop his considerable poetic skills. On his return he made his court at Blois a key literary centre. He invited famous writers and poets, among them François Villon, a 15th-century poet as renowned for the skill of his writing as for his highly disreputable lifestyle. While he was in Blois, Villon won a poetry competition with his work, *"Je Meurs de Soif auprès de la Fontaine"* ("I am Dying of Thirst by the Fountain").

François Rabelais, the racy 16th-century satirist and humanist, was born in 1483 near Chinon (*see pp98–9*) and educated at Angers. He became famous throughout Europe upon the publication of his *Pantagruel* (1532) and *Gargantua* (1535), huge, sprawling works full of bawdy humour and learned discourse in equal measure.

Pierre de Ronsard, born near Vendôme 30 years after Rabelais, was the leading French Renaissance poet, perhaps best known for his lyrical odes and sonnets to "Cassandre", "Hélène" and "Marie" (an Anjou peasant girl). Court poet to Charles IX and his sister Marguerite de Valois, he lived and died at St-Cosme Priory near Tours. Ronsard was also at the head of the Pléiade, a group of seven poets who were determined to revolutionize French poetry through the study of the classics. In the same group was Joachim du Bellay, an Anjou aristocrat and keen advocate of French literature. His *Defence and Illustration of the French Language* (1549) was a prose manifesto of the Pléiade doctrine.

Another famous native of the Loire Valley spearheaded a 17th-century intellectual revolution. Mathematician and philosopher René Descartes, born in Touraine and educated at the Jesuit college in La Flèche (*see p167*), developed a new method of philosophical inquiry involving the simultaneous study of all the sciences. Starting with the celebrated "I think, therefore I am," he developed the

George Sand, the 19th-century novelist

Illumination from the *Roman de la Rose*

rationalist doctrine known as Cartesianism in his most famous work, the *Discourse on Method*.

France's most prolific 19th-century novelist, Honoré de Balzac, often referred to his native Touraine as his favourite province. Tours, Saumur and the Château de Saché feature as settings for some of his best-known novels, all of which are keenly observant of 19th-century French mores. The work of Balzac's contemporary, George Sand (the masculine pen name of Aurore, Baroness Dudevant), is rooted in the landscapes of her native Berry, which also inspired Alain-Fournier's magical *Le Grand Meaulnes*, a romantic vision of his childhood in the region.

The hawthorn hedges and peaceful villages near Chartres provided the unforgettable setting for the early passages of Marcel Proust's impressive sequence of novels, *Remembrance of Things Past*. At the mouth of the Loire, the city of Nantes saw the birth, in 1826, of the ever-popular Jules Verne *(see pp192–3)*, whose pioneering works of science fiction have been enormously influential.

ARTISTS

In 1411, the three Limbourg brothers became court painters to the Duc de Berry in Bourges. He commissioned them to paint some 39 miniatures for *Les Très Riches Heures du Duc de Berry*. This Book of Hours was to become the jewel in the duke's fabled manuscript collection and remains one of the finest achievements of the International Gothic style. Some of these intricate illustrations depict scenes from life in the Loire Valley.

Jehan Fouquet, born in Tours in about 1420, was officially appointed royal painter in 1474. His portraits

A miniature from *Les Très Riches Heures du Duc du Berry*

include the famous image of the royal mistress Agnès Sorel *(see p104)* posing as the Virgin Mary.

A century after Fouquet's birth, François I persuaded the elderly Leonardo da Vinci to settle in the manor house of Cloux (now called Le Clos-Lucé, *see pp110–11)* near the royal château of Amboise. Aged 65, Leonardo was no longer actively painting, although he is known to have made some sketches of court life which have not survived. However, he was engaged in scientific investigations and inventions, the results of which can be seen in a museum in the basement of the château.

At about the time of Leonardo's death in 1519, François Clouet was born in

Henri Rousseau, in a self-portrait that typifies his naïve style

Tours. He succeeded his father, Jean, as court painter to François I and produced a string of truly outstanding portraits. His sitters included François I himself, Elizabeth of Austria and Mary, Queen of Scots. François Clouet's style, which was typical of the French Renaissance, was perpetuated by the artists and artisans in his workshop.

Anjou's most celebrated sculptor is David d'Angers, who was born in 1788. His works include busts and medallions of many of the major historical figures of his day, including a memorial to the Marquis de Bonchamps, which can be found in the church at St-Florent-le-Vieil *(see pp68–9)*.

François Clouet's portrait of Mary, Queen of Scots

Exactly a century later, the Impressionist painter Claude Monet spent several weeks in the village of Fresselines in the Creuse Valley, painting the river as it passed through a narrow gorge *(see p147)*. One of these canvases, *Le Pont de Vervit*, now hangs in the Musée Marmottan in Paris.

Henri Rousseau, the quintessential naïve painter, was born in the town of Laval in 1844. Although he never left France, his best-known works are stylized depictions of lush jungles, home to all manner of wild animals. Part of the château in Laval has been converted into a Museum of Naïve Art *(see p160)* in honour of the artist.

Themed Tours of the Loire Valley

For those who wish to travel independently of tour companies, or who have a special interest in the region, themed tours provide an attractive alternative. Local tourist offices produce information on routes visitors can travel in order to see the best sights on a given theme – including wine, churches, châteaux, historical buildings and beautiful botanical gardens and arboretums. Illustrated brochures and tourist maps describing each route, often in languages other than French, are available, and some of the routes are signposted along the way. Tourist office staff are also able to customize a route for your particular needs.

A la Recherche des Plantagenêts *traces the lives of Henry Plantagenet, his wife, Eleanor of Aquitaine, and their sons (see p50). The evidence of their remarkable lives, including this fortress in Loches, can be seen throughout the region.*

The Route Touristique du Vignoble (Wine Route) *guides the traveller through some of the region's prettiest wine country, including the Coteaux de la Loire. Further information is available from the tourist offices in Angers, Nantes and Saumur.*

Champtoceaux

Nantes   St-Florent-   Chalonnes
          le-Vieil   Cunault   Bou
                                    Saumur
          Clisson   Chir
                           Montreuil
                           -Bellay

The Route de la Vallée des Rois *takes motorists to many former royal residences, such as Azay-le-Rideau, as well as to cathedrals and churches along the part of the Loire known as the Valley of the Kings. Information is available from tourist offices along the route.*

Chaille
Luçon   les Marais
L'Aiguillon-   Maillezais
sur-mer

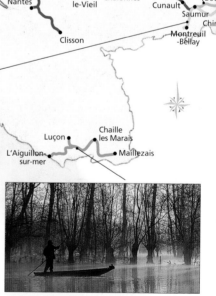

The Sentier Cyclable du Marais Poitevin *is a sign-posted cycle route which takes in the attractions of the south Vendée, including the Marais Poitevin, to give a selection of the varied sights in this area. The tourist office at La-Roche-sur-Yon provides details.*

The Route des Parcs et Jardins *takes visitors to Villandry and many other exquisite châteaux and manor house gardens, contemporary gardens, parks and arboretums in the region. Contact the tourist office in Tours for a brochure.*

The Route Jacques Cœur *leads motorists through some picturesque towns as well as to memorable châteaux, including the Château de Maupas and the Palais Jacques-Cœur in Bourges (see p151), the former home of the wealthy merchant who gives the tour its name. Some of the private châteaux along the route take paying guests (see pp200–1). The tourist office in Bourges provides details of the route.*

Bois Richeux

Villeprévost

Orléans-la-Source
Orléans

Talcy
St-Benoît-sur-Loire
Beaugency
Arboretum des Barres
La Bussière
Gien

Plessis Sasnières

Blois · Chambord

Aubigny-sur-Nère

Chaumont-sur-Loire
Cheverny

Tours
Chenonceaux · Gué-Péan
Villandry
La Verrerie

ay-le-eau
Selles-sur-Cher
Menetou-Salon

Loches · Montrésor
Bouges-le-Château
Bourges
Apremont-sur-Allier

Abbaye de Noirlac

Drulon · Ainay-le-Vieil

Culan

0 kilometres 50

0 miles 50

KEY

— Sentier Cyclable du Marais Poitevin

— Route des Parcs et Jardins

— A la Recherche des Plantagenêts

— Route François I

— Route Jacques Cœur

— Route de la Vallée des Rois

— Route Touristique du Vignoble

The Route François I *explores the châteaux, such as Beauregard. This magnificent château was originally constructed as a hunting lodge for François I (see p54), who held court in Chambord and Blois during the 16th century. Ask at Blois tourist office for details.*

Walking in the Loire Valley

The best way to follow the "most sensual river in France," as Flaubert called it – to appreciate the transformation of the river as it flows through the Sologne forests, carves out the Valley of the Kings, and finally rushes into the ocean – is on foot. The *Grande Randonnée 3* (GR 3) is one of the longest marked walks in France, accompanying the Loire from its source at Gerbier de Jonc to its mouth. The route occasionally strays from the river bank in order to follow the most picturesque paths. For walks lasting a few hours, or several days, ramblers can follow a part of the *Grande Randonnée* or try the region's many shorter, often circular, routes. A Topo-Guide *(see p224)* is a useful companion for detailed information about your walk.

KEY

— Recommended walk

— Grande Randonnée de Pays

— Grande Randonnée

In the charming Alpes Mancelles, on the edge of the Parc Régional Normandie-Maine, there is a variety of walks in the valleys of the Sarthe, the Mayenne and the Orne. *(IGN 1618 OT)*

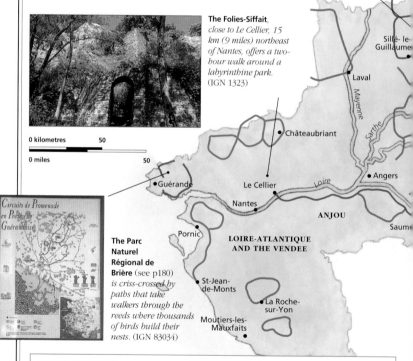

The Folies-Siffait, *close to Le Cellier, 15 km (9 miles) northeast of Nantes, offers a two-hour walk around a labyrinthine park.* (IGN 1323)

0 kilometres 50
0 miles 50

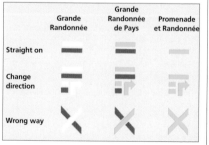

The Parc Naturel Régional de Brière (see p180) *is criss-crossed by paths that take walkers through the reeds where thousands of birds build their nests.* (IGN 83034)

ROUTE MARKERS

All the walking routes are marked with symbols painted onto trees or rocks along the paths. The different colours of the symbols indicate which kind of route you are taking. A red and white mark denotes a *Grande Randonnée* (GR) route, yellow and red are used for a regional route (*Grande Randonnée de Pays*), and local routes (*Promenade et Randonnée*) are marked in a single colour (usually yellow).

	Grande Randonnée	Grande Randonnée de Pays	Promenade et Randonnée
Straight on	▬▬	▬▬	▭▭
Change direction	▬▬ ▪	▬▬ ⬑	▭▭ ⬑
Wrong way	✕	✕	✕

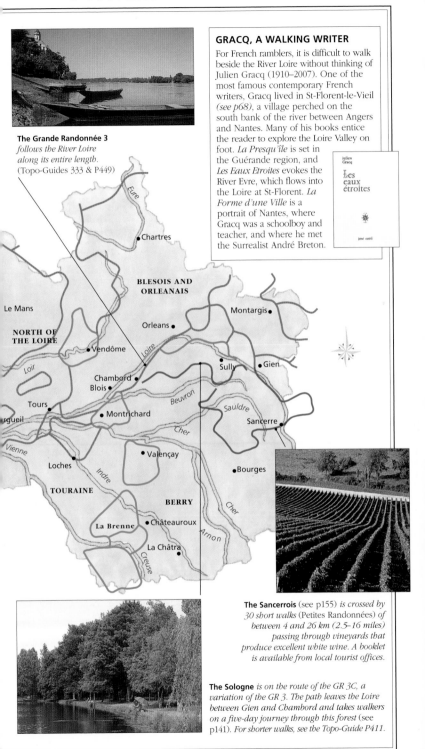

The Grande Randonnée 3
*follows the River Loire
along its entire length.*
(Topo-Guides 333 & P449)

GRACQ, A WALKING WRITER

For French ramblers, it is difficult to walk
beside the River Loire without thinking of
Julien Gracq (1910–2007). One of the
most famous contemporary French
writers, Gracq lived in St-Florent-le-Vieil
(*see p68*), a village perched on the
south bank of the river between Angers
and Nantes. Many of his books entice
the reader to explore the Loire Valley on
foot. *La Presqu'île* is set in
the Guérande region, and
Les Eaux Etroites evokes the
River Evre, which flows into
the Loire at St-Florent. *La
Forme d'une Ville* is a
portrait of Nantes, where
Gracq was a schoolboy and
teacher, and where he met
the Surrealist André Breton.

The Sancerrois (see p155) *is crossed by
30 short walks (Petites Randonnées) of
between 4 and 26 km (2.5–16 miles)
passing through vineyards that
produce excellent white wine. A booklet
is available from local tourist offices.*

The Sologne *is on the route of the GR 3C, a
variation of the GR 3. The path leaves the Loire
between Gien and Chambord and takes walkers
on a five-day journey through this forest (see
p141). For shorter walks, see the Topo-Guide P411.*

Winemaking and Vineyards

The importance of wine to life in the Loire Valley is immediately apparent. Fields of vines stretch along both banks of the river, and roadsides are lined with signs offering *dégustations*, or wine tastings *(see p212)*. Stretching 300 km (186 miles) from Nantes to Pouilly-sur-Loire, the Loire Valley is the third largest wine-producing area by volume in France and offers an unprecedented range of wine styles. The white Sancerres have an excellent reputation

Caricature of a wine maker in "costume"

(see p155), as do some of the rosé wines of Anjou, the sweet and sparkling Vouvrays, the full-bodied reds of Chinon and Bourgueil, and the superb, dry *méthode champenoise* wines of Saumur. There are many more modest wines available, including Muscadet and its younger cousin Gros Plant, which are best served chilled.

Traditional vineyard cultivation

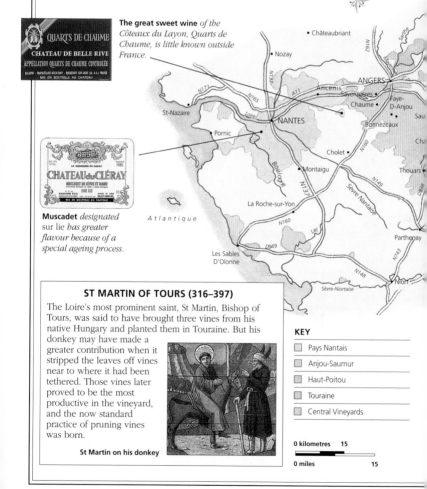

QUARTS DE CHAUME

CHATEAU DE BELLE RIVE
APPELLATION QUARTS DE CHAUME CONTRÔLÉE

The great sweet wine *of the Côteaux du Layon, Quarts de Chaume, is little known outside France.*

CHATEAU du CLÉRAY
MUSCADET DE SÈVRE ET MAINE
SUR LIE

Muscadet *designated sur lie has greater flavour because of a special ageing process.*

Atlantique

ST MARTIN OF TOURS (316–397)

The Loire's most prominent saint, St Martin, Bishop of Tours, was said to have brought three vines from his native Hungary and planted them in Touraine. But his donkey may have made a greater contribution when it stripped the leaves off vines near to where it had been tethered. Those vines later proved to be the most productive in the vineyard, and the now standard practice of pruning vines was born.

St Martin on his donkey

KEY

☐	Pays Nantais
☐	Anjou-Saumur
☐	Haut-Poitou
☐	Touraine
☐	Central Vineyards

0 kilometres   15

0 miles   15

KEY FACTS ABOUT LOIRE WINES

Grape Varieties
The Muscadet grape makes simple, dry whites. The Sauvignon Blanc produces gooseberryish, flinty dry whites. Chenin Blanc is used for the dry and medium Anjou, Vouvrays, Savennières and Saumur, and the famous sweet whites, Vouvray, Quarts de Chaume and Bonnezeaux. Summery reds are made from the Gamay and the Cabernet Franc.

Good Producers (west to east)
Muscadet: Château de la Bretesche, Marquis de Goulaine, Château de Chasseloir. *Anjou* (red): Domaine de Ste-Anne. *Anjou* (rosé): Robert Lecomte-Girault. *Anjou* (dry white): Domaine Richou. *Saumur* (sparkling): Bouvet-Ladunay, Ackerman-Laurance, Gratien & Meyer. *Saumur* (red): Château de Villeneuve. *Saumur* (white): Domaine des Nerleux,

Château de St-Florent. *Bourgueil* (red): Clos du Vigneau. *Chinon* (red): Domaine Réné Couly, Clos de la Dioterie. *Touraine* (white): Domaine Joel Delaunay. *Vouvray*: Clos du Bourg, Le Haut-Lieu, Chevreau-Vigneau, Alain Ferraud, Sylvain Gaudron. *Sancerre*: Domaine de St-Pierre, Domaine Paul Prieur. *Crémant de Loire* (sparkling white): Château de Midouin, Perry de Maleyrand.

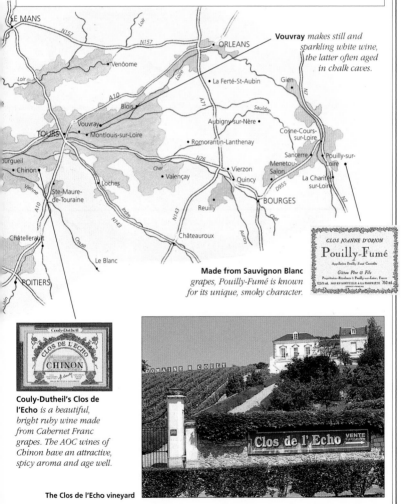

Vouvray *makes still and sparkling white wine, the latter often aged in chalk caves.*

Made from Sauvignon Blanc *grapes, Pouilly-Fumé is known for its unique, smoky character.*

CLOS JOANNE D'ORION
Pouilly-Fumé
Appellation Pouilly-Fumé Contrôlée
Gitton Père & Fils
Propriétaire-Récoltant à Pouilly-sur-Loire, France
12,5% vol.   MIS EN BOUTEILLE À LA PROPRIÉTÉ 750 ml

Couly-Dutheil's Clos de l'Echo *is a beautiful, bright ruby wine made from Cabernet Franc grapes. The AOC wines of Chinon have an attractive, spicy aroma and age well.*

The Clos de l'Echo vineyard

A VIEW OF
THE RIVER LOIRE

A natural highway to the centre of France, the Loire was travelled from the earliest days. The remains of prehistoric canoes have been found along the river; later evidence shows that Celtic tribes and the Romans used the river extensively as a major trade route. In fact, until the development of the railway network during the 19th century, the river was a key transportation route. The growth of the French canal network from the 17th to 19th centuries, connecting the port of Nantes with Paris and the north, enhanced the Loire's importance. **See pages 34–5**

The River Loire can be unpredictable and sometimes dangerous, and it was one of the first rivers that man tried to control. There is evidence that embankments were being built as early as the 12th century – and work continues – but the river remains essentially wild and is still subject to floods, freezes, shifting sands and dangerous currents. Today, the river is no longer used for commerce, except by tour boats giving visitors a unique view of the surrounding landscape. This makes an exploration of the River Loire all the more pleasant. **See pages 36–7**

Sailing boats, with their typical square sails, often travelled in groups of three or more.

Steamers would use powerful winches to dip their smoke-stacks, enabling them to pass under low bridges.

Amboise's bridge traverses the river and the Ile St-Jean.

Château d'Amboise is set on a promontory above the river, safe from possible flooding.

VUE D'AMBOISE
This painting by Justin Ouvrié, now kept in the vaults of the Musée de la Poste in Paris, was painted in 1847. The bustling river scene, which includes several types of vessel, gives an indication of the importance of the River Loire to life and trade in the region, before the railways came to dominate transportation later in the century.

Barges, known in French as *chalands*, did not always have sails – sometimes they were rowed.

Everyday objects *were often decorated with river scenes, such as this 19th-century plate from the Musée de la Marine de Loire in Châteauneuf-sur-Loire.*

◁ **Orléans, with the imposing Cathédrale Ste-Croix, seen from across the river**

River View: St-Nazaire to Montsoreau

A pleasure barge on the River Loire

As the river Loire leaves Touraine and heads through Anjou and the Loire Atlantique, it widens and flows faster, as though rushing towards the Atlantic Ocean. Its waters are also swelled by many tributaries. Some flow alongside, creating a multitude of islands big and small; other tributaries flow north and south through the surrounding countryside. This land is rich in ancient monuments, including the Bagneux dolmen, the largest Neolithic construction of its kind, as well as fortresses built during the Middle Ages.

Champtoceaux
The village of Champtoceaux, on a cliff 80 m (260 ft) above the river, offers panoramic views. A private Renaissance château now occupies the lower part of the bluff, where a medieval citadel once stood.

St-Nazaire
At the mouth of the River Loire, where it flows into the Atlantic Ocean, St-Nazaire (see p190) is the site of a major French industrial zone. Its graceful bridge is the westernmost river crossing.

Ancen

Nantes' Cathédrale
St-Pierre et St-Paul is Gothic style.

Nantes
Nantes was a prosperous port during the 18th and 19th centuries (see pp 190–193), the meeting point between the ocean and the inland river transportation channels.

| 0 kilometres | 20 |
| 0 miles | 20 |

Péage Fortifié du Cul-du-Moulin
This toll station was one of many constructed in the 13th century to collect revenue from passing vessels. This is one of the few remaining river toll stations in France.

THE BRIDGES OF THE LOIRE

There have long been bridges across the River Loire – there was one at Orléans as early as AD 52, which was later destroyed by Julius Caesar's army. Now, with so many options for places to cross the river, it is difficult to imagine what it was like during the Middle Ages, when there were only five, or during the 15th century, when there were just 13. The bridges crossing the river today tell the story not only of the development of bridge building, but also of the region itself, its history and relationships.

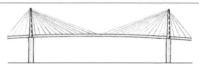

St-Nazaire
At 3,356 m (11,000 ft), St-Nazaire is the longest bridge in France. The central, suspended section is 404 m (1,300 ft) long. It opened for traffic in 1975. Before then, the estuary was crossed by ferry, and the nearest bridge was at Nantes.

St-Florent
Once the church of a Benedictine monastery, the abbey on the promontory was the site of dramatic events during the Vendée Uprising (see p68). More than 40,000 Royalist troops and their supporters crossed the river here.

Montsoreau
Montsoreau, at the confluence of the Loire and Vienne rivers, has a 15th-century turreted château (see p85).

The Château d'Angers, with its massive towers and curtain walls, is on the River Maine, north of the Loire.

Cunault
The impressive Romanesque church in Cunault (see p79) is home to this painted 15th-century statue of St Catherine.

Angers
The Apocalypse Tapestries (see pp76–7), masterpieces of the 14th century, are displayed in the Château d'Angers.

Les Rosiers

Saumur
Saumur is famous for its cavalry school, whose fallen cadets are honoured by this memorial.

The Château de Saumur *(see p82)* rises above the town like a fairytale castle.

Ile Béhuard
This island (see p69) was once a pilgrimage site for sailors, who prayed to a sea goddess to help them navigate the sometimes treacherous waters of the River Loire. The present church was built by Louis XI who had nearly drowned here.

Chinon
Above the River Vienne, Chinon (see pp98 – 100) was home to Henry Plantagenet in the 12th century.

Ancenis
The suspension bridge at Ancenis opened in 1953, replacing one destroyed in 1940. As the town is at the border of Brittany and Anjou, two coats of arms adorn either end of the bridge, one with the three lilies of Anjou and one with the ermine of Brittany.

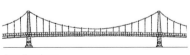

Les Rosiers
The bridge at Les Rosiers is one of the two that cross the Loire at this point. The river is particularly wide here and has an island in the middle. The island is connected to the banks at the towns of Les Rosiers and Gennes by two bridges.

River View: Tours to Nevers

Stained glass in Gien

This is truly the royal Loire Valley. As the river flows through the regions of Touraine, Blésois and Orléanais, it passes beside many Renaissance châteaux. Some, like Chaumont, Amboise and Gien, show their fortress-like exteriors to the river, often concealing courtyard gardens and highly decorated façades. Others, like Sully, glory in their luxury. Throughout Touraine, vineyards gently slope towards the river, while in the west, the lands bordering the river are taken up by the forests that were once the hunting grounds of kings and princes.

Beaugency's massive keep (*see p136*) dates from the 10th century.

Beaugency

Langeais
In the town of Langeais, (see p92) high above the river, there is a massive 15th-century château, still furnished in keeping with its period.

Château d'Amboise (*see p110*) is a 15th-century château, built by Charles VIII.

Blois
On the north bank of the Loire, Blois (see pp124–7) was the seat of the counts of Blois, and then the residence of François I, whose salamander emblem decorates one fireplace.

Pagode de Chanteloup
All that remains of a once-lovely château, this strange pagoda (see p111) is 44 m (145 ft) tall.

Tours
In the heart of the Loire Valley region, Tours (see pp112–17) was always a significant crossing point on the river. The lively place Plumereau, lined with 15th-century buildings, is in the Old Town.

Château de Chaumont
The great fortress of Chaumont (see p128) is softened by Renaissance touches and offers impressive views from its terrace.

Tours
When Tours' original 18th-century bridge was built, the rue Nationale, which links it to the centre of the city, became the major thoroughfare, in place of the road between the cathedral and the Old Town.

Blois
The bridge at Blois was built between 1716 and 1724, replacing a medieval bridge destroyed when a ship crashed into it. It was built to a very high standard, enabling it to survive floods and freezes.

Abbaye de St-Benoît *(see p140)* has one of France's finest Romanesque abbey churches.

Jargeau

An amateur fisherman, one of many attracted to the banks of the Loire

0 kilometres	15
0 miles	15

Château de Sully-sur-Loire
A magnificent 14th-century castle, Sully is set in a moat created from the diverted River Sange.

Orléans
Set strategically at the point where the Loire turns southwards, Orléans (see pp138–9) has been inhabited since the earliest times. It is famous as the town that was liberated by Joan of Arc during the Hundred Years' War.

Briare Bridge-Canal
The elegant Pont-Canal de Briare (see p141) carries the Canal Latéral à la Loire across the river.

Nevers •

Gien
Gien's 15th-century château (see p140) replaced an earlier fortress. The terraces give good views of the river and of the town's 16th-century bridge.

Beaugency
Beaugency's bridge is built in several different styles, because sections of the original 12th-century wooden structure were gradually replaced with stone. The earliest date from the 14th century.

Jargeau
The original bridge was replaced by a wooden suspension bridge in the 19th century. A steel bridge, built in the 1920s, was hit in World War II. The current bridge dates from 1988.

THE LOIRE VALLEY THROUGH THE YEAR

Spring and early summer are often particularly beautiful in the regions bordering the River Loire. But it should not be forgotten that this is the "Garden of France", and that successful gardens need plentiful watering in the main growing season, so be prepared for showery days. In the sultry, humid heat of July and early August, the Loire is usually reduced to a modest trickle between glistening sand banks. The châteaux can be very crowded in the summer. Perhaps the most pleasant season is

Spring asparagus

autumn, when forests gleam red and gold in the mild sunshine, the restaurants serve succulent local game and wild mushrooms, and the grape harvest is celebrated in towns and villages with many colourful festivals. Music festivals are also very popular in the region. Concerts are staged all year round at the Abbaye de Fontevraud (see pp86–7), and Amboise (see p110) holds its Summer Organ Festival between June and August. For more information about any of these festivals, contact the local tourist office (see p231).

SPRING

March sees the reopening of many châteaux after their winter closure, often on the Palm Sunday weekend that marks the beginning of the influx of visitors from the rest of France and abroad. The spring flowers in the meadows, the flowing waters of the Loire and other rivers, swollen by winter rains, and the spring migrations of birds are particularly appreciated by nature lovers.

MARCH

Foire à l'Andouillette (weekend before Easter), Athée-sur-Cher (nr Chenonceau). One of many celebrations of local produce, in this case chitterling sausages. **Foire aux Vins** (third weekend), Bourgueil (nr Chinon). Wine fairs bring together

many local producers to display their latest vintages, but drinking as well as tasting is the order of the day.

APRIL

Le Printemps de Bourges (third week), Bourges (pp150–51). This contemporary music festival starts off the long concert season. **Carnaval de Cholet** (end Apr), Cholet (p69). Carnival ending in a fabulous night-time parade of multi-coloured floats.

MAY

Fête de Jeanne d'Arc (week of 8 May), Orléans (pp138–9). One of France's oldest fêtes, begun in 1435 to celebrate the routing of the English in 1429, takes the form of a huge, colourful costume pageant. **Concours Complet International** (third weekend), Saumur

Horse and rider from Saumur's Cadre Noir display team

(pp80–83). This international horse-riding competition takes place at the famous Cadre Noir riding school, which also hosts tattoo and equestrian displays from April until September. **Jour de Loire** (last weekend), Loiret, Anjou and Touraine. This wide-reaching festival illustrates and celebrates all aspects of life lived alongside the River Loire. **Le Printemps des Arts** (May and Jun), Nantes (pp190–93) and surrounding area. A Baroque dance, theatre and music festival, with performances held in churches and historic buildings in Nantes, Angers and other towns in the western Loire. **Le Festival International des Jardins de Chaumont-sur-Loire** (May–mid-Oct). A celebration of the region's horticultural magnificence.

Farm workers in the fields around Bourgueil

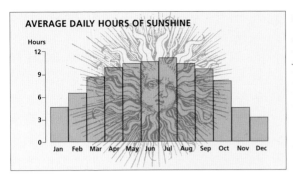

AVERAGE DAILY HOURS OF SUNSHINE

Hours

Jan Feb Mar Apr May Jun Jul Aug Sep Oct Nov Dec

Sunshine Chart
The summer months are generally hot, with the hottest period in July. On the Atlantic coast, cool sea breezes often bring welcome relief from the heat but do not mean that sun-bathers are less likely to burn. In the spring and autumn, river areas can be misty in the mornings.

SUMMER

France's traditional mid-summer celebrations take place on or around the Feast of John the Baptist on 24 June, with fireworks, bonfires, live music and dancing. Towards the end of the month, most of the famous son et lumière *(see pp42–3)* performances begin again, although the long, light evenings of June and July are the peak time for these special events. Many of the small towns and villages hold local fêtes in July and the first half of August, the height of the French tourist season.

JUNE

Les 24 Heures du Mans *(second or third weekend)*, Le Mans *(pp164–7)*. One of France's main events, this international 24-hour car race attracts enormous crowds.
Sardinantes *(second or third Sat)*, Nantes. Savour a plate of grilled sardines accompanied by Celtic music and dancing on the quay in old Nantes. A typical local festival.
Festival d'Anjou *(mid-Jun–mid-Jul)*. This theatre festival is held in historic sites throughout the *département*.
Foire aux Escargots *(last weekend)*, Loché-sur-Indrois (nr Azay-le-Rideau). Snails are served along with local wines in an open-air restaurant.
Fêtes Musicales en Touraine *(last weekend; first weekend in Jul)*, Tours *(pp112–17)*. Started in 1964, this international festival of chamber music is held in a superb medieval tithe barn.

The beach at the popular Atlantic resort, Les Sables d'Olonne

JULY

Bastille Day *(14 Jul)*.
The celebrations for the Fête Nationale, commemorating the Storming of the Bastille in 1789, are the high point of the year in many small communities, where visitors can join in the dancing and wine-quaffing, and enjoy the often-impressive firework displays.
Tous sur le Pont, *(first two weeks)*, Blois.
An open-air celebration of classical and jazz music and theatre culminating in a firework display and dancing on the bridge.
Foire à l'Ail et au Basilic *(26 Jul)*, Tours. The headily scented garlic and basil fair is held every year on the Feast of St Anne *(p117)*.

Festival International d'Orgue *(Sun in Jul and Aug)*, Chartres Cathedral *(pp171–5)*. Renowned organists from all over the world descend on Chartres to participate in this prestigious organ festival.
Les Enfantillages *(last two weeks)*, Cholet. Two afternoons a week, the Parc de Moine features events to entertain children aged 3–12.

AUGUST

Marché Médiéval *(first weekend)*, Chinon *(pp98–100)*. A lively market takes over the whole of the little town, with stallholders dressed in period costume and medieval dishes served in outside taverns.
Foire aux Vins de Vouvray *(around 15 Aug)*, Vouvray. The Feast of the Assumption is marked by numerous local festivities, with wine events predominating.
Foire aux Sorcières *(first Sun)*, Bué (nr Sancerre). The Berry is often said to be a centre of witchcraft and sorcery. On this occasion, children dressed as witches or ghosts parade through the village to a nearby field where crowds play games and watch folk groups performing.

Folk dancers at a festival

Festival de Sablé *(last weekend)*, Sablé-sur-Sarthe *(p162)*. Over a period of five days, musicians perform in churches and manor houses around Sablé.

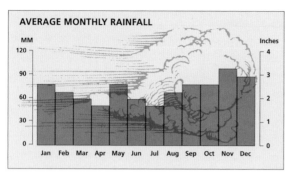

AVERAGE MONTHLY RAINFALL

MM

120

90

60

30

0

Jan Feb Mar Apr May Jun Jul Aug Sep Oct Nov Dec

Inches

4

3

2

1

0

Rainfall Chart
*Spring and autumn
are the wettest times,
with the amount of
rainfall occasionally
causing the River Loire
and its many tribu-
taries to break their
banks. As you head
inland from the coast,
precipitation tends to
increase. During the
summer, rains and
violent storms are
common at night.*

AUTUMN

The golden days of autumn
attract large numbers of
Parisians to the region for
shooting weekends, espe-
cially to the forested eastern
areas. This is also the season
for the *vendanges*, or grape
harvest, and the events and
festivities associated with it,
and for fairs celebrating the
new season's produce.

SEPTEMBER

Les Accroche-Coeurs *(second
week)*, Angers *(pp72–3)*.
During the course of three or
four days, the streets of Angers
are alive with open-air theatre,
dance, circus, concerts and all
manner of performance arts.
Foire aux Melons *(second
Fri)*, Bléré. The fields around
Bléré near Chenonceau are
bright with golden and
orange melons in autumn.
Fête du Pain *(second Sat)*,
Montreuil-en-Touraine *(nr
Amboise)*. The humble bread

loaf, often decorated with
nuts and leaves to celebrate
the arrival of autumn,
becomes a work of art in the
skilful hands of local bakers.
Journées du Patrimoine
(third weekend). For one
weekend a year, châteaux
and other historic buildings
that are usually closed to the
public can be visited, and
concerts, exhibitions and other
cultural events are staged.
Foire aux Rillons *(last Mon in
Sep)*, St-Michel-sur-Loire *(nr
Langeais)*. The Feast of St
Michael is celebrated with a
festival devoted to a delicacy
of Touraine *(see p210)*.

OCTOBER

Celtomania *(first three
weeks)*, Nantes. This lively
celebration of Celtic culture
includes music and theatre
performances.
Foire aux Pommes *(second
weekend)*, Le Petit-Pressigny
(nr Le Grand-Pressigny).
Apple orchards yield their
fruit this month, filling the

**High-quality local produce on sale
at the Saturday market in Saumur**

markets with a wide variety of
apples. Azay-le-Rideau holds
its own Apple Fair during the
last weekend of October.
Foire à la Bernache *(last Sun
Oct or 1st Sun Nov)*, Reugny *(nr
Tours)*. Although it may be an
acquired taste, the *bernache*
(unfermented new wine) is
very popular with the locals.
Foire aux Marrons *(last
Tue)*, Bourgueil *(nr Chinon)*.
Chestnuts are the traditional
accompaniment to new wine,
and for this reason they
feature in many guises here.
Musiques et Patrimoine *(mid-
Sep–mid-Oct)*, Chinon. Six
classical music concerts take
place at weekends in churches
and châteaux in and around
Chinon.

NOVEMBER

Marché de Noël *(last
weekend)*, Château de Brissac
(p78). The Christmas market
in the château, featuring local
artisans and seasonal produce,
marks the beginning of the
Christmas season.

Wine-tasting at Kerhinet in La Grande Brière

AVERAGE MONTHLY TEMPERATURE

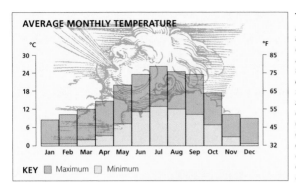

KEY ▪ Maximum □ Minimum

Temperature Chart
It is rare for winter temperatures to fall below freezing in the Loire Valley. In the west, the sea moderates the climate, keeping it mild. Elsewhere, summer temperatures can reach over 30° C (86° F) in the middle of the day, but the evenings are usually cooler and perfect for eating outside on terraces by the river.

WINTER

Winter is the quiet season in the Loire Valley, when a damp chill rather than a frosty cold sets in, and many of the châteaux are closed. A few Christmas markets are held, and a film festival, but in general this is a time when local people prefer the pleasures of home.

DECEMBER

Festival du Film *(first week)*, Vendôme *(pp122–3)*. This celebration of short, animated and experimental films is held at the Minotaure cultural centre. In addition to the competition, there are video installations, exhibitions, debates and retrospectives.
Fête de la St-Nicolas *(first weekend)*, St-Nicolas-de-Bourgueil (nr Chinon). One of many Christmas fairs held throughout the region, selling toys and festive decorations.
Foire de Noël *(first weekend)*, Richelieu *(p102–3)*. This traditional Christmas market

An old windmill in the Anjou countryside

sells gifts, decorations and seasonal food.

JANUARY

La Folle Journée *(last week)*, Nantes and various other towns around the region. As many as 400 classical music concerts take place in 12 different towns, all focusing on a theme that changes every year.

FEBRUARY

Fêtes des Vins d'Anjou *(last weekend)*, Chalonnes-sur-Loire. The winter period is enlivened with wine fairs, such as this gathering of producers of the Saumur and Anjou appellations.

PUBLIC HOLIDAYS

New Year's Day
(1 Jan)
Easter Monday
Ascension (sixth
Thursday after Easter)
Labour Day (1 May)
VE Day (8 May)
Bastille Day (14 Jul)
Feast of the Assumption
(15 Aug)
All Saints' Day
(1 Nov)
Remembrance Day
(11 Nov)
Christmas Day
(25 Dec)

A concert at the Abbaye de Fontevraud

Son et Lumière in the Loire

The Loire Valley was the birthplace of son et lumière (literally "sound and light") shows, and some of the world's finest examples can be found here. The first performances, staged at Chambord in 1952, combined lighting effects and a soundtrack to emphasize the beauty of the building and to conjure up important historical figures. Today many of the shows use lasers and dramatic fireworks, as well as a cast of hundreds (often amateur actors drawn from the local community), to create a spectacular pageant. The following list includes the main regular shows, but it is worth keeping an eye open for posters advertising one-off events. Performance times may vary.

Actor at Amboise

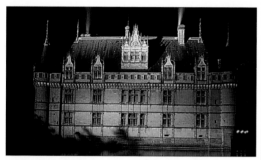

Lighting effects bringing drama to the Château d'Azay-le-Rideau

TOURAINE

Amboise At the Court of King François (1½ hours). *Tel* 02 47 57 14 47. ☐ late Jun–Jul: 10:30pm Wed, Sat; Aug: 10pm Wed, Sat. book in advance. **Translations** Eng. **www**.renaissance-amboise.com

This is a celebration of the life of François I, held at his favourite royal château (see p110). The show is enacted by local residents and re-creates the court, with its sumptuous costumes, thrilling hunts, pleasure gardens and elaborate festivities.

Azay-le-Rideau Dreams & Lights (45 mins). *Tel* 02 47 45 42 04. ☐ Jul: 9:45pm nightly; Aug: 9pm nightly.

During this fascinating promenade production, all the spectators walk around the grounds of this elegant château (see pp96–7), as they observe a succession of stage, sound and lighting effects.

Chenonceau Night-time Promenade (1½ hours). *Tel* 02 47 23 90 07. ☐ Jun: 9:30–11pm Fri, Sat & Sun; Jul & Aug: 9:30–11pm nightly.

The son et lumière production at this beautiful royal residence (see pp106–9) takes the form of a play of light and shadow orchestrated by Pierre Bideau, the designer of the Eiffel Tower illuminations. The walk leads through the gardens designed by Diane de Poitiers and Catherine de Médicis. Corelli's music adds to the romantic atmosphere.

Loches

Les Nuits Royales (approx 3 hours for the two events). *Tel* 05 47 59 01 32. ☐ mid-Jul–mid-Aug: 10pm Tue.

A dramatic nocturnal walk around the floodlit monuments and medieval streets of the town, starting from the Logis Royal. This is followed by a spectacle of fire and dance. It's cheaper to book the two events together.

BLESOIS AND ORLEANAIS

Blois The Story of Blois (45 mins). *Tel* 02 54 90 33 32. ☐ 15 Apr–31 May: 10pm nightly; Jun & Jul: 10:30pm nightly; Aug: 10pm nightly; 1–24 Sep: 9:30pm nightly. **Translations** Eng, Ger, Ital, Spa. English performance on Wed.

Images of key moments in the history of the château (see pp126–7) are projected onto its façade. Included are the visit of Joan of Arc in 1429, the poetry contest between Charles of Orléans and François Villon, and the assassination of the Duc de Guise. Watch the show from the château's courtyard.

Cléry-Saint-André La Révolution Française (1¾ hours). *Tel* 02 38 45 94 06. ☐ last 3 w/ends Jul: 10:30pm. **www**.cleryraconte.com

A cast of hundreds recreates the uprising, struggles and other events of the French Revolution. Afterwards you can sit down to a Republican banquet, starting at 7pm (advanced reservation advised), during which more entertainment is provided.

Faces from the past projected onto the walls of Château de Blois

Fireworks and lighting effects illuminate the château of Puy-du-Fou

BERRY

Valençay *Tel* 📋 *02 54 00 04 42.* **La Visit aux Chandelles** (90 mins) 🕐 *two Fridays in Jul and Aug: 9:30pm.* 📷

The grounds of this château *(see p146)*, including the maze, are illuminated by 3,000 candles on two nights each summer. A troupe of 40 actors in period costume and hunting horns help to recreate a memorable atmosphere. The château also stages a Spectacle Nocturne in the last week of July and the first week of August at 10:30pm.

Aubigny-sur-Nère **Different Franco-Scottish themes** (90 mins). *Tel 02 48 81 50 91(Mairie).* 🕐 *second and third weekend in Jul, around 9:30pm.* 📷 *book in advance.*

Centuries of proud association with the Stuart clan, including a time in the 18th century when Jacobite exiles made their home at Aubigny *(see p154)*, are reflected in this Franco-Scot celebration. The main event takes place over the course of four days around 14 July, comprising a historical re-enactment, plus costume parades, music and dance. On the Saturday the spectacle is complemented by a feast in the gardens of the château, while on the Sunday there is a medieval market. The 14th of July is marked with a big firework display.

LOIRE ATLANTIQUE AND THE VENDÉE

Le Puy-du-Fou **Cinéscénie** (100 mins) *Tel 02 51 64 11 11.* 🕐 *Jun & Jul: 10:30pm Fri & Sat; Aug–early Sep: 10pm Fri & Sat. Arrive one hour earlier.* 📷 *book in advance.* **Translation** *Eng.* **www**.puydufou.com

The Château du Puy-du-Fou *(see p188)* hosts the Ciné-scénie, which bills itself as the world's largest permanent son et lumière spectacle. More than 1,000 actors, 250 horses, countless volunteers and various spectacular high-tech effects combine to trace the turbulent history of the Vendée from the Middle Ages to the end of World War II.

THE MAGICIAN OF THE NIGHT

The master of the modern son et lumière in France is Jean-Claude Baudoin, who is also known as *"le magicien de la nuit"*. Since 1966 he has created the sets for more than 150 musical productions, held at the châteaux of Blois, Loches, Chambord and Valençay, as well as in St-Aignan-sur-Cher, Les Sables d'Olonnes and Chartres.

Producer Jean-Claude Baudoin

The history of the Vendée re-enacted in the Cinéscénie at Le Puy-du-Fou

THE HISTORY OF THE LOIRE VALLEY

The Loire's central role in French history is splendidly displayed in the breadth of its architectural styles, ranging from megalithic structures to royal and ducal châteaux.

Imposing prehistoric monuments testify to the existence of thriving Neolithic cultures as early as the third millennium BC. By the 1st century BC, the conquering Romans found sophisticated Celtic communities already established. Later, as Christianity spread, the ancient Celtic towns at Angers, Bourges, Chartres, Orléans and Tours became well known as centres of learning, and they remain vibrant cultural centres today.

Fleur-de-lys, the royal emblem

A long period of territorial conflict began in the 9th century, first among local warlords and later between France and England, when Henry Plantagenet, count of Anjou and duke of Normandy and Aquitaine, inherited the English crown in 1154. Major battles between the two countries were fought in the region during the Hundred Years' War. The Loire also saw bloodshed during the fierce 16th-century Wars of Religion, which took place between the Catholics and the Protestant Huguenots. Later, the Vendée Uprising of 1793 was the most serious civil threat to the French republic after the 1789 Revolution.

Yet the Loire was also the scene of outstanding cultural achievements and the home of many French kings. By the 17th century, France's political focus had shifted to Paris, although the River Loire remained a key transportation route until the advent of the railway in the late 19th century.

In the 20th century, the impressive architectural evidence of this rich history has led to the growth of the Loire's tourist industry. This balances with a diverse, well-established industrial base and thriving agriculture to make the valley one of the most economically stable regions of France.

16th-century views of Tours, with its cathedral, and Angers, with quarries of *ardoise* slate

◁ **A portrait of François I, the Renaissance king (reigned 1515–47), attributed to Jean Clouet**

Rulers of the Loire

In the course of the Loire's history, the power of the
local nobility often rivalled that of the French throne.
The dukedoms of Anjou and Blois were established
when Charlemagne's territory was divided among his
sons upon his death in 814. Henry Plantagenet, count
of Anjou, duke of Normandy and king of England,
could trace his lineage to Charlemagne. The French
monarchy did not consolidate its authority until
Charles VII moved from the Loire back to Paris in
1436. Another local family, the royal house of Orléans,
saw two of its sons become kings.

KEY

French monarchs

Notable members of local dynasties

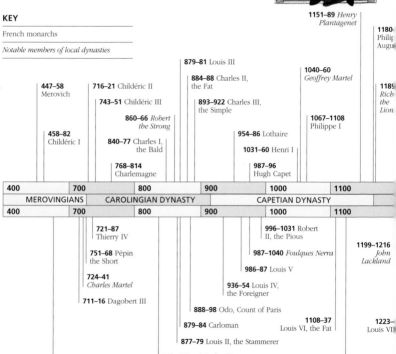

1151–89 *Henry
Plantagenet*

1180
Philip
Augu

879–81 Louis III

884–88 Charles II,
the Fat

893–922 Charles III,
the Simple

1040–60
Geoffrey Martel

1189
*Rich
the
Lion*

447–58
Merovich

716–21 Childéric II

743–51 Childéric III

860–66 *Robert
the Strong*

954–86 Lothaire

1067–1108
Philippe I

458–82
Childéric I

840–77 Charles I,
the Bald

1031–60 Henri I

768–814
Charlemagne

987–96
Hugh Capet

400	700	800	900	1000	1100
MEROVINGIANS	CAROLINGIAN DYNASTY		CAPETIAN DYNASTY		
400	700	800	900	1000	1100

721–87
Thierry IV

996–1031 Robert
II, the Pious

751–68 Pépin
the Short

987–1040 *Foulques Nerra*

1199–1216
*John
Lackland*

986–87 Louis V

724–41
Charles Martel

936–54 Louis IV,
the Foreigner

711–16 Dagobert III

888–98 Odo, Count of Paris

1108–37
Louis VI, the Fat

1223–
Louis VI

879–84 Carloman

877–79 Louis II, the Stammerer

814–40 Louis I, the Pious

482–511 Clovis I

1137–80 Louis VII

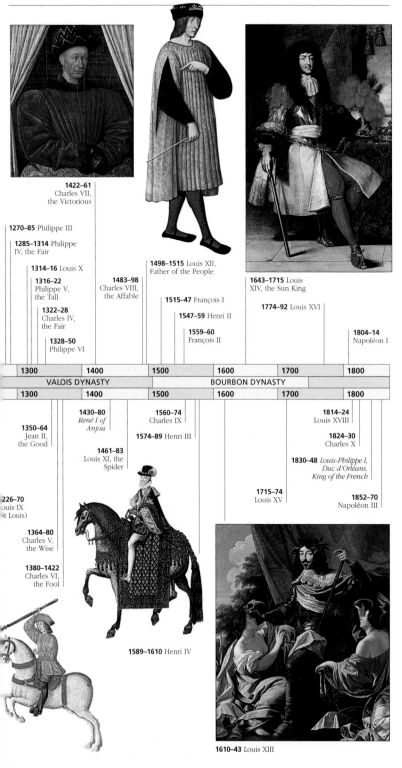

1422–61
Charles VII,
the Victorious

1270–85 Philippe III

1285–1314 Philippe
IV, the Fair

1314–16 Louis X

1316–22
Philippe V,
the Tall

1322–28
Charles IV,
the Fair

1328–50
Philippe VI

1483–98
Charles VIII,
the Affable

1498–1515 Louis XII,
Father of the People

1515–47 François I

1547–59 Henri II

1559–60
François II

1643–1715 Louis
XIV, the Sun King

1774–92 Louis XVI

1804–14
Napoléon I

1300	1400	1500	1600	1700	1800

VALOIS DYNASTY   BOURBON DYNASTY

1300	1400	1500	1600	1700	1800

1350–64
Jean II,
the Good

1430–80
*René I of
Anjou*

1461–83
Louis XI, the
Spider

1560–74
Charles IX

1574–89 Henri III

1814–24
Louis XVIII

1824–30
Charles X

1830–48 *Louis-Philippe I,
Duc d'Orléans,
King of the French*

1226–70
ouis IX
St Louis)

1364–80
Charles V,
the Wise

1380–1422
Charles VI,
the Fool

1715–74
Louis XV

1852–70
Napoléon III

1589–1610 Henri IV

1610–43 Louis XIII

Neolithic and Roman Loire

Neolithic Culture produced some of France's largest prehistoric tombs and sacred sites. Their builders had Central European roots, as did the Celts who established cities along the Loire in the Bronze and Iron Ages. Julius Caesar's conquest of the valley in 51 BC left the Celtic tribes under a light Roman rule, the basis of peace and prosperity for the next 300 years. The spread of Christianity coincided with Rome's military decline and the rise of kingdoms ruled by Visigoths to the south and Germanic Franks to the north. The Frankish king Clovis I converted to Christianity and took power in 507 by routing the Visigoths.

Baptism of Clovis
Frankish chieftain Clovis converted to Christianity at the start of the 6th century to legitimize his rule.

The entrance porch is a distinctive feature of Angevin dolmens.

Palaeolithic Remains
Flint tools made in the Loire basin were traded by Palaeolithic tribes at least 50,000 years ago.

Celtic Art
Celtic art was not dominated by the naturalistic ideals of the occupying Romans. This bronze statuette of a young woman dates from the 1st–2nd century AD.

BAGNEUX DOLMEN
This 5,000-year-old chamber tomb in Saumur is 21 by 7 m (69 by 23 ft). The nine massive uprights were levered onto loose stones, dragged to the site, tilted and sunk into ditches 3 m (10 ft) deep.

TIMELINE

c.2500 Loire dolmens with porches set new style of Neolithic burial chamber

c.800 Celtic Carnutes found settlements at Blois, Chartres and Orléans

57–6 Romans conquer western Loire tribes

51 Julius Caesar ends Gaulish uprising that began in Orléans

Julius Caesar, first to unite Gaul

2500 BC		100 BC	AD 1		AD 100

c.1200 Loire region exports bronze weapons made using local tin resources.

Celtic helmet

31 Roman emperor Augustus sets framework for 300 years of Pax Romana (peace and prosperity) in the Loire

50 Loire Valley flourishes as border link between two Gallo-Roman provinces, Lugdenunsis and Aquitania

Celtic Armour
The warlike Celts were skilled armourers, as this bronze breastplate of 750–475 BC shows. The Romans found them formidable opponents.

An inner pillar, perhaps part of a wall, helps support a 40-tonne capstone.

WHERE TO SEE NEOLITHIC AND ROMAN LOIRE

Anjou is rich in Neolithic sights, mostly on the south bank of the Loire. The largest are at Saumur *(see pp82–3)* and Gennes *(p78)*. Gennes' amphitheatre and the walls at Thésée *(p129)* are two of the few surviving Gallo-Roman monuments. Museums at Orléans *(pp138–9)* and Tours *(pp114–15)* have major Gallo-Roman collections.

Gennes Amphitheatre
Roman gladiatorial combats were held in the amphitheatre at Gennes.

Gallo-Roman Art
This beaten bronze stallion, displayed in the archeology museum in Orléans, was dedicated to Mars, bringer of war and god of agriculture.

Orthostats (walls) were sunk in holes 3 m (10 ft) deep and filled with sand, which was then dug out.

Fresh Water by Aqueduct
Roman pillars near Luynes supported a 2nd-century aqueduct which carried spring water to baths in Caesarodunum (Tours).

50 Gatien, Bishop of ours, among the first Christian evangelists in the Loire

313 Emperor Constantine makes Christianity official Roman religion

372 Martin, Bishop of Tours, leads monastic growth

507 After converting to Christianity, Clovis defeats Visigoths near Poitiers

498 Clovis I takes Orléans

511 Clovis I dies; his sons divide his lands

| 200 | 300 | 400 | 500 |

0 Romans build hitheatre at Gennes

275 Emperor Aurelian gives Orléans independent status

St Martin, Bishop of Tours

451 Visigoth kingdom of Toulouse helps repel Attila the Hun at Orléans

Wine: an early Loire export

473 Visigoths capture Tours

c.550 First record of wine production in the Loire region

The Early Middle Ages

Royal seal of Henry II

In raising the massive keep at Loches, Foulques Nerra of Anjou was typical of the warlords who took power in the Loire after the 9th century. The chains of citadels they built laid the foundations for the later châteaux. The Plantagenets, who followed Nerra as rulers of Anjou, also claimed territory from Normandy to Aquitaine and then inherited the English throne. It was not until the 13th century that the French King Louis IX brought Anjou back under direct control of the crown. Throughout this period the Church was a more cohesive power than the French crown. Its cathedrals and monastic orders established schools and *scriptoria* (where manuscripts were copied and illuminated), and it was to the Church rather than the throne that feudal warlords turned to mediate their brutal disputes.

THE LOIRE AROUND 1180

☐ *French royal domain*

☐ *Other fiefs*

Gregory I codified the liturgical music sung during his reign as pope (590–604).

St Louis
Popularly called St Louis for his piety, Louis IX (1214–70) was the first Capetian monarch to inherit a relatively stable kingdom. A brave crusading knight and just ruler, he forced England to abandon claims to the Loire.

TIMELINE

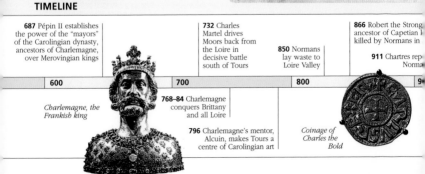

687 Pépin II establishes the power of the "mayors" of the Carolingian dynasty, ancestors of Charlemagne, over Merovingian kings

732 Charles Martel drives Moors back from the Loire in decisive battle south of Tours

850 Normans lay waste to Loire Valley

866 Robert the Strong, ancestor of Capetian killed by Normans in

911 Chartres rep Norma

600 | **700** | **800** | **9**

Charlemagne, the Frankish king

768–84 Charlemagne conquers Brittany and all Loire

796 Charlemagne's mentor, Alcuin, makes Tours a centre of Carolingian art

Coinage of Charles the Bold

Carolingian Ivory
Ivory plaques, reliquaries and book covers are among the most beautiful Frankish decorative objects to survive Norman destructions of the 10th century. Carolingian art usually served a religious or utilitarian purpose.

WHERE TO SEE EARLY MEDIEVAL LOIRE
Early churches such as the one at Cunault *(see p79)* are charged with medieval atmosphere, as are abbeys such as Noirlac *(p149)* or at Solesmes *(p162)* and Fontgombault *(p147)*, where you can hear Gregorian chant. Fortress châteaux such as the one at Loches *(p104)* and ruined towers at Lavardin *(p122)* or Montrichard *(p128)* tell grimmer feudal stories.

Medieval musical notation showed variations in pitch (high and low notes). The length of each note depended on the natural rhythm of the text.

Monastic Arts
The development of the Caroline Minuscule style of calligraphy was led by the monks of Tours' Basilique St-Martin in the 9th century.

Romanesque Capitals
This Romanesque sculpture is on a capital in Cunault church.

Fine Craftsmanship
Many of the finest surviving pieces of medieval craftsmanship are worked in metal. This 13th-century funerary mask was cast in copper from the effigy of a woman and then gilded.

ILLUMINATED MANUSCRIPT
This manuscript is the first page of a 13th-century gradual, a book of plainsong sung during mass. It is typical of the style of illuminated manuscripts that were produced by the abbeys of the Loire Valley. This collection of Gregorian chant was compiled by monks of the strict Cistercian Order *(see p149)*.

Hugh Capet of Orléans
Hugh, depicted here being handed the keys to Laon, was elected king in 987, ending the Carolingian dynasty. He set a precedent for kings to seek refuge in the Loire in troubled times.

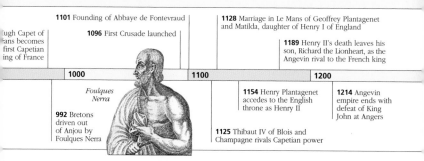

1101 Founding of Abbaye de Fontevraud

1096 First Crusade launched

1128 Marriage in Le Mans of Geoffrey Plantagenet and Matilda, daughter of Henry I of England

Hugh Capet of Orléans becomes first Capetian king of France

1189 Henry II's death leaves his son, Richard the Lionheart, as the Angevin rival to the French king

1000   **1100**   **1200**

Foulques Nerra

992 Bretons driven out of Anjou by Foulques Nerra

1154 Henry Plantagenet accedes to the English throne as Henry II

1125 Thibaut IV of Blois and Champagne rivals Capetian power

1214 Angevin empire ends with defeat of King John at Angers

The Hundred Years' War

14th-century knight

The destructive climax of the Middle Ages was war between the French and English crowns, flaring intermittently from 1337 to 1453. When the English besieged Orléans in 1428, the Loire region became the focus for a struggle that seemed likely to leave France partitioned between England and its powerful ally, Burgundy. Instead, the teenage heroine, Joan of Arc, inspired Orléans to fight off the English and brought the dauphin Charles VII out of hiding in Chinon. Her martyrdom in 1431 helped to inspire a French recovery. In spite of marauding soldiery and the more widespread disaster of the plague known as the Black Death, the Loire knew periods of peace and prosperity, during which medieval court life flourished.

THE LOIRE VALLEY IN 1429

☐ *French territory in the Loire*

▨ *English possessions*

The English longbow was a powerful weapon, requiring strong, skilled archers.

Charles VII
Joan of Arc's dauphin, often portrayed as a weakling, was in fact a crafty man in a difficult situation. Disinherited by the French royal family in 1420, he used Joan's charisma to rally support. However, he distrusted her political judgment.

Cannons could fire stone balls that weighed as much as 200 kg (440 lb).

Jousting Tournament
The sumptuous trappings of their warlike recreations display the wealth of the ruling class in the early 15th century. Jousting was dangerous – Henri II died from a lance blow.

TIMELINE

1341 English support John of Montfort against Charles of Blois in War of Brittany Succession	**1346** English longbows defeat French knights at Crécy	**1352** Loire begins recovery from four years of plague

Black Death depicted in a 15th-century illuminated manuscript

1325	1350	1375

1337 Philippe VI, first Valois king, confiscates English lands in Guyenne, starting Hundred Years' War

Portrait of Philippe VI

1360 Anjou becomes a duchy

Apocalypse
War and the plague made the end of the world a preoccupation of 15th-century art. In this tapestry from Angers (see pp76–7), St John hears the clap of doom.

WHERE TO SEE THE LOIRE OF THE 14TH AND 15TH CENTURIES

Guérande (*p180*) is a well-preserved, 15th-century walled town. Many others, such as Chinon (*pp98–100*), have half-timbered houses. Orléans (*pp138–9*) has a replica of the house in which Joan of Arc lodged. Le Plessis-Bourré (*p70*) exemplifies the shift towards more graceful lifestyles after the end of the Hundred Years' War.

Château de Chinon
This château is strategically positioned on a cliff above the River Vienne.

The halberd was a typical infantryman's weapon.

Siege tower

Joan of Arc
Although shown here in feminine attire, the real Joan (see p137) wore men's dress into battle.

René, Duke of Anjou
René I (1409–80) loved tournaments but was also a painter, scholar and poet. To his people he represented the ideal 15th-century ruler.

THE SIEGE OF ORLÉANS

The English first besieged Orléans in November 1428, and they quickly established their position and built major siegeworks. In February 1429, a French attempt to cut English supply lines was defeated, and it was not until 30 April that Joan of Arc's troops were able to enter the city. Within a week the English were forced to abandon the siege.

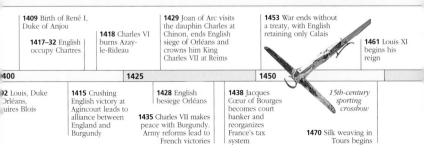

1409 Birth of René I, Duke of Anjou

1417–32 English occupy Chartres

1418 Charles VI burns Azay-le-Rideau

1429 Joan of Arc visits the dauphin Charles at Chinon, ends English siege of Orléans and crowns him King Charles VII at Reims

1453 War ends without a treaty, with English retaining only Calais

1461 Louis XI begins his reign

400　　　　**1425**　　　　**1450**

?2 Louis, Duke Orléans, ?uires Blois

1415 Crushing English victory at Agincourt leads to alliance between England and Burgundy

1428 English besiege Orléans

1435 Charles VII makes peace with Burgundy. Army reforms lead to French victories

1438 Jacques Cœur of Bourges becomes court banker and reorganizes France's tax system

15th-century sporting crossbow

1470 Silk weaving in Tours begins

Renaissance Loire

Catherine de Médicis (1519–89)

The Italian wars of Charles VIII, Louis XII and François I between 1494 and 1525 gave all three kings a taste for Italian art and architecture. At Amboise, Blois and Chambord they made the Loire a centre of court life, establishing the culture of the French Renaissance. François I patronized countless artists and craftsmen who worked in the Italian style, setting an example for the aristocracy throughout France. The Loire suffered 40 years of warfare when his son's widow, Catherine de Médicis, could not persuade Catholics, led by the Guise family, to live in peace with Protestants during the reigns of her sons, Charles IX and Henri III.

Fortress of Faith
The pope is besieged by Protestants in this portrayal of the Wars of Religion.

François I
France's strongest Renaissance king made the Loire his hunting playground. His great confidence is captured here by François Clouet of Tours (see p23).

Colonnades were a feature of the Classical Renaissance style.

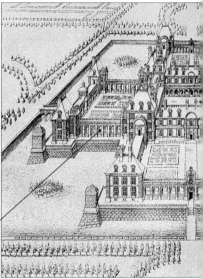

The First Tank Design
Leonardo spent his last years at Le Clos-Lucé (see p111). This tank is a model of one of the inventions he worked on there.

THE IDEAL CHÂTEAU

From Charles VIII (1483–98) onwards, French Renaissance kings dreamt of creating the ideal château. The symmetrical vistas of this plan by Androuet du Cerceau display a late-Renaissance stylistic move towards Classical grandeur.

TIMELINE

1484 Etats Généraux, a national assembly, meets at Tours

1493 Charles VIII redesigns his birthplace, the Château d'Amboise, in Italian style

1498 Duke of Orléans is crowned Louis XII and marries Anne of Brittany

1515 François I conquers Milan and invites Italian artists to the Loire

1532 Treaty binds Brittany and Nantes to France

1475	1500	1525

Charles VIII, France's first Renaissance king

1508 Louis XII remodels Blois as Renaissance royal capital

Cellini's saltcellar for François I (1515–47)

1491 Marriage of Charles VIII to Anne of Brittany links autonomous Brittany to French crown

1519 François I begins building Chambord. Leonardo da Vinci dies at Le Clos-Lucé *(see p111)*

Henri IV
Brave, astute and likeable, Henri IV of Vendôme and Navarre skilfully reasserted the authority of the crown over a disintegrating kingdom within 10 years of his accession in 1589. Rubens (1577–1640) shows him receiving a betrothal portrait of Marie de Médicis.

WHERE TO SEE RENAISSANCE LOIRE

Fine Renaissance buildings can be seen throughout the region. Older châteaux that reflect the Italian influence include Amboise *(p110)* and Blois *(pp126–7)*. The most delightful achievements of the French Renaissance are Chenonceau *(pp106–9)* and Azay-le-Rideau *(pp96–7)*. Smaller examples, such as Beauregard *(pp130–31)*, are widespread. Undoubtedly the most spectacular is Chambord *(pp132–5)*.

Château de Chambord
This impressive château sits on the banks of the River Cosson.

High roofs and dormers show the persisting French influence.

An arcaded central courtyard formed the basis of 15th-century palaces in the Italian style.

Anne of Brittany's Reliquary
By marrying successively Charles VIII and Louis XII, Anne of Brittany, whose reliquary is in Nantes (see p191), welded her fiercely independent duchy to France.

Diane de Poitiers
The mistress of Henri II was flatteringly portrayed as Diana, the Roman goddess of the hunt.

1559 Death of Henri II begins power struggle between his widow, Catherine de Médicis, and anti-Protestant followers of the Duc de Guise

1572 Court moves to Fontainebleau after St Bartholomew's Day massacre of Protestants

1576 Henri, Duc de Guise, founds pro-Catholic Holy League. Meeting of Etats Généraux at Blois fails to find a peace formula

1598 Edict of Nantes establishes Protestant rights of worship

1550

1575

1547 Henri II begins reign and gives Chenonceau to his mistress, Diane de Poitiers

1562 Wars of Religion start with major battles and massacres along the Loire

1588 Holy League virtually takes over government. Henri III has Duc de Guise and his brother murdered at Blois

Coin of Henri IV "the Great"

1594 Henri IV crowned at Chartres after becoming a Catholic to end the Wars of Religion

Growth and Prosperity

The Loire lost its central role in French politics when the focus of court life moved to the Paris region at the end of the 16th century. The Vendée, however, was the centre during the French Revolution of a violent popular uprising against Republican excesses, including rising taxes, the persecution of priests and conscription. River trade remained important, especially for the increasingly wealthy port of Nantes. In the 17th century, work had begun on canals to connect Nantes and the Loire directly with Paris, of which Eiffel's bridge-canal at Briare was the aesthetic high point. Although industry grew slowly, the region remained predominantly agricultural.

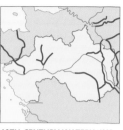

19TH-CENTURY WATERWAYS

— *Rivers*

— *Canals built before 1900*

Cardinal Richelieu
As Louis XIII's chief minister between 1624 and 1642, Cardinal Richelieu helped to establish orderly government in France.

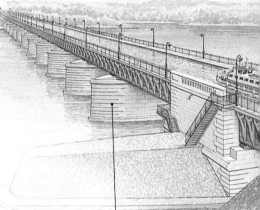

The 15 granite piers supporting the structure were bedded using early compressed-air techniques.

Winemaking in the Loire
Winemaking in the 18th century remained a pastime for the idle rich, who used badly paid peasants to harvest and press the grapes.

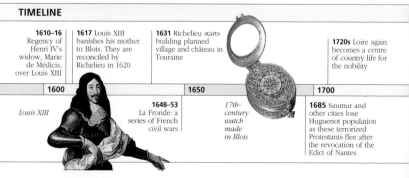

TIMELINE

1610–16 Regency of Henri IV's widow, Marie de Médicis, over Louis XIII

1617 Louis XIII banishes his mother to Blois. They are reconciled by Richelieu in 1620

1631 Richelieu starts building planned village and château in Touraine

1720s Loire again becomes a centre of country life for the nobility

1600

Louis XIII

1648–53 La Fronde: a series of French civil wars

17th-century watch made in Blois

1650

1685 Saumur and other cities lose Huguenot population as these terrorized Protestants flee after the revocation of the Edict of Nantes

1700

Vendée Hero
Bonchamps' plea to spare Republican prisoners (see p187) was depicted in stone by David d'Angers.

Loire "Inexplosibles"
Faced by competition from the railways, 19th-century steamboats were a last attempt to maintain the Loire's role as France's greatest trade route.

Graceful lamps above the wide pavements provide a Parisian boulevard touch.

Passage Pommeraye
The elegance of this 19th-century shopping arcade reflected the wealth of Nantes.

BRIARE BRIDGE-CANAL
Gustave Eiffel designed this 662-m (725-yd) bridge to carry canal traffic safely across the Loire. Opened in 1896, it completed a grand waterway system begun in the 17th century linking the Seine and Rhône rivers. The metal structure used new steel technology.

Steam Omnibus
In 1873, Amédée Bollée's l'Obéissante *was the first car to be built in Le Mans.*

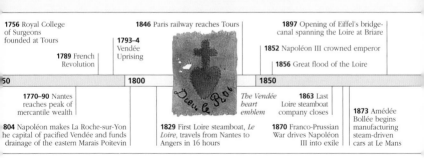

1756 Royal College of Surgeons founded at Tours

1789 French Revolution

1770–90 Nantes reaches peak of mercantile wealth

1804 Napoléon makes La Roche-sur-Yon the capital of pacified Vendée and funds drainage of the eastern Marais Poitevin

1793–4 Vendée Uprising

1846 Paris railway reaches Tours

50

1800

1829 First Loire steamboat, *Le Loire*, travels from Nantes to Angers in 16 hours

The Vendée heart emblem

1897 Opening of Eiffel's bridge-canal spanning the Loire at Briare

1852 Napoléon III crowned emperor

1856 Great flood of the Loire

1850

1863 Last Loire steamboat company closes

1870 Franco-Prussian War drives Napoléon III into exile

1873 Amédée Bollée begins manufacturing steam-driven cars at Le Mans

The Modern Era

Fruits of the Loire Valley

Although ship-building reached a peak at Nantes and St-Nazaire in the 1920s, and light industry expanded steadily around Orléans, Le Mans and Angers, the region did not become prosperous until after World War II. Its larger cities were occupied by the Germans in 1940 and many were bombed in 1944. Since the 1960s, when the recovery gathered momentum, tourism has supplemented the Loire's traditional strength as the "Garden of France". Private châteaux have been opened to the public, and the state has funded major restoration schemes, as at the Abbaye de Fontevraud.

Wilbur Wright
The pioneer US flying ace galvanized European aviation when he demonstrated this commercial prototype near Le Mans in 1908.

Dramatic fireworks
light up the night sky.

TGV Links
With stops at Vendôme, Tours, Angers and Nantes, the Loire is well served by France's TGV (Train à Grande Vitesse) network.

Orléans, 1944
Bridges across the River Loire were prime bombing targets at both the beginning and the end of World War II.

SON ET LUMIERE
Puy-du-Fou's Cinéscénie laser spectacle updates a tradition begun at Chambord in 1952 by Robert Houdin, son of a famous Blois magician. Evening performances draw thousands to Blois, Chenonceau, Cheverny and other great châteaux (*see pp42–3*).

TIMELINE

1900	1910	1920	1930	1940	1950
1905 Loire farming in decline as falling wheat prices follow damage to vines from phylloxera	**1908** Wilbur Wright stages test flights at Auvours near Le Mans		**1936** Renault opens Le Mans factory	**1944** Liberation of Loire cities ends four-year German occupation	**1959** André Malraux m Minister of Cultural Aff He speeds up restora work on Loire monume
		1920 Cheverny opens to the public	**1923** First 24-hour race at Le Mans		
Alain-Fournier (1886-1914)	**1914** World War I begins. Among the first dead is the writer Alain-Fournier (*see p23*)		**1929** Town of La Baule builds promenade and becomes one of France's top beach resorts	**1940** German advance forces temporary government to move from Paris to Tours	**1952** First son et lumière perform-ance at Chambor

Earth Day Ecology Protests on the Loire
Environmentally aware locals are committed to preserving the rich natural resources of the great river.

Nuclear Power
The Loire was an early resource for cooling nuclear reactors. Avoine, near Chinon, opened in 1963.

Computer-controlled lighting effects, lasers and water jets add a modern twist.

Le Vinci
The sensitive modernization of Tours city centre shows how old and new architectural styles can be combined.

More than 2,000 local residents volunteer as performers, security patrols and guides at each Cinéscénie evening.

Le Mans
The renowned 24-hour race at Le Mans attracts motor enthusiasts from around the world.

1963 First French nuclear power station, Avoine near Chinon

1970s Loire wine exports, especially of Muscadet, soar

1989–90 Inauguration of TGV Atlantique high-speed services brings Angers within a mere 90 minutes of Paris

2007 Nicolas Sarkozy wins the presidential election. He appoints François Fillon from the Sarthe as Prime Minister

1970	1980	1990	2000	2010	2020

Muscadet, produced east of Nantes

1994 Government dismantles dam at Maisons Rouges on the River Vienne to allow salmon to reach spawning grounds

2002 The euro replaces the Franc as France's currency

2000 The Loire Valley from Chalonnes-sur-Loire to Sully-sur-Loire is inscribed on UNESCO's World Heritage list

THE LOIRE
VALLEY
AREA BY AREA

The Loire Valley at a Glance

Rich in history and architecture, the Loire Valley is best known for its sumptuous Renaissance châteaux, such as Chambord and Chenonceau. But the region has also retained the wealth of earlier ages, from Bronze Age dolmens to medieval keeps, such as the Château d'Angers, and an impressive heritage of religious architecture, including the Gothic marvels of Chartres and Bourges cathedrals. Visitors who desire a break from the past can revel in the beauty of the landscape, which contains natural surprises such as the lush Marais Poitevin. In a region packed with delights, those shown here are among the very best.

The Gothic spires of Chartres Cathedral, which tower over an attractive town *(see pp172–5)*

The Château d'Angers, protected by its formidable curtain walls *(see pp74–7)*

NORTH C
THE LOIR

Angers •

ANJOU

• Nantes

• Cholet

LOIRE-ATLANTIQUE
AND THE VENDEE

La Roche-
sur-Yon •

Abbaye de Fontevraud, the largest medieval abbey complex in France *(see pp86–7)*

0 kilometres   50

0 miles   50

The Marais Poitevin, a labyrinth of shady canals contrasting with rich fields of painstakingly reclaimed land *(see pp182–5)*

◁ Tree-lined avenue at the Château de Blanville

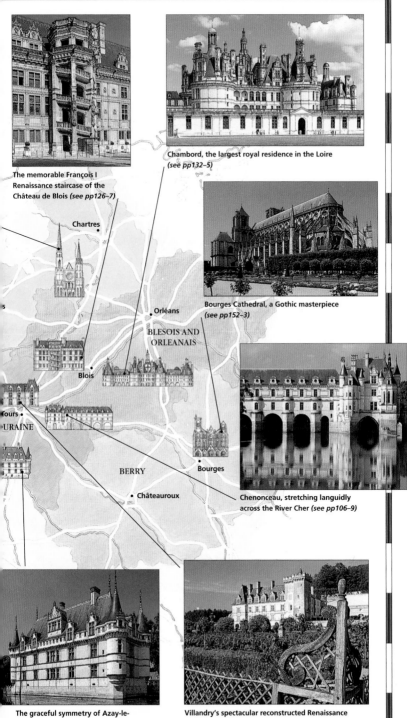

The memorable François I Renaissance staircase of the Château de Blois *(see pp126–7)*

Chambord, the largest royal residence in the Loire *(see pp132–5)*

Bourges Cathedral, a Gothic masterpiece *(see pp152–3)*

BLESOIS AND ORLEANAIS

Chartres

Orléans

Blois

Tours

URAINE

BERRY

Bourges

Châteauroux

Chenonceau, stretching languidly across the River Cher *(see pp106–9)*

The graceful symmetry of Azay-le-Rideau *(see pp96–7)*

Villandry's spectacular reconstructed Renaissance gardens *(see pp94–5)*

ANJOU

The landscape of Anjou is as gentle and pleasant as its climate and its people. The region's rolling plains are intersected by a network of rivers, which help to irrigate the already fertile land. North of the city of Angers, the confluence of the Sarthe, Mayenne and Loir rivers forms a great flood-plain in the winter months and is a regular port of call for thousands of migrating birds.

The creamy limestone, or tufa, used to build the great châteaux of Anjou, combines with grey roof slates to give Angevin architecture its distinctive look. Tufa quarrying has created hundreds of caves. Many are now used for growing mushrooms, and others have been transformed into troglodyte dwellings, some of which are open to visitors.

Some of the Loire Valley's finest fruits and vegetables are grown here. Trees and flowers also flourish: white magnolias, mimosas and palms decorate the region's parks, and the rose gardens of Doué are legendary. The region's vines produce the sparkling wines of Saumur and St-Cyr-en-Bourg. Visitors can see the complicated process of the *méthode champenoise* firsthand by visiting the major wine houses around Saumur.

Anjou is steeped in the history of the powerful rival dynasties of medieval France. Then, as now, Angers, dominated by its barrel-chested fortress, was the centre of the region. The city was the feudal capital of the Plantagenets, among them Henry of Anjou, who became Henry II of England. Fifteen of the family, including Henry II, his wife, Eleanor of Aquitaine, and their sons, Richard the Lionheart and John Lackland, are buried at Fontevraud Abbey. Nearby, Saumur's château formed the fairy-tale backdrop to the "September" miniature in the 15th-century masterpiece, *Les Très Riches Heures du Duc de Berry*. Other impressive châteaux in this region include Brissac, the tallest château in the Loire, and Le Plessis-Bourré, a charming pre-Renaissance château.

Château de Saumur, towering above the town and the River Loire

◁ Cattle resting in an Anjou meadow

Exploring Anjou

Northern Anjou is crossed by the Mayenne, Sarthe and Loir rivers, flowing southwards to their convergence in the River Maine. Angers, the geographical and administrative centre of the region, straddles the Maine 8 km (5 miles) before it flows into the Loire. Anjou's most famous châteaux, antiquities and troglodyte sites are located around Angers and Saumur, 50 km (30 miles) up the Loire. But there are also dozens of lesser-known châteaux, clustered around Segré in the northwest and Baugé in the northeast.

SEE ALSO

• *Where to Stay* p202

• *Where to Eat* pp214–15

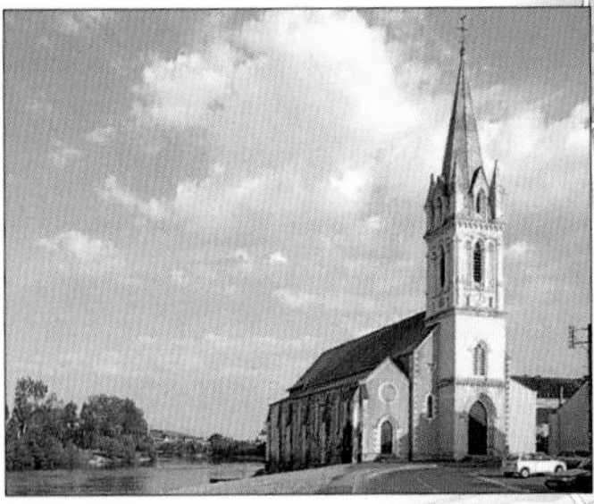

**Eglise St-Maurille,
Chalonnes-sur-Loire**

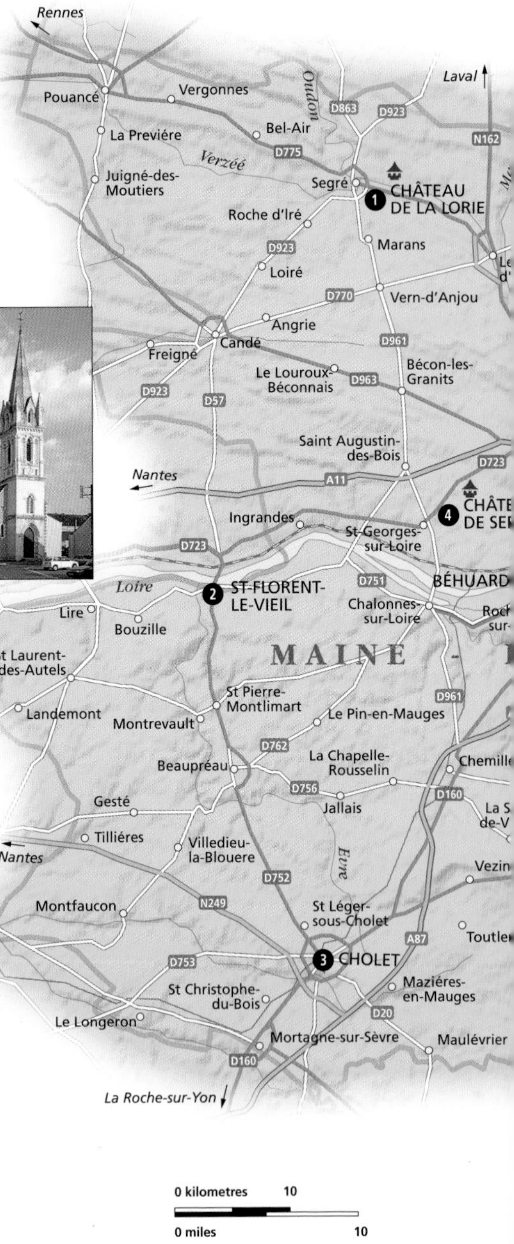

SIGHTS AT A GLANCE

| 0 kilometres | 10 |
| 0 miles | 10 |

The Loire in full flood in Anjou

GETTING AROUND

Angers is 90 minutes from Paris by TGV. *L'Océane* autoroute (A11) via Le Mans is the fastest road access from Paris. Tours and Angers are linked by the A85 motorway. The D751 from Saumur follows the south bank of the Loire and is the most pleasant drive towards Angers. It continues as the Corniche Angevine, providing splendid views of the Loire on the road to Champtoceaux. Leisurely boat cruises are available on the Oudon and Mayenne tributaries.

One of Angers' lively pavement cafés

KEY

— Motorway

— Major road

— Secondary road

┅ Minor road

= = Scenic route

— Main railway

┅ Minor railway

─ Regional border

St-Florent-le-Vieil's 18th-century church, on a hill above the old town

Château de la Lorie ❶

Road map B3. 🚌 *Segré, then taxi.*
Tel *02 41 92 10 04.* ◯ *Jul–mid-Sep:*
Wed–Mon; groups by appt. 📷 ♿
www.chateaudelalorie.net

Elegant gardens in the 18th-century French style introduce this dry-moated château, 2 km (1 mile) southeast of the old town of Segré on the River Oudon. The original building,

which is embellished by a statue of the Roman goddess Minerva over the central door, was built during the 17th century by René le Pelletier, provost-general of Anjou.

A century later, two wings were added to form a court-yard, together with an ornate marble ballroom. This *pièce de résistance* is crowned with a musicians' gallery located in an overhead rotunda. It was completed by Italian craftsmen in 1779, only a few short years

before the French Revolution put an end to these types of extravagant shows of wealth and personal power.

St-Florent-le-Vieil ❷

Road map B3. 🏚 *2,700.* 🚇
Varades, then taxi. 🚌 🛈 *4 pl de la Févrière (02 41 72 62 32).* 🗓 *Fri pm.* 🎵 *Festival de Musique, Les Orientales (late Jun–early Jul).*
www.ville-saintflorentlevieil.fr

A walk through the narrow streets of the old town, lined with buildings dating from the 16th to the 18th centuries, ends atop a hill on which stands a large, 18th-century church, the scene of dramatic events during the Vendée Uprising. The Uprising began in the square outside the church in March 1793, with a mass revolt against conscription into the Republican army.

Seven months later, the Royalist army, beaten at Cholet, crossed the Loire here with 40,000 troops and at least as many supporters. They planned to kill more than 4,000 Republicans held in the church, but were stopped by one of their leaders, the Marquis de Bonchamps, who cried, "Spare the prisoners," as he lay dying. Among those

---

THE CORNICHE ANGEVINE

One of the most scenic routes in the region, the Corniche Angevine (D751) curves along the cliffs above the south side of the Loire, offering lovely views of the islands that break up the river in this area, and of the opposite bank, with its fertile vineyards and beautiful manor houses. The road is never more than hilly and has a pleasantly rural feel as it runs alongside the Louet (a tributary of the Loire), passing though villages and flanked by vineyards and fields.

Chalonnes-sur-Loire, at the western end, is an ancient village with a graceful church, the Eglise St-Maurille, parts of which date back to the 12th century. The quay beside the church is a good place to stop for a picnic. Further along, La Haie Longue has particularly pretty views across the river. At the eastern end of the Corniche Angevine, the town of Rochefort-sur-Loire has a 15th-century bell-tower and a square of old turreted houses. Powerful fortresses once stood on outcrops of rock below the village, and the ruins of some of them can be explored.

The view across the river at La Haie Longue

---

saved was the father of the sculptor David d'Angers, whose marble statue of Bonchamps was placed in the church in 1825 (*see p57*). Stained-glass windows in the chancel recount the story, as does the **Musée d'Histoire Locale et des Guerres de Vendée**.

🏛 **Musée d'Histoire Locale et des Guerres de Vendée**
Place J et M Source.
***Tel** 02 41 72 50 03.* ☐ *Easter–Jun & Oct: Sat & Sun pm only; Jul–Sep: daily pm.*

Emile Boutigny's 1899 depiction of the Vendée Uprising in Cholet

Cholet ❸

Road map B4. 👥 57,000. 🚉 🚌
ℹ️ *14 av Maudet (02 41 49 80 00).*
📅 Sat. 🎭 *Carnaval de Cholet (Apr); Festival des Arlequins (Apr–May); L'Eté Cigale (Jun–mid-Sep).*
www.ot-cholet.fr

Capital of the Mauges region and second city of Anjou, Cholet was a thriving town until 1793 when it lost half its population in the Vendée Uprising (*see p187*). Its revival was testimony to the strength of the area's

The tomb of the Marquis de Vaubrun in Serrant's chapel

textile industry. Cholet's red handkerchiefs with white borders are souvenirs of a crucial battle. The Vendée Uprising is commemorated in the portraits, battle scenes and models in the city's **Musée d'Art et d'Histoire**.

🏛 **Musée d'Art et d'Histoire**
27 av de l'Abreuvoir. ***Tel** 02 41 49 29 00.* ☐ *Wed–Sun.*
● *1 Jan, 1 May, 25 Dec.* ♿

Château de Serrant ❹

Road map B3. 🚉 *Angers, then taxi.*
***Tel** 02 41 39 13 01.* ☐ *mid-Mar–mid-May: Wed–Mon; mid-May–end Sep: daily; end Sep–mid-Nov: Wed–Mon.*
www.chateau-serrant.net

The most westerly of the great Loire châteaux, the privately-owned Serrant was begun in 1546 and developed in an entirely harmonious style over the next three centuries. Its pale tufa and dark schist façades, with massive corner towers topped by cupolas, create an air of dignity. Inside, the central pavilion contains one of the most beautiful Renaissance staircases in the region. The château also has

a fine collection of 18th-century furniture and Flemish tapestries, and a library of some 12,000 books.

Serrant's most famous owner was the Marquis de Vaubrun, whose death in battle (1675) is commemorated by a magnificent tomb in the chapel, sculpted by Antoine Coysevox. The Irish Jacobite family of Walsh, shipowners at Nantes, owned Serrant in the 18th century, and the château displays a painting of Bonnie Prince Charlie bidding farewell to Anthony Walsh, whose ship took the prince to Scotland.

In 1830 Serrant passed to the Duc de la Trémoille. His descendents still own it today.

A statue of the Madonna, set in the church wall at Béhuard

Béhuard ❺

Road map C3. 👥 110. 🚌 *Baiche Maine, then taxi.* ℹ️ *Angers tourist office (02 41 23 50 00).*

The narrow lanes of the medieval village on this delightful island in the Loire were made for pilgrims visiting a tiny church fitted into an outcrop of rock. Since pagan times, prayers have been offered on this site for the safety of sailors navigating the often treacherous river.

The church, moving in its simplicity, was built during the 15th century under the protection of Louis XI, who was himself saved from shipwreck on the Loire. The aisle that bisects the little nave is hollowed from the rock.

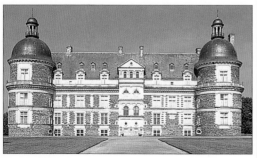

The south façade of Château de Serrant, with huge corner towers

Château du Plessis-Bourré ❻

Road map C3. 🚉 *Angers, then taxi.* **Tel** *02 41 32 06 72.* ⏰ *Feb, Mar, Oct & Nov: Thu–Tue pm only; Apr–Jun & Sep: Fri–Tue, pm Thu; Jul–Aug: daily.* ⏰ *Oct–Jan.* 🎫 🚫 ♿ *grd flr only.*
www.plessis-bourre.com

Set in a moat so wide it looks more like a lake, Château du Plessis-Bourré, with its silvery-white walls and dark slate roofs, seems to float on the water. Built in five years from 1468, it is the least altered and perhaps even the most perfect example of the work of Jean Bourré, whose home it was.

As advisor and treasurer to the king of France, Bourré also oversaw the creation of Langeais (*see p92*) and Jarzé and was influential in the transformation of Loire castles from fortresses into pleasure palaces. The Château du Plessis-Bourré itself is well defended, but its fortifications do not interfere with a design that is orientated towards gracious living. Its wonderful condition stands as a testament to the quality of the materials used in its construction and to the skills of the craftsmen who created it.

After crossing a long, seven-arched bridge, visitors enter

Ceiling of the Salle des Gardes

the château's arcaded courtyard by one of four working drawbridges. The state rooms are surprisingly light and airy, with finely carved stone decoration. A superb painted ceiling in the Salle des Gardes depicts many allegorical and alchemical scenes, including a lively representation of the demonwolf Chicheface, emaciated because she could eat only wives who always obeyed their husbands. Some furniture, mainly dating from the 18th century, is displayed. During the French Revolution, coats of arms on the library fireplace were defaced, and graffiti can still be seen.

Château du Plessis-Bourré, set in its wide moat

BIRD-WATCHING IN THE BASSES VALLÉES ANGEVINES

At the confluence of the Sarthe, Loir and Mayenne rivers, some 4,500 ha (11,100 acres) of land, the Basses Vallées Angevines, are flooded between October and May each year. Thousands of migrating birds visit the area, making it an exceptional bird-watching site.

Perhaps the rarest visitor is the elusive corncrake, which arrives in the grasslands during April. There are more than 300 breeding pairs in the area, making it one of the best sites in western Europe. Protection of this species is aided by enlightened local farming methods, such as late hay harvests.

Insects in the meadows, ditches and rivers attract swifts, hobbys, whinchats and yellow wagtails. In early summer the Basses Vallées resound with birdsong and in the evenings the strange call of the corncrake can be heard.

The flood-plains of Anjou at twilight

For hotels and restaurants in this region see p202 and pp214–15

Château de Montgeoffroy ❼

Road map C3. *Angers or Saumur, then taxi.* **Tel** *02 41 80 60 02.* *mid-Mar–mid-Nov: daily.* *restricted.*

Montgeoffroy is a masterpiece of late 18th-century style, built for the Maréchal de Contades by the architect Nicolas Barré between 1773 and 1775, and beautifully preserved by his descendants. The château is a model of balance, with subtle blue and grey harmonies of stone and paintwork, tall French windows and a lovely park.

The central building is flanked by flat-roofed pavilions, which connect two side wings to the main house. The wings are both rounded off with towers built in the 16th century. One tower houses a harness room smelling of fresh Norwegian spruce, leading to magnificent stables and a fine display of carriages. The chapel in the opposite wing is also 16th-century.

The symmetrical façade of the Château de Montgeoffroy

Hérault de Séchelles by Hubert Drouais

Next to the main house, the kitchen has a collection of 260 copper and pewter pots.

The charming principal rooms are alive with pictures, tapestries and furniture made especially for the château. An innovation in the dining room is a porcelain stove fashioned in the shape of a palm tree, brought from Strasbourg where the *maréchal* (marshal) was governor. His crossed batons are used as a decorative motif in the superbly positioned Grand Salon. The marshal's "friend", Madame Hérault, had her own rooms, where a portrait of their "natural" grandson, Marie-Jean Hérault de Séchelles, can be seen.

Montgeoffroy's stables, where the collection of carriages is housed

Snipe

Lapwing

BIRD SPECIES

In winter, resident ducks, coots and cormorants are joined by geese and swans at the margins and golden plovers in the fields. February sees the arrival of the black-tailed godwits. Pintail ducks, greylag geese, lapwings and black-headed gulls also appear for a time, as do waders such as ruff, snipe, redshank and dunlin. In summer, the meadows dry out, and things are quieter.

Golden plover

BIRD-WATCHER'S CHECKLIST

Road map C3. *Angers, then taxi or hire car.* *Ligue pour la Protection des Oiseaux, Maison de la Confluence, 10 rue de Port-Boulet, Bouchemaine (02 41 44 44 22).* *Day, night and week-end outings.* *Reservations are required for LPO programmes.* **www**.lpo-anjou.org

Best viewing area (Feb–late Jul): confluence of Loir and Sarthe rivers, southwest of Briollay. Take the D107 from Angers to Cantenay-Epinard. Turn right just before the village and follow signs for Le Vieux Cantenay. Return to the D107 via Vaux. Continue north to Noyant, where all of the little roads across the meadows lead to the River Sarthe. Return to Noyant and head for Les Chapelles and Soulaire-et-Bourg. Then take the D109 to Briollay if the road is passable.

Angers ⑧

Situated on the River Maine, only 8 km (5 miles) before it joins the Loire, Angers was once the power base for Foulques Nerra *(see pp50–51)* and the other notorious medieval counts of Anjou. By the 12th century, under the rule of the Plantagenets, Angers became the regional capital of an empire stretching as far as Scotland. Today, it is a thriving university town, with wide boulevards, beautiful public gardens and narrow older streets evocative of its long history.

Angers Cathedral carving

Exploring Angers

Angers is divided into two sections by the River Maine. The oldest part is on the left bank of the river, guarded by the fortress-like 13th-century **Château d'Angers** *(see pp74–5)*. Shielded inside the château's massive walls are the Apocalypse Tapestries, the oldest and largest of France's tapestries, dating from the 14th century *(see pp76–7)*. The **Cathédrale St-Maurice** is just a short walk from the château.

Angers has 46 timber-framed houses, most of them found in the old streets near the cathedral. The best of these is the **Maison d'Adam**, on place Ste-Croix. This 15th-century merchant's house is decorated with carved wooden figures of sirens, musicians and lovers tucked into every angle. The extravagant decoration was a display of the owner's prosperity. Maison d'Adam now houses a craftshop, but its exterior is its main charm.

On the right bank of the River Maine, the old quarter of **La Doutre** (*"d'outre*

Maine", or "the other side of the Maine") is well worth a visit. Formerly an area of tradesmen's establishments, inhabited only by the poor, the district has now been restored and contains a number of well-preserved timber-framed buildings.

A rewarding stroll from rue Gay-Lussac to place de la Laiterie passes many of La Doutre's historic buildings. Included among them are the elegant **Hôtel des Pénitentes** (once a refuge for reformed prostitutes), a 12th-century **apothecary's house** and the restored church of **La Trinité**, which adjoins the ruins of Foulques Nerra's Romanesque **Abbaye du Ronceray** – a Benedictine abbey reserved for daughters of the nobility.

🔒 Cathédrale St-Maurice
pl Freppel. *Tel 02 41 87 58 45.*
◯ *daily.*
This striking cathedral was built at the end of the 12th century, although the central lantern tower was added during the Renaissance period. The façade's Gothic sculptures are still impressive,

Maison d'Adam, the best of Angers' timber-framed houses

although they have become heavily worn over the years and are shell-pocked.

The elegant Angevin vaulting in the nave and the transept is one of the best, and earliest, examples of its kind, and gives a dome-like shape to the high ceiling. The interior is lit through glowing stained glass, which includes a stunningly beautiful 15th-century rose window in the northern transept.

🏛 Musée des Beaux Arts
14 rue du Musée. *Tel 02 41 05 38 00.*
◯ *Oct–May: 10am–noon, 2–6pm Tue–Sun; Jun–Sep: 10am–6:30pm daily.* ● *pub hols.* 📷 ♿

The museum is arranged according to two themes: the history of Angers told through works of art from Neolithic to modern times; and fine arts from the 14th century. Don't miss the intriguing display of religious antiquities on the first floor, including a lapidary Cross of Anjou and a beautiful 13th-century copper-gilt mask of a woman.

🔒 Collégiale St-Martin
23 rue St-Martin. *Tel 02 41 81 16 00.* ◯ *Jun–Sep: 10am–7pm daily; Oct–May: 1–6pm Tue–Sun.* 📷 ♿
www.collegiale-saint-martin.fr
This 9th-century church was reopened in 2006 after 20 years of restoration. It now houses a superb collection of religious statues dating from the 14th century, including a delightful representation of the Virgin preparing to suckle the infant Jesus.

One of the many beautiful public gardens in Angers

COINTREAU

Angers, the city of Cointreau, produces some 15 million litres of the famous liqueur every year. The distillery was founded in 1849 by the Cointreau brothers, local confectioners well known around Angers for their exotic, curative tonics. But it was Edouard, the son of one of them, who created the original recipe. The flavour of this unique colourless liqueur is artfully based on sweet and bitter orange peels.

VISITORS' CHECKLIST

Road map C3. 🙣 *157,000.*
🚉 pl de la Gare.
🚌 pl Molière. 🛈 pl Kennedy
(02 41 23 50 00).
🗓 Wed & Sat.
🎭 Festival d'Anjou (Jul).
www.angersloiretourisme.com

🏛 Galerie David d'Angers

33 bis, rue Toussaint. **Tel** 02 41 05 38 90. ◯ Oct–May: 10am–noon, 2–6pm Tue–Sun; Jun–Sep: 10am–6:30pm daily. ● public hols. 🏷 ♿

The glassed-over ruins of the 13th-century abbey church of Toussaint are filled with plaster casts of the work of local sculptor Pierre-Jean David (1788–1856), known as David d'Angers. His idealized busts and figures were much in demand as memorials for people such as the Marquis de Bonchamps (see p57). Enhanced by the well-lit gallery, they are forceful examples of Academic art.

Sculpture by David d'Angers

🏛 Musée Jean Lurçat et de la Tapisserie Contemporaine

4 bd Arago. **Tel** 02 41 24 18 45. ◯ Oct–May: 10am–noon, 2–6pm Tue–Sun; Jun–Sep: 10am–6:30pm daily. ● public hols. 🏷 ♿

A Gothic masterpiece in La Doutre, this graceful building functioned as a hospital until 1875, the oldest surviving one in France. It was founded in 1175 by Henry II of England, and the Plantagenet coat of arms is displayed with the Anjou heraldry inside the entrance to the grounds. A reconstruction of the dispensary occupies one corner of the Salle des Malades, and a chapel and 12th-century cloisters can be reached through a door at the far end of the gallery. The Hôpital St-Jean now houses the works of the 20th-century artist Jean Lurçat, namely *Le Chant du Monde*, his masterpiece, and many of his vivid tapestries (see p77).

🏛 Musée Cointreau

Bd des Brétonnières, St. Barthélémy d'Anjou. 🚌 **Tel** 02 41 31 50 50. ◯ May–Oct: 11am–6pm daily; Nov–Apr: 11am–6pm Tue–Sat. ● Jan, 25 Dec. 🏷 ♿

From a walkway high above the alambics and bottling machines, visitors can observe the production processes involved in the creation of Cointreau here. The 90-minute tour takes you round the distillery, in the St. Barthélémy district of Angers, ending up with a *dégustation* of the famous orange-flavoured liqueur. Thousands of objects, documents, photos, publicity posters and films illustrate the long history of the company and its famous square bottle.

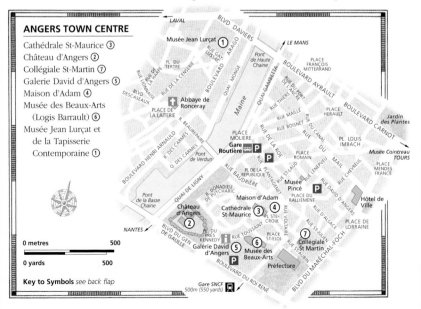

ANGERS TOWN CENTRE

Cathédrale St-Maurice ③
Château d'Angers ②
Collégiale St-Martin ⑦
Galerie David d'Angers ⑤
Maison d'Adam ④
Musée des Beaux-Arts
    (Logis Barrault) ⑥
Musée Jean Lurçat et
    de la Tapisserie
    Contemporaine ①

0 metres   500
0 yards   500

Key to Symbols see back flap

Château d'Angers

The huge drum towers and curtain walls of this powerful feudal fortress were built on the site of Count Foulques Nerra's stronghold between 1228 and 1240. The work was begun at the behest of Blanche of Castille, the mother of Louis IX and regent during his youth. Within the 650-m (2,100-ft) perimeter, later nobles developed a château lifestyle in almost playful contrast to the forbidding schist and limestone towers. The last duke of Anjou, King René I, added charming buildings, gardens, aviaries and a menagerie. After several centuries as a prison, the citadel-château now houses France's most famous tapestries.

The Logis du Gouverneur was built in the 15th century and modified in the 18th century. It is now a restaurant.

★ Moat Gardens
The dry moat, which is a remarkable 11 m (36 ft) deep and 30 m (98 ft) wide, is now filled with a series of geometric flower beds.

Fortress Towers
The 17 towers rise up to 40 m (131 ft) in height. They lost their pepper pot roofs and were shortened as a delaying tactic, following royal orders to demolish them completely during the 16th century.

Formal gardens have been planted in the great courtyard.

The drawbridge leading to the Porte de la Ville (Town Gate) is the entrance to the château.

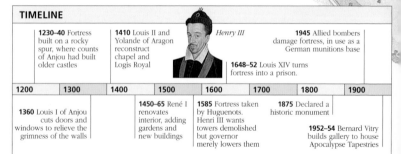

TIMELINE

1230–40 Fortress built on a rocky spur, where counts of Anjou had built older castles	**1410** Louis II and Yolande of Aragon reconstruct chapel and Logis Royal	*Henry III*		**1945** Allied bombers damage fortress, in use as a German munitions base			
			1648–52 Louis XIV turns fortress into a prison.				

1200	1300	1400	1500	1600	1700	1800	1900

1360 Louis I of Anjou cuts doors and windows to relieve the grimness of the walls		**1450–65** René I renovates interior, adding gardens and new buildings	**1585** Fortress taken by Huguenots. Henri III wants towers demolished but governor merely lowers them	**1875** Declared a historic monument		**1952–54** Bernard Vitry builds gallery to house Apocalypse Tapestries	

★ **Apocalypse Tapestries**
*Bernard Vitry's modern
Galerie de l'Apocalypse
displays the Apocalypse
Tapestries (see pp76–7).*

The Roi Window depicts René I,
king of Naples, and his wife,
Jeanne de Laval, kneeling before
the Virgin.

VISITORS' CHECKLIST

Prom du Bout du Monde. 🚌
Tel *02 41 86 48 77.* ⬚ May–
Aug: 9:30am–6:30pm daily; Sep–
Apr: 10am–5:30pm. ⬤ 1 Jan, 1
May, 1 Nov, 11 Nov, 25 Dec. 🎫
📷 ⚒ 🔟 **www**.angers.
monuments-nationaux.fr

**Walkways along the wide
walls** stretch for more than a
kilometre (¾ mile). There are
fine views of the town, as well
as some beautiful gardens.

The towers
are ascended
by spiral
staircases.

The Logis Royal
is where the beautiful
Mille Fleurs tapestries
(see p77) are displayed.

★ **Châtelet**
*Built in 1450 by René I, the
gatehouse still retains its
charming pepper pot roofs.*

★ **Ducal Oratory**
*The ducal oratory
overlooks the Chapelle
St-Geneviève. Equipped
with a fireplace and
decorated with statues
of past owners of the
château, it was used
by the duke and
members of his family.*

STAR FEATURES

★ Apocalypse
Tapestries

★ Ducal Oratory

★ Moat Gardens

★ Châtelet

The Tapestries at Angers

The Apocalypse Tapestries, made in the 14th century for Duke Louis I of Anjou, illustrate the visions of St John from the Book of Revelation. In the turmoil of the French Revolution, the tapestries were thrown out, cut up and used for anything from bed canopies to horse blankets. Restoration began in the mid-19th century. Acclaimed as a masterpiece, the surviving sections of this work stretch for 103 m (338 ft) along a specially-built gallery in the Château d'Angers. Nearly 600 years after their creation, they inspired Jean Lurçat to design his own tapestry sequence, called *Le Chant du Monde*.

Detailed Work
Each of the devils devouring Babylon has a distinct character. The tapestries were woven so skilfully that the front and the back are almost mirror images.

St John appears as the narrator of each vision.

An angel dictates to St John in one of the best-preserved scenes. Elsewhere, the green textiles have faded to beige.

THE FALL OF BABYLON

The Apocalypse Tapestries were woven in 1375–83 in Parisian workshops. Designed by Hennequin de Bruges, who was inspired by Carolingian manuscript illuminations, they depict the end of the world and the coming of a New Jerusalem. The original 90 panels were arranged in 6 chapters, each with an introductory panel and 14 scenes. Scene 66 depicts the Fall of Babylon: "Babylon the Great is fallen, is fallen, and is become the habitation of devils" (Rev. 18:2).

Water is changed to poisonous wormwood at the blowing of the third trumpet in this cataclysmic scene.

Mille Fleurs Tapestries
Displayed in the Logis Royal, these late 15th-century Flemish tapestries are still vibrantly coloured.

Le Chant du Monde

The vast, vaulted interior of the Musée Jean Lurçat *(see p73)* provides a stunning background to *The Song of the World*. This piece, which stretches for 79 m (260 ft) around three sides of the hall, was Lurçat's response to the Apocalypse Tapestries, which he saw for the first time in 1937. The

Jean Lurçat (1892–1966)

ten panels are 4 m (13 ft) high and were woven from wool at workshops in Aubusson between 1957 and 1963. Thematically, the images move from the horrors of Nazi genocide and the bombing of Hiroshima to the conquest of space, conceived as the dawning of a new age.

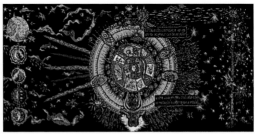

"Ornamentos Sagrados" from Lurçat's *Le Chant du Monde* tapestry

The tumbling towers of Babylon reveal a nest of demons.

Blue backgrounds alternate with red, providing continuity through the series.

THE ART OF TAPESTRY

In medieval times, tapestries were a symbol of luxury, commissioned by royal and noble families to adorn châteaux and churches. Hung on the thick stone walls, they helped to keep the vast rooms warm by preventing drafts.

Medieval tapestry weaver

Paris and Flanders were the centres of tapestry work in the 14th century, where highly skilled weavers followed an artist's full-size drawing, called a "cartoon". Threads were stretched vertically (the warp) on a loom to the length of the finished piece, then coloured threads (the weft) were woven horizontally across them.

Tapestry-making declined from the 16th century, but the 20th century has seen a revival, with artists such as Pablo Picasso and Henri Matisse experimenting in the medium.

Coloured tapestry threads at the Manufacture St-Jean in Aubusson

Brissac's wine cellars

Château de Brissac **9**

Brissac-Quincé. **Road map** C3.
🚉 Angers, then taxi. 🚌 **Tel** 02 41
91 22 21. ⬤ Apr–Jun & Sep–Oct:
Wed–Mon; Jul–Aug: daily; Nov–
Mar: by appointment only. ⬤ Jan,
25 & 31 Dec. 🎦 📷 🐾 🎦
www.brissac.net

The château of the dukes of Brissac, towering above the River Aubance 18 km (11 miles) southeast of Angers, is the tallest along the Loire, and is perhaps the grandest still in private hands. Ownership has passed down a line going back to Charles de Cossé, governor of Paris and marshal of France. His death in 1621 halted the completion of a programme to build a vast palace set upon on the ruins of an earlier fortress.

On the entrance façade, an ornate, 17th-century, domed pavilion soars to 37 m (120 ft) between two 15th-century towers. Fifteen of the 204 rooms are open to the public and are filled with furniture, paintings and tapestries. Among the most striking is the Salle des Gardes, which is decorated with Aubusson tapestries and gilded ceilings. The room is lit through the distinctive paned windows that are a feature of architect Jacques Corbineau's work.

Other memorable rooms are Louis XIII's bedroom and an 1883 opera theatre, still used for concerts. In the château's picture gallery hangs

a 19th-century portrait of Madame Clicquot, matriarch of the famous champagne house and a distant ancestor of the present duke. At the end of the visit, the duke's own wines can be tasted in cellars dating from the 11th century.

Gennes **10**

Road map C3. 🏘 2,000. 🚉 Saumur
or Les Rosiers-sur-Loire. 🛈 square de
l'Europe (02 41 51 84 14). 🛒 Tue.
www.gennes.fr

During the Gallo-Roman period *(see pp48–9)* Gennes, on the south bank of the River Loire, was an important religious and commercial centre. The largest **amphi-theatre** in western France was built on a hillside here more than 1,800 years ago and was used from the 1st to the 3rd centuries for gladiatorial contests. A restoration project in the 1980s revealed the sandstone walls and brick tiers of a stadium that seated at least 5,000 spectators and included changing rooms and an efficient drainage system. In front of the arena, which measures 2,160 sq m (2,600 sq yds), marshlands on the Avort river were probably flooded for aquatic combats and displays.

The area around Gennes is also very rich in Neolithic sites. Among the 20 ancient burial chambers and menhirs nearby is the **Dolmen de la Madeleine**, one of the largest in France. Used as a bakery

The medieval Eglise St-Vétérin in the town of Gennes

until recently, it can be found 1 km (1100 yds) east, past Gennes' medieval **Eglise St-Vétérin** on the D69.

There is a lovely panoramic view over the Loire from **St-Eusèbe**, a ruined church dating from the 11th to the 15th centuries, sited on a knoll above the village. Beside the old nave is a moving memorial to cadets of the Saumur cavalry school *(see p83)* who died trying to prevent the German army crossing the Loire in June 1940.

A bronze statue of Mercury has been discovered on the hill, and this seems to suggest that a temple to the Roman god may have stood here in the Gallo-Roman period.

🏛 Amphithéâtre
Tel 02 41 51 94 70.
⬤ groups only and only by appointment. 🎦

🏛 Dolmen de la Madeleine
⬤ daily. 🐾 restricted.

The Neolithic Dolmen de la Madeleine, near Gennes

Environs

At L'Orbière, 4 km (2½ miles) from Gennes, the sculptor Jacques Warminsky has created a monumental work, named *L'Hélice Terrestre* (*The Earth's Helix*). Occupying a surface area of 875 sq m (1,050 sq yds), this spiralling labyrinth has been cut into the soft limestone hillside. Warminsky and his assistants have carved out a series of galleries, some reaching 14 m (46 ft) below the surface, which expand or contract into organic and mineral forms.

The helix continues its path out to the exterior, where it becomes a spiral assemblage of reversed forms. The two spaces are complementary and represent the universal philosophy of the artist.

Artist Jacques Warminsky at work on *L'Hélice Terrestre*

🏛 **L'Hélice Terrestre**
L'Orbière, St-Georges-des-Sept-Voies. **Road map** C3. 🚉 *Saumur,* then taxi. **Tel** *02 41 57 95 92.* ⏰ *May–Sep: daily; Oct–Apr: daily, pm only (by appt).* 🎫

Cunault ⓫

Road map C3. 🏚 *1,000.* 🚌 *Saumur.* ℹ *Gennes (02 41 51 84 14).* 🎭 *Mois de L'Orgue (May); Les Heures Musicales (Jul & Aug).*

Cunault's pale limestone priory church, the **Eglise Notre-Dame**, has rightly been called the most majestic of all the Romanesque churches in Anjou, if not the whole of the Loire Valley. In the 12th century, Benedictine monks from Tournus in Burgundy built the church in this small village on the south bank of the Loire. They incorporated the bell-tower, dating from the 11th century, from an earlier building. A short spire was added in the 15th century.

Cunault is the longest Romanesque church without a transept in France. Inside, the first impression is of simplicity and elegance. The height of the pillars is impressive; they are topped with 223 carved capitals, decorated with fabulous beasts, demons and religious motifs, and are placed high enough so as not to interfere with the pure architectural lines. Binoculars are needed to see details.

Three aisles of equal width were made to accommodate the crowds of pilgrims who travelled to the church to see its relics, which include one revered as the wedding ring of the Virgin Mary, and the floor is deeply worn beside a 12th-century marble stoup at the foot of the entrance steps. Towards the chancel, the ambulatory is floored with scalloped terracotta tiles. Traces of 15th-century frescoes remain, including a figure of St Christopher.

Other treasures include some impressive furniture in oak and ash, a 13th-century carved wooden reliquary and a painted 15th-century statue representing St Catherine.

The central aisle of Cunault's majestic 12th-century church

CULTIVATED MUSHROOMS

Around 75 per cent of French cultivated mushrooms come from Anjou. The damp, dark caves in the tufa cliffs along the Loire are the perfect environment for the *champignons de Paris*, so called because they were first cultivated in disused quarries in the Paris region before production began in the Loire Valley in the late 19th century. Today, mushroom cultivation is a thriving business, employing around 5,000 people in the region. Growers have been diversifying in recent years, cultivating more exotic mushrooms such as *pleurottes* and *shiitake*, in response to demand from food-lovers.

Oyster mushrooms, known as *pleurottes*

Street-by-Street: Saumur ⑫

The storybook château is set on a hill high above the
town, making it easy for visitors to locate Saumur's
old quarter, which lies mainly between the château, the
river and the main street running straight ahead from
the central bridge over the Loire. The twisting streets
that wind up and down the hill on which the château is
built merit exploration. Saumur's modest size, which
suits sightseeing on foot, is only one of the many
charms of this friendly town.

Theatre
*Saumur's theatre, which opened in
the late 19th century, was modelled
on the Odéon in Paris.*

Rue St-Jean is the heart of
Saumur's main shopping area.

The Hôtel des Abbesses de Fontevraud, at No. 6
rue de l'Ancienne-Messagerie, was built in the 17th
century and has a marvellous spiral staircase.

Maison du Roi
*This pretty Renaissance building at No. 33
rue Dacier once housed royalty but is
now the headquarters of the Saumur Red
Cross. In the courtyard is a plaque to
the much-loved René I of Anjou, who
often held court at Saumur.*

STAR SIGHTS

★ Château de Saumur

★ Eglise St-Pierre

0 metres 50

0 yards 50

Hôtel de Ville

The town hall was originally a manor house forming part of the city's fortified river wall. Built in 1508, subsequent restorations and additions have been in keeping with its Gothic style.

VISITORS' CHECKLIST

Road map C3. 🏠 30,000.
🚉 av David d'Angers. 🚌 square Balzac. 🅿️ pl de la Bilange (02 41 40 20 60). 🔄 Sat.
🎠 Carrousel de Saumur (Jul).
www.saumur-tourisme.com

Place St-Pierre

Saumur's oldest half-timbered houses, dating from the 15th century, are situated in place St-Pierre (Nos. 3, 5 and 6).

★ Eglise St-Pierre

First erected in the 12th and 13th centuries, and completed during the 15th and 16th centuries, this church has a fascinating collection of tapestries.

Maison des Compagnons

is a 15th-century building at the top of La Montée du Fort, which has been restored by a guild of stonemasons whose apprentices can be seen at work.

★ Château de Saumur

Saumur's château is situated next to the Butte des Moulins, a small hill that was once covered with windmills. Views of the town and the Loire and Thouet rivers can be seen from the top of the watchtowers.

KEY

— — — Suggested route

Exploring Saumur

Today, Saumur is best known for its sparkling wines, mushrooms and fine horse riders. It was a centre of Protestant scholarship in the 16th and 17th centuries, until the revocation of the Edict of Nantes in 1685 forced many Protestants to leave. This rich legacy can be seen during a walk through the attractive streets of the old quarter. An excellent self-guided walking tour is available from the tourist office.

Panel from the 15th-century choir stalls in the Eglise St-Pierre

The old quarter

At the heart of Saumur's old quarter stands the **Eglise St-Pierre**, which was built in the late 12th century. Its treasures include the beautifully carved 15th-century wooden stalls in the choir, and the magnificent 16th-century tapestries of the lives of Sts Peter and Florent. The latter was an influential figure in the monastic history of the region. He is depicted being rescued from Roman

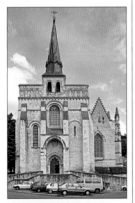

The façade of the Eglise Notre-Dame de Nantilly

persecution, slaying a dragon and founding a monastery.

Nearby, the **Grande Rue**'s limestone and slate houses reflect Saumur's prosperity in the late 16th century under Protestant rule. The "Huguenot Pope", Philippe Duplessis-Mornay, who governed the town between 1589 and 1621, owned the house at No. 45.

The oldest church in Saumur, **Notre-Dame de Nantilly**, was the town's principal place of worship for centuries. It too has a collection of 16th-17th-century tapestries, as well as carved capitals and an epitaph composed by the poet-king René I (*see p53*) to his childhood nurse inscribed on the third pillar on nave's south side.

🏛 La Distillerie Combier

48 rue Beaurepaire.
Tel 02 41 40 23 00. ⭘ Apr, May & Oct: Wed–Sun; Jun–Sep: daily; Nov–Mar: by appt.
🖼 🅿 🛗
www.combier.fr

Since 1834 this distillery has been producing liqueurs according to traditional methods. The recipes remain a well-kept secret, but you can see the process and then have a tasting.

♞ Château de Saumur

Tel 02 41 40 24 40. ⭘ Tue–Sun (only the inner courtyard and exhibition rooms can be visited). 🖼 🅿
The famous miniature of this château in Les Très Riches Heures du Duc de Berry (see p23) shows a white fairy-tale palace. The château was built by Louis I, Duke of Anjou, in the second half of the 14th century. It was constructed on the base of an earlier fortification. The glittering mass of chimney

Skyline of the Château de Saumur

stacks and pinnacles was later simplified to a more sturdy skyline of shortened pencil towers, but the shape of the château remains graceful. The powerful-looking outbuildings that surround the château recall its later, although less pleasant, roles as a Protestant bastion, state prison and finally army barracks.

The château houses two very different museums. The **Musée des Arts Décoratifs** is a collection formed by Count Charles Lair, a native of Saumur, who left it to the château in 1919. It includes paintings, many fine tapestries, furniture, statuettes and ceramics that date from the 13th up to the 19th century. Horse-lovers will find a great deal to delight them in a second museum, the **Musée du Cheval**, founded by a veterinarian at Saumur's cavalry school. Its exhibits trace the development of the horse and its relationship with man from prehistoric times to the present day. They include the skeleton of the unbeaten Flying Fox, winner of the 1899 Epsom Derby, and a collection of beautiful saddles from all around the world.

The château is undergoing extensive renovation following the collapse of part of the ramparts in 2001. The two museums are currently closed, but you can still visit the courtyard and exhibition rooms.

Statuette from the Musée des Arts Décoratifs

🏛 Musée des Blindés

1043 rte de Fontevraud.
Tel 02 41 83 69 95. 🗓 daily.
📷 1 Jan, 25 Dec. 🗌 ♿
www.musee-des-blindes.asso.fr

Owned by the Cavalry and Armoured Vehicles School, this barn-like museum has on display more historic tanks and armoured personnel carriers in working order than any other international military collection.

Beginning with a FT 17 Renault dating from 1917 and moving through the German World War II panzers to the monsters produced today, the museum offers a chance to see at close quarters these veterans of many conflicts.

🏛 Dolmen de Bagneux

56 rue du Dolmen, Bagneux. **Tel** 02 41 50 23 02. 🚉 Saumur. 🚌 🗓 Sep–Jun: Thu–Tue; Jul & Aug: daily. 📷 ♿ www.saumur-dolmen.com

Saumur's main street leads to the suburb of Bagneux. Here, in a local bar's garden, one unexpectedly finds one of the most impressive Neolithic burial chambers in Europe. Visitors can sip drinks in the garden, absorb the impact of the dolmen and marvel at the massive sandstone slabs, some weighing 40 tonnes, that were dragged, tilted and wedged into position 5,000 years ago *(see p48–9)*.

A signpost for the Bagneux dolmen

Environs

The village of St-Hilaire-St-Florent, 2 km (1½ miles) northwest of Saumur on the D751, is well worth a visit for its museums and the famous

A 1917 Renault tank in the collection of the Musée des Blindés

Cadre Noir riding school. It also has a number of wine cellars where visitors can taste and buy the famous Saumur Brut, a sparkling wine that is produced by the *champagne method*. The chalky tufa stone, contained in the soil on which local grapes are grown, is said to add to the wine's natural tendency to sparkle.

🏛 Musée du Champignon

Route de Gennes, St-Hilaire-St-Florent. **Tel** 02 41 50 31 55. 🗓 Feb–mid-Nov: daily. 📷 ♿ www.musee-du-champignon.com

This unique museum takes visitors through a network of limestone caves. Displays show how mushrooms that are grown from spores in bagged or boxed compost thrive in the high humidity and constant temperature of this environment *(see p79)*. The museum has an excellent collection of live mushroom species, as well as of fossils found during quarrying. On offer, and worth tasting, is a local speciality, *gallipettes farcies*, large mushrooms stuffed with a variety of fillings.

🏛 Parc Miniature Pierre et Lumière

Route de Gennes, St-Hilaire-St-Florent. **Tel** 02 41 50 70 04. 🗓 Feb–mid-Nov: 10am–7pm daily. 📷 mid-Nov–Jan. 🗌 ♿ www.pierre-et-lumiere.com

The gallery of a former underground quarry is now the setting for 20 scale models carved from the tufa rock. They represent some of the most famous – and a few less well-known – monuments, towns and villages of the Loire Valley. Among the highlights are Fontevraud Abbey, Tours cathedral and the Château d'Amboise. The models are the work of self-taught sculptor Philippe Cormand.

🏛 Ecole Nationale d'Equitation

Terrefort, St-Hilaire-St-Florent. **Tel** 02 41 53 50 60. 🗓 Apr–mid-Oct: Mon pm–Sat am; Oct–Mar: groups only, by appt. Mornings: show (usually Thu am from Apr–Oct) and buildings; afternoons: buildings only. 📷 ♿ www.cadrenoir.fr

The National Riding School, founded in 1814, is world famous for its team, known as the Cadre Noir because of the riders' elegant black and gold ceremonial uniforms. The Cadre Noir's horses are trained in a distinctive style of dressage, which was first practised in the 19th century. They are taught perfect balance and control and learn choreographed movements that show their natural grace.

During the summer months, visitors can enter the academy team's quarters and watch a training session. There are also regular performances of the spectacular show.

The 5,000-year-old Bagneux dolmen near Saumur

Montreuil-Bellay ⑬

Road map C4. 🏠 *4,500.* 🚌 *Saumur*
🚍 ℹ️ *pl du Concorde (02 41 52 32
39).* 🛒 *Tue am (all year), Sun (May–
Sep).* **www**.ville-montreuil-bellay.fr

Combining an ancient village
and a fascinating feudal
château, Montreuil-Bellay, 18
km (11 miles) south of Saumur,
is one of the most attractive
towns in Anjou. The château
complex occupies a site
which was first fortified in the
11th century by Foulques
Nerra and besieged by Geoffrey Plantagenet during the
following century. In the 13th
century it was surrounded by
strong walls, with a grand tow-
ered entrance (known as the
Château-Vieux) and 11 other
towers. Inside the ramparts is
a collection of mainly late 15th-
century buildings, looking over

**Frescoes in the oratory of the
Château de Montreuil-Bellay**

landscaped terraces falling
to the pretty River Thouet.
The Château-Neuf is an
elegant Renaissance-fronted
building, begun in the late
15th century. The turret was

made famous by the infamous
French noblewoman, Anne
de Longueville (1619–79),
who rode her horse to the
top of its spiral staircase.
The interior of the château
is superbly furnished and has
a number of fireplaces in the
Flamboyant style as well as
splendid painted and carved
ceilings. The 15th-century
frescoes adorning the oratory
are currently under long-term
restoration, but the guided
tour still takes in the medieval
kitchens, with much of their
18th-century cooking equipment. The kitchens are said
to be modelled on those of
the earlier Fontevraud Abbey
(see pp86–7).

🏰 **Château de
Montreuil-Bellay**
Tel *02 41 52 33 06.* ⬜ *Apr–Jun, Sep,
Oct: Wed–Mon; Jul, Aug: daily.* 📷 🎫

Troglodyte Tour ⑮

Caves, cut into the Tufa cliffs beside
the Loire and other limestone-rich
areas in Anjou, are used as dovecotes,
chapels, farms, wine cellars and even
homes. These so-called "troglodyte"
dwellings are extremely old, with some
dating back to the 12th century, and
have hardly changed over the
centuries. They are now
fashionable again as
résidences secondaires for
wealthy Parisians. Life in
and among these caves
is the subject of this
fascinating tour.

0 kilometres   3

0 miles   3

Dénézé-sous-Doué ⑥
In these underground
caves, carved by
Protestant stonemasons
during the 16th-century
Wars of Religion, more
than 400 figures are
chiselled into the walls,
floors and ceilings.

La Fosse ⑦
This inhabited troglodyte
farmhouse is open
to visitors.

**Carved figures at Dénéz
sous-Doué**

GENNES

Montfort

Troglodyte houses at Rochemenier

Rochemenier ⑤
This former troglodyte
farming community has
been turned into a
museum displaying
underground
farmyards, barns,
houses and a simple
rock chapel.

Doué-la-Fontaine ④
The rue des Perrières was
excavated from a stratum of shell
marl *(faluns)*; its "cathedral"
vaults were dug vertically from
the top. The town also has an
amphitheatre cut from the rock
and an outstanding zoo in the
old quarries.

Château de Montsoreau ⓮

Road map C3. 🚂 *Saumur, then taxi.* 🚌 **Tel** *02 41 67 12 60.* ⏰ *Apr: daily pm; May–Sep: daily; Oct–mid-Nov: daily pm.* 🎫 ♿
www.chateau-montsoreau.com

A forbidding battlemented wall is all that remains of the four-sided château built in 1455 for Jean de Chambes and his wife, Jeanne Chabot, heiress to the village of Montsoreau. The view from within the château's former courtyard, however, is far from forbidding: a beautiful octagonal palm-vaulted staircase was added to the northeast of the courtyard around 1520. It carries a frieze, featuring monkeys labouring at its construction, under the heading, *Je le feray*, or, *I will make it*. In Alexandre Dumas'

Château de Montsoreau on the River Loire

novel, *La Dame de Montsoreau*, the jealous Count, Charles de Chambes, forces his wife to lure her lover, the governor of Anjou, Bussy d'Amboise, to the château, where he is brutally murdered. The story is true: the characters lived in the château de Montsoreau. The murder itself, however, took place at a château on the opposite bank of the river, now long-since vanished.

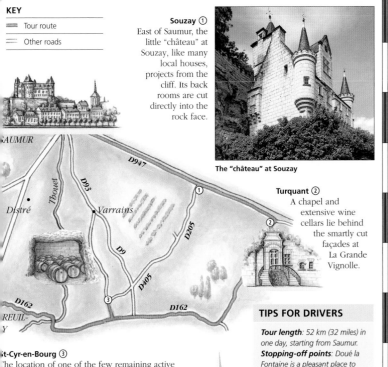

KEY

▬ Tour route

══ Other roads

Souzay ①
East of Saumur, the little "château" at Souzay, like many local houses, projects from the cliff. Its back rooms are cut directly into the rock face.

The "château" at Souzay

SAUMUR

D947

D93

Thouet

Distré ● ● *Varrains*

D205

D9

D405

D162

REUIL-Y

D162

St-Cyr-en-Bourg ③
The location of one of the few remaining active tufa quarries, this vast underground network of galleries is owned by the St-Cyr wine co-operative, which makes a full range of Saumur appellations in these caves.

Turquant ②
A chapel and extensive wine cellars lie behind the smartly cut façades at La Grande Vignolle.

TIPS FOR DRIVERS

Tour length: 52 km (32 miles) in one day, starting from Saumur.
Stopping-off points: Doué la Fontaine is a pleasant place to stop for lunch: Restaurant Le France and Auberge le Bienvenue are excellent restaurants.

Abbaye de Fontevraud 🔟

Stained glass in church

Fontevraud abbey, founded in 1101 by the hermit Robert d'Arbrissel for both women and men, is the largest and most extraordinary of its kind in France. It was run for nearly 700 years by aristocratic abbesses, almost half of them royal-born. They governed a monks' priory outside the main walls, and four distinct communities of nuns and lay sisters, ranging from rich widows to repentant prostitutes, as well as a leper colony and an infirmary. Restoration work has diligently removed traces of the ravages of the Revolution and the subsequent 150 years, when this "queen of abbeys" was used as a prison.

The grand refectory, with its Renaissance ribbed vaulting, is 60 m (200 ft) long.

Nursing sisters of the St Benoît order cared for invalids in this section of the abbey.

★ Chapter House Paintings
The paintings in the Chapter House date from the 16th century. However, some figures were added later.

★ Plantagenet Effigies
These four effigies (gisants), each a realistic portrait, are displayed in the nave of the abbey church.

Grand-Moûtier
The cloisters of the main convent are the largest, and possibly the finest, in France. They have Gothic and Renaissance vaulting and upper galleries built in the 19th century.

STAR FEATURES

★ Plantagenet Effigies

★ Chapter House Paintings

★ Romanesque Kitchens

THE RESTING PLACE OF THE PLANTAGENETS

The medieval painted effigy of Henry Plantagenet, count of Anjou and king of England (1133–1189), lies beside that of his wife, Eleanor of Aquitaine, who died here in 1204. With them are the effigies of their son, King Richard the Lionheart (1157–1199), and Isabelle, wife of his brother, King John. In all, 15 of the family are buried here.

Effigies of Eleanor of Aquitaine and Henry II

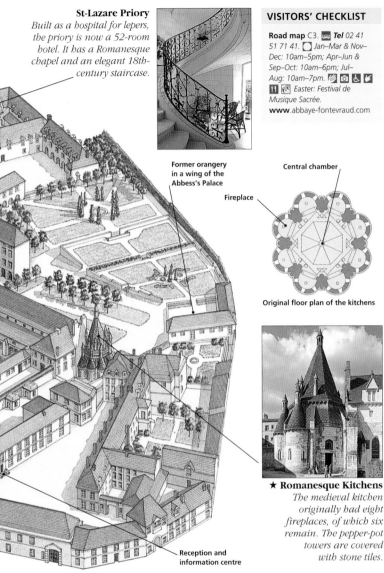

St-Lazare Priory
Built as a hospital for lepers, the priory is now a 52-room hotel. It has a Romanesque chapel and an elegant 18th-century staircase.

Former orangery in a wing of the Abbess's Palace

Central chamber

Fireplace

Original floor plan of the kitchens

★ **Romanesque Kitchens**
The medieval kitchen originally had eight fireplaces, of which six remain. The pepper-pot towers are covered with stone tiles.

Reception and information centre

TIMELINE

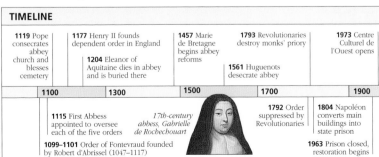

1119 Pope consecrates abbey church and blesses cemetery

1177 Henry II founds dependent order in England

1204 Eleanor of Aquitaine dies in abbey and is buried there

1457 Marie de Bretagne begins abbey reforms

1793 Revolutionaries destroy monks' priory

1561 Huguenots desecrate abbey

1973 Centre Culturel de l'Ouest opens

1100	1300	1500	1700	1900

1115 First Abbess appointed to oversee each of the five orders

17th-century abbess, Gabrielle de Rochechouart

1099–1101 Order of Fontevraud founded by Robert d'Arbrissel (1047–1117)

1792 Order suppressed by Revolutionaries

1804 Napoléon converts main buildings into state prison

1963 Prison closed, restoration begins

TOURAINE

Touraine is known chiefly for the magnificent white châteaux strung out along the broad Loire and its tributaries. Added to these are its rich history and fertile landscape, making it the archetypal Loire Valley region. The rolling terrain and lush forests that once attracted the kings and queens of France continue to work their charm over visitors from all around the world today.

The feudal castles that still exist, at Loches and Chinon for example, remind visitors that this now tranquil region was once a battleground on which the warring counts of Blois and Anjou staged many an epic encounter. It was also here, at Chinon, that Joan of Arc managed to bully the future Charles VII into raising the army that she would lead to victory over the English.

François I brought the influence of the Italian Renaissance to France and set a fashion in architecture that produced the unforgettable châteaux of this region. The most magical – the delicate Azay-le-Rideau, the majestic Chenonceau, and Villandry with its extraordinary formal gardens – were built during this period. At the end of the 16th century, however, Touraine ceased to be a playground for the aristocracy, and its people then settled into the peaceful, unhurried routine that still prevails.

Tours, at the heart of the region, makes a natural base for visitors, who can enjoy its sensitively restored, medieval old town and marvel at the Cathédrale St-Gatien, a Gothic masterpiece.

The rolling terrain and gentle climate of Touraine encourage outdoor pursuits, including hiking, boating and fishing. The area is also famous for its *primeurs*, early fruit and vegetables, such as white asparagus, grown on its low-lying, fertile soils. Its many wines, including the well-known *appellations* of Bourgueil, Chinon and Vouvray, are the perfect accompaniment to the region's excellent cuisine.

A view of the Château de Chinon, on a cliff above the River Vienne

◁ The rooftops of Le Grand-Pressigny, as seen from high on the hill on which the town is built

Exploring Touraine

Criss-crossed by rivers great and small, Touraine sits regally at the heart of the Loire Valley. Châteaux are distributed along the paths of the rivers: Langeais and Amboise by the Loire itself; Ussé, Azay-le-Rideau and Loches by the gentle Indre; and Chenonceau gracefully straddling the Cher. Tours, the main town in the region, is also on the Loire. The Gâtine Tourangelle to the north of the river was once a magnificent forest but was felled progressively from the 11th century by local people in search of wood and arable land. However, small pockets of woodland remain, delightful for walking and picnicking.

Candes-St-Martin, with its 12th- to 13th-century church

KEY

===	Motorway
===	Major road
===	Secondary road
:::	Minor road
===	Scenic route
—	Main railway
—	Minor railway
===	Regional border

GETTING AROUND

Tours is the natural hub of the region. The TGV from Paris takes an hour to St-Pierre-des-Corps, followed by a five-minute shuttle service to the centre of Tours. It is possible to rent a car either from Tours or St-Pierre-des-Corps. The A10 is the fastest route from Paris by car. The D952, running east–west along the north bank of the Loire, is the easiest way to get across the region. The smaller D751 along the south bank passes through attractive countryside. The prettiest drives, however, follow the banks of the Indre.

SEE ALSO

- *Where to Stay* pp203–4
- *Where to Eat* pp215–16

One of Touraine's renowned vineyards

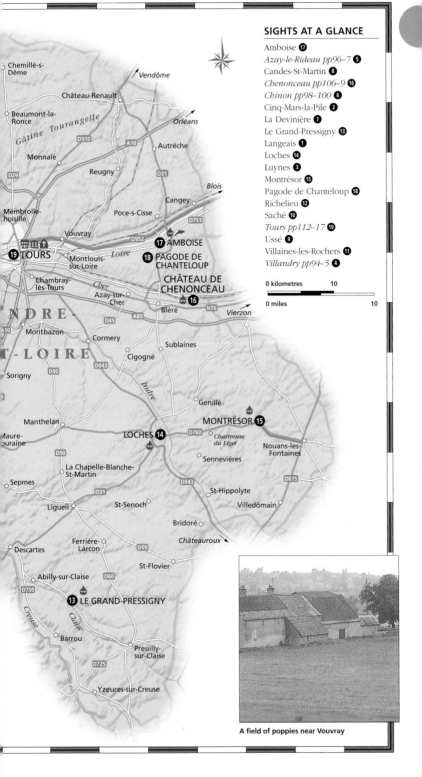

SIGHTS AT A GLANCE

```
0 kilometres        10
▬▬▬▬▬▬▬▬▬
0 miles             10
```

A field of poppies near Vouvray

Chapel of the Château de Langeais, with its curved, wood ceiling

Château de Langeais ❶

Road map D3. 🚉 **Tel** 02 47 96 72 60. ☐ daily. 🌐 ☑
www.chateau-de-langeais.com

The feudal Château de Langeais, looming up in the centre of the small town, was built for King Louis XI between 1465 and 1490 by his treasurer, Jean Bourré. It stands on the site of an earlier fortress built by the fearsome Foulques Nerra (see p50), of which only the rectangular keep remains.

Langeais' forbidding outer walls, towers, drawbridge and heavily machicolated sentry walk contrast strongly with its elegant interior courtyard. The whole has remained virtually unaltered over the centuries. Unlike many of the châteaux in the region, Langeais is largely furnished in keeping with its period, offering a fascinating picture of aristocratic life in the late Middle Ages and Renaissance. Its collection of 15th- and 16th-century furniture, paintings and tapestries was amassed in the late 19th century by its last private owner, the Alsace banker and philanthropist, Jacques Siegfried.

Among the treasures in the castle is the wedding chest brought by the 14-year-old Anne of Brittany when she married the tiny, hunchbacked Charles VIII here in the early hours of 6 December 1491. A waxwork tableau re-creates this clandestine event – both were already betrothed to others – and includes a copy of Anne's cloth-of-gold wedding gown, lined with 160 sable skins.

From the castle's parapets visitors can view the small town below, which has a good Sunday morning food market selling the delicious local melons in season.

The Gallo-Roman tower near Cinq-Mars-la-Pile

Château de Cinq-Mars-la-Pile ❷

Road map D3. 🚉 **Tel** 02 47 96 40 49. ☐ Apr–Jun & 16 Sep–Oct: Sat & Sun; Jul & Aug: Wed–Mon. 🌑 Nov–Mar. 🌐

The most famous inhabitant of the castle of Cinq-Mars was Henri Ruzé d'Effiat, Marquis de Cinq-Mars, and the eponymous hero of a novel by the Touraine writer Alfred de Vigny. The marquis, a favourite of King Louis XIII, rashly became involved in a plot against Louis' minister, Cardinal Richelieu, and was beheaded in 1642, aged 22. Richelieu ordered the castle at Cinq-Mars to be truncated – it is said that even the trees had their crowns chopped off. A pair of towers remain, each with three vaulted chambers, surrounded by an extremely wide moat. The château's fragrant, romantic gardens are adorned with topiary.

The *Pile* in the town's name refers to a strange Gallo-Roman brick tower, more than 30 m (98 ft) high, on a

Towers of the Château de Cinq-Mars-la-Pile

For hotels and restaurants in this region see pp203–4 and pp215–16

Luynes' imposing château, dominating the village below

ridge just east of the village. The south side of the tower, whose purpose and precise date are a mystery, was decorated with 12 multi-coloured brick panels, laid out in a geometric design, four of which are still intact today.

Luynes ❸

Road map D3. 🏘 *5,000.* 🚋 *Tours, then bus.* 🏛 *9 rue Alfred Baugé (02 47 55 77 14).* 🛒 *Sat.* **Château Tel** *02 47 55 67 55.* 🕐 *Apr–Sep: daily.* 🎫 🌐 *www.luynes.fr*

Brooding over this pretty little village is a château, originally called Maillé after the noble owners who rebuilt it in the early 13th century. It is still inhabited by descendants of the first Duc de Luynes, who bought it in 1619, and furnished with Renaissance and 17th-century pieces. The old town developed to the south of the château, and its 15th-century wooden market hall remains.

The remaining 44 arches of a **Gallo-Roman aqueduct** can be seen 1.5 km (1 mile) northeast of Luynes. Standing in isolation amid fields, they are a striking sight.

The wealthy Maillé family also owned a feudal castle on the site of the **Château de Champchevrier**, 10 km (6 miles) northwest of Luynes. The present Renaissance manor house, with various 18th-century additions, is set in a lush forest. Its elegant rooms are beautifully furnished, with particularly fine family portraits and Beauvais tapestries. A pack of hounds is kept at the château.

♣ **Château de Champchevrier** Cléré-les-Pins. **Tel** *02 47 24 93 93.* 🕐 *Mid-Jun–mid-Sep: Mon–Sat, Sun pm only; mid-Sep–mid-Jun: groups by appt.* 🎫 🗺 🚫 *grd flr only.* *www.champchevrier.com*

The Chambre du Roi in the Château de Champchevrier

LIFE IN A MEDIEVAL CHÂTEAU

During times of peace, life in a medieval château took on a pleasant routine. To fill the long winter days, nobles played board games, such as chess and draughts, or cards. Ladies, when they were not playing music or embroidering, had dwarves to entertain them, while the court jester kept banquet guests amused by making fun of everyone, even the king. Mystery plays (dramas based on the life of Christ) were very popular and cycles of these plays often lasted for several weeks. Outdoor pursuits enjoyed during the summer included bowling, archery and ball games, but it was the tournaments, with jousting and sword-play, that provoked the most excitement. Hunting was also favoured by kings and nobles and much practised in the woods and forests of the Loire Valley.

The illumination for August from *Les Très Riches Heures du Duc de Berry*

Château de Villandry ❹

Jeune Infante by Pantoja de la Cruz

The Château de Villandry, dating from the late Renaissance (1536), has an almost Classical elegance. But it is most famous for its superb gardens, which have been restored since the estate was bought in 1906 by the Spanish Carvallo family. Working from 16th-century designs, skilful gardeners mixed flowers and vegetables in strictly geometric patterns. The result is a fascinating insight into a typical Renaissance garden. The garden is on three levels: a water garden at the top, fringed by ancient lime trees; a flower garden level with the château; and, below it, the world's largest ornamental kitchen garden. There is also a play garden for children.

★ **Garden of Love**
Flower designs here symbolize four types of love: tragic, adulterous, tender and passionate.

A collection of Spanish paintings is housed in the château.

Herb garden

Gardeners
Ten full-time gardeners look after the 60,000 vegetables and 45,000 bedding plants in the kitchen garden and the ornamental flower garden.

Maze

Jardin du Soleil

Culture d'Été 2009 du Potager de Villandry

STAR FEATURES

★ Garden of Love

★ Ornamental Kitchen Garden

★ **Ornamental Kitchen Garden**
The current state of the garden can be studied in the plan pinned up near the moat. The plant and vegetable names for each square are listed and the colours shown.

RENAISSANCE KITCHEN AND HERB GARDENS

A 16th-century French treatise on diet reveals that the melons, artichokes, asparagus and cauliflower that fill Villandry's kitchen gardens today all also commonly appeared on Renaissance dinner tables. Herbs were widely used both for their medicinal and culinary applications. They formed the borders in the kitchen gardens of monasteries, such as that at Solesmes *(see p162)*, which were the first to feature geometric planting. Villandry has a *jardin des simples* (herb garden) on its middle level.

Knautia dipsacifolia, from a 16th-century manual on plants

VISITORS' CHECKLIST

Road map D3. **Tel** 02 47 50 02 09. 🚉 *Savonnières, then taxi.* 🕐 *daily from 9am. Feb, mid-Oct–mid-Nov: to 5pm; Mar: to 5:30pm (gardens to 6pm); Apr–Jun & Sep–mid-Oct: to 6pm (gardens to 7pm); Jul–Aug: to 6.30pm (gardens to 7:30pm).* 🖼 📷 ♿ **www**.chateauvillandry.com

Shaped Pear Trees
In Villandry's gardens, nature is completely controlled. The pear trees are carefully pruned to form neat oval shapes.

The elegant stone balustrades above the kitchen garden have been restored.

The pool for irrigating the gardens is shaped like a gilt-framed mirror.

The flower gardens, including the garden of love, level with the south façade of the château

Decorative Cabbage
Ornamental Japanese cabbages were introduced by the mother of the present owner to provide year-round colour in the kitchen garden.

Château d'Azay-le-Rideau

Memorably described by Honoré de Balzac as a "faceted diamond set in the Indre", Azay-le-Rideau is one of the most popular châteaux in the Loire. Its graceful silhouette and richly decorated façades are mirrored in the peaceful waters of its lake, once a medieval moat. Azay was built from about 1514 by Gilles Berthelot, only to be confiscated by François I in 1527. The unknown architect, influenced by Italian design and innovative in his use of a straight staircase, took the defensive elements of an earlier, more warlike age and transformed them into charming ornamental features. Furnished in 16th–19th-century styles, the château has some notable tapestries and a famous portrait said to be of Henri IV's mistress, Gabrielle d'Estrées.

Kitchen
The kitchen, situated in the west wing, has rib vaulting and a huge open fireplace.

La Dame au Bain
Henri IV's haughty mistress Gabrielle d'Estrées is said to feature in the château's finest painting, done in the style of François Clouet.

STAR FEATURES

★ Central Staircase

★ South Façade

AZAY'S CREATORS

Treasurer to François I and mayor of Tours, Gilles Berthelot bought Azay-le-Rideau in 1510. With the help of his wife, he immediately began transforming the medieval ruins into a Renaissance palace befitting his station. The emblems of François I and Claude de France were engraved in stone above various doors in the château in an attempt to flatter the sovereigns. But flattery did not save Berthelot's career – about to be accused of embezzlement, he was forced to flee Azay before the building was completed.

François I's salamander emblem

The elegant turrets
adorn the château's façade rather than protect it, as the sturdy towers of medieval fortresses had done in the past.

Entrance Façade
The entrance façade is dominated by the galleried stairwell topped by a tall gable. Its decoration, full of shells, medallions and candelabras, was influenced by Italian Renaissance artists.

Entrance

VISITORS' CHECKLIST

Road map D3.
Tel *02 47 45 42 04.*
🚃 🅿 *Apr–Jun & Sep: 9:30am–6pm daily; Jul & Aug: 9:30am–7pm; Oct–Mar: 10am–12:30pm, 2–5:30pm.* ⬤ *1 Jan, 1 May, 25 Dec.* ♿ ☑
📷 *Son et Lumières (Jul & Aug: 9:45pm–midnight nightly.*
www.azay-le-rideau.
monuments-nationaux.fr

Red Room
This striking room is the antechamber to the Chambre du Roi *(the King's Bedroom). The walls are hung with portraits of, among others, François I, Henri II and Henri III.*

★ Central Staircase
Azay's most significant design feature is its central staircase, consisting of three straight flights with landings, rather than the spiral staircase that was usual for the period.

Ballroom with Flemish tapestries

★ South Façade
Symmetry is the underlying motif of the exterior design, with its matching turrets and its stripe of decoration imitating machicolations.

Street-by-Street: Chinon ❻

The Château de Chinon stands on a golden-coloured cliff above the River Vienne. Below it, Chinon's old crooked streets resonate with history. The travel-weary Joan of Arc *(see p137)* arrived in the town on 6 March 1429, dismounting by a well in the Grand Carroi. It was here that she began her transformation from peasant girl to the warrior-saint shown sitting astride a charger in a statue in the marketplace. In the nearby Maison des Etats-Généraux, now the Musée d'Art et d'Histoire, Richard the Lionheart lay in state in 1199. His father, Henry Plantagenet, had died a few years earlier in the château, from which he had ruled England as well as much of the Loire Valley.

Tour de l'Horloge
This 14th-century clock-tower, which now houses a small exhibition on the life of Joan of Arc, is the entrance to the château.

0 metres   50
0 yards   50

★ Château
The long walls enclose three separate citadels, some entirely ruined, with magnificent views over the river. Here, in the Great Hall, Joan of Arc recognized the dauphin (see p52), a scene beautifully represented in a fine 17th-century tapestry.

RUE HAUTE ST-MAURICE

RUE BE

QUAI CHARLES VI

Eglise St-Maurice
Henry II rebuilt this church with Angevin vaults, retaining the Romanesque lower part of what is now the steeple.

Ramparts
The château's ramparts are an impressive sight from the opposite bank of the River Vienne.

★ Musée d'Art et d'Histoire
Now a museum of local history, this building was once the scene of France's first attempt at a parliament, which met in an upper room to fund the war against the English in 1428.

VISITORS' CHECKLIST

Road map D3. 🚉 9,000. 🚏 bd
Gambetta. 🚌 bd Gambetta.
ℹ️ pl Hofheim (02 47 93 17 85).
📅 Thu. www.chinon.com

Hôtel Torterue de Langardière's Classical façade is ornamented with wrought-iron balconies.

Caves Painctes were originally dug under the château in the 15th century.

Musée Animé du Vin
Animated figures show 19th-century winemaking and coopering techniques.

Maison Rouge, a superbly restored medieval house, has sculpted beams across its red-brick façade.

Grand Carroi
This crossroads, at the heart of the old fortified town, is where Joan of Arc is said to have dismounted at a well.

François Rabelais
A bronze statue, made in 1882 by Emile Hébert, celebrates the famous satirist.

STAR SIGHTS

★ Château

★ Musée d'Art et d'Histoire

KEY

‒ ‒ ‒ Suggested route

Exploring Chinon

A walk through the narrow streets to the east of
the château shows how much Chinon has to offer.
High above the place Jeanne d'Arc is the remarkable
Chapelle de Ste-Radegonde, carved into the limestone
cliff. Behind this 12th-century frescoed chapel are
ancient hermit caves (now displaying traditional crafts)
and dizzying steps to an underground well. Lower
down the hill, the important Romanesque monastery
of St-Mexme is Chinon's oldest building. Rue Jean-
Jacques Rousseau, leading to the 15th-century
church of St-Etienne, has medieval houses.

♜ Château de Chinon
Tel 02 47 93 13 45.
◯ daily all year. ● 1 Jan, 25 Dec.
▨ ✓
This atmospheric château is
currently undergoing a
major restoration
programme, although
parts can still be
visited. It was built
largely by Henry II,
count of Anjou, who
became Plantagenet king
of England in 1154. It
consists of three castles
– Fort St-Georges,
Château du Milieu and
Fort du Coudray – separated
by moats.
   The main focus of interest is
the Tour de l'Horloge, in
which there are displays on
the life of Joan of Arc. Further
on, in the Logis Royaux, the
west wall is all that remains
of the Great Hall where, in
the light of 50 smoking flares,
Joan picked out the dauphin
from among his courtiers.
   The views of Chinon
from the westerly Fort du
Coudray are delightful.

Statue of Joan of Arc by Jules Roulleau

🏛 Musée d'Art et d'Histoire
44 rue Haute St-Maurice. **Tel** 02 47
93 18 12. ◯ Jun–Sep: daily pm;
Oct–May: Mon–Fri pm. ▨
Among the treasures found in
this intriguing museum of local
history are a fine portrait of
Rabelais by Eugène Delacroix
(1798–1863), and the "Cope of
St. Mexme", the first large Arab
tapestry brought to France.

🏛 Caves Painctes
Impasse des Caves Painctes
Tel 02 47 93 30 44. ▨ only. Jul &
Aug: 11am, 3pm, 4:30pm, 6pm
Tue–Sun. ▨

Oenology and literature come
together in these wine cellars,
which occupy a subter-
ranean quarry dug under
the château in the 15th
century. They are the
headquarters of the
*Confrérie des Bons
Etonneurs Rebelaisiens*,
a brotherhood of wine
growers who meet four
times a year to cele-
brate Chinon wine
and commemorate
Rebelais's humanism and
joie de vivre. The caves are
allegedly inspired by the
author's description of the
Temple of the Divine
Bottle. The price of a
visit includes a wine
tasting session.

🏛 Musée Animé du Vin et
de la Tonnellerie
12 rue Voltaire. **Tel** 02 47 93
25 63. ◯ 15 Mar–15 Oct:
daily; 15 Oct–15 Mar: groups
by appt. ● 1 Jan, 25 Dec. ▨
Here you can taste sharp, dry,
strawberry-like Chinon red
wine, while watching automated models demonstrate the
various stages in wine- and
barrel-making (both are
important Chinon industries)
using some of the museum's
19th-century implements.

FRANÇOIS RABELAIS (1483–1553)

Priest, doctor, humanist and supreme *farceur* of French
literature, François Rabelais is everywhere present in
"Rabelaisie", as the area around La Devinière has become
known. Rabelais enthusiasts will recog-
nize in the old farmhouse the castle of
Grandgousier, besieged by the hordes
of King Picrochole, but saved by the
arrival of giant Gargantua on his mare,
who drowns most of them by
creating a flood with her pro-
digious urination. Rabelais'
thirst for knowledge
imbued his *Gargantua*
and *Pantagruel (see p24)*
with a wealth of learning
that sits surprisingly
easily alongside a ribald
joie de vivre.

The infant Gargantua

**The Tour de l'Horloge, leading to
the middle castle**

View of the Château d'Ussé from the bridge crossing the River Indre

Musée de la Devinière ❼

Road map D3. 🚊 *Chinon, then taxi.* **Tel** *02 47 95 91 18.* ⬜ *Wed–Mon (Jul & Aug: daily).* ⬤ *1 Jan, 25 Dec.* 🖼 🎞

The 16th-century writer François Rabelais was probably born in this pleasant, modest farmhouse, 2 km (1½ miles) southwest of Chinon. It now houses a small museum devoted to the man, his work, and that of his contemporaries.

A dovecote, with its pigeonholes carved into the wall, and some troglodyte rooms add to the interest.

La Devinière farmhouse

Candes-St-Martin ❽

Road map C3. 🚶 *230.* 🚊 *Chinon or Port Boulet, then taxi.* 🛈 *Chinon (02 47 93 17 85).*

Beautifully situated overlooking the shimmering waters where the Loire and Vienne rivers converge, picturesque Candes is famous as the place where St Martin died in 397. Stained glass in the 12th-century church depicts the saint's body being secretly rowed to Tours for burial. The porch of the church was fortified in the 15th century and is adorned with carved heads. Inside, the ceiling is a fine example of Angevin vaulting.

Château d'Ussé ❾

Road map D3. 🚊 *Chinon, then taxi (15km/9 miles).* **Tel** *02 47 95 54 05.* ⬜ *mid-Feb–mid-Nov: daily.* 🖼 ♿ *park & grd flr only.*

With its countless pointed turrets gleaming white against the sombre trees of the Forêt de Chinon, the Château d'Ussé is said to have inspired 17th-century French author Charles Perrault to write the fairy tale *The Sleeping Beauty*. The fortified château was begun in 1462 by Jean de Bueil on the foundations of a medieval castle. In 1485 it was sold to the Espinay family, chamberlains to both Louis XI and Charles VII, who softened the courtyard façades with Renaissance features that blend with its Gothic ancestry.

In the 17th century the north wing was demolished, opening up the main courtyard to views of the River Indre and the Loire Valley. Formal gardens were planted in terraces to the river and an orangery was added, completing the transformation from fortress to aristocratic country house *(see p19)*.

The interior of the château, which is still lived in, is also decorated in a variety of styles. In the tower, visitors can see a waxwork tableau of *The Sleeping Beauty.*

On the edge of the forest is a lovely late-Gothic chapel, with some Renaissance decoration. Inside is a terracotta Virgin sculpted by Luca della Robbia (1400–82).

The late-Gothic exterior of Ussé's chapel

**Mobile by Alexander Calder
(1898–1976) in Saché**

Saché ⑩

Road map D3. 🏃 *1200.* 🚉 *Azay-le-Rideau, then taxi.* ℹ *Azay-le-Rideau (02 47 45 44 40).*

The pretty village of Saché is notable for having been second home to both a writer and an artist of world fame: the 19th-century novelist Honoré de Balzac and the 20th-century American sculptor Alexander Calder, one of whose mobiles adorns the main square.

Admirers of the work of Balzac make pilgrimages to the **Musée Balzac** in the Château de Saché. The plain but comfortable manor house, built in the 16th and 18th centuries, was a quiet place to work and a source of inspiration for many of the writer's best-known novels. The house has been well restored – one of the reception rooms has even been redecorated with a copy of the bright green wallpaper with a Pompeiian frieze that was there in Balzac's day.

It is full of busts, sketches and memorabilia of the great man, including the coffee pot that kept him going during his long stints of writing. There are manuscripts and letters, as well as portraits of the women in Balzac's life: his pretty, but casual, mother; his first love, Madame de Berny; and his loyal friend, Madame Hanska, whom he finally married shortly before his death in 1850.

⛪ Musée Balzac
Château de Saché. *Tel 02 47 26 86 50.* ◯ *daily.* ● *Tue (Oct–Mar); 1 Jan, 25 Dec.* 🎦 ♿ *park.*

Villaines-les-Rochers ⑪

Road map D3. 🏃 *930.* 🚉 *Azay-le-Rideau, then taxi.* ℹ *Azay-le-Rideau (02 47 45 44 40).*

Since the Middle Ages, willows from the local river valleys have been made into baskets in this peaceful town. Production has been on a more substantial scale since the mid-19th century, when the local priest organized the craftsmen into one of France's first cooperatives. Everything is still hand made by the many wickerworkers *(vanniers)* in the town. This explains the relatively high prices of the attractive furniture and baskets on sale in the **cooperative**'s shop. Craftsmen and women can be watched at work in the adjoining studio. In the summer, you can also visit a small museum with displays on the subject of basket-making, the **Musée de l'Osier et de la Vannerie**.

🧺 Coopérative de Vannerie de Villaines
1 rue de la Cheneillère. *Tel 02 47 45 43 03.* ◯ *daily (Sat, Sun: no work in progress).* ● *1 Jan, 25 Dec.* ♿
🏛 Musée de l'Osier et de la Vannerie
22 rue des Caves-Fortes. *Tel 02 47 45 23 19.* ◯ *Apr–Sep: Tue–Sun, pm only; Oct–Sep: groups by appt.* 🎦

A wickerworker in Villaines

Richelieu ⑫

Road map D4. 🏃 *2,000.*
🚉 *Chinon, then bus.*
ℹ *7 pl Louis-XIII (02 47 58 13 62).*
🗓 *Mon, Fri.* **www**.cc-richelieu.com

It would be difficult to find a better example of 17th-century urban planning than the town of Richelieu, on the border between Touraine and Poitou. Its rigid design was the brainchild of Armand Jean du Plessis who, as Cardinal Richelieu and chief minister, was the most powerful man in the kingdom, not excepting his monarch, Louis XIII.

The Cardinal was determined to build a huge palace near his modest family estate of Richelieu. In 1625 he commissioned the architect Jacques Lemercier to draw up the plans and, in 1631, he received permission from the king to proceed, not only with the palace, but also with the creation of a new walled

The Château de Saché, often visited by Honoré de Balzac

town. Lemercier had already designed the Palais Royal and the Church of the Sorbonne in Paris, and would later be appointed chief royal architect. His brothers, Pierre and Nicolas, were put in charge of the building work, which kept nearly 2,000 labourers busy for more than a decade.

The resulting town is a huge rectangle, surrounded by walls and moats (mostly taken up with gardens today) and entered through three monumental gates. The Grande Rue, running from north to south through the centre of the town and linking two large squares, is lined with identical Classical mansions. In the south square, place du Marché, the buildings include the Classical **Eglise Notre-Dame**, the market building with its superb timber framework, and the former law courts, in which the **Hôtel de Ville** (town hall) and a small **history museum** are now housed. In the north square, the place des Religieuses, stands a convent and the Royal Academy, founded by Richelieu in 1640.

Richelieu clearly intended that his palace should be incomparably luxurious, and that vision was impressively realized. It was filled with priceless furniture and works of art, including paintings by

Richelieu's timber-framed market hall

Caravaggio and Andrea Mantegna. Michelangelo's *Dying Slaves*, statues that were originally designed for the tomb of Pope Julius II (now housed in the Louvre in Paris), adorned one of the courtyard façades.

Extremely fearful of competition, Richelieu ordered many of the châteaux in the area to be razed. While his town survived the ravages of the French Revolution intact, the palace, ironically, was confiscated, damaged and then dismantled. Today, only a few garden buildings remain intact, scattered around the 475-ha (1,174-acre) **Domaine du Parc de Richelieu**, though visitors can get an inkling of its former glory from the virtual

Cardinal Richelieu (1585–1642)

presentation, **Visite en 3D du Château de Richelieu** (Tel: 02 47 58 13 62), which takes place at 28 Grand Rue.

🏛 **Musée de l'Hôtel de Ville**
Place du Marché.
Tel 02 47 58 10 13. ⬤ Mon, Wed–Fri (Jul & Aug: daily). ⬤ public hols. 🌐

🌿 **Domaine du Parc de Richelieu**
5 pl du Cardinal. **Tel** 02 47 58 10 09. ⬤ daily. 🚫 restricted.

Environs

Champigny-sur-Veude, 6 km (4 miles) to the north of Richelieu, was one of the châteaux demolished on Richelieu's orders. All that is left is the Renaissance church of **Ste-Chapelle**, with its superb stained glass.

🔒 **Ste-Chapelle**
Champigny-sur-Veude. **Tel** 02 47 95 73 48. ⬤ May–Jun: Thu–Sun pm; Jul–Aug: daily pm; Sep: Mon & Wed–Sun pm. 🌐

BALZAC AT SACHÉ

Honoré de Balzac's (1799–1850) regular stays at the Château de Saché between 1829 and 1837 coincided with the most productive period in his highly industrious career as a writer. Here, hidden well away from his creditors, he would work at least 12 hours a day. Despite starting in the early hours of the morning, he remained able to entertain his hosts, Monsieur and Madame de Margonne, and their guests in the evenings by reading aloud the latest chunk of text from his novels, acting out all the characters as he did so.

Two of Balzac's major novels, *Le Père Goriot (Father Goriot)* and *Le Lys dans la Vallée (The Lily of the Valley)*, were written at Saché. The latter is set in the Indre valley, which can be seen from the house and does indeed have something of that "intangibly mysterious quality" to which Balzac refers with typical eloquence.

Balzac's bedroom at Saché

Le Grand-Pressigny ⑬

Road map D4. 🔼 *1,100.*
🚉 *Châtellerault, then taxi.*
🚌 *Tours.* 🛈 *pl de Savoir Villars
(02 47 94 96 82)* 🔲 *Thu.*

Perched high above the hilly streets of the town, the **Château du Grand-Pressigny** has lovely views over the peaceful Claise and Aigronne valleys.

The château is part medieval ruins, part 15th-century castle and part Renaissance residence. The rectangular, 12th-century ruined keep contrasts dramatically with the elegant 16th-century Italianate wing.

Important prehistoric finds have been made in the area, and various excavations have revealed that the site was a key centre for the large-scale production of flint implements, such as blades, which were then exported as far afield as Switzerland and even Great Britain.

Many of these finds are displayed at the **Musée de la Préhistoire**, which has been built in the château ruins. The collection includes examples of tools and other objects from all the prehistoric eras, along with rock flints, large blocks of obsidian and multi-coloured jasper. Particularly impressive are the yellowish flint blocks known familiarly as "pounds of butter". The museum is also home to an important collection of plant and animal fossils, some of which date back

60 million years. The museum also has a room dedicated to temporary exhibitions and an educational workshop on the ground floor.

On summer afternoons you can visit the **Archéolab**, 6 km (4 miles) northwest at Abilly-sur-Claise, where a transparent dome covers a site that was inhabited by stone cutters between 2800 and 2400 BC.

♣ **Château du Grand-Pressigny**
Tel 02 47 94 90 20. 🔲 *Gardens
Call for opening times.* ♿

♫ **Archéolab**
Abilly-sur-Claise. *Tel 02 47 59 80 82 or 02 47 91 07 48.* 🔲 *mid-Jun–mid-Sep: daily, pm only.* 🗓 🛈

Neolithic tool from the Musée de la Préhistoire

Loches ⑭

Road map D3. 🔼 *7,000.* 🚉 🚌
🛈 *pl de la Marne (02 47 91 82 82).*
🔲 *Wed, Sat.* **www.**loches-tourainecotesud.com

Its medieval streets lined with picturesque houses, the peaceful town of Loches lies beside the River Indre on the edge of the Forêt de Loches. Thanks to its strategic location, it became an important citadel

Agnès Sorel as the Virgin, painted by Jehan Fouquet

in the Middle Ages, with an 11th-century keep begun by Foulques Nerra *(see p50)*. The **château** remained in the hands of the counts of Anjou until 1194, when John Lackland gave it to King Philippe Augustus. John's brother, Richard the Lionheart, recaptured Loches in a surprise attack in 1195. It took Philippe Augustus nearly ten years to retake the castle by force, and eventually it became a French royal residence. It was in the 15th-century **Logis Royal** that Joan of Arc, fresh from her Orléans triumph, persuaded the dauphin to travel to Rheims and be crowned king of France as Charles VII. This event is commemorated in the tapestry-hung Salle Jeanne d'Arc.

Also in the Logis Royal is the tiny, late Gothic private chapel of twice-queen Anne of Brittany, whose ermine tail emblem recurs in the decoration. Also on show in the Logis Royal are a fine *Crucifixion* triptych by Tours painter Jehan Fouquet (c.1420–80) or one of his pupils, and a copy of his colourful *Virgin with Child*, which was modelled on Agnès Sorel, another woman of influence in Charles VII's life.

The massive keep with its surrounding towers is famous for its torture chambers. Prisoners are said to have been locked for years into small wood-and-iron cages. One of the most famous was Lodovico Sforza, the duke of Milan, who died as a prisoner in the **Tour Martelet**, where the tempera wall paintings

Renaissance façade of the Gallery, Château de Grand-Pressigny

For hotels and restaurants in this region see pp203–4 and pp215–16

he made can still be seen.

Beside the château is the Collégiale St-Ours, a church with four pyramid-like spires and a Romanesque portal. Inside is the Gothic marble tomb of Agnès Sorel. The famous beauty is shown with lambs resting at her feet.

Near the Porte Royale lies the **Maison Lansyer**, the birthplace of the 19th-century painter Emmanuel Lansyer. Some of his canvases are on display, along with his collection of Japanese armour and prints. It also houses a folklore museum, exhibiting typical 19th-century interiors.

♠ Château de Loches
Tel **Logis Royal** 02 47 59 01 32; **Donjon** 02 47 59 07 86. ☐ daily. ☐ 1 Jan, 25 Dec. ☒ ☒ Spectacle Nocturne (Aug), phone the Logis Royal to make a reservation.

⌂ Maison Lansyer
1 rue Lansyer. *Tel* 02 47 59 05 45. ☐ Apr–Oct: Wed–Sat; Jun–Sep: Wed–Mon. ☒

Montrésor **⑮**

Road map E3. ⛰ 415. ☐ Loches, then taxi. ℹ Maison du Pays (02 47 92 70 71).

The turreted **Château de Montrésor**, largely built in the 15th and 16th centuries, stands on the site of medieval fortifications built by Count Foulques Nerra (*see p50*). It was bought in the mid-19th century by Count Branicki, an émigré Polish financier closely linked to the future Napoleon III. Still owned by Branicki's descendants, the château's Second Empire decor remains virtually unaltered.

As well as a fine collection of early Italian paintings and some elegant portraits, there are many gold and silver pieces. The rooms, with their mounted stags' and wolves' heads and dark panelling, retain a somewhat Central European feel. The château terrace and informal gardens offer fine views of the river.

An estate building, which used to house the château's wine press, has been converted into the Maison du Pays, an information centre

and showcase for the Indrois Valley and its products.

The village's small Gothic and Renaissance church was built by Imbert de Bastarnay, lord of Montrésor, adviser to François I and grandfather of Diane de Poitiers (*see p108*). On the beautiful marble Bastarnay tomb lie *gisants* (effigies) of the lord, his lady and their son, guarded by angels and with their feet resting on greyhounds. The tomb, believed to be the work of the Renaissance sculptor Jean Goujon (c.1510–68), is decorated with statues of the apostles. There are also some wonderful Flemish and Italian paintings in the church, and a 17th-century *Annunciation* by Philippe de Champaigne (1602–74), the Baroque painter who worked on the Luxembourg palace in Paris with Nicolas Poussin.

In a lovely forest setting, 4 km (2½ miles) west of the village of Montrésor, are the ruins of the **Chartreuse du Liget**, a Carthusian monastery founded by the Plantagenet king Henry II of England in

Farm buildings and poppy fields near the village of Montrésor

expiation for the murder of Archbishop Thomas à Becket. The nearby Chapel of **St-Jean-du-Liget** is decorated with 12th-century frescoes.

♠ Château de Montrésor
Tel 02 47 92 60 04. ☐ Apr–Oct: daily; Nov–Mar: Sat & Sun pm. ☒ ☒ ☒ park and ground floor only.

♠ Chapelle St-Jean-du-Liget
Tel 02 47 92 60 02 (Chartreuse du Liget). ☐ phone first. ☒

Château de Montrésor, built on medieval fortifications

Château de Chenonceau ⓰

Chenonceau, stretching romantically across the River
Cher, is considered by many the loveliest of the Loire
châteaux. Surrounded by formal gardens and wooded
grounds, this pure Renaissance building was transformed over the centuries from a modest manor into
a palace designed solely for pleasure. Visitors can
wander freely through the beautifully furnished rooms,
using a multilingual iPod as a guide. A small waxworks museum illustrates the château's history, and the
site also includes a restaurant in the old stables and a
miniature train ride down the lovely tree-lined drive.
Wines from Chenonceau's own vineyards are on sale.

★ **Cabinet Vert**
*The walls of Catherine de
Médicis' study were originally
covered with green velvet.*

Chapelle
*The chapel has a vaulted
ceiling and pilasters
sculpted with acanthus
leaves and cockle
shells. The stained
glass, ruined by a
bomb in 1944, was
replaced in 1953.*

Louise de Lorraine's room
was painted black and
decorated with monograms,
tears and knots in white after
the death of her husband.

The Tour des Marques
survives from the 15th-century
castle of the Marques family.

STAR FEATURES

★ Cabinet Vert

★ Grande Galerie

★ Formal Gardens

The Three Graces
*Painted by Charles-André
Van Loo (1705–65),* The
Three Graces *depicts the
pretty Mailly-Nesle sisters,
all royal mistresses.*

Tapestries
As was the practice in the 16th century, Chenonceau is hung with Flemish tapestries that both warm and decorate its well-furnished rooms.

VISITORS' CHECKLIST

Road map D3.
Tel 02 47 23 90 07.
Chenonceaux.
daily. Jul, Aug: 9am–8pm; Nov–Jan: 9am–5pm; Feb–Jun, Sep & Oct: 9am–6pm.
Promenade Nocturne (Jun: 9:30–11pm Sat & Sun; Jul & Aug: 9:30–11pm daily).
www.chenonceau.com

CHÂTEAU GUIDE

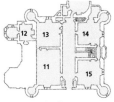

Ground floor

First floor

1 Vestibule
2 Salle des Gardes
3 Chapelle
4 Terrasse
5 Librairie de Catherine de' Médicis
6 Cabinet Vert
7 Chambre de Diane de Poitiers
8 Grande Galerie
9 Chambre de François I
10 Salon Louis XIV
11 Chambre des Cinq Reines
12 Cabinet des Estampes
13 Chambre de Catherine de Médicis
14 Chambre de Vendôme
15 Chambre de Gabrielle d'Estrées

★ Grande Galerie
Catherine de Médicis added this elegant gallery to the bridge designed by Philibert de l'Orme in 1556–9 for Diane de Poitiers.

Chenonceau's Florentine-style gallery, which stretches across the River Cher for 60 m (197 ft)

The Creation of Chenonceau

Chenonceau reflects the combined influence of five women, who brought a feminine touch to this graceful building. First came Catherine Briçonnet, wife of the royal chamberlain, who supervised the construction of the château. Later, Diane de Poitiers, Henri II's mistress, created a formal garden and built a bridge over the Cher. After Henri's death, his widow, Catherine de Médicis, reclaimed the château and topped the bridge with a gallery. Chenonceau survived the 1789 Revolution – because of local respect for Louise Dupin, wife of a tax collector – to be restored by Madame Pelouze in the 19th century.

Sphinxes
Inscrutable stone sphinxes guarding the entrance to the gardens came from the Château de Chanteloup, which was destroyed in the 19th century (see p111).

Diane de Poitiers
Henri II's mistress, here painted by François Clouet, created a large, formal garden, as well as the bridge across the Cher.

★Formal Gardens
The current designs of the formal gardens of Diane de Poitiers and Catherine de Médicis date from the 19th century.

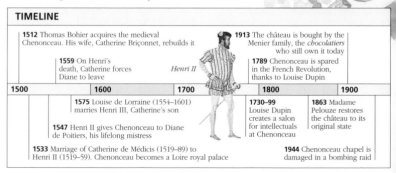

TIMELINE

1512 Thomas Bohier acquires the medieval Chenonceau. His wife, Catherine Briçonnet, rebuilds it

1559 On Henri's death, Catherine forces Diane to leave

Henri II

1575 Louise de Lorraine (1554–1601) marries Henri III, Catherine's son

1547 Henri II gives Chenonceau to Diane de Poitiers, his lifelong mistress

1533 Marriage of Catherine de Médicis (1519–89) to Henri II (1519–59). Chenonceau becomes a Loire royal palace

1913 The château is bought by the Menier family, the *chocolatiers* who still own it today

1789 Chenonceau is spared in the French Revolution, thanks to Louise Dupin

1730–99 Louise Dupin creates a salon for intellectuals at Chenonceau

1863 Madame Pelouze restores the château to its original state

1944 Chenonceau chapel is damaged in a bombing raid

1500		1600	1700		1800	1900

Catherine de Médicis
After ousting Diane de Poitiers, Catherine de Médicis made her own mark on Chenonceau's design. She built the Grande Galerie over the Cher and added a formal garden to rival Diane's.

Louise Dupin
A well-read beauty with huge brown eyes, Louise Dupin entertained all the literary lions of her day, including Montesquieu and Voltaire. One guest, Jean-Jacques Rousseau, stayed on to tutor her children and famously praised Chenonceau's cuisine, claiming he had become "as plump as a monk".

Catherine de Médicis' emblem

Madame Pelouze bought Chenonceau in 1863 and restored it to Catherine Briçonnet's original design. Fortunately, she stopped short of taking down the Grande Galerie.

Court Festivities
Catherine de Médicis staged lavish balls and festivities at Chenonceau, some featuring plaster triumphal arches and statues designed by Francesco Primaticcio, others with living "nymphs" leaping out of the bushes chased by "satyrs".

Louise de Lorraine
Catherine de Médicis left Chenonceau to her daughter-in-law, Louise de Lorraine. Louise had her room redecorated in black upon the death of her husband, Henri III.

Catherine Briçonnet supervised the creation of an innovative château design, with rooms leading off a central vestibule on each floor.

The Château d'Amboise, high above the town and the River Loire

Amboise ⑰

Road map D3. 🏠 *13,000.* 🚊
🛈 *quai du Général de Gaulle
(02 47 57 09 28).* 🚌 *Fri, Sun.*
www.amboise-valdeloire.com

The bustling little town of
Amboise is mostly visited
for its château, but this is not
the town's only attraction.

⚜ Château d'Amboise
***Tel** 02 47 57 00 98.* 🔲 *daily.* ● *1
Jan, 25 Dec.* 🎫 🔲 *(underground
rooms and towers).* 🎭 *A la Cour du
Roy François (Jul & Aug: Wed & Sat).*
www.chateau-amboise.com

The late-Gothic Chapelle St-Hubert, with its
highly ornate roof and spire

While much of the château
has been destroyed, it is still
possible to see the splendour
that prevailed
when first
Charles VIII and
then François I
brought the Italian
love of luxury and
elegance to the
French court.
    Amboise has
also played a
tragic part in
history. In 1560 a
Protestant plot to gain
religious concessions
from the young King
François II was un-
covered, and 1,200
conspirators were
slaughtered, their
bodies strung up
from the castle and
town walls, from
trees, and even
from the balcony
on the Logis du Roi.
    This horrifying
episode was to spell
the end of Amboise's
glory, and over the
years that followed,
the château was
gradually disman-
tled. The enchanting,
late-Gothic **Chapelle
St-Hubert**, where
Leonardo da Vinci
is said to be buried,
has fortunately sur-
vived, perched on
the ramparts of the
château. Carvings on
the exterior lintel of

**Sculpted detail from the
Logis du Roi**

the chapel depict St Hubert
and St Christopher. Some of
the guard rooms and state
rooms in the part-Gothic, part-
Renaissance **Logis du Roi** are
open to visitors, along with
fascinating 19th-century
apartments once
occupied by King
Louis-Philippe.
Flanking the Logis
du Roi is the **Tour
des Minimes**, the
original entrance to
the château, with
its impressive spiral inner
ramp, up which horsemen
could ride.

⚜ Château du Clos-Lucé
2 rue du Clos-Lucé. ***Tel** 02 47 57 00
73.* 🔲 *daily.* ● *1 Jan, 25 Dec.* 🎫
🔲 *restricted.* www.closluce.com
This graceful Renaissance
manor house on the outskirts
of Amboise was the last home
of Leonardo da Vinci. In 1516
François I enticed Leonardo
to the royal court at Amboise
and the following year settled
him at Le Clos-Lucé (called
Cloux at the time), where he
lived until his death in 1519.
    While here, Leonardo
almost certainly conceived
the plans for the Château de
Chambord *(see pp132–5)*. He
is known to have made various
drawings of double staircases,
similar to the one that was built
there. His bedroom, reception
room, study, kitchen and a
small chapel built for Anne of
Brittany by Charles VIII are
open to visitors. There are

models made from Leonardo's astonishing technical drawings in the basement.

🐟 Aquarium du Val de Loire

Lussault-sur-Loire. **Tel** 02 47 23 44 57. ☐ daily. ● 3 wks Jan, 2 wks Nov. ☒ ☒
www.aquariumduvaldeloire.com
With more than 10,000 fresh-water fish on display in its 53 tanks, it is the largest such collection in Europe.

Environs

Behind the Renaissance Château de la Bourdaisière, now also a hotel (*see p203*), hides a *potager* with 500 varieties of tomato, 150 kinds of lettuce and over 200 different herbs. Sample its produce at the Tomato Festival (mid-Sep).

⛪ Château et Jardins de la Bourdaisière

Montlouis-sur-Loire. **Tel** 02 47 45 16 31. ☐ May–Oct: daily. ☒ ☒
www.chateaulabourdaisiere.com

Leonardo da Vinci's bedroom at the Château du Clos-Lucé

Pagode de Chanteloup 🔞

Forêt d'Amboise. **Tel** 02 47 57 20 97. ☐ Apr–Sep & school hols: daily. ☒ ☒ park only.
www.pagode-chanteloup.com

In the forest of Amboise, south-west of Amboise itself, stands this Chinese-style pagoda, more than 44 m (140 ft) high and built in seven stories, linked by steep spiral stair-cases. Each layer is smaller than the preceding one and contains an airy, octagonal room with a domed ceiling.

LEONARDO DA VINCI (1452–1519)

François I, who developed a love of Italian Renaissance art during his military campaigns there, persuaded Leonardo to join his court at Amboise, offering him an annual allowance and free use of the manor house at Clos-Lucé. The great Italian painter arrived in Amboise in 1516 with some precious items in his luggage – three major paintings, in leather bags tied to a mule. One of them was the *Mona Lisa*, which François was to buy and place in the royal collection (hence its presence today in the Louvre in Paris).

Leonardo spent the last three years of his life at Le Clos-Lucé as the *Premier Peintre, Architecte, et Mécanicien du Roi* (first painter,

Engraving of Leonardo da Vinci

architect and engineer to the king), mainly writing and drawing. As he was left-handed, the paralysis that affected his right hand was not a major handicap. Fascinated by hydrology, he produced plans to link the royal residences of the Loire Valley via waterways and even proposed rerouting the river. He also organized a series of elaborate court festivities, planning them down to the last detail with the same meticulous care he lavished on his scientific designs.

A model of Leonardo's prototype for a "car"

Seven avenues lead into the forest from the pagoda, which is reflected in a large lake.

This is all that is left of a splendid château built by Louis XV's minister, the Duc de Choiseul (1719–85). In the 1770s, Choiseul fell out with the king's mistress, Madame du Barry – he had been a protégé of her predecessor Madame de Pompadour – and was exiled from Versailles. He retreated to the château he had bought at Chanteloup in 1761 and rebuilt it. He spent his time entertaining on a large scale and dabbling in farming. After his death, the château was abandoned and then pulled down in 1823.

An exhibition in the pavilion explains the history of the once magnificent château and, for those brave enough to climb, there are impressive views of the Loire Valley from the top of the tower.

The Pagode de Chanteloup, in the heart of the forest of Amboise

Street-by-Street: Tours ⑲

The medieval old town, Le Vieux Tours, is full of narrow streets lined with beautiful half-timbered houses. Now sensitively restored, it is a lively area crammed with little cafés, bars and restaurants that attract locals as well as tourists. There are also numerous chic fashion boutiques and small shops devoted particularly to craft work and to stylish kitchen equipment. At its heart is the attractive place Plumereau, which in fine weather is filled with parasol-shaded café tables.

| 0 metres | 50 |
| 0 yards | 50 |

★ Maison de Tristan
The brick-and-stone 15th-century Maison de Tristan is renowned for its vaulted spiral staircase.

Musée du Gemmail
Inside the vine-covered Hôtel Raimbault, a museum displays jewel-like works of art made from stained glass.

Place Pierre-le-Puellier
A Gallo-Roman and medieval cemetery has been excavated in this square, which once formed part of a Renaissance cloister.

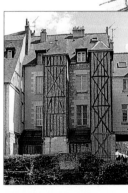

STAR SIGHTS

★ Place Plumereau

★ Maison de Tristan

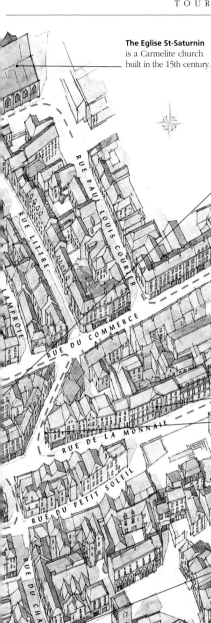

The Eglise St-Saturnin
is a Carmelite church
built in the 15th century.

★ Place Plumereau
*The lively square is surrounded by tall,
half-timbered buildings dating from
the 15th century.*

Hôtel de la Monnaie
*This 18th-century mansion, at
No. 5 rue de la Monnaie,
stands in a street of mainly
17th-century houses.*

Carved Posts
*The wooden
posts on the
twin-gabled
house at the
corner of
the rue du
Change are
adorned with
carved figures
and scenes.*

Tour Charlemagne
*A terracotta relief depicting
St Martin can be seen on
the Tour Charlemagne, one
of two towers that have
survived from the medieval
Old Basilica of St-Martin.*

KEY

– – – Suggested route

Exploring Tours

The pleasant Cathedral city of Tours, popular with foreign students eager to learn the country's purest French, is a perfect base for exploring Touraine's impressive châteaux. But Tours itself, its medieval heart imaginatively restored, repays exploration, too. Once a major Gallo-Roman centre and later filled with pilgrims flocking to St Martin's tomb, it has remained prosperous over the centuries. Yet despite the rapid expansion beyond the Loire and Cher rivers, it has kept its unhurried, provincial charm.

Tours's Pont Wilson, recently rebuilt, spanning the Loire

Tours Town Center

The area of the town close to the magnificent **Cathédrale St-Gatien** *(see pp116–17)* was part of the original Roman settlement. In the 3rd century AD, it was enclosed by a wall, the shape of which can still be seen in the rue des Ursulines, circling the cathedral and the Musée des Beaux Arts. The rue du Général-Meunier, a curving cobbled street of elegant houses once occupied by the clergy, follows the line of a Roman amphitheatre.

On the west side of Tours, a religious community grew up around the sepulchre of St Martin *(see p49)*. The saint's tomb now lies in the crypt of the late 19th-century New Basilica, which was built on the site of the considerably larger, medieval Old Basilica. Two stone towers – the **Tour Charlemagne** and the **Tour de l'Horloge** – on either side of the rue des Halles, survive from the earlier building. Not far from the towers, the **place Plumereau**, with its charming medieval houses and tempting cafés, attracts locals, foreign students and tourists in large numbers.

The half-timbered house at No. 39 rue Colbert bears a wrought-iron sign dedicated to the *Pucelle Armée* (the armed maid), recalling that Joan of Arc *(see p137)* bought her suit of armour from a workshop here, before setting out to liberate Orléans in 1429. Nearby is the **place Foire-le-Roi**, a square where, thanks to a permit granted by the king in 1545, regular fairs were once held. The main merchandise was the silk that had been a key factor in the town's economy since the middle of the previous century. Of the gabled houses that line the square, the finest is the Renaissance Hôtel Babou de la Bourdaisière, named after the

finance minister to François I, who lived there. Slightly to the west, the 13th-century **Eglise St-Julien** stands on the site of an abbey founded in the 6th century.

The central bridge crossing the Loire, the **Pont Wilson**, is known locally as the *pont de pierre* (stone bridge). It is an exact replica of the town's original 18th-century bridge, which collapsed suddenly in 1978, making national headlines. It was rebuilt following the original design after a referendum of local residents backed the idea.

⛫ Musée des Beaux-Arts
18 pl François-Sicard. **Tel** *02 47 05 68 73.* ◻ *Wed–Mon.* ● *1 Jan, 1 May, 14 Jul, 1 & 11 Nov, 25 Dec.* ▨
The Museum of Fine Arts, conveniently situated next to the Cathédrale St-Gatien, is shaded by a cedar of Lebanon nearly two centuries old and fronted by attractive formal gardens. Once the Archbishop's Palace, the building dates mainly from the 17th and 18th centuries.

Its collections of paintings range from the Middle Ages to contemporary artists and include two celebrated altarpiece panels by Andrea Mantegna, *The Resurrection* and *Christ in the Olive Grove*, which were painted between 1456 and 1460 for the church of San Zeno in Verona.

To the right of the entrance courtyard is an outbuilding housing a huge stuffed circus elephant that died in Tours in the early 20th century.

Christ in the Olive Grove (1456–1460) by Andrea Mantegna

The Hôtel Goüin's elaborate Renaissance façade

🏛 Hôtel Goüin & Musée Archéologique

25 rue du Commerce. *Tel 02 47 66 22 32.* ⬤ temporarily closed for renovation, call before visiting. 🖼

This fine example of early Renaissance architecture, its highly ornamented façade beautifully re-created following World War II destruction, now houses the city's archaeological museum. The collection, which commences with the prehistoric era and continues to the 18th century, includes an interesting group of Celtic

coins from the Chartres area, whose different values are denoted not by numerals but by pictures of animals. The most famous exhibit in the museum, however, is a set of scientific instruments collected in 1743 by the owner of Chenonceau château.

🏛 Musée des Vins de Touraine

16 rue Nationale. *Tel 02 47 61 07 93* ⬤ Wed–Sun. ⬤ public hols. 🖼

The vaulted cellars and parts of the cloisters of the 13th-century **Eglise St-Julien** now form a wine museum, with a huge Renaissance winepress, displays on early viticultural

history, and collections of wine making tools dating from the Middle Ages to the 19th century. In an adjacent courtyard there is an original Gallo-Roman winepress, which was discovered near Azay-le-Rideau in 1946.

Exhibits in the Musée des Vins de Touraine

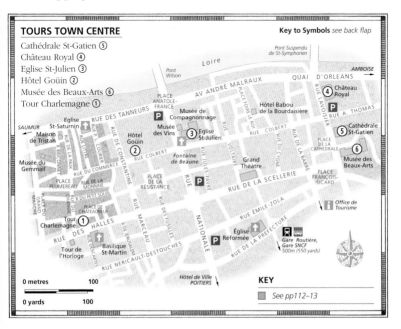

TOURS TOWN CENTRE

Key to Symbols *see back flap*

KEY

☐ See pp112–13

0 metres 100

0 yards 100

Tours: Cathédrale St-Gatian

The foundation stone of Tours' Gothic cathedral, named after St Gatian, a 3rd-century bishop, was laid in the early 13th century. Because building work continued until the mid-16th century, the cathedral provides an illustration of how the Gothic style developed over the centuries. The Early Gothic chancel was the first area to be completed, while the nave and transept represent the Middle or High Gothic period and the highly decorated west façade is Flamboyant (or Late) Gothic.

★ West Façade
The richly carved Flamboyant west façade has three portals surmounted by a fine rose window.

Cloître de la Psalette
The cloisters, which lead off the north aisle, are made up of three galleries dating from the mid-15th and early 16th centuries.

Inside the North Tower is the elegant 16th-century "royal staircase".

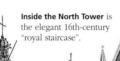

Colombe tomb

The narrow nave has a vaulted ceiling, dating from the late 15th century.

★ Colombe Tomb *(1499)*
The marble tomb of Charles VIII's and Anne of Brittany's infant sons features lifelike effigies by Michel Colombe or one of his pupils.

Fresco
This 14th-century fresco, restored in 1993, shows St Martin giving half his cloak to a beggar.

For hotels and restaurants in this region see pp203–4 and pp215–16

VISITORS' CHECKLIST

Pl de la Cathédrale. *Tel 02 47 70 21 00.* 9am–8pm daily (to 7pm in winter). 11am, 6:30pm Sun.

Colombe Statue
This statue of Tours' famous sculptor, Michel Colombe, stands in a square near the cathedral.

In the chancel, the stained-glass windows, depicting Christ's Passion and the legends of St Martin and other saints, date from around 1265.

★ Stained-Glass Windows
The stained glass is notable for its rich, strong colours and for the paler stained panels, or grisailles, *which let in more light than ordinary stained glass.*

STAR FEATURES

★ Colombe Tomb

★ Stained-Glass Windows

★ West Façade

⚓ Château Royal de Tours
25 ave André Malraux. *Tel 02 47 70 88 46.* 2–6pm Tue–Sun. **Atelier Histoire de Tours** (entry from church square). *Tel 02 47 70 88 59.* 2–6pm Wed & Sat. public hols.

The château, which served as a royal residence in the 13th and 15th centuries, was erected on top of the ancient Gallo-Roman walls, parts of which are still visible.

The buildings, including the 18th-century Logis de Mars, used to house a waxworks museum of historic figures. However, this has recently closed down and given way to a contemporary art centre hosting a broad range of exhibitions.

Though only occasionally open to the public, the Tour de Guise can still be admired from the outside. The tower is named after the Duc de Guise, who made a daring escape while being held as a prisoner here following the assassination of his father at the Château de Blois in 1588 *(see pp126–7)*.

In the Renaissance Logis des Gouverneurs, the exhibitions of the **Atelier Histoire de Tours** explain the city's long urban history using three-dimensional models and plans.

⛪ Musée du Compagnonnage
8 rue Nationale. *Tel 02 47 21 62 20.* mid-Sep–mid-Jun: Wed–Mon; mid-Jun–mid-Sep: daily. public hols.

Housed in part of the abbey once attached to the medieval **Eglise St-Julien**, this unusual museum is devoted to crafts-manship. It has a fascinating collection of "master pieces" made by members of a guild of itinerant *compagnons* (journeymen) who applied to be awarded the prestigious title of Master Craftsman. Displays cover many trades, ranging from the work of stonemasons to that of clog makers, and even include some extraordinary spun-sugar creations.

A barrel on display in the Musée du Compagnonnage

GARLIC AND BASIL FAIR

On 26 July, the Feast of St Anne, the place du Grand-Marché in the Old Town, near the colourful covered market *(Les Halles)*, is the scene of the traditional Garlic and Basil Fair *(Foire à l'Ail et au Basilic)*. Pots of basil form a green carpet, and stalls are garlanded with strings of garlic heads, purple onions and grey or golden shallots.

Stalls laden with garlic and basil in the place du Grand-Marché

BLESOIS AND ORLEANAIS

hese two closely-linked regions are excellent starting points for an exploration of the central Loire Valley. The area's forests and marshlands have attracted nature lovers for centuries. During the Renaissance, magnificent hunting lodges were built by kings and nobles throughout the area, including the great Chambord, the sumptuously furnished Cheverny and the charming Beauregard.

Blésois and Orléanais remain richly forested, with abundant game, including rabbits and hares, deer and wild boar. The great forest of Orléans, still magnificent, contrasts with the heaths and marshy lakes of the Sologne, a secretive region of small, quiet villages and low, half-timbered brick farmhouses. Although a paradise for hunters and fishermen, other visitors rarely venture into the depths of this area.

The northern stretch of the Loire flows through towns whose names resound throughout the history of France. Bridges and castles at Gien, Orléans, Beaugency and Blois all assumed strategic significance during wars from the Middle Ages to the 20th century.

It was at Orléans in 1429 that Joan of Arc, lifting the English siege of the town, galvanized the spirit of the French army engaged in the Hundred Years' War. The modern city's proximity to Paris has led to its growth as a commercial centre, but careful reconstruction after the devastation of World War II has meant that a sense of the past survives in the old *quartier*.

During the Wars of Religion, the château at Blois was sunk in political intrigue. Now restored, its walls still echo with the events of 1588, when the Duc de Guise was assassinated on the orders of the king, Henri III.

To the west of the region, the River Loir, smaller than its majestic sound-alike, flows through the countryside of the Vendômois and also through Vendôme itself, one of the most attractive towns in the region. Vendôme's cathedral, La Trinité, is only one of the memorable churches in Blésois and Orléanais, many of them decorated with early frescoes and mosaics.

Anglers taking part in a competition on a local canal

◁ **The nave of the Cathédrale Ste-Croix in Orléans**

Exploring Blésois and Orléanais

Orléans, the largest city in Blésois and Orléanais, lies at the northernmost point of the River Loire. To the west is the Petite Beauce, fertile, wheat-growing land, while to the east is the great forest of Orléans, dense and teeming with wildlife. Blois, downstream from Orléans, is also surrounded by forests. To the south, the Sologne is a land of woods and marshes, scattered with small lakes, or *étangs*. The River Cher marks its southern border, as it flows through charming villages.

One of the region's stone farmhouses

SIGHTS AT A GLANCE

Beaugency ⑭
Beauregard ⑪
Blois pp124–7 ⑤
Briare-le-Canal ⑳
Chambord pp132–5 ⑬
Chamerolles ⑯
Chaumont-sur-Loire ⑥
Cheverny ⑩
Gien ⑲
Lavardin ②
Meung-sur-Loire ⑮
Montrichard ⑦
Orléans pp138–9 ⑰
St-Aignan-sur-Cher ⑧
St-Benoît-sur-Loire ⑱
Sologne ㉑
Talcy ④
Thésée ⑨
Trôo ①
Vendôme ③
Villesavin ⑫

KEY

═══	Motorway
═══	Major road
───	Secondary road
═══	Minor road
───	Scenic route
───	Main railway
───	Minor railway
═══	Regional border

SEE ALSO

• *Where to Stay* pp204–5

• *Where to Eat* pp216–17

Map labels: Droué, Chartres, Mondoubleau, Ouzouer-le-Marché, D357, Coul, Le Mans, D357, Epuisay, N10, Morée, Binas, Marchenoir, MEUNG-SUR-LOIRE ⑮, TRÔO ①, Montoire-sur-le-Loir, ③ VENDÔME, CHÂTEAU DE TALCY ④, D917, D917, A10, ⑭ BEAUGEN, Loir, D957, LAVARDIN ②, LOIR-ET-CHER, Mer, N152, D951, St-Amand-de-Vendôme, N10, Herbault, Loire, ⑬ CHÂTEAU DE CHAMBORD, BLOIS ⑤, Tours, CHÂTEAU DE BEAUREGARD ⑪, D923, CHÂTEAU DE VILLESAVIN ⑫, N, sur-Be, D952, Beuvron, ⑩ CHÂTEAU DE CHEVERNY, CHÂTEAU DE CHAUMONT ⑥, Contres, Mur-de-So, Pontlevoy, D675, D765, D956, Romorantin Lanthena, MONTRICHARD ⑦, ⑨ THÉSÉE, A85, Cher, D976, Villefranc, sur-Cl, ⑧ ST-AIGNAN-SUR-CHER, Châtillon

GETTING AROUND

The fastest route by car from Paris is *L'Aquitaine* autoroute (A10), which passes through Orléans and Blois. Some Paris-to-Tours TGVs stop at Vendôme, only a 45-minute journey. The Corail express train from Paris takes one hour to Les Aubrais (a suburb of Orléans with a connecting train to the city centre) and a further 30 minutes to Meung-sur-Loire and Blois via Beaugency. From Tours, a local line follows the Cher, stopping at Montrichard, Thésée and St-Aignan. Bus services between towns are extremely limited, especially during the school holidays. The drive along the D976, which parallels the River Cher, is very scenic, and the roads through the cool, forested areas of the region are tranquil and pleasant.

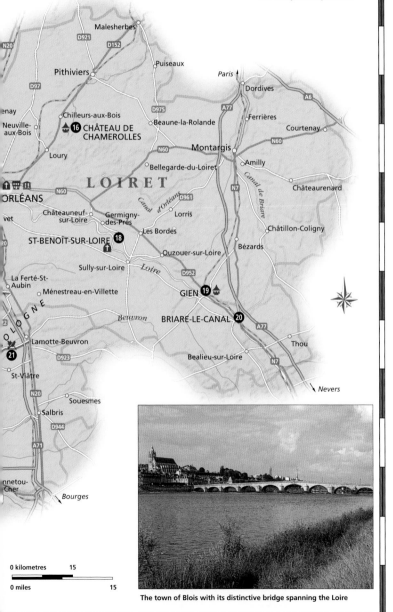

The town of Blois with its distinctive bridge spanning the Loire

Trôo's "speaking well"

Trôo **1**

Road map D3. 🏛 *320.* 🚌 *Vendôme, then taxi.* 🚃 **ℹ** *Mairie (02 54 73 55 00).*

On a cliff above the Loir, this village should be entered from the top through its ruined medieval gate. To the left of the gate is a covered "speaking well"; at 45 m (150 ft) deep, it produces a very clear echo.

During the Middle Ages, a massive fortress stood here. It was fought over at the end of the 12th century by Richard the Lionheart, who lost it to the French king, Philippe Augustus. In 1590, the uncrowned Henri IV ordered the fortress to be dismantled. All that remains today is a mound, or *motte*, from the top of which there is a good view of the valley below.

Parts of the **Eglise St-Martin**, nearby, date from the 11th century, including the nave walls. The windows in the square Angevin tower are decorated with ornamental columns.

Steep paths wind down the hill towards the attractive **Château de la Voûte**, passing on the way the pretty flower gardens of a group of troglodyte dwellings, some of which are open to visitors. At the bottom of the hill is the

Grotte Pétrifiante, a cave full of stalactites that have been developing for more than 4,000 years.

Across the river, the little church at **St-Jacques-des-Guérets**, built in the 12th century, is justly famous for its 13 murals, painted in a distinctive Byzantine style. They were rediscovered in 1890 during restoration work. The *Christ in Majesty* in the apse is particularly beautiful.

St-Gilles chapel in nearby Montoire-sur-le-Loir is also worth a visit. It has some even finer 12th–century murals, remarkable for the range of colours used.

Lavardin **2**

Road map D3. 🏛 *250.* 🚌 *Vendôme, then taxi.* 🚃 **ℹ** *Montoire-sur-le-Loir (02 54 85 23 30).*

The remaining fortifications of Lavardin's ruined **château**, towering above the reconstructed medieval bridge leading to the village, are an impressive sight. Situated on the boundary between the Capetian and Angevin kingdoms, the fortress was for centuries a key stronghold in battles between the French crown and the Plantagenet

Delicate murals in Lavardin's Eglise St-Genest

dynasty. In 1590, like the castle at Trôo, it was partly destroyed on the orders of Henri IV.

Memorable buildings in the town include the 11th-century town hall and the stone houses in the route de Villavard. Lavardin's treasure is the Romanesque **Eglise St-Genest** with its fragile and charmingly naïve murals dating from the 12th–16th centuries. Scenes from the life of Christ are alongside astrological symbols. Among the oldest of the frescoes is the *Baptism of Christ*, which is found at the entrance to the left chapel, together with the *Passion* and *Christ in Majesty*.

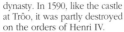

⛪ **Château de Lavardin**
Tel *02 54 85 07 74 (Mairie).* ◯ *May: Sat & Sun; Jun–Sep: Tue–Sun.* 🧳 🖼

Vendôme **3**

Road map D3. 🏛 *18,000.* 🚉 🚌 **ℹ** *47–49 rue Poterie. (02 54 77 05 07).* 🍷 *Fri & Sun.*

One of France's most scenic towns, Vendôme is built over a group of islands in the Loir, its bridges, water gates and old stone buildings forming a delightful tableau. Now that it is just 45 minutes from Paris by rail, it has become a popular weekend retreat for many Parisians.

Situated on the border between the French and English feudal territories, the town changed hands many times. During the Hundred Years' War, it passed to the Bourbons in 1371, eventually becoming a duchy in 1515.

Later, held by the Holy League during the Wars of Religion, it was recaptured by Henri IV in 1589; the skulls of his leading Catholic opponents are by far the most grisly exhibit in the **Musée de Vendôme**. Set in an old abbey's cloisters, the museum also has a harp said to have been played by the ill-fated

Ornate façade of Abbaye de la Trinité in Vendôme

Marie-Antoinette, and some frescoes in the adjoining chapter house.

Vendôme's jewel is the abbey church of **La Trinité**, founded in 1034 by Geoffroy Martel, son of Foulques Nerra. It stands beside a 12th-century Romanesque bell-tower, with a spire reaching more than 80 m (260 ft). The church's bold, ornate façade was created by Jean de Beauce, who also designed the Old Bell-tower of Notre-Dame de Chartres. Its flame-like tracery is a typically virtuoso statement of the Flamboyant Gothic style.

Inside, beyond the transept, which dates from the 11th century, are choir stalls carved with amusing figures. To the

Wooden carving from La Trinité

left of the altar, a pretty latticework base with teardrop motifs once held a cabinet displaying a famous relic, which was said to be the tear supposedly shed by Jesus on the grave of Lazarus.

Shopping is centred around the place St-Martin, with its 15th-century clock-tower and carillon, and a statue of the count of Rochambeau, who commanded the French forces during the American Revolution. There is also a graceful, *fin-de-siècle* covered market just off rue Saulnerie.

The best views of the town's old fortifications are from the square Belot. Also visible from here is the Porte d'Eau, a water gate built during the 13th and 14th centuries, which once controlled the water for the town's mills and tanneries.

In the centre of town is the Parc Ronsard, with its 15th-century wash house, the Lavoir des Cordeliers, and the Old Oratorians College, which dates from the 17th and 18th centuries. Vendôme's ruined château stands on a bluff above the town, with the 12th-century Tour de Poitiers at one corner. The garden offers some delightful panoramic views of the town.

🏛 **Musée de Vendôme**
Cloître de la Trinité. **Tel** 02 54 77 26 13. ☐ Wed–Mon. ● Sun (Nov–Mar); 1 Jan, 1 May, 25 Dec. 🎥

Talcy's 300-year-old wine press, still in working order

Château de Talcy ❹

Road map E3. 🚆 *Mer, then taxi.* **Tel** 02 54 81 03 01. ☐ Apr–Sep: daily; Oct–Mar: Wed–Mon. ● 1 Jan, 1 May, 25 Dec. 🎥 🎫 also night tours Jul–Aug. 🎪 events change every year. **www**.monum.fr

After the grander châteaux of the Loire Valley, Talcy comes as a delightful surprise: a fascinating, human-scale home, hiding behind a stern façade. The original building, a donjon, dates from the 15th century. It was transformed by Bernardo Salviati, a Florentine banker and cousin of Catherine de Médicis, who bought it in 1517 and added to the building significantly.

In 1545, the poet Pierre de Ronsard *(see p24)* fell in love with Salviati's 15-year-old daughter, Cassandre. Over the following decade, his love for her inspired the sonnets of his famous collection, known as *Amours de Cassandre*.

Bernardo Salviati gave Talcy its feudal look, adding the crenellated sentry walk and fake machicolations to the gatehouse. In the first courtyard, with its arcaded gallery, is an elegant domed well. A 3,000-bird dovecote in the second courtyard, dating from the 16th century, is the best-preserved in the Loire.

A huge wooden wine press, over 300-years-old but still in working order, is worth a look. The château's vineyards are no longer productive, so the press is not in use. The grounds also contain old flower gardens.

Inside the château, the charming rooms have retained their original 17th- and 18th-century furnishings.

The Lavoir des Cordeliers in Vendôme's Parc Ronsard

Street-by-Street: Blois **5**

A powerful feudal stronghold in the 12th century, Blois rose to glory under Louis XII, who established his court here in 1498. The town remained at the centre of French royal and political life for much of the next century. Now an important commercial centre for the agricultural districts of the Beauce and Sologne, Blois, with its harmonious combination of white walls, slate roofs, and redbrick chimneys, is the quintessential Loire town. The hilly, partly pedestrianized old quarter, bordered by the river, the château, and the cathedral, is full of architectural interest.

Hôtel d'Alluye
Blois' outstanding Renaissance mansion was built in 1508 by Florimond Robertet, treasurer to three kings.

Façade des Loges, the château's most theatrical side, has Renaissance window bays rising in tiers to a gallery.

★ Château de Blois
The rich history of the Château de Blois is reflected in its varied architectural styles.

Blois as seen from the Loire, with the three spires of the Eglise St-Nicolas in the centre

★ Eglise St-Nicolas
This striking, three-spired church once belonged to a 12th-century Benedictine abbey. Its high, narrow Gothic nave leads to an apse of magical beauty, sheltered by elegant Corinthian columns and lit through lovely blue glass.

KEY

– – – Suggested route

Escalier Denis-Papin
Named after the native son (1647–1714) who invented the pressure cooker, these stairs provide a remarkable view over the town and the river.

VISITORS' CHECKLIST

Road map E3. 🚅 *51,000.* 🚉
🚌 *pl de la Gare.* ℹ️ *23 pl du Château (02 54 90 41 41).* 🍷
Tue & Sat. 🎭 *Son et Lumière: Château de Blois (mid-Apr–mid-Sep: daily); Tous sur le Pont (music & theatre; early Jul).*
Musée d'Histoire Naturelle
Couvent des Jacobins. **Tel** *02 54 90 21 00.* ⏰ *Tue–Sun pm.*
⬤ *1 Jan, 1 May, 1 Nov, 25 Dec.*
📷 ♿ **Musée d'Art Religieux**
Couvent des Jacobins. **Tel** *02 54 78 17 14.* ⏰ *Tue–Sat pm.* ⬤
1 Jan, 1 May, 1 Nov, 25 Dec. ♿

Cathédrale St-Louis
Most of the original building was destroyed by a hurricane in 1678. The present cathedral was erected during the reign of Louis XIV.

Maison des Acrobates, in the place St-Louis, has carvings of medieval characters on its posts.

Couvent des Jacobins now houses museums of religious art and natural history.

★ Quartier Vieux Blois
This well-preserved area of Blois has some marvellous 16th-century buildings. This galleried town house is at the top of rue Pierre de Blois.

STAR SIGHTS

★ Château de Blois

★ Eglise St-Nicolas

★ Quartier Vieux Blois

Château de Blois

Home to Kings Louis XII, François I and Henri III, no other Loire château has such a sensational history of skulduggery at court. It culminated with the stabbing, on the order of Henri III, of the ambitious Duc de Guise, leader of the Catholic Holy League *(see pp54–5)*. This macabre event, which took place in the king's own bedroom, marked the end of the château's political importance. The building itself juxtaposes four distinct architectural styles dating from the 13th century, through the Gothic and Renaissance periods, to the Classical. The château has benefited from major restorations, which began in 1989.

Porcupine emblem of the House of Orléans

Gaston d'Orléans Wing
The simplicity of the Classical design of this wing, as shown in the ceiling of the entrance hall, marked a departure from the rich decor of the Renaissance.

King Louis XII
A statue of Louis XII (1462–1515) is the centrepiece of the entrance archway. Known as "Father of the People", he was popular for his benevolent domestic policies.

The Tour du Foix remains from the ramparts that surrounded the 13th-century feudal fortress.

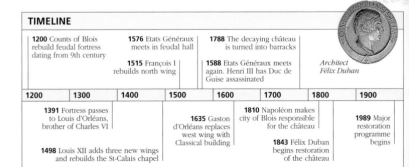

STAR FEATURES

★ François I's Staircase

★ Cabinet de Catherine de Médicis

★ Salle des Etats Généraux

TIMELINE

1200 Counts of Blois rebuild feudal fortress dating from 9th century			**1576** Etats Généraux meets in feudal hall		**1788** The decaying château is turned into barracks		
			1515 François I rebuilds north wing		**1588** Etats Généraux meets again. Henri III has Duc de Guise assassinated	*Architect Félix Duban*	

1200	1300	1400	1500	1600	1700	1800	1900
	1391 Fortress passes to Louis d'Orléans, brother of Charles VI			**1635** Gaston d'Orléans replaces west wing with Classical building	**1810** Napoléon makes city of Blois responsible for the château		**1989** Major restoration programme begins
	1498 Louis XII adds three new wings and rebuilds the St-Calais chapel					**1843** Félix Duban begins restoration of the château	

★ **Cabinet de Catherine de Médicis**
The queen's room has 237 carved panels, four with secret cupboards for her jewels, works of art or, some believed, poisons.

VISITORS' CHECKLIST

Pl du Château. 02 54 90 33 32. daily. Jan–Mar: 9am–noon; Apr–Jun: 9am–6:30pm; Jul–Aug: 9am–7pm; Sep: 9am–6:30pm; Oct: 9am–6pm, Nov–Dec: 9am–12:30pm. 1 Jan, 25 Dec. *Ainsi Blois vous est conté (see p42).*

The nave of the St-Calais chapel was pulled down during the 17th century to make way for Gaston d'Orléans' wing, leaving only the chancel standing today.

The Salle d'Honneur, previously partitioned, has a sumptuous west fireplace bearing the salamander and ermine emblems of François I and his wife, Claudia.

The Gothic Louis XII wing has intricate, decorative brickwork.

Statue of Louis XII

★ **François I's Staircase**
Enclosed in an octagonal well, the staircase, with its highly ornate carving, is a Renaissance tour de force. From its open balconies, the royal family could watch events in the courtyard.

★ **Salle des Etats Généraux**
Used for royal receptions and Etats Généraux meetings (see pp54–5), the 13th-century room survives from the original fortress.

Château de Chaumont, towering above the town

Château de Chaumont ⑥

Chaumont-sur-Loire.
Road map D3. 🚉 *Onzain, then taxi.* 🛈 02 54 51 26 26.
⬜ *daily.* ⬛ *1 Jan, 1 May, 1 & 11 Nov, 25 Dec.* 🎫 Festival International des Jardins (May–mid-Oct). **www**.monum.fr

Seen from the south, Chaumont, set on a wooded hill above the river, appears like a fantasy of a feudal castle. Its tall, white donjon and round towers, built between 1466 and 1510, were never tested in battle and have thus remained in immaculate condition.

The main entrance, with its double drawbridge and elaborate machicolated parapets, is beautiful. Emblems carved on the towers include the crossed Cs of Charles II d'Amboise, whose family had owned a previous 12th-century fortress on the site.

When Charles inherited Chaumont in 1481, he undertook several major alterations. These were early examples of the Renaissance architectural style in France and included the east wing, with its elaborate frieze, and the south wing, with its entrance towers.

At one end of the south wing, the projecting octagonal tower, enclosing the main spiral staircase, predates those at Blois and Chambord *(see pp126–7 and pp132–5).*

Catherine de Médicis, wife of Henri II, acquired the château in 1560. Legend has it that Catherine's astrologer, Ruggieri, used the tower connected to her room as an observatory. Here he is said to have shown the queen the fate of her three royal sons in a magic mirror. Catherine's chamber also has a balcony adjoining the attractive chapel, which was restored towards the end of the 19th century. In 1562 Catherine gave Chaumont to Diane de Poitiers, mistress of the late Henri II, after forcing her out of Chenonceau *(see pp108–9).* Diane's entwined Ds and hunting motifs are carved on the machicolations of the entrance and on the east wing.

Stained glass from the dining room at Chaumont

Subsequent owners either neglected the château or altered it, sometimes radically, to their own purposes. One 18th-century owner, abandoning the fortress design, demolished the north wing so that the whole courtyard was opened up to the river views.

Sweeping improvements began in 1875 when Prince Amédée de Broglie came to live in the château with his wife Marie, a sugar heiress. Their lavish lifestyle can be sensed in the handsome stables, which once housed an elephant, given to them on a visit to the Maharajah of Kapurtala in India.

The council room has tapestries by Reymbouts and majolica floor tiles, brought from a 17th-century Palermo palace, while the library has medallions made in the château by Jean-Baptiste Nini in the 1700s. The château's park was landscaped in 1884 by Achille Duchêne and closely follows the lines of an English country garden.

Montrichard ⑦

Road map D3. 🏘 3,500. 🚉 🚌 🛈 1 rue du Pont (02 54 32 05 10). 🛒 Mon pm, Fri am. **www**.montrichard.fr

This small village built of tufa rock is dominated by the

Montrichard, seen from across the River Cher

ruins of its **château**. The 11th-century drawbridge, archers' tower and the remains of its Renaissance apartments remain, and the keep houses the small **Musée du Donjon** on local life.

Adjoining the château is the **Eglise Ste-Croix**. Here, in 1476, the future Louis XII reluctantly wed Jeanne, the tragically deformed daughter of Louis XI. The marriage was later annulled so Louis could marry Anne of Brittany.

♣ **Château de Montrichard & Musée du Donjon**
Tel 02 54 32 57 15.
⬜ *Easter–Sep: daily.* 🎟
📷 *events and times change every year; call 02 54 32 05 10 for more information.*

White tiger from Beauval Zoological Park

St-Aignan-sur-Cher ❽

Road map E3. 🏠 *3,700.* 🚉 *St-Aignan-Noyers-sur-Cher.* 🚌
ℹ️ *02 54 75 22 85.* 🗓 *Sat.* **www.tourisme-valdecher-staignan.com**

Once a river port, St-Aignan is now an engaging summer resort for boating, swimming and fishing. The town is dominated by the Renaissance château of the dukes of Beauvillier and the collegiate church of St-Aignan, a marvel of Romanesque art.

The château interior is not open to the public, but visitors can climb 19th-century stairs to look at its two elegant wings and enjoy the views from its courtyard terrace as a reward for their exertions. Ruined towers and walls remain from a feudal fortress built by the counts of Blois. In rue Constant-Ragot, leading to the château and church, there is a fine half-timbered Renaissance house on the corner with rue du Four.

The **Collégiale de St-Aignan**, with its two impressive bell-towers, was begun around 1080. Its majestic chancel and sanctuary are built over an earlier Romanesque church, which now forms the crypt. Once used as a cowshed, the crypt still retains its Romanesque feel. Among the important frescoes to survive here are a portrayal of the miracles of St Gilles in the southern chapel and a rare 11th-century *Christ in Majesty* on the chancel vault.

Some of the 250 sculpted capitals in the main church are carved with scenes from the Old and New Testaments as well as allegories of sin and punishment. Others are worked with decorative motifs. In the Chapel of Our Lady of Miracles, the 15th-century ceiling paintings are equally fascinating.

The **Beauval Zoological Park**, 2 km (1¼ miles) south of the village, is among France's best. It contains

St-Aignan's Chapel of Our Lady of Miracles

some 4,000 animals, a superb jungle house, a lagoon of piranhas, and impressive landscaped enclosures for big cats, including several magnificent prowling white tigers.

🐾 **Beauval Zoological Park**
Tel 02 54 75 50 00. ⬜ *daily.* 🎟 ♿

Thésée ❾

Road map E3. 🏠 *1,300.* 🚉 ℹ️ *St Aignan (02 54 75 22 85); Mairie (02 54 71 40 20).* 🗓 *Thu.*

Just outside the charming little wine village of Thésée is the most important Gallo-Roman site in the Loire-et-Cher *département*, Les Maselles.

Impressive ruined walls with brick courses testify to the skills of stonemasons who, in the 2nd century AD, built Tasciaca. This settlement was a major staging post and ceramic-making centre on the road between Bourges and Tours. The **Musée Archéologique** within the town hall displays a quite dazzling and instructive array of jewels, coins, pottery and other interesting artifacts from this little-known site.

🏛 **Musée Archéologique**
Hôtel de Ville.
Tel 02 54 71 40 20.
⬜ *Wed–Mon, pm only.* 🎟

Fresco of *Christ in Majesty*, from the Eglise de St-Aignan

Classical façade of the Château de Cheverny

Château de Cheverny ⑩

Road map E3. *Tel* 02 54 79 96 29.
⬜ daily. 🎫 ♿ grd floor & park only.
www.chateau-cheverny.fr

The elegance of Cheverny's white tufa façade, with its pure Louis XIII lines, was achieved in a single phase of construction between 1620 and 1634, with all the finishing touches completed by 1648.

Initiating a new architectural style for the châteaux of the Loire Valley, Cheverny has no defensive elements, such as large turreted towers or formidable entrances. Instead, its Classical façade is striking in its simplicity. The château stands on the site of a previous castle, owned by the Hurault family. Henri Hurault, with his wife, Marguerite, led the château's reconstruction, and the family has retained its ownership.

Jean Mosnier worked on the interior for ten years, using gilded beams, panels and ceilings. His finest work is in the dining room, with its scenes from Don Quixote's travels, and in the king's bedroom, where the combined effect of wall-hangings, painted ceilings and a bed canopied in Persian silk is stunning. The château's largest room, the Salle des Armes, displays a collection of arms and armour and is adorned with Mosnier's paintings and a large Gobelins tapestry, the *Abduction of Helen*.

Paintings in the château include a portrait of Cosimo de' Médici by Titian and Pierre Mignard's striking portrait of the Countess of Cheverny above the fireplace in the Grand Salon. There is a collection of fine portraits by Jean Clouet and Hyacinthe Rigaud in the adjoining gallery. The Tapestry Room, with pieces of work designed by David Teniers, also features a tortoise-shell commode and a fascinating balance-wheel clock showing phases of the moon, both of

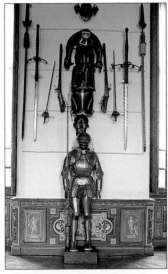

Arms and armour on display in Cheverny's Salle des Armes

which are in the distinctive Louis XV style. The château inspired Hergé to create Marlinspike Hall for his *Tintin* stories.

The Cheverny hunt, which rides twice a week in winter, is famous throughout the Sologne. A visit to the kennels (open Apr–mid-Sep) is a highlight of the château, especially at 5pm, when 70 hounds wait their turn to eat. The Trophy Room, with 2,000 pairs of antlers mounted on the walls and ceiling, is currently closed to the public.

A contemporary garden has been planted on the site of the original French-style gardens.

The Trophy Room at Cheverny

Château de Beauregard ⑪

Cellettes. **Road map** E3. 🚉 Blois, then taxi. *Tel* 02 54 70 40 05.
⬜ Feb–Mar, Oct–Nov school hols: Thu–Tue; Apr–Sep: daily. ● Dec & Jan. 🎫 **www**.beauregard-loire.com

Beauregard stands in a well-tended park on the edge of the Russy forest. Originally built at the beginning of the 16th century as a hunting lodge for François I, it was transformed into a graceful private manor house more than a century later by Jean du Thier, scholarly secretary of state to Henri II. It was du Thier who commissioned the king's Italian cabinet-maker, Scibec de Carpi, to make him an exquisite study panelled in gilded oak, the Cabinet des Grelots. This little room is

Detail from Beauregard's portrait gallery

decorated with the bells, or *grelots*, found on du Thier's crest, and has some charming paintings from the studio of Niccolo dell'Abate.

The portrait gallery, the château's most spectacular feature, was added in the 17th century by Henry IV's former treasurer, Paul Ardier. A complete catalogue of famous European faces from 1328 to 1643 – kings, queens, saints, explorers – is arranged in three rows around the gallery. Adding to the impact of these 327 portraits are beautiful beams and panels painted by Jean Mosnier and the largest

delft-tiled floor in Europe, which depicts an army on the move in Louis XIII costume.

Other delights include the southern gallery, with its rich Brussels tapestry and carved furniture, and the kitchen, with its flag-stone floors and a table built around the central column. Above the ratchet-operated spit, a motto on the chimney breast advises that those who keep promises have no enemies.

One of Villesavin's antique carriages

Château de Villesavin ⑫

Villesavin. **Road map** E3. 🚉 *Blois, then taxi.* **Tel** *02 54 46 42 88.* ⏰ *Mar: Fri–Wed; Apr–mid-Nov: daily.* ⚫ *mid-Nov–Feb.* 📷 ♿ *grd flr only.* 🖥 *www. chateau-de-villesavin.com*

Villesavin, built between 1527 and 1537 by Jean Breton, was his home while he supervised works at Chambord (*see pp132–5*) nearby. Stone carvers from the royal château ornamented Villesavin and presented Breton with the beautiful Florentine basin made of Carrara marble that stands proudly in the entrance courtyard.

This is one of the least altered of the many late-Renaissance châteaux in the Loire Valley. Villesavin, with its low walls and unusually high roofs, was built around three very spacious courtyards. The elegant southern façade ends with a large dovecote, which has 1,500 pigeonholes and a revolving ladder.

The château's essentially domestic spirit is also evident in the service court, overlooked by a spacious kitchen with a working spit. The interesting collection of old carriages on display here includes an 18-m (59-ft) long *voiture de chasse* with four rows of seats, from which ladies could watch the hunt.

Environs
Situated on the southern banks of the Beuvron river, Bracieux is worth a visit for its grand covered market, which was built during the reign of the Renaissance king François I (1515–47). At that time, the town acted as an important staging post on the routes between the towns of Tours, Chartres and Bourges.

The market is built of brick, stone and wood, with an upper tithe barn. Its original oak posts were strengthened during the 19th century. There are also 17th-and 18th-century houses.

Garden façade of the Château de Villesavin

Château de Chambord ⑬

Henry James once said: "Chambord is truly royal – royal in its great scale, its grand air, and its indifference to common considerations." The brainchild of the extravagant François I, the château began as a hunting lodge in the Forêt de Boulogne. In 1519 the original building was razed and Chambord begun, to a design probably initiated by Leonardo da Vinci. By 1537 the keep, with its towers and terraces, had been completed by 1,800 men and two master masons. The following year, François I began building a private royal pavilion on the northeast corner, with a connecting two-storey gallery. His son Henri II continued the west wing with the chapel, and Louis XIV completed the 440-roomed edifice in 1685.

Statue of Diana in the Salle de Diane

The Château de Chambord with the Cosson, a tributary of the Loire, in the foreground

The roof terraces include miniature spires, stair turrets, sculpted gables and cupolas.

★ Skyline
Chambord's skyline is its most astonishing feature – a bizarre jumble of different forms, likened to an overcrowded chess board.

Salamander
François I's emblem appears more than 700 times in the château. It symbolizes patronage of the good and destruction of the bad.

The central keep, with its four circular towers, forms the nucleus of the château.

Chapel
Begun by François I shortly before his death in 1547, the chapel was given a second storey by Henri II. Later, Louis XIV embellished the roof.

STAR FEATURES

★ Skyline

★ Grand Staircase

François I Staircase
The external spiral staircase located in the northeastern courtyard was added at the same time as the galleries, starting in 1538.

VISITORS' CHECKLIST

Road map E3. 🚃 Blois, then bus or taxi. **Tel** 02 54 50 40 00.
🕐 Oct–Mar: 9am–5:15pm daily; Apr–Sep: 9am–6:15pm daily.
🔴 1 Jan, 1 May & 25 Dec.
🎫 ♿ 📷 🎦 Spectacle d'Art Equestre **Tel** 02 54 20 31 01 for reservations (May–Sep daily). 🎫 Other shows change every year, call ahead to check times and dates. **www**.chambord.org

The lantern tower, 32 m (105 ft) high, is supported by flying buttresses.

The guardrooms, which were once the setting for royal balls and plays, have ornate, vaulted ceilings.

François I's bedchamber in the east wing, as it was at his death in 1547.

Cabinet de François I
The king's barrel-vaulted study (cabinet) in the outer north tower was turned into an oratory in the 18th century by Queen Catherine Opalinska, wife of Stanislas Leszczynski (Louis XV's father-in-law and the deposed king of Poland).

★ Grand Staircase
Seen here from the guardrooms, this innovative double staircase was supposedly designed by Leonardo da Vinci. Two flights of stairs spiral around each other.

Louis XIV's Bedchamber
The Sun King's state apartments are the grandest in the château.

The History of Chambord

Chambord, the largest château in the Loire, was a *folie de grandeur* of the young François I, whose ruling passions were hunting and flirting. "He is forever chasing, now stags, now women," the Venetian ambassador once said of him. The king personally supervised the enclosure of the game park surrounding Chambord with the most extensive wall in France – nearly 32 km (20 miles) long and 2.5 m (8 ft) high. At one point, he even suggested diverting the Loire to flow in front of his château, but instead settled for redirecting the nearer Closson to fill his moat.

Louis XIV portrayed as Jupiter, conquering La Fronde

François I as a young man, with various symbols of his kingship

After François I

On his father's death, Henri II took charge of François I's ambitious project. Subsequent owners – Louis XIII, who had no great love of hunting, and his brother Gaston d'Orléans – continued to modify the château. By the 17th century, Chambord comprised 440 rooms and had 365 chimneys, 14 main staircases and 70 smaller stairways.

Louis XIV, whose chief youthful amusement was hunting, took Chambord very seriously. His full court retinue visited the château numerous times. With balls, plays by Molière and operatic ballets, he re-created the glittering lifestyle of François I.

Louis XV also hawked at Chambord, but by 1725 he was ready to relinquish the château to his father-in-law, Stanislas Leszczynski. The exiled King of Poland is reported to have disliked the winter draughts. Certainly, he filled in the moats to prevent malarial fevers.

The last owner to enjoy Chambord's theatricality was the Maréchal de Saxe, victor over the English troops at the Battle of Fontenoy in 1745.

As well as lodging his actress mistress here, Saxe also kept two cavalry regiments whose mock battles he watched from the roof terraces.

During the second half of the 18th century, Chambord fell into neglect. Stripped during the French Revolution, the château was hardly used by the Bourbon pretender, Henri, Duc de Bordeaux, to whom it was given by public subscription in 1821. It was sequestered by the state in 1915, which bought it in 1930. A restoration programme was begun in the 1970s.

A view of Chambord (detail) by PD Martin (1663–1742)

TIMELINE

1547–59 Henri II adds the west wing and second storey of the chapel

1560–74 Charles IX continues tradition of royal hunting at Chambord and writes *Traité de la Chasse Royale*

Maréchal de Saxe

1840 Chambord declared a *Monument Historique*

1500	1600	1700	1800	1900

1670 Molière's *Le Bourgeois Gentilhomme* staged at Chambord

1519–47 The Count of Blois' hunting lodge is demolished by François I and the château created

1748 Acquired by the Maréchal de Saxe. On his death the château falls into decline

1725–33 Inhabited by exiled king of Poland

1685 Louis XIV completes the building

1970s Under Giscard d'Estaing, Chambord is restored and refurnished and the moats redug

Royal Hunting at Chambord

Under the influence of François I and his heirs, hunting and hawking were the foremost pastimes of the court during the 16th century. A Tuscan nobleman complained that the king only stayed in a place "as long as the herons last". They were quick prey for the 500 falcons that travelled with the rest of the royal retinue.

St Hubert, patron saint of hunting

Within his vast oak forests, the king rode out at dawn to a prepared picnicking spot, there to feast and await the selection of a red deer tracked by his beaters. The quarry flushed, he would ride at full tilt in pursuit, sometimes for hours. For ladies of the court, Chambord's

roof terraces offered matchless views of these exertions.

François' son Henri II and grandson Charles IX were also keen and practised hunters, sometimes pursuing quarry on foot. Louis XIV favoured the English sport of following packs of hounds, but falconry was preferred by Louis XV.

Hunting was regarded as an art by the court, and its tools – weapons, horns and costumes – were carefully designed and crafted. For centuries, it was also a favourite subject for painters and tapestry designers, whose works were used to decorate palaces and hunting lodges.

Matchlock

Engraved barrel

Arquebus, an early form of musket, dating from the 16th century

Wild boar was a favourite beast of the chase because of its strength and ferocity. Its head was considered a delicacy.

The crossbow was a popular hunting weapon thanks to its versatility and rapid rate of fire.

Greyhounds, prized for their speed and keen eyesight, were used as hunting dogs.

The Boar Hunt *comes from the* Traités de Fauconnerie et de Vénerie *(1459), one of many treatises on falconry and hunting to hounds. In the foreground, beaters and dogs chase their quarry. Behind them, animals and men witness the end of the hunt.*

Beaugency 🔟

Road map E3. 🏘 *8,000.* 🚉 🚌
ℹ️ *3 pl de Docteur Hyvernaud (02
38 44 54 42).* 🛍 *Sat.* 🎭 *Festival de
Beaugency (first & second w/end Jul).*

With the Loire racing
beneath its famous 23-
arch bridge, the medieval
town of Beaugency makes a
delightful base for exploring
the Orléanais area. The town
is surprisingly well preserved,
although its bridge, the best
on the Loire between Orléans
and Blois, has attracted the
attentions of a number of
armies over the centuries.
Restored in the 16th century,
the bridge was damaged
again in 1940 when the Allied
army blew up its southern
end to prevent the Nazis
from crossing the river.

On the place Dunois at the
top of rue de l'Abbaye stands
a massive 11th-century keep.
Opposite is the Romanesque
abbey church of **Notre-
Dame**, where Eleanor of
Aquitaine's marriage to Louis
VII was annulled in 1152,
leaving her free to marry the
future Henry II of England.

Higher up is the 16th-
century Tour St-Firmin, near
an equestrian statue of Joan
of Arc. Next to the keep, her
companion-in-arms, Jean
Dunois, Bastard of Orléans
and Lord of Beaugency, built
the **Château Dunois**, which
houses the Musée Regional de
l'Orléanais. Nearby, in rue des

Beaugency's 11th-century clock-
tower, once gateway to the town

Trois Marchands, is a
medieval clock-tower and
the Renaissance façade of
the Hôtel de Ville. A flower-
lined stream runs through
the old mill district.

⛪ **Château Dunois**
Pl Dunois.
Tel *02 38 44 55 23.*
⬜ *call for opening times.* 🈲

Meung-sur-Loire 🔟

Road map E3. 🏘 *6,300.* 🚉 🚌
ℹ️ *7 rue des Mauves (02 38 44 32
28).* 🛍 *Sun am, Thu pm.*

This pretty little village,
sloping down to the Loire,
was the birthplace of Jean de
Meung *(see p24)*, one of the

authors of the 13th-century
masterpiece *Le Roman de
la Rose.* There has been a
town on this site since Gallo-
Roman times, when it was
known as Magdunum.

Beside the impressive
Romanesque church of **St-
Liphard**, built from the 11th
to the 13th century, rise the
feudal towers of the **Château
de Meung**. Frequently altered
from the 12th century to the
18th century, the château
was built in a variety of
styles. The 18th-century wing
has an interesting collection
of furniture, paintings and
tapestries put together by
the current owner.

More intriguing are the
underground passages and
dungeons of the older castle,
dating from the 12th to 13th
centuries and used for 500
years by the bishops of
Orléans as a prison. In 1461,
the poet François Villon *(see
p24)*, renowned for his life of
disrepute as well as his fine
writing, spent five months
fighting with the other
condemned criminals on a
ledge above a cesspool in
the château's claustrophobic
oubliette. Thanks to a royal
pardon from Louis XI, he
was the only prisoner ever
to emerge alive from there.

⛪ **Château de Meung**
Tel *02 38 44 36 47.*
⬜ *Mar–Oct: daily; Nov–Feb: Sat,
Sun pm.* 🈲
♿ *grd flr only.*

Beaugency's medieval bridge, the Tour St-Firmin and the keep rising above the trees

The entrance to the Château de Chamerolles

Château de Chamerolles ⑯

Chilleurs-aux-Bois. **Road map** E2.
🚉 Orléans, then taxi. **Tel** 02 38
39 84 66. ◯ Wed–Mon.
◗ Jan, 25 Dec. 🎫

On the edge of the huge forest of Orléans, this Renaissance château was built between 1500 and 1530 by Lancelot du Lac, Governor of Orléans (who was named after the legendary Arthurian knight).

Although it was built in the form of a fortress, with a drawbridge crossing a moat and a courtyard enclosed by turreted wings, Chamerolles was designed as a pleasant personal residence. Pretty Renaissance gardens, accurately reconstructed, extend to a gazebo offering views back to the château across a "mirror" lake. There is an area of rare aromatic plants, many of which were used during the 1500s for making medicines and perfumes.

A museum in the château traces the development of perfumery through the centuries, covering the variety of uses for perfumes as well as the refinement of the science of making them. This includes the laboratories of perfumers and naturalists and glittering displays of bottles, as well as a charming gift shop.

Baccarat perfume bottle, Chamerolles' museum

JOAN OF ARC

Joan of Arc is the supreme national heroine, a virgin-warrior, patriot and martyr whose shining self-belief turned the tide of the Hundred Years' War against the English. Nowhere is she more honoured than in the Loire Valley, scene of her greatest triumphs.

Responding to heavenly voices telling her to "drive the English out of France", Joan left her home soon after her 17th birthday in 1429 and travelled via Gien to Chinon to see the dauphin, the as yet uncrowned Charles VII. He

Joan of Arc, pictured in a medieval tapestry

faced an Anglo-Burgundian alliance on the verge of capturing Orléans. Joan convinced him she could save the city, armed herself in Tours, had her standard blessed in Blois and entered Orléans with a small force on 29 April. Galvanized by her leadership, the French drove the English off on 7 May. The people of Orléans have celebrated 8 May as a day of thanksgiving almost ever since. Joan returned to Gien to urge Charles forward to Reims for his coronation in July. In 1430 she was captured and accused of witchcraft. Handed over to the

Stained-glass portrait of Charles VII from Loches

English, she was burned at the stake at the age of 19. Joan's piety, patriotism and tragic martyrdom led to her canonization almost 500 years later, in 1920.

Joan of Arc Entering Orléans by Jean-Jacques Sherrer (1855–1916)

Orléans ⑰

Orleans was the capital of medieval France and a royal duchy until the 18th-century French Revolution, when it became staunchly Republican. Its historical fame might, at first glance, seem submerged by its 20th-century role as a rail junction, food processing and business centre, especially as the old quarter of the city was badly damaged during World War II. However, an area of the old town near the river, now reconstructed, is full of interest for the visitor, and there are many beautiful gardens in this "city of roses".

Heroic Joan of Arc

Exploring Orléans

A sense of grandeur lingers in Vieil Orléans, the old quarter bounded by the cathedral, the River Loire and the **place du Martroi**. Dominating this square is Denis Foyatier's statue of the city's heroine, Joan of Arc, whose festival on 8 May is a highlight of the year. The plinth of the statue, which was erected in 1855, is beautifully sculpted with the events of her life. Two splendid Classical buildings, the Chancellery and the Chamber of Commerce, are also found in the square.

A few medieval buildings have survived in the narrower streets around rue de Bourgogne, a partly pedestrianized shopping street with an astonishing range of ethnic restaurants. Other delightful and often inexpensive restaurants can also be found close to the **Nouvelles Halles**, the city's covered market. The most sophisticated shopping street is the rue Royale, which leads to the 18th-century bridge, the Pont George V.

🏛 Maison de Jeanne d'Arc

3 pl de Gaulle. **Tel** 02 38 52 99 89. ☐ May–Oct: Tue–Sun; Nov–Apr: Tue–Sun pm only.
● public hols. 🖼
A reconstruction of the half-timbered house that lodged the warrior-saint for ten days in 1429, the Maison de Jeanne d'Arc presents scenes from her life as well as mementos, costumes and banners.

The evocative audiovisual dioramas include one that shows Joan's assault on the English-held Tourelles fort.

Orléans' Renaissance Hôtel Groslot, once a private residence

🏰 Hôtel Groslot

Pl de l'Etape. **Tel** 02 38 79 22 30.
☐ Mon–Sat. ● public hols. 🖼
The most handsome of the many Renaissance buildings in the city, the Hôtel Groslot, built between 1549 and 1555, served until recently as the town hall.

Built out of red brick crossed with black, this was a grand residence, with scrolled staircase pillars, caryatids and an ornately tooled interior. It was once considered fine enough to lodge the kings of France. Here, in 1560, the sickly, young François II died after attending a meeting of the Etats Généraux with his child bride, Mary, later Queen of Scots. The beautiful

statue of Joan of Arc guarding the steps was sculpted by Princess Marie d'Orléans in 1840. Walk through the building to visit a charming little park, backed by the re-erected façade of the 15th-century Flamboyant Gothic chapel of St-Jacques.

⛪ Cathédrale Ste-Croix

Pl Ste-Croix. **Tel** 02 38 24 05 05 (tourist office). ☐ daily. 🖼 🖼
The cathedral, set on a spacious esplanade, was begun in the 13th century. The original building was completely destroyed by Huguenots in the 16th century and then restored in a supposedly Gothic style between the 17th and 19th centuries. Behind the ornate façade, the towering nave is lit by the radiating spokes of the rose window dedicated to the "Sun King", Louis XIV. The chapel of Joan of Arc, whose martyrdom is portrayed in stained glass, features a kneeling sculpture of Cardinal Touchet, who fought for her canonization. The cathedral's most famous painting, a masterly rendition of *Christ Bearing the Cross*, by the Spanish religious painter Francisco de Zurbarán (1598–1664), has temporarily been removed for restoration.

The nave of the Cathédrale Ste-Croix

The peaceful Parc Floral in Orléans-la-Source

🏛 Musée des Beaux-Arts

Place Ste Croix. **Tel** 02 38 79 21 55.
◯ Tue–Sat, Sun am. 🟢 8 May,
public hols. 🖼 🚻
The high standard of the
collection, which includes a
self-portrait by Jean-Baptiste-
Siméon Chardin (1699–1779)
and *St Thomas* by the young
Diego Velázquez (1599–1660),
represents the strength of
European painting from the
14th to the early 20th century.
There is a charming collection
of miniature enamelled
statuettes on the second floor,
a contrast to the richness of
the 19th-century paintings.

🏛 Musée Historique et Archéologique

Square de l'Abbé Desnoyers.
Tel 02 38 79 25 60. ◯ May–Jun
& Sep: Tue–Sun pm only; Jul–Aug:
Tue–Sun; Oct–Apr: Wed & Sun pm.
🟢 public hols. 🖼
The chief treasures of this
museum are the Celtic statues
discovered at Neuvy-en-
Sullias in 1861, which include
a fine horse from the 2nd
century AD *(see p49)*. The
museum also has a beautiful
painted stone head of Joan
of Arc and a pleasing variety
of arts and crafts from the
Middle Ages onwards.

VISITORS' CHECKLIST

Road map E2. 🏘 *116,000.*
🚉 *ave de Paris.* 🚌 *rue Marcel
Proust.* 🛈 *2 pl de L'Etape (02
38 24 05 05).* 🍴 *Tue–Sun.*
🎭 *Fête Jeanne d'Arc: 7–8 May;
Festival de la Loire: Sep.*
www.tourisme-orleans.com

Environs

The suburbs of Orléans are
pleasant places to relax after
a day spent sightseeing in
the city centre. In Olivet, for
example, it is possible to go
boating on the River Loiret.
This river also provides
opportunities for pretty walks.
A tributary of the Loire, the
Loiret flows underground
from near the town of St-
Benoît-sur-Loire *(see p140)*
and rises in the grand **Parc
Floral** of Orléans-la-Source. A
nature reserve, the park is a
mass of blooms from April.
Adjoining the park is the 17th-
century Château de la Source.

🌺 Parc Floral

Orléans-la-Source. **Tel** 02 38 49
30 00. ◯ Apr–Oct: 10am–7pm
daily; Nov–Mar: 2–5pm daily.
🟢 1 Jan, 25 Dec. 🚻 🚻
www.parc-floral-la-source.com

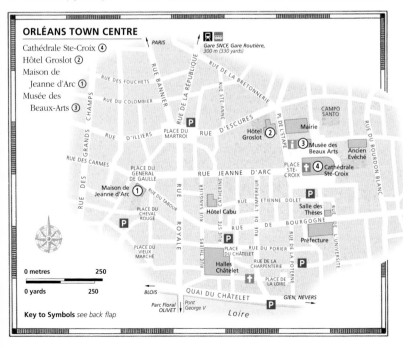

ORLÉANS TOWN CENTRE

Cathédrale Ste-Croix ④
Hôtel Groslot ②
Maison de
  Jeanne d'Arc ①
Musée des
  Beaux-Arts ③

Gare SNCF, Gare Routière,
300 m (330 yards)

0 metres   250
0 yards   250

Key to Symbols *see back flap*

The Romanesque façade of the abbey church of St-Benoît

St-Benoît-sur-Loire ⑱

Road map F3. 🏠 *2,800.* 🚌
🛈 *44 rue Orléanaise (02 38 35 79 00).* **www**.saint-benoit-sur-loire.fr

This quiet town has one of the finest Romanesque abbey churches in France, constructed between 1067 and 1108. The most appealing feature of the façade is the belfry porch, probably built early in the 11th century by Abbot Gauzlin, son of the first Capetian king, Hugh. On the capitals of its 50 golden pillars are carved figures, including beasts and goblins.

Inside, thickset columns separate the side aisles from the rib-vaulted Gothic nave. The chancel, dating from the earlier Romanesque period, has blind arcades and a mosaic floor brought from Rome. The bas-relief head of a Norman raider is carved on the wall of the north transept. Its cheeks are pierced to expel its pagan spirit.

In the crypt, a lamplit casket contains the relics of St Benedict, the 6th-century father of Western monasticism. They were spirited here in 672 from Benedict's own monastery of Monte Cassino in Italy. By the 11th century, when the present building was begun, the Benedictine order was rich and St-Benoît-sur-Loire was renowned for its scholarship as well as its purloined relics. St-Benoît is a living monastery, and one of the best ways to experience the spirit of the place is to attend midday mass sung in Gregorian chant.

The 9th-century church of **St Germiny-des-Prés** lies 5 km (3 miles) along the D60 from St-Benoît-sur-Loire. The small cupola of the east apse has an enchanting mosaic of angels bending over the Ark of the Covenant – a composition made up of 130,000 coloured-glass cubes probably assembled during the 6th century.

Gien ⑲

Road map F3. 🏠 *16,000.* 🚉 🚌
🛈 *pl Jean-Jaurès (02 38 67 25 28).*
🗓 *Wed, Sat.* **www**.gien.fr

Sensitively restored after being devastated during World War II, Gien is considered one of the Loire's prettiest towns. From its handsome quays and 16th-century bridge, houses of brick, slate and pale stone rise steeply to a château. It was built for Anne de Beaujeu, who acted as regent for her brother Charles XIII at the end of the 15th century.

Only the steeple tower of the **Eglise Ste-Jeanne d'Arc**, next to the château, survived the destruction of the war, but a remarkable church replaced it in the 1950s. Warm facings, composed of bricks made in Gien's famous pottery kilns, blend with the patterned red and black brickwork of the château. The interior glows with stained glass by Max Ingrand and the faïence that is a speciality of the area. A museum of fine china and earthenware is open daily (except Sundays and public holidays) at the factory, which was founded in 1821 *(see p221).*

The **château** of Anne de Beaujeu, built between 1484 and 1500 on the site of one of the Loire's oldest castles, sheltered the young Louis XIV and the Queen Mother during the Fronde civil war (1648–53). Its grand beamed halls and galleries now house a superb museum of hunting, tracing the sport's development since prehistoric times. The collection covers the weaponry, costumery, techniques and related artistry of almost every associated activity, from falconry to the royal chase. The memorable entrance hall of the château features a 17th-century painting of St Hubert, the patron saint of hunting, depicting his conversion by the vision of a resurrected

Max Ingrand's stained glass

Gien's château and its 16th-century bridge across the Loire

stag carrying a crucifix between its horns. An Italian crossbow and a powder horn decorated with images of the mythical and tragic encounter between Diana and Actaeon are beautiful examples of 17th-century carving. Other prominent artists on display here include the 20th-century sculptor Florentin Brigaud, the Flemish etcher, Stradanus, and François Desportes, whose fine paintings dominate the spectacular trophy hall.

♣ **Château et Musée International de la Chasse**
Tel 02 38 67 69 69. ○ *Wed–Mon (Jul & Aug: daily).* ● *Jan, 25 Dec.* 🖼

A pleasure boat crossing Briare's elegant bridge-canal

Briare-le-Canal ⓴

Road map F3. 🏠 6,000. 🚌 🚏
🛈 *pl Charles-de-Gaulle (02 38 31 24 51).* ▲ *Fri.*

This small town, with its attractive marina, is the setting for a sophisticated engineering masterpiece – the longest bridge-canal in Europe *(see pp56–7).* With stonework and wrought-iron flourishes designed by Gustave Eiffel (1832–1923), the structure crosses the Loire, linking the Briare-Loing canal with the Canal Latéral. These waterways in turn join the Seine and the Rhône rivers respectively. Visitors can stroll its length, lined in the style of a Parisian boulevard with elegant lampposts, or cruise across the 662-m (2,170-ft) bridge in a *bateau-mouche.*

Fishing on one of the peaceful *étangs* of the Sologne

The Sologne ㉑

Road map E3. 🚌 🚏 *Romorantin-Lanthenay.* 🛈 *(02 54 76 43 89).*

Between Gien and Blois, the Loire forms the northern boundary of the Sologne, a vast area of flat heathland, marshes and forests covering nearly 500,000 ha (1,235,000 acres). The area is dotted with *étangs*, broad lakes teeming with fish, which are magnets for migratory birds and waterfowl. The forests are just as attractive to hunters and nature lovers now as they were during the Renaissance, when members of royalty chose to build their grand hunting lodges here. Much of the land is privately owned, although there are some public paths.

Romorantin-Lanthenay is the "capital" of the Sologne. With its 17th- to 19th-century buildings and its medieval quarter, it is pleasant to visit. The town is also home to the **Musée de Sologne**, whose

exhibits explain the economy and wildlife of the area.

St-Viâtre, just north of Romorantin-Lanthenay, is a centre for bird-watching on the *étangs* of Brosses, Grande Corbois, Favelle, Marcilly and Marguilliärs. The **Maison des Etangs** at St-Viâtre gives guidance on ornithology.

For game, there are observation hides in the park of Chambord *(see pp134–5),* where deer can often be seen – and heard in the autumn rutting season. Another large, public nature reserve is the **Domaine du Ciran**, 25 km (15 miles) south of Orléans, near Ménestreau-en-Villette.

🏛 **Musée de Sologne**
Tel 02 54 95 33 66. ○ *daily.* ● *Tue, Sun am; 1 Jan, 1 May, 25 Dec.* 🖼 &

🦌 **Maison des Etangs**
Tel 02 54 88 23 00. ○ *daily (Nov–Mar: Wed, Sat, Sun & pub hols, pm only).* ● *1 Jan, 25 Dec.* 🖼

🦌 **Domaine du Ciran**
Ménestreau-en-Villette. 🚌 *La Ferté-St-Aubin, then taxi.* 🛈 *02 38 76 90 93.* ○ *daily.* ● *Tue (Oct–Mar).* 🖼

A typical, half-timbered building of La Sologne

BERRY

B*erry lies in the very centre of France, south of the Paris Basin and just north of the Massif Central. It is a varied land of wheat fields, pastures and vineyards, ancient forests, rolling hills and lakes, peaceful villages and elegant manor houses. Mainly off the beaten tourist track, the region gives visitors an opportunity to experience the rural heart of France.*

Bourges, the principal town of Berry, was one of the capitals of Aquitaine in the Gallo-Roman period. It then enjoyed another moment of glory in the 14th century, with the administration of Jean, Duc de Berry. This warmongering patron of the arts built a splendid palace in the city (now destroyed) and collected paintings, tapestries, jewellery and illuminated manuscripts.

In the 1420s, when Charles VII was fighting for the French crown *(see pp52–3)*, Bourges was his campaign base. Afterwards, his treasurer Jacques Cœur did much to make the kingdom financially secure. The Palais Jacques-Cœur in Bourges competes with the city's magnificent cathedral in drawing crowds of admiring visitors.

Berry is ideal for those who love the outdoors, whether walking in the many well-tended forests, fishing or bird-watching in La Brenne, or sailing and canoeing on its rivers and lakes. Among the region's literary associations are George Sand's novels *(see p24)* and Alain-Fournier's evocative tale *Le Grand Meaulnes* (1913), which combines his childhood memories of the Sologne in the north and the rolling country of the south.

The culinary highlights of Berry include dishes made from local game and wild mushrooms. To the northeast, the renowned Sancerre wine district *(see p155)* is also known for its excellent goats' cheeses, such as the famous Crottin de Chavignol.

A river view by the village of Argenton-sur-Creuse

◁ **The vineyards of Sancerre**

Exploring Berry

Bourges is the natural starting point for exploring the heart of France. From here it is only a short drive to the edge of the Sologne (see p141) in the north or La Brenne in the southeast, both havens for wildlife. Below Bourges is the Champagne Berrichonne, a vast agricultural region producing wheat, barley and oil-rich crops such as rape and sunflowers. The River Loire forms the ancient border between Berry and Burgundy to the east as it flows through the vineyards of the Sancerrois hills.

The Palais Jacques-Cœur in Bourges

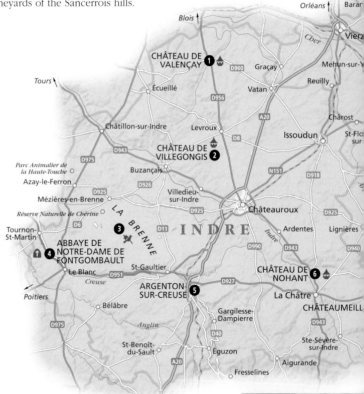

GETTING AROUND

The A71 autoroute from Orléans passes through Vierzon, Bourges and St-Amand-Montrond and is an excellent way of travelling from north to south. The TGV does not stop in the region, but Corail trains from Gare d'Austerlitz in Paris take around two hours to either Bourges or Châteauroux. There are also frequent trains between Bourges and Tours. Public transport to the more isolated sights is limited and a car is a great advantage, especially when touring the Sancerre wine estates or La Brenne nature reserves.

A riverside scene, typical of the Berry region's gentle landscape

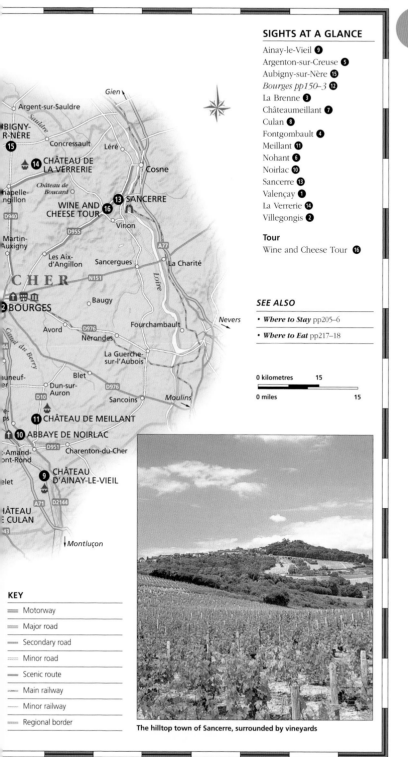

Argent-sur-Sauldre

Gien

AUBIGNY-SUR-NÈRE ⑮

Concressault

Léré

Cosne

⑭ CHÂTEAU DE LA VERRERIE

Château de Boucard

⑬ SANCERRE

WINE AND CHEESE TOUR ⑯

Chapelle-Angillon

D940

Vinon

D955

Martin-Auxigny

Les Aix-d'Angillon

Sancergues

La Charité

CHER

N151

Baugy

BOURGES

Avord

D976

Nérondes

La Guerche-sur-l'Aubois

Fourchambault

Nevers

Canal du Berry

Blet

D976

Dun-sur-Auron

Sancoins

Moulins

⑪ CHÂTEAU DE MEILLANT

⑩ ABBAYE DE NOIRLAC

St-Amand-Mont-Rond

D951

Charenton-du-Cher

⑨ CHÂTEAU D'AINAY-LE-VIEIL

Drevant

A71

D2144

CHÂTEAU DE CULAN

D43

↓ Montluçon

SIGHTS AT A GLANCE

Ainay-le-Vieil ❾
Argenton-sur-Creuse ❺
Aubigny-sur-Nère ⓯
Bourges pp150–3 ⓬
La Brenne ❸
Châteaumeillant ❼
Culan ❽
Fontgombault ❹
Meillant ⓫
Nohant ❻
Noirlac ❿
Sancerre ⓭
Valençay ❶
La Verrerie ⓮
Villegongis ❷

Tour
Wine and Cheese Tour ⓰

SEE ALSO

• *Where to Stay* pp205–6

• *Where to Eat* pp217–18

0 kilometres   15

0 miles   15

KEY

━ Motorway

━ Major road

━ Secondary road

┅ Minor road

━ Scenic route

⌁ Main railway

─ Minor railway

━ Regional border

The hilltop town of Sancerre, surrounded by vineyards

A resident peacock in front of the Château de Valençay

Valençay ❶

Road map E4. 🏰 *2,800.* 🚌 🚃
Valençay. 🛈 *2 ave de la Résistance
(02 54 00 04 42).* 🏪 *Tue.* **Château
& Park Tel** *02 54 00 10 66.*
◯ *Apr–Oct: daily.* 🎭 ♿ *restricted.*
🎭 *There are plays at the château in
summer; themes and dates vary.*
*Son et Lumière: Valençay aux
Chandelles (mid-Jun–Aug).* **Musée
de l'Automobile Tel** *02 54 00 07
74.* ◯ *Apr–Oct: daily.* 🎭 ♿
www.pays-de-valencay.fr;
www.chateau-valencay.com

From its tree-lined approach,
the Château de Valençay is a
fine sight. Started in 1510, it
took more than 300 years to
complete, but its Renaissance
and Classical elements are
convincingly blended. In
1803, it was bought by
Bonaparte's foreign minister,
Charles-Maurice de Talleyrand
Périgord. Until his death in
1838, the famous statesman
entertained many of Europe's
dignitaries here.

Valençay's rooms are richly
furnished, mostly in the
Empire style, and they display
many *objets d'art* connected
with Talleyrand. Indeed, in
summer, visitors can spend
time in the great man's
company, with members of
his entourage, portrayed by
actors, including his famous
chef, Carême. Formal gardens
extend in front of the château,
while the park itself houses
an enormous labyrinth.

Next to the château, the
Musée de l'Automobile has a
private collection of motoring
memorabilia and vintage cars
(all in working order).

Château de Villegongis ❷

Road map E4. 🚃 *Châteauroux, then
taxi.* **Tel** *02 54 36 63 50 (Mairie).*
◯ *closed to public.* 🎭

Elegant and moated, the
Château de Villegongis
was probably built by Pierre
Nepveu, one of the master
masons for Chambord (see
pp132–5). Since the 15th
century, ownership has stayed
in the same family. Barely
touched since that time, it is
one of the purest examples of
the French Renaissance style.

The château's most striking
features are its richly decorated chimneys, which suggest
the link with Chambord, and
its cylindrical towers at either
end of the main building.

The interior is exceptionally
well furnished, with some fine
17th- and 18th-century pieces.
There is also a remarkable
carved stone staircase.

La Brenne ❸

Road map E4. 🚃 *Mézières-en-
Brenne, then taxi.* 🛈 *Maison du
Parc, Rosnay (02 54 28 12 13);
Mézières-en-Brenne (02 54 38 12
24).* **www**.parc-naturel-brenne.fr

The Parc Naturel Régional
de la Brenne, covering
165,000 ha (407,700 acres), is
better known as the *Pays des
Mille Etangs* (The Land of a
Thousand Meres). A beautiful
region of lakes and wooded
hills, La Brenne is a paradise
for nature lovers. It has been
estimated that more than 260
of the 450 bird species known
in Europe can be seen here.

Several specialist reserves
are open to visitors, such
as the **Réserve Naturelle de
Chérine**, good for spotting
European pond tortoises,
and the **Parc Animalier de la
Haute-Touche**, home to many
endangered species. The
town of Mézières-en-Brenne
houses the **Maison de la
Pisciculture**, whose aquaria
display local fish species.

🦌 **Réserve Naturelle de
Chérine**
St-Michel-en-Brenne. 🛈 *02 54 28
11 00.* **Observatory** ◯ *Apr–Sep:
Wed–Mon am.* 🎭 *by appt only,
Apr–Jul: Thu pm.* 🎭

🦌 **Parc Animalier de la
Haute-Touche**
Obterre. **Tel** *02 54 02 20 40.*
◯ *Apr–Sep: daily, Oct–mid-Nov:
Wed, Sat, Sun & pub hols.* 🎭 ♿

🦌 **Maison de la Pisciculture**
Mézières-en-Brenne. **Tel** *02 54
38 12 24.* ◯ *Apr–Oct: Mon &
Wed–Sat, pm only; Nov–Mar:
by appt.* 🎭 ♿ *grd flr only.*

One of the many idyllic lakes in La Brenne

Abbaye de Notre-Dame de Fontgombault ❹

Road map E4. **Tel** 02 54 37 12 03. Hotel: 02 54 37 30 98. ☐ daily. ✝ Mass: 10am daily; Vespers: 6pm Mon–Sat, 5pm Sun. ♿

The beautiful Benedictine abbey, famous for its Gregorian chant, was founded in 1091 but, by 1741, when the number of monks had dwindled to just five, it was abandoned. Restored by a local priest in the 19th century, it now houses monks from Solesmes (see p162).

The church, with its five radiating chapels, has a richly decorated doorway, carved capitals and a much-venerated 12th-century statue known as Notre-Dame du Bien-Mourir, believed to comfort the dying. Gregorian chant is still sung during services and is more prominent in the morning service. The monks run a pottery, whose products can be bought. Accommodation is available, call the number above for details.

The radiating chapels of the Abbaye de Notre-Dame de Fontgombault

Old houses overhanging the river in Argenton-sur-Creuse

Argenton-sur-Creuse ❺

Road map E4. 🚶 5,500. ☐ ➤ ✱ pl de la République (02 54 24 05 30). ✿ Thu & Sat. ✪ International Folklore Festival, biennial (Jul). **www**.ot-argenton-sur-creuse.fr

Argenton-Sur-Creuse is a pretty town along the river, which winds from Fresselines to Argenton, passing through deep gorges. Streets of picturesque houses climb the hillside to Argenton's chapel of Notre-Dame-des-Bancs, dominated by its 6-m (20-ft) gilded statue of the Virgin Mary. There are fine views from here and from the Vieux Pont, a medieval bridge.

In the 19th century, the town became an important centre for the clothing industry. The informative collections of the **Musée de la Chemiserie et de l'Elégance Masculine** honour this heritage.

🏛 **Musée de la Chemiserie et de l'Eléga nce Masculine** **Tel** 02 54 24 34 69. ☐ mid-Feb–Dec: Tue–Sun; Jul–Aug: Mon pm. ♿ ♿

Château de Nohant ❻

Road map E4. **Tel** 02 54 31 06 04. 🚉 🚌 Châteauroux. ☐ daily. ⬤ public hols. ✪ ✪ Fêtes Romantiques de Nohant (Jun); Rencontres Internationales Frédéric Chopin (Jul). ✱ 02 54 31 0737.

George Sand, the nom de plume of the novelist, Baroness Aurore Dudevant (1804–76), was largely brought up in this charming manor house beside a tiny Romanesque church. She frequently returned here during her eventful and unconventional life, to enjoy the calm and beauty of her beloved Berry countryside.

Many of George Sand's novels, including La Mare au Diable (The Devil's Pool) and La Petite Fadette (The Little Fairy), are set here (see p24). Sand's admirers can view the boudoir where she first wrote, at a desk inside a cupboard; the stage on which she and her guests acted out her plays; the puppets made by her son, Maurice; the bedroom used by her lover, Frédéric Chopin; and the room in which she died in 1876.

MONET AT FRESSELINES

In 1889 the Impressionist painter Claude Monet travelled to the village of Fresselines, perched high above the Creuse. He visited a local beauty spot, with views plunging down into the river gorge, was captivated, and painted a series of canvases showing the scene in different lights. In February, bad weather forced him to stop painting and wait for spring. He then found that new growth had changed the view and had to pay the owner of an oak featured in five of his paintings to strip the tree of its new leaves.

***Valley of the Petite Creuse* by Claude Monet**

Châteaumeillant **7**

Road Map F4. 🏘 2,150. 🚋
Chateauroux, then bus. 🚌 **ℹ** *rue de
la Libération (02 48 61 39 89).* 🛒 *Fri.*
www.ot.chateaumeillant.free.fr

The chief glory of this town
is the Romanesque **Eglise
St-Genès**, built between 1125
and 1150, with its elegant pink
and grey west façade. The interior is exceptionally airy, due
not only to its great height, but
also to its very wide chancel
with six apsidal chapels and
side passages that are separated by graceful double bays to
create a cloisters effect.

Châteaumeillant was once an
important Gallo-Roman centre.
The **Musée Emile-Chenon**,
based in a 15th-century
manor house, contains
Roman artifacts and local
medieval finds.

🏛 **Musée Emile-Chenon**
ℹ *rue de la Victoire (02 48 61 49
24).* 🕐 *Mon pm, Wed am, Thu–Sat
(Jun–Sep: daily).* 🔴 *pub hols.* 📷 📹

Château de Culan **8**

Road Map F4. **Tel** *02 48 56 66 66.*
🕐 *Apr–mid-Nov: daily.* 📷 📹
www.culan.fr

Strategically positioned on
an escarpment above the
River Arnon, this medieval
fortress dates from the 13th
and 14th centuries. Its three
conical towers are topped
by wooden siege hoardings.
A series of furnished rooms
relate the castle's long history,

The interior courtyard of the Château d'Ainay-le-Vieil

recalling famous visitors who
have stayed here, including
the Admiral of Culan, who
was a comrade-in-arms of
Joan of Arc (who also stayed
here in 1430), and the writers
George Sand (see p24) and
Madame de Sévigné, and
telling of an attack during the
17th-century Fronde uprising.

Lovely views over Culan's
newly replanted gardens and
the pastoral Arnon Valley
can be enjoyed from the
terrace of the château.

Château d'Ainay-le-Vieil **9**

Road Map F4. 🚉 *St-Amand-Mont-
rond, then taxi.* **Tel** *02 48 63 50 03.*
🕐 *Feb: Wed–Mon pms; Mar, Oct
& Nov: Wed–Mon; Apr–Sep: daily.*
📷 📹

From the outside, Ainay-le-
Vieil has the appearance of
a fortress, with formidable
walls and its nine massive
towers, lit only by thin arrow

slits. The octagonal enclosure,
surrounded by a moat, is
entered through a huge, 13th-
century postern gate. The
exterior belies the fact that
hidden inside is a graceful
Renaissance château designed
for an elegant lifestyle, with
its richly decorated façade
enlivened by sunny loggias.

The castle changed hands
many times during its early
history. In the 15th century,
it belonged briefly to Charles
VII's treasurer Jacques Cœur
(see p151), but in 1467 it was
bought by the Seigneurs de
Bigny whose descendants still
live here today.

The Grand Salon was dec-
orated in honour of a visit by
Louis XII and Anne of Brittany
around 1500. It has a painted
ceiling and a monumental fireplace, which is said to be one
of the most attractive in the
Loire Valley. On display is a
portrait of Louis XIV's chief
minister Jean-Baptiste Colbert
and portraits of other family
members, as well as an amber
pendant that belonged to
Queen Marie-Antoinette and
several *objets de vertu*, friend-
ship gifts given by Napoleon
to General Auguste Colbert.

The tiny Renaissance chapel
has some beautiful, late 16th-
century wall paintings, which
were discovered under 19th-
century decoration. Its stained-
glass windows were made by
an artist who also worked on
the Cathédrale St-Etienne in
Bourges (see pp152–3).

In the park is a delightful
and sweet-smelling rose
garden. Some of the varieties
of roses which are grown here
date back to the 15th century.

The Château de Culan, set high above the River Arnon

Abbaye de Noirlac ⑩

Road map F4. 🚊 St-Amand-Montrond, then taxi. **Tel** 02 48 62 01 01. ◯ daily. ● 23 Dec–Jan. 📷 ✉ 🎵 Les Traversées (music festival in Jul). **www**.abbayedenoirlac.com

The Cistercian Abbaye de Noirlac, founded in 1136, is a fine example of medieval monastic architecture. The Cistercian Order's austerity is reflected in the pure lines of the partly 12th-century church and visually echoed in its sober, modern stained glass.

The chapter house, where the monks' daily assemblies were held, and the *cellier*, where the lay brothers were in charge of the food, wine and grain stores, were also built in this plain but elegant style. The cloisters, with their graceful arches and decorated capitals, date from the 13th and 14th centuries, which was a less severe period.

At **Bruère-Allichamps**, 4 km (2½ miles) northwest of the abbey, a Gallo-Roman milestone marks the alleged exact central point of France.

The austere lines of the Abbaye de Noirlac

Château de Meillant ⑪

Road map F4. 🚊 St-Amand-Montrond, then taxi. **Tel** 02 48 63 32 05. ◯ Mar–mid-Nov: daily. 📷 ✉ 🚻 grd flr only. **www**.chateau-de-meillant.com

Sumptuously furnished rooms and elaborate carved ceilings complement the rather exuberantly decorated façade of this well-preserved Berry château. Built for Charles d'Amboise in 1510 by skilful Italian craftsmen, the château represents a fine combination of late Gothic and early Renaissance architecture. It is dominated by the *Tour de Lion* (Lion's Tower), an octagonal three-storey staircase tower. The plainer west façade, mirrored in a moat, dates from the early 1300s.

A small grotesque carving in Meillant

Other highlights of a visit include the château's graceful chapel and its surrounding grounds in which peacocks strut. The grounds also feature **La Mini'stoire**, an interesting miniature park, where models of buildings depict the ways in which architectural styles have varied over the centuries.

🏛 **La Mini'stoire**
Tel 02 48 63 32 05.
◯ Mar–mid-Nov: daily.

LIFE IN A CISTERCIAN ABBEY

The rules of the Cistercian Order were based on the principles of austerity and simplicity. Abbeys were divided into two communities, which did not mix. Lay brothers, not bound by holy vows, ensured the self–sufficiency of the abbey by managing the barns, tilling the fields, milling corn and welcoming guests. The full, or choir, monks were the only ones allowed into the cloister, at the heart of the complex, and could not leave the abbey without the permission of the abbot.

The monks' days started at 2am and ended at 7pm and were regularly punctuated by religious devotions, which included prayers, confession, meditation and mass. The strict rule of silence was broken only to read from the Bible or from the Rules of the Order. Many monks were literate, and monasteries played a leading role in copying manuscripts.

A Cistercian monk labouring in the fields

Bourges ⑫

The heart of modern Bourges, once the Roman city of Avaricum, is the network of ancient streets around its magnificent cathedral. Despite a dramatic fire in 1487, the city was an important religious and arts centre in the Middle Ages and, by the late 19th century, it was a prosperous industrial town. Today Bourges has a quiet atmosphere that complements its excellent museums, housed in superb old buildings. It comes to life in the spring during the *Printemps de Bourges*, a rock festival attracting a large, predominantly young audience.

The 16th-century *Concert Champêtre*, displayed in the Hôtel Lallemant

🏛 Hôtel des Echevins & Musée Estève

13 rue Edouard Branly. **Tel** *02 48 24 75 38.* ◯ *Mon, Wed–Sat; Sun pm only.* ● *1 Jan, 1 May, 1 & 11 Nov & 25 Dec.* ♿

The Hôtel des Echevins (the house of the aldermen), which is remarkable for its intricately carved octagonal tower, was built in 1489 and served as the seat of the city council that governed Bourges for more than three centuries.

The building was classified an historic monument in 1886. In 1985 work to renovate the building began, and in 1987 it became the Musée Estève, displaying paintings by the self-taught artist Maurice Estève, who was born in Culan in the south of Berry (see p148). The collection is mainly made up of Estève's powerful, brightly coloured canvases. However, this permanent display is augmented by temporary exhibitions of his watercolours, collages and line drawings. The collection is arranged in chronological order on three levels, connected by elegant stone spiral staircases. This modern work seems surprisingly at home in the spacious Gothic rooms.

Samsâra by Maurice Estève (1977)

🏛 Hôtel Lallemant & Musée des Arts Décoratifs

6 rue Bourbonnoux. **Tel** *02 48 57 81 17.* ◯ *Tue–Sat; Sun pm only.* ● *1 Jan, 1 May, 1 & 11 Nov & 25 Dec.*

This Renaissance mansion, built for a rich merchant family originally from Germany, houses the city's decorative arts museum. It still has the little chapel used by the Lallemant family, its coffered ceiling carved with alchemical symbols, and an elegant, restored courtyard. On display is a fine collection of tapestries, clocks, ceramics, glass, paintings and furniture, including a beautiful 17th-century ebony inlaid cabinet. In another part of the mansion, there is a collection of toys dating from the 17th century to the present.

🏛 Musée du Berry

4–6 rue des Arènes. **Tel** *02 48 70 41 92.* ◯ *Mon, Wed–Sat; Sun pm only.* ● *1 Jan, 1 May, 1 & 11 Nov & 25 Dec.* ♿ *grd flr only.*

The Musée du Berry, housed in the Renaissance Hôtel Cujas, concentrates on local history. The collections include a large display of Gallo-Roman arti-facts, many of which were unearthed in the area. There is some wonderful Gothic sculpture, especially Jean de Cambrai's weeping figures from the base of the tomb of Jean, Duc de Berry, the upper section of which can be seen in the crypt of the Cathédrale St-Etienne (see pp152–3).

On the upper floor of the museum is a permanent exhibition of Berry's rural arts, crafts, and everyday objects, including the distinct-ive stoneware made in La Borne near Sancerre.

Jehan Fouquet's Angel Ceiling in the Palais Jaques-Cœur

JACQUES CŒUR

The son of a Bourges furrier, Jacques Cœur (c.1400–56) became one of the richest and most powerful men in medieval France. With his merchant fleet he sailed to the eastern Mediterranean and Far East, bringing back luxury goods such as silks, spices and precious metals, until Charles VII appointed him head of the Paris Mint, then treasurer of the Royal Household.

In 1451 he was accused of fraud and falsely implicated in the death of the king's mistress, Agnès Sorel. He was arrested, tortured and imprisoned, but escaped to Rome. There he took part in the pope's naval expedition against the Turks and died on the Greek island of Chios.

The merchant Jacques Cœur

The fireplace in the south gallery of the Palais Jacques-Cœur

🏛 Palais Jacques-Cœur

Rue Jacques-Cœur. **Tel** 02 48 24 79 42. ☐ daily. ● 1 Jan, 1 May, 1 & 11 Nov, 25 Dec. 🎫

This splendid palace, built on the remains of the city's Gallo-Roman walls, is among the finest secular Gothic buildings in Europe. It was constructed at great expense between 1443 and 1451 for Jacques Cœur, one of the most fascinating men in medieval France.

The palace has a number of innovations remarkable for their period. Rooms open off corridors instead of leading into each other, as they did in most buildings at the time, and a stone lavatory shows that sanitation was a consideration. Appealingly, each room is "labelled" over the doorway with carved scenes that illustrate its function.

From *trompe l'oeil* figures peeping out from the turreted entrance façade to the mysterious, possibly alchemical, symbols carved everywhere, the palace offers a feast of interesting details. Hearts are a common motif – the newly ennobled Jacques Cœur naturally had hearts, *cœurs* in French, on his coat of arms.

Other features are a large courtyard, wooden vaulting in the galleries, and the beautiful ceiling in the chapel, painted by Jehan Fouquet *(see p25)*.

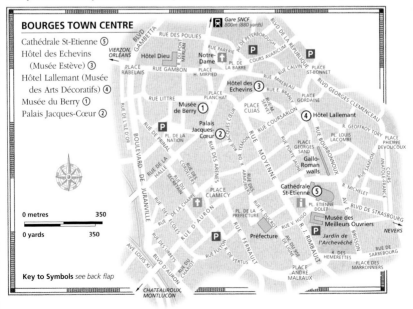

BOURGES TOWN CENTRE

Cathédrale St-Etienne ⑤
Hôtel des Echevins (Musée Estève) ③
Hôtel Lallemant (Musée des Arts Décoratifs) ④
Musée du Berry ①
Palais Jacques-Cœur ②

0 metres 350
0 yards 350

Key to Symbols see back flap

Bourges: Cathédrale St-Etienne

Stained-glass window detail

St-Etienne, one of France's finest Gothic cathedrals, was built mainly between 1195 and 1260. The unknown architect designed St-Etienne without transepts, which, combined with the interior's unusual height and width, makes it seem much lighter than most Gothic cathedrals. This effect is beautifully enhanced by the brilliant hues of the medieval stained glass. Also unusual are the asymmetrical west front; the double row of flying buttresses rising in pyramid-shaped tiers; and a "crypt", a lower, window-lit church, created because the ground is 6 m (20 ft) lower at the east end.

Vast Interior
The interior is 124 m (400 ft) long and 37 m (120 ft) high.

The Tour Sourde
(Deaf Tower) is so called because it has no bell.

★ **Astrological Clock**
Dating from the 1420s, this fascinating clock was designed by Canon Jean Fusoris, a mathematician.

Entrance

THE LAST JUDGMENT

The tympanum on the central portal of the west façade depicts Archangel Michael weighing souls. Those found wanting are hustled by devils into the mouth of Hell, while the elect are gathered into the bosom of Abraham. The youthful, naked dead lift up their tombstones in a dramatic Resurrection scene.

The Last Judgement portal of the Cathédrale St-Etienne

The Grand Housteau is a striking rose window, donated by the renowned patron of the arts Jean, Duc de Berry.

The five portals of the west front are surrounded by carved scenes. The doorways vary in size and shape, adding to the asymmetry of the façade.

★ **Stained-Glass Windows**
The medieval stained glass in the choir was sponsored by local guilds, whose members are depicted practising their crafts at the bottom of each window.

The Chapelle Jacques-Coeur has a glorious Annunciation window.

Praying Figures
In the crypt are statues of the Duc and Duchesse de Berry. During the Revolution the statues were decapitated and the existing heads are copies.

The crypt, or lower church, was built in the earlier Gallo-Roman moat.

The Romanesque portal on the cathedral's south side is decorated with a *Christ in Majesty* and the 12 apostles.

★ **St Sépulcre**
This dramatic sculpture of the Entombment *of Christ was placed at the far end of the lower church in 1540.*

STAR FEATURES

★ Astrological Clock

★ Stained-Glass Windows

★ St Sépulcre

Jean, Duc de Berry
The recumbent marble effigy of Jean, Duc de Berry, his feet resting on a bear, was originally part of his tomb.

A Sancerre vineyard

Sancerre ⑬

Road map F3. ⌖ 1,800. ▦
🛈 esplanade Porte-César (02 48 54
08 21). 🚌 Tue & Sat. ⚑ Foire aux
Crottins (goat's cheese fair, early May);
Foire aux Vins (wine fair, Whitsun);
Foire aux Vins de France (French wine
fair, late Aug). **www.**ville-sancerre.com

The ancient Berry town of
Sancerre is perched on a
domed hill, a rare sight in the
flat landscape of the Loire
Valley. Its narrow streets
boast interesting 15th- and
16th-century houses. All that
remains of the medieval castle
that once dominated the town
is the **Tour des Fiefs**, which
gives a superb view of the
River Loire. The town and
surrounding area are famous
for their dry white wines.

Located in a lovely pastoral
setting, 10 km (6 miles) to the
west of Sancerre, the **Château
de Boucard** is part medieval
in origin, but has an elegant
Renaissance courtyard.

⋔ Tour des Fiefs
⊡ Apr–Nov: 10am–12:30pm,
2–6pm Mon–Fri, 2–6pm Sat & Sun.

⚜ Château de Boucard
Le Noyer. **Tel** 02 48 58 75 49.
⊡ Easter–Nov: Fri–Wed. 🔲

Château de la Verrerie ⑭

Road map F3. 🚉 Gien, then taxi.
Tel 02 48 81 51 60. ⊡ Easter–Nov:
Sat, Sun (Jul, Aug: daily); Dec–Easter:
by appointment only. 🔲 🎫 🍴 See
Where to Stay, p205.

This fine, early Renaissance
château is on the edge of the
Forêt d'Ivoy. The land was

given to the Scot Sir John
Stewart of Darnley by Charles
VII, in thanks for defeating the
English at the battle of Baugé
in 1421. John's son, Béraud
Stewart, began to build the
château several decades later.
It was completed by Béraud's
nephew, Robert.

La Verrerie reverted to the
French crown in 1670. Three
years later Louis XIV gave the
château to Louise de Kéroualle.
She lived here until her death
in 1734 at the age of 85.

La Verrerie has a lovely
Renaissance gallery with 16th-
century frescoes. The chapel
also has fine frescoes. In the
19th-century wing are four
beautiful alabaster statuettes
from the tomb of the Duc de
Berry (see pp152–3).

The grounds have a good
restaurant and 12 of the
château's rooms are available
for visitors to stay overnight.

**Alabaster statuettes in the Château
de la Verrerie's 19th-century wing**

Aubigny-sur-Nère ⑮

Road map F3. ⌖ 6,000. ▦ 🛈 rue
de l'Eglise (02 48 58 40 20). 🚌 Sat.
⚑ Fête Franco-Ecossaise (mid-Jul).
www.aubigny-sur-nere.fr

Attractive Aubigny is proud of
its association with the
Scottish Stewart clan. In
1423 the town was
given by Charles VII
to Sir John Stewart
of Darnley, along
with nearby La
Verrerie. After a
major fire in 1512,
the Stewarts rebuilt
Aubigny in the
Renaissance style
and also constructed
a new château.

In 1673 Louis XIV
gave the duchy of
Aubigny to Louise de
Kéroualle. Although
she spent most of her

time at La Verrerie, Louise
had a large garden created
at the Château d'Aubigny.
The Aubusson tapestries
presented to her by the king
are displayed in the château,
which now serves as the
town hall and also houses
two museums. The unusual
Mémorial de l'Auld Alliance is
devoted to the Auld Alliance,
the town's long ties with Scotland: Jacobite refugees settled
here during the 18th century.

The 13th-century **Eglise St-
Martin**, in transitional Gothic
style, was largely rebuilt by
the Stewarts. It has a beautiful
wooden Pietà and a moving
16th-century Entombment.

Berry has a reputation for
sorcery, a tradition well illustrated in Concressault's lively
Musée de la Sorcellerie, 10
km (6 miles) east of Aubigny.
Here waxworks bring to life
the history of herbalism, heal-
ing and magic, and portray
the gruesome fate of those
accused of witchcraft during
the Inquisition.

**🏛 Mémorial de l'Auld
Alliance & Musée Marguerite-
Audoux**
Château d'Aubigny. **Tel** 02 48 81
50 07. ⊡ Easter–Jun & mid-Sep–
Oct: Sat, Sun & public hols pms only;
Jul–mid-Sep: daily; Nov–Easter:
Sun pm & public hols. 🔲 🔲
Mémorial de l'Auld Alliance only.

🏛 Musée de la Sorcellerie
La Jonchère, Concressault. **Tel** 02
48 73 86 11. ⊡ Easter–Oct: daily.
🔲 🔲 www.musee-sorcellerie.fr

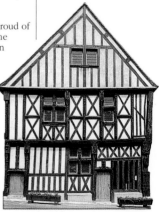

**The Maison de François I, one of the many
old houses in Aubigny-sur-Nère**

Wine and Cheese Tour ⓰

The Sancerrois in eastern Berry is renowned for its wines and goat's cheese. Gourmets can visit the top-class Sancerre cellars and taste the fresh and fragrant white wines made from the Sauvignon grape, or charming light reds and rosés made from the Pinot Noir. The flavours combine beautifully

Sancerre wine

with the sharp little goat's cheeses called Crottins de Chavignol, which are also produced locally. This rural route passes by gently hilly vineyards and fields of grazing red goats. The tour takes in many of the major producers, as well as a few local museums that explain the long history of both wine and cheese.

Verdigny ⑥
The Musée de la Vigne et du Vin charts the history of winemaking in the area. Exhibits include an ancient wooden wine press. By appointment only, call 02 48 79 31 03.

Goat's cheese label

Chavignol ⑤
This pretty town gives its name to the little cheeses. An exhibition at the cheese shop Dubois-Boulay relates the history of the cheese.

Sancerre ①
At the Maison des Sancerre, visitors can learn about the different varieties of Sancerre and get information about local producers.

Ménétréol-sous-Sancerre ②
At the Chèvrerie de Chamons, Crottins de Chavignol can be tasted and the cheese-making process watched. Call 02 48 79 93 30 to book a visit.

Vinon ③
Wine growers around this typical Sancerre village offer guided tours in English, as well as tastings.

Bué ④
Many vintners are based in and around this important *commune viticole*, including Crochet, Balland and Roger.

Bannon

TIPS FOR DRIVERS

Tour length: 30 km (19 miles).
Stopping-off points: Motorists should have little trouble spotting places to stop and sample wine and cheese. Les Augustins and La Pomme d'Or (see p218) in Sancerre are recommended.

KEY

 Tour route

═══ Other roads

| 0 kilometres | 1 |
| 0 miles | 1 |

For additional map symbols see back flap

NORTH OF THE LOIRE

The peaceful Mayenne and Sarthe regions seem worlds away from the tourist-frequented château country of the central Loire Valley. A grouping of districts with little common history, the area north of the Loire has very different attractions from the former royal domains to the south. The rivers, hills, forests and plains abound with opportunities for fishing, boating and country walks.

River boats cruise along the quiet Sarthe, through pretty wooded scenery and meadowlands, to Sablé-sur-Sarthe, near the Abbaye de Solesmes, famous for its tradition of superb Gregorian chant.

The more dramatic scenery of the Mayenne valley, from Laval southwards, with steep cliffs and villages perched on wooded hills, makes a pleasant spot for a restful break from château-visiting. The river, studded with locks, runs into the Maine and then into the Loire, a pattern also followed by the Loir (Le Loir, which is not to be confused with La Loire).

The valley of the Loir is also very pretty, the slow-moving river flowing through peaceful villages. It is a perfect place for relaxing and enjoying the countryside. The valley also offers a few spectacular sights of its own, including the château at Le Lude, with its four imposing corner towers and the stern-faced château of Châteaudun further upstream, which was once a stronghold of the counts of Blois. Le Mans, world famous for its 24-hour car race, also has an attractive old centre. East of Le Mans, gentle scenery gives way first to the wooded hills of the Perche and then to the vast wheat-fields on the plain of the Beauce, which is dominated by the magnificent cathedral at Chartres. Two lovely châteaux, Anet and Maintenon, were homes to royal mistresses: Diane de Poitiers *(see p55)*, mistress of Henri II, retreated to Anet, and Madame de Maintenon was the mistress of Louis XIV. Like Chartres Cathedral, these great houses stand on the edge of the Ile de France, the region around Paris, so they attract many day visitors from the country's capital.

Clog-making at the woodwork centre in Jupilles in the Forêt de Bercé

◁ The River Sarthe near the village of St-Céneri-le-Gérei

Exploring the North of the Loire

Consisting of the *départements* of Mayenne, Sarthe and Eure-et-Loire, the region north of the Loire borders Brittany, Normandy and the Ile de France. It combines characteristics of all these regions with those of the central Loire Valley. In the north, the hills of the Alpes Mancelles have more in common with the landscapes of Normandy than they do with the rolling fields further south. The rivers traversing the region – the Loir, Sarthe and Mayenne – are smaller and gentler than the mighty Loire but still very scenic. The largest towns in the region are Chartres, Le Mans and Laval, all of them worth a visit.

One of Chartres' winding, cobbled streets

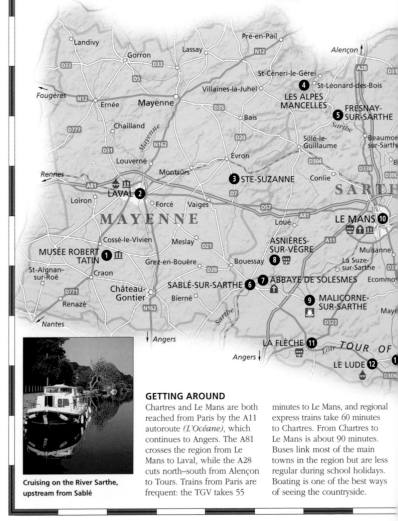

Cruising on the River Sarthe, upstream from Sablé

GETTING AROUND

Chartres and Le Mans are both reached from Paris by the A11 autoroute *(L'Océane)*, which continues to Angers. The A81 crosses the region from Le Mans to Laval, while the A28 cuts north–south from Alençon to Tours. Trains from Paris are frequent: the TGV takes 55 minutes to Le Mans, and regional express trains take 60 minutes to Chartres. From Chartres to Le Mans is about 90 minutes. Buses link most of the main towns in the region but are less regular during school holidays. Boating is one of the best ways of seeing the countryside.

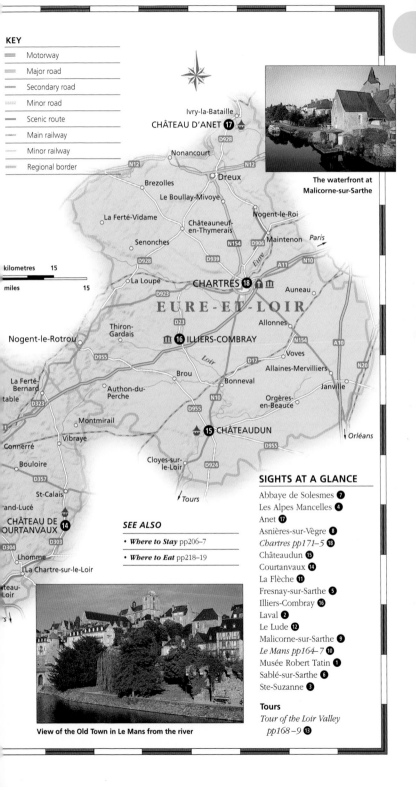

KEY

══	Motorway
──	Major road
──	Secondary road
┄┄	Minor road
──	Scenic route
┈┈	Main railway
──	Minor railway
══	Regional border

kilometres   15

miles   15

The waterfront at Malicorne-sur-Sarthe

Ivry-la-Bataille

CHÂTEAU D'ANET ⑰

D928

Nonancourt

N12   N12

Dreux

Brezolles

Le Boullay-Mivoye

La Ferté-Vidame

Châteauneuf-en-Thymerais

Nogent-le-Roi

Senonches

Maintenon   *Paris*

N154   D906

Eure

A11   N10

La Loupe

CHARTRES ⑱

Auneau

D923

EURE-ET-LOIR

D23

Thiron-Gardais

Allonnes

Nogent-le-Rotrou

ILLIERS-COMBRAY ⑯

Loir

N154   A10

Voves

D955

D17

Allaines-Mervilliers

N20

La Ferté-Bernard

Brou

Bonneval

Authon-du-Perche

Janville

-table   D323

N10

Orgères-en-Beauce

Montmirail

D955

Vibraye

CHÂTEAUDUN ⑮

Orléans

Connerré

Bouloire

D955

D357

St-Calais

Cloyes-sur-le-Loir

D924

-and-Lucé

CHÂTEAU DE COURTANVAUX ⑭

Tours

D304   D303

Lhomme

La Chartre-sur-le-Loir

-teau-Loir

View of the Old Town in Le Mans from the river

SEE ALSO

- *Where to Stay* pp206–7
- *Where to Eat* pp218–19

Musée Robert Tatin ❶

Road map B2. La Frênouse.
🚉 *Laval.* 🚌 *Cossé-le-Vivien.*
Tel *02 43 98 80 89.* 🔲 *daily
(Oct–Mar: pm only).* ⬤ *Jan, 25 Dec.*
📷 📹 ♿ www.musee-robert-
tatin.fr

The multi-talented artist
Robert Tatin (1902–83)
devised an extra-
ordinary museum, in the
little village of La Frênouse,
near Cossé-le-Vivien. The
building is approached
via the Allée des Géants
(Giants' Avenue): lining
the path are huge,
strange concrete
figures, depicting
people who
impressed Tatin,
including Pablo
Picasso, Toulouse-
Lautrec, Joan
of Arc and the
Gallic warrior,
Vercingetorix. Beyond them, a
statue of a huge dragon with
gaping jaws stands guard.

**Tatin's statue of Picasso
at the Musée Robert Tatin**

In the museum is a cross-
section of Tatin's work:
paintings, sculpture, frescoes,
mosaics and ceramics. Tatin
was also a cabinet-maker and
much else besides. He was
influenced by the megalithic
monuments in Brittany and
the traditional costumes worn
by Breton men and women,
as well as by Aztec art – he
lived and travelled in South
America for five years.

Laval ❷

Road map C2. 🏠 *54,000.*
🚉 🚌 🛈 *1 allée du Vieux St-Louis
(02 43 49 46 46).* 🗓 *Tue, Sat.*
www.laval-tourisme.com

Laval straddles the River
Mayenne, which can be
crossed via the humpbacked
Gothic Vieux Pont (Old
Bridge). Beside it on the west
bank is the **Vieux Château**.
This castle dates from the
early 11th century, when the
region was under the sway
of Foulques Nerra, Count of
Anjou – it formed one link
in his chain of fortresses
designed to keep out the
invading Bretons and

Normans. Although it has
been heavily rebuilt and
added to over the centuries,
the original medieval round
keep has survived. The
flower-filled courtyard, with a
terrace offering good river
views, has an attractive
Renaissance façade.
   The château has a collection
of the equipment used
by Laval native,
Ambroise Paré (1510–
c.1592), known as "the
father of modern
surgery". It is best
known, however, for its
Musée d'Art Naïf
(Museum of Naïve Art)
which was inspired
in part by Henri
Rousseau *(see p25).*
He was known
as *Le Douanier,*
his nickname
deriving from the
period when he
worked as a
customs officer.
His Paris studio, complete
with piano, has been well

reconstructed here. Although
the museum has only two
works by Rousseau, there
are many gems in its 450-
strong collection, including
a painting of the ocean
liner *Normandie* by Jules
Lefranc (1887–1972).
   Laval's old town has
attractive houses as well as
the **Cathédrale de la Ste-
Trinité**, with its Aubusson
tapestries. Laval also has one
of France's few surviving
bateaux-lavoirs, **Bateau-Lavoir
St-Julien**, now a museum.
Such floating laundries first
appeared in the mid-19th
century on the banks of rivers
in the western Loire Valley.

🏛 **Château & Musée du
Vieux Château**
Pl de la Trémoille.
Tel *02 43 53 39 89.*
⬤ *for restoration, but castle keep
is open Tue–Sun.* 📷 📹

🏛 **Bateau-Lavoir St-Julien**
Quai Paul-Boudet.
Tel *02 43 49 46 46 (tourist office).*
⬤ *for restoration until 2011.* 📹

Le Lancement du Normandie by Jules Lefranc, at the Musée d'Art Naïf

Ste-Suzanne ❸

Road map C2. 🏯 *1,000.* 🚉 *Evron, then taxi.* 🛈 *Office de Tourisme des Coëvrous, 1 rue du Bueil (02 43 01 43 60).* **www**.sainte-suzanne.com

This village, high on a hill, is still partly surrounded by the fortifications designed as a defence against marauding Normans in the 10th century – it was sturdy enough to withstand an attack by William the Conqueror, whose former encampment site can be seen just 3 km (2 miles) outside the town. Although much of the original castle was pulled down by the English in the early 15th century, a 10th-century keep has withstood the ravages of time. The present castle, the **Château des Fouquet de la Varenne**, constructed of white tufa and grey slate, dates from the early 17th century.

The village has a museum, the **Musée de l'Auditoire**, which covers local history, with reconstructions of events and vignettes of daily life.

🏛 **Château des Fouquet de la Varenne**
Promenade de la Poterne. **Tel** *02 43 01 40 77.* ⬜ *May–Sep: daily; Oct–Apr: Tue–Sun.* ⬤ *1 Jan, 25 Dec.* 🅿️ ✔

🏛 **Musée de l'Auditoire**
7 Grande Rue. **Tel** *02 43 01 42 65.* ⬜ *Apr–Jun: Sat–Sun; Jul & Aug: daily.* 🅿️

Les Alpes Mancelles ❹

Road map C2. 🚉 *Alençon.* 🚌 *Fresnay-sur-Sarthe.* 🛈 *19 av du Dr Riant, Fresnay-sur-Sarthe (02 43 33 28 04).*

The name of this region of wooded hills and green meadows, between Fresnay-sur-Sarthe and Alençon, means "Alps of Le Mans". Although certainly an exaggeration, there is something faintly alpine in the landscape, with its

St-Céneri-le-Gérei's Romanesque church, perched on a hill

streams winding through gorges, sheep, fruit trees and heather-clad hillsides. A large part of the area is now incorporated into the regional natural park of Normandie-Maine. The prettiest villages are **St-Céneri-le-Gérei**, which has a Romanesque church containing 12th- and 14th-century frescoes, and **St-Léonard-des-Bois**, also with a Romanesque church. There are walks through the countryside and along the River Sarthe, and the area is popular for all sorts of sports *(see pp224–7).*

Church doorway, St-Léonard-des-Bois

Fresnay-sur-Sarthe ❺

Road map C2. 🏯 *2,400.* 🚉 *Alençon, Sillé-le-Guillaume, La Hutte.* 🚌 🛈 *19 av du Dr Riant (02 43 33 28 04).* 🛒 *Sat am.*

From the 16th to the 19th century, Fresnay-sur-Sarthe was an important centre for cloth weaving, and its outskirts remain rather industrial. The centre of Fresnay, however, still retains a somewhat medieval feel. There were originally three rings of walls surrounding the town, and fragments of them are still visible from the river.

The castle, which is strategically located on a rocky spur above the Sarthe, was besieged by William the Conqueror in 1073. During the Hundred Years' War *(see pp52–3),* this was the last fortress in the region to be surrendered by the English. The remains of the castle now stand as a reminder of more turbulent times, commemorated by a small museum of medieval history, the **Musée Médiéval**, in the 14th-century postern. Around the castle ruins spread acres of pleasant parkland.

Situated at the end of the avenue du Dr Riant, the **Eglise Notre-Dame**, with both Romanesque and Gothic elements, has an unusual tower with an octagonal base and a beautiful, intricately carved, old oak door.

The tourist office organises a free guided walk of the village that takes place on one day of the week in summer; check with the office for dates and times.

🏛 **Musée Médiéval**
Pl Bassum. **Tel** *02 43 20 87 55 (Fresnay tourist office).* ⬜ *by appointment only.* 🅿️

The River Sarthe from the town of Fresnay-sur-Sarthe

Sablé-sur-Sarthe ⑥

Road map C2. 🏛 *13,000*.
🚉 🚌 ℹ️ *pl Raphaël-Elizé (02 43 95
00 60).* 🛒 *Mon, Fri–Sat.* 🎵 *Festival
de la Musique Baroque (late Aug).*
www.tourisme.sablesursarthe.fr

A good base from which
to take river cruises along
the Sarthe, Sablé is pleasant,
although fairly industrial.
There is some surprising
modern sculpture in this
traditional setting: in the cobbled place Raphaël Elizé in
the town centre stands a contemporary sculpture entitled
Hymne à l'Amour, by local
sculptor Louis Derbré, and
around the square are several
piles of "cannon balls", a
rather curious modern
installation that was inspired
by an 18th-century fashion.

Sablé has some attractive
shops in the pedestrian rue de
l'Ile and in the nearby square,
where the Maison du Sablé
sells the famous shortbread-like
biscuits to which the town has
given its name.

The town's château, which
was built in the early 18th
century by a nephew of Louis
XIV's chief minister, Jean-
Baptiste Colbert, now houses
workshops for restorers of old
books and manuscripts of the
Bibliothèque Nationale, the
national library of France.

**The Entombment of Our Lord, part of the "saints of Solesmes" group of
stone carvings in the church of the Abbaye de Solesmes**

Although the château cannot
be visited, the pleasant park
that surrounds it is open.

On the route de Solesmes,
opposite the summer swim-
ming pool, is the Jardin Public,
from which there are views of
the Abbaye de Solesmes.

Abbaye de
Solesmes ⑦

Road map C2. 🚉 *Sablé-sur-Sarthe,
then taxi.* **Tel** *02 43 95 03 08.*
Abbey Church ⭕ *daily.* ✝ *10am
daily; vespers: between 4 and
5:30pm, depending on the season.*
♿ **www**.solesmes.com

Services at the Benedictine
Abbaye de St-Pierre, part of
the Abbaye de Solesmes, attract
visitors who come from far and
wide to listen to the monks'
Gregorian chant. For over a
century, the abbey has been
working to preserve and
promote this ancient form of
prayer. Books and recordings
produced by the monks are
sold, outside church service
times, in the shop near the
entrance to the abbey.

Originally founded in 1010
as a priory, the abbey was
substantially rebuilt in the late
19th century in a somewhat
forbidding, fortress-like style.

The interior of the **abbey
church** has an austere beauty.
Its nave and transept are both
Romanesque, while the 19th-
century choir imitates the
medieval style. Both arms of
the transept are adorned with
groups of stone carvings made
in the 15th and 16th centuries
and known collectively as the
"saints of Solesmes". The
chapel to the left of the high
altar contains *The Entombment
of Our Lord*, with the haunting
figure of Mary Magdalene
kneeling at Christ's
feet, deep in prayer. In
*The Dormition of the
Virgin*, which can be
seen in the chapel on
the right, the lower
scenes illustrate the
Virgin Mary's death
and burial, while the
scenes above depict
her Assumption and
heavenly Coronation.

The little **parish
church**, which is locat-
ed beside the entrance
to the abbey, is worth
visiting for its interesting modern stained-
glass windows.

The imposing Abbaye de Solesmes, reflected in the River Sarthe

For hotels and restaurants in this region see pp206–7 and pp218–19

Asnières-sur-Vègre ❽

Road map C2. 🏠 380. 🚉 *Sablé-sur-Sarthe, then taxi.* 🚌 *Sablé-sur-Sarthe (02 43 95 00 60).*

This pretty village of old houses and water mills, with a 12th-century hump-backed bridge, is largely built in pinkish-yellow stone. Its tiny church has lively wall paintings, dating from the 12th and 15th centuries. In warm ochre and terracotta tones, they depict scenes from medieval life and moral warnings in the shape of the damned being herded into hell by huge, slavering hounds. The 13th-century **Cour d'Asnières** is an impressive Gothic building, built as a meeting place for the canons of the Cathédrale St-Julien in Le Mans.

Nearby **Juigné** is situated on the old road from Le Mans to Sablé-sur-Sarthe. Its château was rebuilt in the early 17th century. Although private, its park and terraces, with their panoramic views of the river, are open to the public. It is possible to hire boats from Juigné's tiny harbour, from which there are good views of the church perched on the cliff above.

Detail from the frescoes in Asnières' church

The 12th-century humpbacked bridge in Asnières-sur-Vègre

🏛 **Cour d'Asnières**
Manoir de la Cour. **Tel** *02 43 92 40 47.* ⬤ *for restoration.* 📷 *(of exterior).* ♿

Malicorne-sur-Sarthe ❾

Road map C3. 🏠 *2,000.* 🚉 *Noyen-sur-Sarthe, La Suze-sur-Sarthe.* 🚌 🏢 *pl Bertrand Du Gesclin (02 43 94 74 45).* 🛍 *Fri.* **www**.ville-malicorne.fr

The chief claim to fame of this little town on the Sarthe is its faïence (tin-glazed earthenware). Jean Loiseau, a potter, first set up here in 1747. At the **Faïenceries d'Art du Bourg-Joly** visitors can buy the open-work ware known as *Faïence de Malicorne*. The **Faïenceries d'Art de Malicorne**, (pottery) just outside the village, also has a factory shop, while the **Malicorne Espace Faïence**, in the centre of town, boasts an extensive pottery museum.

Malicorne's small harbour is a popular spot for boaters, and both cruises and the hire of small motorboats are possible. The village also boasts the pretty **Château de Malicorne**, dating from the 18th century, as well as a charming Romanesque church.

🏺 **Faïenceries d'Art du Bourg-Joly**
16 rue Carnot. **Tel** *02 43 94 80 10.* **Shop** ⬤ *Mon–Sat & Sun pm.*

🏺 **Faïenceries d'Art de Malicorne**
18 rue Bernard Palissy. **Tel** *02 43 94 81 18.* **Workshop** ⬤ *Apr–Sep: Tue–Sat.* **Shop** ⬤ *Mon–Sat.* 📷 ♿ 📋

🏺 **Malicorne Espace Faïence**
Rue Victor Hugo. **Tel** *02 43 48 07 17.* ⬤ *Apr–Oct: daily; Nov–Mar: Wed–Mon.* 📷 ♿

🏰 **Château de Malicorne**
Tel *02 43 94 80 03.* ⬤ *Jul–Aug: Wed–Sun; Sep–Jun: groups by appointment only.* 📷 ♿ 📋

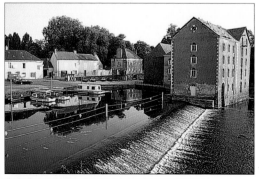

The harbour at Malicorne, surrounded by former water mills

Street-by-Street: Le Mans ⑩

The hilly, picturesque old town (La Cité Plantagenêt) can be explored only on foot. Its narrow, cobbled streets are lined by 15th- and 16th-century half-timbered houses interspersed with Renaissance mansions. Several of the finest buildings served as temporary residences for France's kings and queens, although the one named after Richard the Lionheart's queen Bérengère, or Berengaria, was built two and a half centuries after her death. The quarter is bounded to the northwest by the old Roman walls, which run beside the River Sarthe.

Carving on house in rue des Chanoines

Maison d'Adam et Eve
The carvings on this doctor's house illustrate the importance of astrology in 16th-century medicine.

Hôtel d'Argouges
Louis XI is said to have stayed in this 15th-century turreted mansion in 1467.

The Roman walls are among the best-preserved in Europe.

```
0 metres      50
0 yards       50
```

Hôtel Aubert de Clairaulnay
The sundial on the side of this late 16th-century mansion was placed there in 1789 by Claude Chappe, the inventor of semaphore.

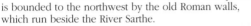

QUAI LOUIS-BLANC
RUE DE VAU
RUE DE LA VERRERIE
GRANDE RUE
RUE ST-FLACEAU
RUE DES FOSSE
RUE ST-BENOIT
RUE DE LA
AVENUE DE ROST SUR-LE-DO

KEY

– – – Suggested route

Le Grabatoire is a 16th-century mansion, built on the site of an infirmary for sick canons.

RUE DES CHAPELAINS

RUE DES CHANOINES

R. DE LA REINE BÉRENGÈRE

RUE WILBUR

WRIGHT

IERRE

VISITORS' CHECKLIST

Road map C2. 🏙 *150,000.*
🚆 *bd de la Gare.* 🚌 *ave du Général Leclerc.* 🛈 *Hôtel des Ursulines, rue de l'Etoile (02 43 28 17 22).* 🗓 *Wed, Fri, Sun.* 🎭 *Europa Jazz Festival (Apr); Son et Lumière (Jul & Aug, Tue–Sat).*
www.lemanstourisme.com

Menhir
Tradition has it that visitors should make a wish while placing their fingers in one of the little cavities in the menhir, a prehistoric standing stone, resting against the west front of the cathedral.

The Maison de la Reine Bérengère houses a museum of local history.

★ Cathédrale St-Julien
This magnificent cathedral, renowned for its intricate flying buttresses, combines Romanesque and Gothic elements.

★ Rue des Chanoines
Among the historic buildings in this attractive street is the 12th-century St Martin's Priory at No. 11.

★ Maison des Deux Amis
This building is named for its carving of two friends holding a coat of arms.

STAR SIGHTS

★ Rue des Chanoines

★ Maison des Deux Amis

★ Cathédrale St-Julien

Exploring Le Mans

Although best known for its gruelling 24-hour motor race, Le Mans has many other attractions, not least of which is the magnificent Cathédrale St-Julien. The city's history stretches back to Roman times. The walls surrounding the old town, once the Roman city of Vindunum, date from the late 3rd and early 4th centuries. They originally stretched for some 1,300 m (1,400 yards). Eleven towers are still standing, all but one on the river side, and their massive walls are decorated with geometric patterns created by using courses of brick alternating with undressed stone in various colours. Outside the city walls, Le Mans has developed into a bustling, modern city with several memorable museums and a number of attractive churches.

The Plantagenet Enamel (1150) displayed in the Musée de Tessé

🏛 Cathédrale St-Julien

Pl St Michel. *Tel 02 43 28 28 98.*
⬜ *daily.* ♿

The best view of Cathédrale St-Julien's dramatic flying buttresses, unlike those of any other cathedral in their complex arrangement, is from the place des Jacobins. The cathedral is something of a hybrid: the 12th-century nave is essentially Romanesque, and the transepts were built a century later than the pure Gothic choir, one of the tallest in France, which dates from the 13th century. From the entrance via the Romanesque south portal, there is a striking view of the pillars in the choir. These used to be decorated with 16th-century tapestries that provided a splash of colour echoed in the medieval stained glass. These days, the tapestries are displayed only a few months a year.

The Curate's Meal (1786), from the Musée de la Reine Bérengère

🏛 Musée de la Reine Bérengère

Rue de la Reine Bérengère. *Tel 02 43 47 38 51.* ⬜ *May–Sep: Tue–Sun; Oct–Jun: Tue–Sun, pm.* ● *public hols.* 📷

This museum is set in three attractive half-timbered houses in the old town, their wooden façades lively with carved figures. Its collections of art and local history include faïence and pottery from many periods, with some examples of Malicorne ware (*see p163*). The museum also shows furniture made in the region. On the second floor, the 19th-century paintings by local artists show how relatively little the town of Le Mans has changed over the years. Also of note is Jean Sorieul's dramatic canvas, *The Battle of Le Mans of 13 December, 1793.*

🏛 Musée de Tessé

2 av de Paderborn. *Tel 02 43 47 38 51.* ⬜ *Tue–Sun.* ● *pub hols.* 📷 ♿

The bishop's palace was converted in 1927 into Le Mans' art museum, devoted to the fine and decorative arts, as well as archaeology. The permanent collection of paintings on the ground floor ranges from the late Middle Ages to the 19th century, and the archaeology section is mainly Egyptian and Greco-Roman, with two replica Pharaonic tombs. The Tessé's most famous exhibit is the vivid Plantagenet Enamel, a medieval enamelled panel depicting Geoffroy V, known as Le Bel (The Handsome). Geoffroy's son, King Henry II of England, was born in Le Mans in 1133.

🏛 Musée de 24 Heures

Circuit des 24-Heures. *Tel 02 43 72 72 24.* ⬜ *Mar–May, Sep–Dec: Tue–Sun; Jun–Aug: daily.* ● *Jan, Feb.* 📷 ♿

Near Le Mans' famous race track is this museum, which displays a dazzling range of vintage, classic and modern racing cars and motorbikes. It includes some of the early designs of Amédée Bollée, an industrialist whose first pioneering car design dated from 1873. Bollée's family made the city famous for car design decades before the first 24-hour race (*see p57*).

16th-century tapestry hanging in the Cathédrale St-Julien

For hotels and restaurants in this region see pp206–7 and pp218–19

La Flèche ⓫

Road map C3. 🏠 16,000. 🚌 🚉
blvd de Montréal (02 43 94 02 53).
🏪 *Wed, Sat & Sun.* 🎭 *Festival
des Affranchis (2nd weekend Jul).*
www.tourisme-paysflechois.fr

La Flèche's chief glory is the
Prytanée Militaire, the French
military academy. Founded
as a Jesuit college in 1604 by
Henri IV, it was assigned its
present function by
Napoléon in 1808.

The entrance to the academy
is through a large Baroque
doorway, the Porte d'Honneur,
which leads into the Cour
d'Austerlitz. The Chapelle
St-Louis is in the central
courtyard. Its interior is
richly decorated, and urns
containing the ashes of the
hearts of Henri IV and Marie
de Médicis are displayed. The
academy's gardens, with
spectacular views over the
river, are open to the public.

On the opposite bank
of the river is Port Luneau,
from where Jérôme le Royer
de la Dauversière and his
companions set off for the
New World. Nearby, the
bustling place Henri IV, with
a statue of the king, is lined
with cafés.

At the heart of the town,
the 15th-century **Château des
Carmes**, the former town hall
(now hosting art exhibitions),
is reflected in the River Loir.

🏛 **Prytanée Militaire**
Rue du Collège. **Tel** 02 43 48 59
06. ⏰ Jul & Aug: daily; Sep–Jun:
groups by appt. 🎟

Place Henri IV in La Flèche, with the statue of the king in the centre

Le Lude ⓬

Road map C3. 🏠 4,200. 🚌
🈺 *pl F-de-Nicolay (02 43 94 62
20).* 🏪 *Thu.* 🎭 *Marché Nocturne
(night market; 3rd weekend in Jul).*
www.ville-lelude.com

The oldest section of this
market town is the area
surrounding the **Château du
Lude**, where houses dating
from the 15th to 17th centuries line the narrow streets.
Although the site has been
fortified for more than 1,000
years, the present château
dates from the 15th century.
Over the next 300 years the
building's originally square
layout and four corner towers
were transformed as its function changed to that of a
country house.

The interior is beautifully
furnished, largely in the 19th-
century style, although there
are some pieces from the 17th
and 18th centuries, including
French and Flemish tapestries.
The Oratory is decorated with
16th-century frescoes, which

depict Old Testament scenes.
The formal gardens lead
down to the River Loir.

🏰 **Château du Lude**
Tel 02 43 94 60 09. ⏰ Apr–Sep:
Thu-Tue, pm only (mid-Jun–Aug: daily
pm). **Park** Apr–Sep: daily. Oct–Mar:
groups by appt. 🎟 🎟 🎟 ground
floor. 🎭 Le Weekend des Jardinières
(1st w/end Jun). **www**.lelude.com

The imposing towers of the
Château du Lude

LES 24 HEURES DU MANS

The name of Le Mans is known throughout
the world, thanks to its famous 24-hour car
race. Since it began on 26 May 1923, the
event has attracted huge crowds every June,
both from France and abroad – these days,
more than 230,000 spectators and 2,500
journalists watch the race. The circuit is to
the south of the city and is 13.6-km (8½-
miles) long, including some stretches on
ordinary roads. Nowadays, drivers can cover
some 5,300 km (3,300 miles) within the time
limit. Within the course is the Hunaudières
track where, in 1908, Wilbur Wright staged
the first aeroplane flight in France.

One of the early races in Le Mans

Tour of the Loir Valley ⑬

Between Poncé-sur-le-Loir and La Flèche, the River
Loir passes through peaceful, unspoiled countryside and picturesque villages. An unhurried tour of
the valley takes two days and allows time to try some
of the numerous riverside and forest walks. Families
may enjoy the sailing, riding, angling and cycling
facilities available in the area, while art lovers can
seek out little-known churches adorned with delicately
coloured Romanesque frescoes. Wine buffs will be
interested in trying some of the area's wines, which
can be sipped from locally blown glass – the Loir
Valley also has an excellent reputation for its crafts.

**The banks of the tranquil Loir,
ideal for fishing and walking**

La Flèche ①

The home of the Prytanée
Militaire (military academy,
see p167), La Flèche is a
charming town with
wonderful views across
the River Loir.

**Entrance to the
Prytanée Militaire**

Vaas ④

The Moulin de Rotrou, on the edge of
this pretty village, is a working flour mill
and museum of breadmaking. In Vaas,
the Eglise Notre-Dame de Vaas has fine
17th-century paintings.

N23

Loir

D306

D307

D305

D141

Zoo de la Flèche ②

Just outside the town, this zoo
is one of the largest in France,
with nearly 1,200 inhabitants.

D307

D306

SAUMUR

TIPS FOR DRIVERS

Tour length: 103 km (64 miles).
Stopping-off points: The forests
and riverbanks along the Loir are
ideal for picnicking, and shops in
the region sell delicacies to make
a cold meal very special. This will
be a doubly satisfying experience
if you buy local produce from a
market, such as that in Le Lude,
first. If you prefer to eat in a
restaurant, La Fesse d'Ange in
La Flèche has local dishes on
the menu. For those wishing
to stay overnight, Le Relais
Cicéro, also in La Flèche, is
recommended.

Le Lude ③

This market town is known mainly for its
spectacular château (see p167).

The entrance to the Château du Lude

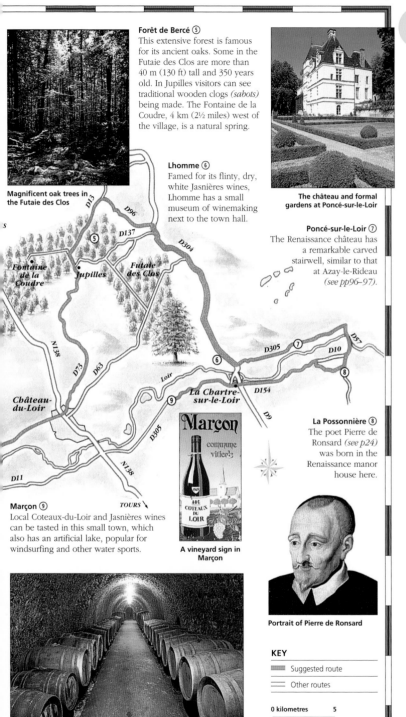

Forêt de Bercé ⑤
This extensive forest is famous
for its ancient oaks. Some in the
Futaie des Clos are more than
40 m (130 ft) tall and 350 years
old. In Jupilles visitors can see
traditional wooden clogs (*sabots*)
being made. The Fontaine de la
Coudre, 4 km (2½ miles) west of
the village, is a natural spring.

Magnificent oak trees in
the Futaie des Clos

The château and formal
gardens at Poncé-sur-le-Loir

Lhomme ⑥
Famed for its flinty, dry,
white Jasnières wines,
Lhomme has a small
museum of winemaking
next to the town hall.

Poncé-sur-le-Loir ⑦
The Renaissance château has
a remarkable carved
stairwell, similar to that
at Azay-le-Rideau
(*see pp96–97*).

La Possonnière ⑧
The poet Pierre de
Ronsard (*see p24*)
was born in the
Renaissance manor
house here.

Marçon ⑨
Local Coteaux-du-Loir and Jasnières wines
can be tasted in this small town, which
also has an artificial lake, popular for
windsurfing and other water sports.

A vineyard sign in
Marçon

Portrait of Pierre de Ronsard

Rows of barrels in a Marçon wine cellar

KEY

▦ Suggested route

═ Other routes

0 kilometres   5

0 miles   5

The Château de Courtanvaux with its towering walls

Château de Courtanvaux ⑭

Bessé-sur-Braye. **Road map** D3. **Tel** 02 43 35 34 43. ◯ Easter–mid-Sep: Tue–Sun. ● for private events. ⬛ Park ◯ daily.

Although difficult to find and unpromisingly approached through an ugly industrial estate, this large Gothic and Renaissance private château, restored in 1815, is a romantic sight as it looms up at the end of a tree-lined drive. Turrets surmount the towering walls and the impressive gateway, and willows weep gracefully over the moat.

From the 15th century until 1978, when its Renaissance gateway was officially classed as an historical monument, the château was never sold – its ownership was transferred either through inheritance or through marriage. The formal gardens are home to a tiny Gothic chapel, and visitors are free to explore the woods and pools of its 63 ha (156 acres) of pleasant parkland.

Châteaudun ⑮

Road map E2. 🏠 14,500. 🚊 🚌
ℹ️ 1 rue de Luynes (02 37 45 22 46). 🅰️ Thu. 🎪 Foire aux Laines (medieval fair, early Jul).
www.ville-chateaudun.com

Dominated by its fierce-looking **château**, the town of Châteaudun is situated above the River Loir

where the Beauce plain meets the Perche district. Châteaudun was owned at one time by the aristocratic poet Charles d'Orléans (see p24), who then handed it on to his half-brother Jean Dunois, known as the bastard of Orléans and one of Joan of Arc's loyal companions-in-arms (see p137). It was Jean who began the château's south wing in 1460, and built the beautiful late Gothic chapel, adorned with murals and life-size statues. The other wing was built half a century later.

Both wings are hung with wonderful tapestries, which date from the 16th and 17th centuries. Visitors can tour the château's living rooms, kitchens and the massive keep.

Châteaudun's Old Town has a number of picturesque buildings, as well as several interesting churches: the Romanesque **Eglise de la Madeleine**, built in stages and now restored after damage sustained in 1940, and **St-Valérien**, with its tall square belfry. Situated on the far bank of the River Loir, the **Eglise St-Jean-de-la-Chaine** is also Romanesque.

***Remembrance of Things Past* by Proust**

⚜️ **Château**
Tel 02 37 94 02 90. ◯ daily.
● 1 Jan, 1 May, 25 Dec. ⬛ ⬛
♿ restricted. **www**.monum.fr

Illiers-Combray ⑯

Road map E2. 🏠 3,300. 🚊
ℹ️ 5 rue Henri Germond (02 37 24 24 00). 🅰️ Fri. 🎪 Journée des Aubépines (Proustian May Day, May).

The little market town of Illiers has added the word "Combray" to its name in honour of Marcel Proust's magnificent novel, *Remembrance of Things Past*, in which it is depicted as Combray (see p25). As a child, Proust spent many happy summer holidays in the town, walking by the banks of the River Loir, which he later portrayed in his work, as the "Vivonne". With its quiet church square, it seems surprisingly unspoilt to the author's admirers, who make pilgrimages to the places described in the novel. They can also visit the house once owned by Proust's uncle Jules Amiot, **La Maison de Tante Léonie**. The house is now a small and touching museum, with displays about the famous writer's life, complete with the kitchen where the "Françoise" of the novel (who was actually Ernestine, the family cook) reigned supreme.

🏛️ **La Maison de Tante Léonie**
4 rue du Dr Proust. **Tel** 02 37 24 30 97. ◯ Tue–Sun. ● mid-Dec–mid-Jan. ⬛ ⬛

A view of Châteaudun's castle from across the River Loir

Carved hounds and stag on the gateway of the Château d'Anet

Château d'Anet ⑰

Road map E1. 🚃 *Dreux, then taxi.*
Tel *02 37 41 90 07.* ⬜ *Feb–Mar & Nov: Sat–Sun pm; Apr–Oct: Wed–Mon pm.* ⬤ *Dec–Jan.* 🎫
♿ *restricted* 📷

When the mistress of Henri II, Diane de Poitiers, was banished from Chenonceau after the king's accidental death in 1559, she retired to Anet, which she had inherited from her husband, and remained here until her death in 1566. It had been rebuilt for her by Philibert de l'Orme, who also designed the bridge over the Cher at Chenonceau (*see pp106–7*). The château was superbly decorated and furnished, as befitted the woman who reigned over a king's heart for nearly 30 years.

The château was sold after the Revolution and, in 1804, the new owner pulled down the central apartments and the right wing. However, you can still admire the magnificent entrance gate (the bronze relief of Diane by Benvenuto Cellini is a copy), the chapel,

decorated with bas-reliefs by the Renaissance sculptor Jean Goujon (c.1510–68), and the richly furnished west wing. Just beside the château stands the mausoleum where Diane de Poitiers is buried.

Chartres ⑱

Road map E2. 🏛 *42,000.* 🚃 🚌
ℹ *pl de la Cathédrale (02 37 18 26 26).* 🛒 *Sat.* 🎵 *Festival d'Orgue (organ music; Jul–Aug).*
www.chartres-tourisme.com

Surrounded by the wheat fields of the Beauce plain, Chartres was for many years a major market town. Visitors who come to see the Gothic cathedral (*see pp172–3*) should explore the town's old streets, particularly the rue Chantault, the rue des Ecuyers, the rue aux Herbes and, over the Eure, the rue de la Tannerie (which took its name from the tanneries that once lined the river).

The **Musée des Beaux-Arts**, occupying the elegant 18th-century building that was once the bishop's palace, is to the north of the cathedral. It has some fine Renaissance enamel plaques, a portrait of Erasmus in old age by Holbein, and many 17th- and 18th-century paintings, by French and Flemish artists. There is also a collection of 17th- and 18th-century harpsichords and spinets.

Beautiful stained glass is not restricted to the cathedral: the Gothic **Eglise St-Pierre** beside the river has lovely windows dating from

Half-timbered houses in the rue Chantault in Chartres

the 14th century, those in **St-Aignan** date from the 17th century.

The **Centre International du Vitrail**, a stained glass centre, is housed in the converted attics of the Cellier de Loëns, which was part of the cathedral's chapter house. Visitors can enjoy temporary exhibitions of old and new stained glass, as well as changing exhibitions on the theme of stained glass.

🏛 **Musée des Beaux-Arts**
29 cloître Notre–Dame. **Tel** *02 37 90 45 80.* ⬜ *Wed–Mon.* ⬤ *Sun ams & public hols.* 🎫

🏛 **Centre International du Vitrail**
5 rue du Cardinal Pie. **Tel** *02 37 21 65 72.* ⬜ *daily.* ⬤ *1 Jan, 25 Dec (and between exhibitions).* 🎫 ♿
www.centre-vitrail.org

🏛 **Conservatoire de l'Agriculture**
Le Compa, pont de Mainvilliers.
Tel *02 37 84 15 00.* ⬜ *Tue–Sun.*
⬤ *1 Jan, 1 May, 1 Nov & 25 Dec.*
🎫 ♿

IN THE FOOTSTEPS OF PROUST

No visit to Illiers-Combray is complete without retracing the hallowed walks of Marcel Proust's childhood holidays. When he stayed with his Aunt and Uncle Amiot, he would join in the family walks that became, in *Remembrance of Things Past*, "Swann's Way" and "Guermantes Way".

The first takes the walkers towards the village of Méréglise, crossing the Loire and passing through a park that was once Uncle Jules' Pré Catelan and appears in the novel as "Tansonville Park". The "Guermantes" walk covers a few kilometres towards St-Eman, following the river to its source, now trapped unromantically in a wash house in the village. The walks are signposted and guides are available at the local tourist office.

Illiers-Combray's "Tansonville Park"

Chartres: Cathédrale Notre-Dame

According to art historian Emile Male, "Chartres is the mind of the Middle Ages manifest". The Romanesque cathedral, begun in 1020, was destroyed by fire in 1194; only the south tower, west front and crypt remained. Inside, the sacred Veil of the Virgin relic was the sole treasure to survive. In a wave of enthusiasm, peasant and lord alike helped to rebuild the church in just 25 years. There were few alterations after 1250 and, unlike other cathedrals, Chartres was unscathed by the Wars of Religion and the French Revolution. The result is a Gothic cathedral with a true "Bible in stone" reputation.

Part of the Vendôme Window

Elongated Statues
These statues on the Royal Portal represent Old Testament figures.

The taller of the two spires dates from the start of the 16th century. Flamboyant Gothic in style, it contrasts sharply with the solemnity of its Romanesque counterpart.

STAR FEATURES

★ Royal Portal

★ South Porch

★ Stained-Glass Windows

Gothic Nave
As wide as the Romanesque crypt below it, the nave reaches a record height of 37 m (121 ft).

★ Royal Portal
The central tympanum of the Royal Portal (1145–55) shows Christ in Majesty.

The lower half of the west front is a survivor of the earlier Romanesque church, dating from the 11th century.

Labyrinth

THE LABYRINTH

The 13th-century labyrinth, inlaid in the floor of the nave, was a feature of most medieval cathedrals. As a penance, pilgrims used to follow the tortuous route on their knees, echoing the Way of the Cross. The journey of 262 m (860 ft), around 11 bands of broken concentric circles, took at least an hour to complete.

VISITORS' CHECKLIST

Pl de la Cathédrale. *Tel 02 37 21 75 02.* ◻ 8:30am–7:30pm daily. ✝ 11:45am Mon–Sat; 6:15pm Mon–Fri; 7pm Sun–Fri; also 9am Fri; 6pm Sat; 11am & 6pm Sun. 📷 ♿ 📷 Easter–Oct: 10:30am Tue–Sat & 3pm daily; Nov– Easter: 2:30pm daily. English: noon, 2:45pm. 📷 (tours).

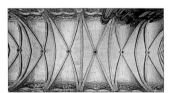

Vaulted Ceiling
A network of ribs supports the vaulted ceiling.

St-Piat Chapel
Built between 1324 and 1353, the chapel houses the cathedral treasures, including the Veil of the Virgin relic and fragments of the fragile 13th-century rood screen dismantled in 1763.

★ **Stained-Glass Windows**
The windows cover a surface area of over 3,000 sq m (32,300 sq ft).

★ **South Porch**
Sculpture on the South Porch (1197–1209) reflects New Testament teaching.

Crypt
This is the largest crypt in France, most of it dating from the early 11th century. It comprises two parallel galleries, a series of chapels and the 9th-century St Lubin's vault.

The Stained Glass of Chartres

Donated by the guilds between 1210 and 1240, this glorious collection of stained glass is world-renowned. Over 150 windows illustrate biblical stories and daily life in the 13th century (bring binoculars if you can). During both World Wars the windows were dismantled piece by piece and removed for safety. Some windows were restored and releaded in the 1970s, but much more remains to be done.

Stained glass above the apse

Redemption Window
Six scenes illustrate Christ's Passion *and death on the Cross (c.1210).*

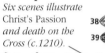

★ **Tree of Jesse**
This 12th-century stained glass shows Christ's genealogy. The tree rises up from Jesse, father of David, at the bottom, to Christ enthroned at the top.

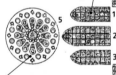

★ **West Rose Window**
This window (1215), with Christ seated in the centre, shows the Last Judgment.

KEY

1 Tree of Jesse	**12** Noah	**22** St Anthony and St Paul	**33** St Theodore and St Vincent
2 Incarnation	**13** St John the Evangelist	**23** Blue Virgin	**34** St Stephen
3 Passion and Resurrection	**14** Mary Magdalene	**24** Life of the Virgin	**35** St Cheron
4 North Rose Window	**15** Good Samaritan and Adam and Eve	**25** Zodiac Window	**36** St Thomas
5 West Rose Window	**16** Assumption	**26** St Martin	**37** Peace Window
6 South Rose Window	**17** Vendôme Chapel Windows	**27** St Thomas à Becket	**38** Modern Window
7 Redemption Window	**18** Miracles of Mary	**28** St Margaret and St Catherine	**39** Prodigal Son
8 St Nicholas	**19** St Apollinaris	**29** St Nicholas	**40** Ezekiel and David
9 Joseph	**20** Modern Window	**30** St Remy	**41** Aaron
10 St Eustache	**21** St Fulbert	**31** St James the Greater	**42** Virgin and Child
11 St Lubin		**32** Charlemagne	**43** Isaiah and Moses
			44 Daniel and Jeremiah

For hotels and restaurants in this region see pp206–7 and pp218–19

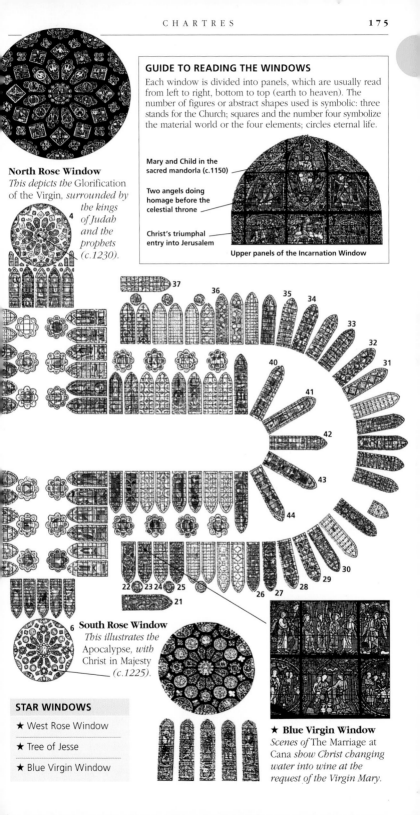

North Rose Window
This depicts the Glorification of the Virgin, *surrounded by the kings of Judah and the prophets (c.1230).*

GUIDE TO READING THE WINDOWS

Each window is divided into panels, which are usually read from left to right, bottom to top (earth to heaven). The number of figures or abstract shapes used is symbolic: three stands for the Church; squares and the number four symbolize the material world or the four elements; circles eternal life.

Mary and Child in the sacred mandorla (c.1150)

Two angels doing homage before the celestial throne

Christ's triumphal entry into Jerusalem

Upper panels of the Incarnation Window

South Rose Window
This illustrates the Apocalypse, *with Christ in Majesty (c.1225).*

STAR WINDOWS

★ West Rose Window

★ Tree of Jesse

★ Blue Virgin Window

★ **Blue Virgin Window**
Scenes of The Marriage at Cana *show Christ changing water into wine at the request of the Virgin Mary.*

LOIRE-ATLANTIQUE AND THE VENDEE

T *he region stretching from Guérande in the north to the Marais Poitevin in the south turns away from the Vallée des Rois, the land of châteaux, to face the sea. Pale limestone gives way to darker granite and, beyond the hilly, wooded areas to the east, plains stretch into marshlands and estuaries inhabited by clouds of birds.*

Here, people have for centuries won their living either from the land or from the sea. Local communities were until quite recently isolated, conservative, religious and fiercely independent. Their loyalties were the basis of the Vendée Uprising *(see p187)* which, at the end of the 18th century, threatened the new French Republic and ended in the devastation of an entire region south of the Loire. Until the 1790s, Nantes, the capital of the Loire-Atlantique, and its environs were part of Brittany, one of the last French duchies to be brought under the crown.

Nantes itself grew prosperous on the wealth generated by its maritime trade to become the seventh largest city of France in the 18th and 19th centuries. With its fine museums and elegant 18th-century *quartiers*, it remains a fascinating and likeable city.

The coast and islands of the Loire-Atlantique to the north, and the Vendée – as the region to the south is known – now draw thousands of summer visitors. Part of their charm is that most of the holiday-makers are French, since the rest of the world has barely begun to discover the beauty of the rocky headlands of Le Croisic or the beaches of golden sand that stretch from La Baule to Les Sables d'Olonne. In the south, dry summers and warm winters on the Ile de Noirmoutier have given it an almost Mediterranean look, with its whitewashed houses and Roman tiles.

In contrast, the Marais Poitevin, at the southern tip of the Vendée, is one of France's most fascinating natural environments. This land has been won back from rivers and the sea through the construction of dykes, canals and dams over hundreds of years.

An oyster gatherer in the Bay of Aiguillon

◁ Romanesque capitals in the nave of the Collégiale St-Aubin in Guérande

Exploring Loire-Atlantique and the Vendée

The mighty river Loire finally reaches the sea at St-Nazaire, in the west of the Loire-Atlantique *département*. To the northwest lies the Guérandaise Peninsula, where long expanses of sandy, south-facing beaches give way to the dramatic, rocky Atlantic coastlines. The best Atlantic beaches stretch along the Vendée coastline, from the Ile de Noirmoutier to the Marais Poitevin in the south. The Marais Poitevin, 96,000 hectares (237,000 acres) of marshland, is networked with canals. To the east lie the Vendée Hills, where the roads wind gently through towns and along the hillsides, giving lovely views of the surrounding area.

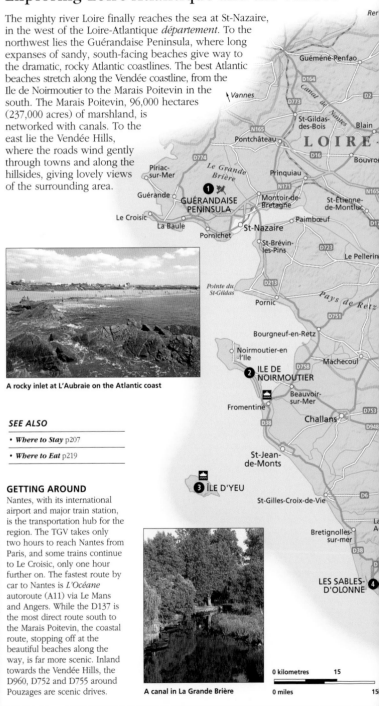

A rocky inlet at L'Aubraie on the Atlantic coast

SEE ALSO

- *Where to Stay* p207
- *Where to Eat* p219

GETTING AROUND

Nantes, with its international airport and major train station, is the transportation hub for the region. The TGV takes only two hours to reach Nantes from Paris, and some trains continue to Le Croisic, only one hour further on. The fastest route by car to Nantes is *L'Océane* autoroute (A11) via Le Mans and Angers. While the D137 is the most direct route south to the Marais Poitevin, the coastal route, stopping off at the beautiful beaches along the way, is far more scenic. Inland towards the Vendée Hills, the D960, D752 and D755 around Pouzages are scenic drives.

A canal in La Grande Brière

0 kilometres 15

0 miles 15

SIGHTS AT A GLANCE

Clisson **12**
Fontenay-le-Comte **8**
Goulaine **13**
Guérandaise Peninsula **1**
Ile de Noirmoutier **2**
Ile d'Yeu **3**
Luçon **7**
Marais Poitevin *(pp182–5)* **5**
Nantes *(pp190–93)* **14**
Pouzauges **10**
Puy-du-Fou **11**
La Roche-sur-Yon **6**
Les Sables d'Olonne **4**
Vouvant **9**

Harvesting salt the traditional way near
Guérande

KEY

━━━ Motorway

━━━ Major road

━━━ Secondary road

┄┄┄ Minor road

━━━ Scenic route

╾╼╾ Main railway

━━━ Minor railway

━━━ Regional border

Guérandaise Peninsula **❶**

Road map A3. 🚘 *Le Croisic, La Baule.* 🚌 *Le Croisic, La Baule, Guérande.* 🛈 *Le Croisic (02 40 23 00 70), La Baule (02 40 24 34 44), Guérande (02 40 24 96 71).*

La Baule, one of the grandest seaside resorts of the late 19th century, has a superb 8-km (5-mile) sweep of golden sand, now dominated by apartment blocks. However, in the pines behind the modern buildings, there is a fascinating assortment of eccentric turn-of-the-century villas. The resort of Pornichet, which adjoins La Baule, also retains some older villas beyond a modern marina crammed with yachts.

Le Croisic, reaching into the Atlantic on the west, has a wilder charm. Beyond the lively main port are miles of salty headlands with small beaches, pounding surf and wind-sculpted pines. The **Océarium** near the port is one of France's largest, privately owned aquaria.

The medieval walled town of Guérande grew rich on its *fleur de sel* – gourmet Breton salt "farmed" on extensive marshlands between here and Le Croisic. Exhibitions and a video in the **Musée des Marais Salants** at Batz-sur-Mer give an excellent idea of the painstaking techniques used to maintain its quality.

Guérande is protected by its ramparts, which are entered through four 15th-century gateways. The main gatehouse, St-Michel, houses a regional museum. In the centre of the town is the **Collégiale St-Aubin**, a church first built in the 1100s and later renovated. It has stained glass from the 14th and 16th centuries and Romanesque capitals depicting scenes from the lives of martyrs, mythology and arts.

Just 10 km (6 miles) to the east of Guérande is the **Parc Naturel Régional de**

Porte St-Michel gatehouse, one of the entrances to Guérande

A traditional thatched house in the Brière regional park

Brière, a park of 40,000 hectares (100,000 acres) of marshlands. Information about guided tours by flat-bottomed boat or on foot, bicycle or horseback is available from the tourist office in what was once a clog-maker's house in La Chapelle-des-Marais. Kerhinet, a village of 18 restored cottages, has displays on regional life.

🎣 Océarium
Av de St-Goustan, Le Croisic. **Tel** *02 40 23 02 44.* ⏲ *daily.* ● *first 3 weeks Jan.* 🎟 🕹 **www**.ocearium-croisic.fr

🏛 Musée des Marais Salants
Batz-sur-Mer. **Tel** *02 40 23 82 79.* ⏲ *Sat & Sun (Jun–Sep, school hols: daily).* ● *1–21 Dec, pub hols.* 🎟 🕹

🎣 Parc Naturel Régional de Brière
Road map A3. 🚘 *La Baule, Le Croisic, Pontchâteau, St Nazaire.* 🚌 🛈 *La Chapelle-des-Marais (02 40 66 85 01).*

Ile de Noirmoutier **❷**

Road map A4. 🚌 *Noirmoutier-en-l'Ile.* 🛈 *Noirmoutier-en-l'Ile (02 51 39 80 71).* **www**.ile-noirmoutier.com

Whitewashed Midi-style beach villas on a long, low island of fertile polders (land reclaimed from the sea) give Noirmoutier a unique character. The adventurous visitor arrives along a bumpy causeway nearly 5 km (3 miles) long, which is above the sea for only three hours at low tide. Cockle-collecting locals park their cars in the mud, but those who flirt with the tides sometimes have to climb to safety on platforms (*balises*) along the causeway. Crossing periods are posted on the road at Beauvoir-sur-Mer. There is also a bridge from Fromentine.

The island's mild climate, fishing industry and salt marshes were the basis of its wealth. Now summer tourists come to visit its long dunes, pretty beaches on the northeast and the neat main village of Noirmoutier-en-l'Ile. The dry-moated **Château de Noirmoutier** dates from the 12th century. It has displays on aspects of local history, including the bullet-riddled chair in which the Duc d'Elbée was executed during the Vendée Uprising *(see p187)*. There is also an **aquarium** and the **Musée de la Construction Navale**, illustrating boat-making techniques and maritime traditions. **Parc Océanile**, a water park that opened in 1994, includes water chutes and slides, pools with artificial waves, torrents and hot geysers.

⚓ **Château de Noirmoutier**
Pl d'Armes. *Tel 02 51 39 10 42.*
◯ *Wed–Mon (mid-Jun–mid-Sep: daily).* 🏛 📷

🐟 **Aquarium-Sealand**
Rue de l'Ecluse. *Tel 02 51 39 08 11.*
◯ *mid-Feb–mid-Nov: daily.* 🏛 ♿

🏛 **Musée de la Construction Navale**
Rue de l'Ecluse.
Tel 02 51 39 24 00. ◉ *closed for restoration until 2011.* 🏛 ♿

🏊 **Parc Océanîle**
Site des Oudinières, route de Noirmoutier. *Tel 02 51 35 91 35.*
◯ *late Jun–early Sep: daily.*
🏛 ♿ 🍴

***Polyprion americanas**, one of the fish in Noirmoutier's aquarium*

Ile d'Yeu ❸

Road map A4. 🏠 *5,000.* 🚢 *from Fromentine to Port-Joinville.* 🏨 *Rue du Marché, Ile d'Yeu (02 51 58 32 58).* **www**.ile-yeu.fr

The sandy coves and rocky coastline of this island, only 10 by 4 km (6 by 2½ miles), attract summer visitors. Near the old fishing harbour of Port-de-la-Meule are a ruined 11th-century **castle** and the **Pierre Tremblante**, a giant Neolithic stone said to move when pressed at a critical spot.

The fishing village of La Chaume, near Les Sables d'Olonne

Les Sables d'Olonne ❹

Road map A4. 🏠 *16,000.* 🚆 🚌
🏨 *1 promenade Marechal Joffre (02 51 96 85 85).* 🛒 *Tue–Sun.* **www**. lessablesdolonne-tourisme.com

The justifiable popularity of the fine, curving sands has helped to preserve the most elegant beach promenade in western France. Behind the 18th-century esplanade, hilly streets lead to a lively port on the sea channel. Opposite, the fishing village of La Chaume has a chic marina.

In Les Sables itself, attractions include the morning market at Les Halles (Tue–Sun; daily mid-Jun–mid-Sep), near the church of **Notre-Dame-de-Bon-Port**. Running between Les Halles and the rue de la Patrie lies France's narrowest street, rue de l'Enfer, which is only 53 cm (21 in) wide at the entrance on rue de la Patrie.

Masterly views of Les Sables in the 1920s by Albert Marquet are in the **Musée de l'Abbaye Ste-Croix**. Built as a convent in the 1600s, this now houses mainly modern paintings and Surrealist multimedia works.

🏛 **Musée de l'Abbaye Ste-Croix**
Rue de Verdun. *Tel 02 51 32 01 16.* ◯ *mid-Jun–Sep: Tue–Sun; Oct–mid-Jun: Tue–Sun pm only.* ◉ *public hols.* 🏛 *not first Sun of every month.*

THE BEST ATLANTIC COAST BEACHES

Les Sables d'Olonne hosted both the European surfing championship in 1987 and the world windsurfing championship in 1988. It also offers family bathing at the Grande Plage. Surfers enjoy the bigger waves at Le Tanchet (Le Château d'Olonne) and L'Aubraie (La Chaume). Other good surfing beaches are Sauveterre and Les Granges (Olonne-sur-Mer) and, further north, La Sauzaie at Brétignolles-sur-Mer. Apart from Les Sables, major esplanades and beaches with fine sands and good facilities include the Grande Plage at La Baule and Les Demoiselles at St-Jean-de-Monts.

The wide, sandy beach of L'Aubraie at La Chaume

Marais Poitevin ⑤

Kingfisher

The vast regional park of the Marais Poitevin stretches 96,000 ha (237,000 acres) across the south of the Vendée. In Roman times, most of it was under water. One thousand years of dyke building and drainage, first started by medieval monks, have produced the agricultural plains of the western Marais Desséché (dry marsh), which are protected from river floods inland by a complex network of canals. The enchanting aquatic mosaic of the Marais Mouillé (wet marsh), also known as the Venise Verte (Green Venice), lies to the east. Here, summer visitors punt or paddle along quiet, jade-coloured waterways under a canopy of willow, alder, ash, and poplar.

White Charolais Cattle
Prized for their meat, these cows are often transported by boat.

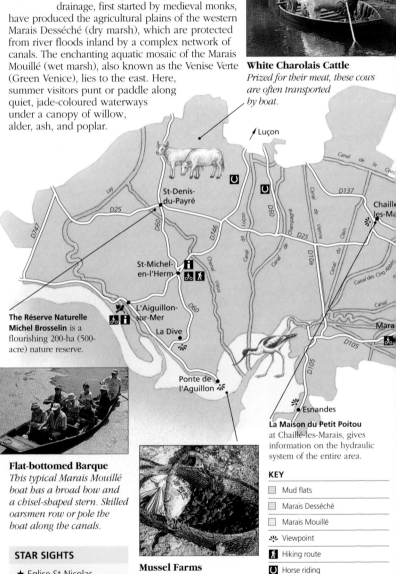

The Réserve Naturelle Michel Brosselin is a flourishing 200-ha (500-acre) nature reserve.

La Maison du Petit Poitou at Chaillé-les-Marais, gives information on the hydraulic system of the entire area.

Flat-bottomed Barque
This typical Marais Mouillé boat has a broad bow and a chisel-shaped stern. Skilled oarsmen row or pole the boat along the canals.

Mussel Farms
Mussels are farmed on the coast around L'Aiguillon-sur-Mer. The larvae are placed on ropes strung between posts embedded in the silt, exposed to the tide's ebb and flow.

KEY

☐	Mud flats
☐	Marais Desséché
☐	Marais Mouillé
❊	Viewpoint
🚶	Hiking route
⛑	Horse riding
ℹ	Tourist information
⛵	Boating
🚲	Bicycles for rent
✗	Wildlife reserve

STAR SIGHTS

★ Eglise St-Nicolas, Maillezais

★ Coulon

★ Arçais

★ **Eglise St-Nicolas, Maillezais**

The 12th-century Eglise St-Nicolas is in the town of Maillezais, which is situated at the heart of the Marais Poitevin. The church has a Romanesque façade and an unusually spacious interior. To the left of the choir is a beautiful stone statue of the Virgin and Child, *dating from the 14th century. The town also has an attractive, ruined 10th-century abbey.*

VISITORS' CHECKLIST

Road map B5. 🚆 *Niort.*
ℹ️ *Maillezais (02 51 87 23 01); Coulon (05 49 35 99 29). Good embarkation points for boating: Coulon, Maillezais, Arçais, Sansais, La Garette, St-Hilaire-la-Palud, Damvix; Tourist train: Coulon (05 49 35 02 29). Facilities for hiking tours, renting bicycles, caravans and horses.*
www.parc-marais-poitevin.fr

| 0 kilometres | 5 |
| 0 miles | 5 |

Le Poiré-sur-Velluire is a small village where the annual opening of the common grazing rights is celebrated at the end of April.

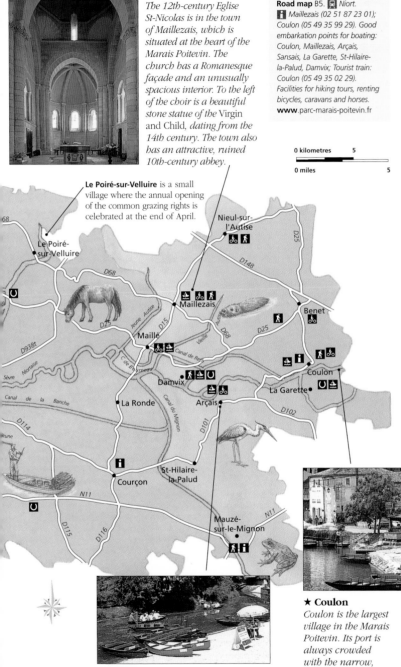

★ **Arçais**
This village in the Venise Verte has a small, stylish port and a 19th-century château.

★ **Coulon**
Coulon is the largest village in the Marais Poitevin. Its port is always crowded with the narrow, flat-bottomed boats that are traditional in this area.

Exploring the Marais Poitevin

Sign advertising trips in a barque

Early Dykes, built to hold back the tide, did nothing to solve the problem of the rivers' annual flooding of the marshlands. So large canals were dug in the 12th and 13th centuries, under the supervision of monks who had acquired land rights to marshy areas. The Marais Mouillé (wet marsh) and the Marais Desséché (dry marsh) are still separated by one of these canals: the 13th-century Canal des Cinq Abbés, south of Chaillé-les-Marais, which was a joint effort by five abbeys. Peasants labouring for the monks were rewarded with common grazing rights, some of which are still in force. During the 17th century, Henri IV brought in Dutch engineers to improve the canals, hence the "Dutch Belt" *(La Ceinture des Hollandais)* southeast of Luçon. Current measures to control flooding on lands below high-tide level range from pressure-operated dam gates to bung holes that let water into the plains of the marais in summer.

Eastern Marais

The best way to see this area is by boat. Guided tours are available from a number of towns in the region, and braver souls can hire their own boats from Arçais, Coulon, Damvix, La Garette or Maillezais.

Coulon

Road map B5. 👥 *2,300.* 🚌 *Niort.* 🛈 *31 rue Gabriel Auchier (05 49 35 99 29).* 🍴 *Fri & Sun.* **www**.marais-poitevin.fr

With its narrow streets of old whitewashed houses and imposing 12th-century church,

Coulon is the main entry point to the Marais Mouillé. The quay on the Sèvre Niortaise river is lively in summer with punt tours and crews embarking on their day's negotiation of the maze of canals. **Coulontourisme** organises accompanied or go-as-you-please boat trips and cycle hire. You can book online. Exhibits explaining local ways of life and the history of reclamation are displayed at the **Maison des Marais Mouillés**.

🚣 Coulontourisme
6 rue d'Eglise. **Tel** *05 49 35 14 14.* **www**.coulontourisme.com

🏛 Maison des Marais Mouillés
Pl de la Coutume. **Tel** *05 49 35 81 04.* ☐ *Apr–Oct: daily; Nov–Mar: groups by appointment only.* ♿

Maillezais

Road map B5. 👥 *1,000.* 🚌 *Fontenay-le-Comte, then taxi.* 🛈 *rue du Dr-Daroux (02 51 87 23 01).* **www**.maraispoitevin-vendee.com

Maillezais was one of the most important inhabited islands in the former Gulf of Poitou. Whether from a canal boat or

---

WILDLIFE OF THE MARAIS POITEVIN

An area of diverse natural habitats, including flood-plains, copses, reclaimed agricultural land and estuaries, the Marais Poitevin supports a rich array of wildlife. It is a paradise for bird-watchers, featuring around 130 different species of nesting bird and more than 120 species of migrating and wintering birds. It also supports some 40 species of mammal, 20 species of snake, 30 species of fish and hundreds of insect species.

The stands of elms, alders, willows and hawthorns supply herons with nest sites. Birds of prey such as the European kestrel and the common buzzard are present all year round, as well as breeding pairs of black kites, hobbys and, less commonly, honey buzzards in spring and summer. At night, long-eared and tawny owls scour the marshes for small rodents.

Reed warbler

For bird-watchers, the real interest of the area lies in migratory waders and wildfowl. These can be seen on the water meadows of the Marais Mouillé, on the drier expanses of the Marais Desséché and, especially, on the wide mud flats of the Bay of Aiguillon where the Sèvre Niortaise river reaches the sea. Birds to be seen here in autumn and winter include the common redshank, black-tailed godwit and whimbrel, and rare species such as the spotted crake.

The Marais Desséché is also an ideal winter refuge for frogs, toads and grass snakes, and its wide canals, bordered by thick vegetation, are home to two rare species of warbler: the great reed warbler and savi's warbler. Small numbers of another rare species, Montagu's harrier, hunt field voles in the area's reclaimed agricultural land.

The kestrel, one of the Marais' birds of prey

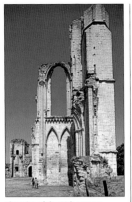

The ruins of the 10th-century Abbaye St-Pierre at Maillezais

from a viewpoint within the town, the great ruined **Abbaye St-Pierre**, founded in the 10th century, is a dramatic sight. Much of the monastery was destroyed in 1587 by the Protestant armies. The church retains decorated capitals in the 11th-century narthex, the north wall of the nave and the Renaissance transept.

The abbey refectory is still standing, as is the kitchen, now a museum. From 1524 to 1526, Rabelais sought refuge with the monks here. To the right of the entrance is a small château, built in 1872 on the ruins of the bishop's palace.

🔒 **Abbaye St-Pierre**
Tel 02 51 87 22 80. ☐ *daily.*
⬤ *3 weeks Jan.* 🎫 🔶 *restricted.*

Chaillé-les-Marais

Road map B5. 🏘 *1,800.* 🚌
🛈 *rue de l'An VI (02 51 56 71 17).*
📅 *Thu.*

This village, beside cliffs once washed by the tide, was a centre for the reclamation works that established the fields of dark soil in the Marais Desséché. The techniques are explained at the **Maison du Petit Poitou**, a museum covering different aspects of the Marais Poitevin.

Long-haired Poitou donkey

🏛 **Maison du Petit Poitou**
Tel 02 51 56 77 30.
☐ *Apr, Jun & Sep: daily pm;*
May: public hols only; Jul & Aug:
pm daily.
⬤ *Oct–Mar.* 🎫 🔶

Western Marais

Much of the early drainage work in the *marais* was led by the monks of **St-Michel-en-l'Herm**. The Benedictine abbey on this former island was originally founded in 682, but has been destroyed and rebuilt several times since then. Its 17th-century chapter house and refectory are the most important remnants.

A short drive to the south, on the River Lay estuary, are the ancient fishing port of **L'Aiguillon-sur-Mer** and the Pointe d'Aiguillon, with its 19th-century Dutch-built dyke. From here, there are marvellous views across the bay to the Ile de Ré and La Rochelle. Shellfish farming, especially mussels and oysters, is a leading industry along this part of the coast as well as in the estuaries of the western *marais*. Mussels are grown on a forest of posts, which are visible at low tide, or on ropes hung from rafts in the Bay of Aiguillon.

Male garganey duck

HABITATS

The Marais Mouillé's extensive network of canals provides an ideal refuge for otters, while its many trees provide an ample choice of nest sites for the purple heron. Migrating birds, such as garganey ducks, and waders, such as the lapwing, thrive in the Marais Desséché.

Otter

A nesting purple heron

A lapwing wintering in the Marais Poitevin

Statue of Napoléon in the main square in La Roche-sur-Yon

La Roche-sur-Yon ❻

Road map B4. 👥 54,000. 🚉 🚌
ℹ️ rue Georges Clemenceau (02 51 36 00 85). 🏪 Tue–Sat. 🎭 Café de l'Eté, open-air free concerts (mid-Jul–mid-Aug). **www**.ot-roche-sur-yon.fr

In 1804, La-Roche-sur-Yon was plucked from obscurity by Napoleon, who made it the administrative and military capital of the Vendée region.

The town's rectangular grid layout was centred on a very large parade ground, which is now called **place Napoléon**. In the middle of the square is a statue of the emperor seated astride his horse. As if to deflate these imperial pretensions, a fountain made of squashed oil cans stands playfully outside the Classical theatre building on the place du Théâtre. The 19th-century **Eglise St-Louis** is the largest church in the area.

Restored buildings of the old village are grouped around the place de la Vieille-Horloge. In summer, the oldest of these, **La Maison Renaissance**, hosts an exhibition on the history of La Roche told through models, maps and photographs.

🏛 **La Maison Renaissance**
Rue du Vieux-Marché. **Tel** 02 51 36 00 85. ⬜ Jul & Aug: Mon–Sat pm.

Luçon ❼

Road map B4. 👥 10,000. 🚉 🚌
ℹ️ square Edouard Herriot (02 51 56 36 52). 🏪 Wed & Sat. 🎭 Les Nocturnes Océanes (every other year, mid-Jul). **www**.lucon.fr

Luçon, once a marshland port, was described by its most famous inhabitant, Cardinal Richelieu (see p56) as the muddiest bishopric in France. Sent there as a 23-year-old bishop in 1608, he went on to reorganize first the town and then the kingdom. Richelieu's statue stands in the square south of the **Cathédrale Notre-Dame**.

The cathedral has an impressive Gothic nave with Renaissance side chapels. One of these contains a pulpit and two canvases painted by Richelieu's gifted successor as bishop, Pierre Nivelle, a naturalist painter. The beautiful cloisters date from the 16th century.

Painted pulpit in Luçon cathedral

Fontenay-le-Comte ❽

Road map C4. 👥 15,000. 🚉 Niort. 🚌 ℹ️ 8 rue du Grimouard (02 51 69 44 99). 🏪 Sat.

Fontenay, sloping down to the River Vendée, was the proud capital of Bas–Poitou until the French Revolution. Napoléon downgraded it in favour of a more centrally-placed administrative centre, La Roche-sur-Yon, from which he could easily control the Royalist Vendée.

Although the city's castle and fortifications were destroyed in 1621, following repeated conflicts in the Wars of Religion, much of its Renaissance quarter survived, and a prosperous postwar town has sprung up around it.

The **Eglise Notre-Dame**, with its commanding spire, is a good place to begin threading through the old streets that lead down from the place Viète. The building with the corner turret at No. 9 rue du Pont-aux-Chèvres was once the palace of the bishops of Maillezais. Many Renaissance luminaries, including the poet Nicolas Rapin and François Rabelais (see p100), lived in rue Guillemet, rue des Jacobins and the arcaded place Belliard. Rabelais was later to satirize soirées he attended here during his five years as an unruly young priest in the Franciscan friary (1519–24).

Fontenay's motto "A fountainhead of fine spirits" is incised on the **Quatre-Tias** fountain in the rue de la Fontaine, which was built in the 16th century and embellished in 1899 by Octave de Rochebrune, a local artist and intellectual.

In the **Musée Vendéen**, displays range from Gallo-Roman archaeology to an excellent scale model of Fontenay during the Renaissance. Several 19th-century portraits convey the suffering of the Vendée in the wake of the 1793 insurrection. There are also displays on daily life in the bocage, the wooded region bordering the city.

Once a manor house, the **Château de Terre-Neuve** on the rue de Jarnigande, was converted into something

The high Gothic nave of the Cathédrale Notre-Dame in Luçon

The medieval walls surrounding Vouvant, reflected in the River Mère

more imposing for Nicolas Rapin, poet and grand provost, at the beginning of the 17th century. Two hundred years later, Octave de Rochebrune added decorative flourishes, including statues of the Muses.

The interior of the château has beautiful ceilings and two wonderful fireplaces together with a collection of fine art, furniture, panelling and a door brought from the royal study in the Château de Chambord.

Musée Vendéen
Pl du 137e Régiment d'Infanterie. ***Tel*** *02 51 69 31 31.* *May–Sep: Tue–Sun, pm only; Oct–Apr: Wed, Sat & Sun, pm only.*

Château de Terre-Neuve
Rue de Jarnigande. ***Tel*** *02 51 69 99 41, 02 51 69 17 75.* *May–Sep: daily; Oct–Apr: groups by appt.*

Vouvant ❾

Road map B4. *850.* *Fontenay-le-Comte.* *Luçon.* *pl du Bail (02 51 00 86 80).* *Fête Folklorique (2nd Sun in Aug).*

The Romanesque **Eglise Notre-Dame** in the medieval village of Vouvant has a fantastically carved twin-portal doorway, from which rows of sculptures look down on an arch decorated with a Romanesque bestiary. On the tympanum, Samson wrestles a lion as Delilah advances with her shears.

Vouvant is a starting point for tours of the popular Mervant-Vouvant forest with its signposted walks, biking trails, grottoes and folklore surrounding the serpent-fairy Mélusine: she tried to lead a life as a woman, but once a week her lower half would turn into a serpent's tail. The **Tour Mélusine** has splendid views of the River Mère.

The twin portals of Vouvant's Eglise Notre-Dame

Portrait of Cathelineau (1824) by Anne-Louis Girodet-Trioson

THE VENDÉE UPRISING

Although it may at times seem a footnote to the French Revolution, the Vendée Uprising has never been forgotten in this region. The Revolution outraged the conservative, Royalist people here. Rising taxes, the persecution of Catholic priests and the execution of Louis XVI in January 1793 were then followed by attempts to conscript locals for the Republican army. This triggered a massacre of Republican sympathizers in the village of Machecoul on 11 March by a peasant mob. As the riots flared, peasant leaders, such as the wagoner Cathelineau and the gamekeeper Stofflet, took charge. They were joined by nobles including Charette, Bonchamps and La Rochejaquelain under the emblem of the sacred heart.

Using guerilla tactics, the Grand Royal and Catholic Army (Whites) took nearly all the Vendée plus Saumur and Angers by June 1793. They won several battles against Republican armies (Blues) but lost at Cholet on 17 October. Nearly 90,000 Whites fled, vainly hoping for reinforcements to join them. The Blues laid waste to the Vendée in 1794, massacring the populace. More than 250,000 people from the Vendée died.

Detail from the frieze in the church in Pouzauges

Pouzauges ⑩

Road map C4. 👥 5,500.
🚉 La Roche. 🚌 ℹ️ 28 pl de
l'Eglise (02 51 91 82 46). 🛒 Thu.
www.paysdepouzauges.fr

This small town's ruined
12th-century castle was
one of several in the
Vendée owned by Gilles
de Rais in the 15th century.
Once Marshal of France, de
Rais' distinguished military
career ended in charges
of abduction and murder,
and he later came to be
associated with the story
of Bluebeard.

The little **Eglise Notre-
Dame du Vieux-Pouzauges**,
with its 13th-century frescoes
uncovered in 1948, is one of
the treasures of the Vendée.
The frescoes depict charming
scenes from the life of the
Virgin Mary and her family.
A short audio-visual

programme describes the
paintings. On the left, 4 m
(12 ft) from the ground,
a bestiary frieze, also
discovered in 1948, illustrates
the months of the year.

Château du Puy-du-Fou ⑪

Road map B4. 🚉 to Cholet,
then taxi. **Tel** 02 51 64 11 11.
www.puydufou.com

The brick-and-granite
Renaissance château of
Puy-du-Fou is 2 km (1 mile)
from the little village of Les
Epesses. Partly restored after
its destruction in the Vendée
Uprising of 1793–4, it now
houses an ambitious theme
park, and is the backdrop
to the **Cinéscénie**, a thrilling
son et lumière spectacle
(see pp58–9).

The large theme park, **Le
Grand Parc**, offers plenty of
entertainment. It has two
reconstructed villages, one
medieval and one 18th-
century, with costumed
"villagers" and artisans,
and a market town of 1900
along the same lines. Other
features include wooded
walks, lakes, aquatic organ
pipes and puppet theatre.
Each day Le Grand Parc
stages five "spectacles".
These range from gladiatorial
battles and a Viking assault
to lively displays of jousting
and stunt-riding. But the
highlight of the events is
the falconry display, during

which falcons, eagles and
vultures skim over the heads
of seated spectators.

🎭 **Cinéscénie**
Tel 02 51 64 11 11.
🕐 Jun–early Sep: Fri & Sat.
Spectacle begins: Jun & Jul:
10:30pm; Aug–early Sep:
10pm (arrive 1 hour earlier);
reservations required. 🔴 early
Sep–May. 🎟 ♿

🎭 **Le Grand Parc**
🕐 May: Fri–Sun & public hols; Jun:
Wed–Mon; Jul & Aug: daily; Sep:
Sat & Sun. 🔴 Oct–Apr. 🎟 ♿

**Château de Clisson, a feudal
fortress now in ruins**

Clisson ⑫

Road map B4. 👥 7,000. 🚉
ℹ️ pl du Minage (02 40 54 02 95).
🛒 Tue, Wed, Fri. 🎭 Les Médiévales
(last weekend Jul).
www.clisson.com

Clisson, perched on two
hills straddling the Sèvre
Nantaise river, is notable for
its Italianate beauty. After
much of the town was
destroyed in 1794 by punitive
Republican forces following
the collapse of the Vendée
Uprising, Clisson was rebuilt
by two brothers, Pierre and
François Cacault, working
with the sculptor Frédéric
Lemot. Lemot's country
home is now the **Parc de
la Garenne Lemot**, which
celebrates the style of ancient
Rome with grottoes and
tombs, including Lemot's own.

The evolution of defensive
strategies can be followed in
the massive, ruined **Château
de Clisson**, dating from the
12th century and gradually

"Villagers" at work in Puy-du-Fou's Grand Parc

strengthened in stages up to the 16th century. This was a key feudal fortress for the dukes of Brittany.

Visitors can peer into the dungeons, and into a well with a grisly story behind it: in the vengeful aftermath of the Vendée's defeat, Republican troops butchered and flung into it 18 people who were trying to make bread in the ruins. Next to the château is a fine Renaissance covered market, which survived the destruction because it was used as Republican barracks.

♣ **Parc de la Garenne Lemot & Maison du Jardinier**
Tel 02 40 54 75 85. ☐ *Park* daily.
Maison du Jardinier Tue–Sun pm
(Jul & Aug: daily). ♿ restricted.

♣ **Château de Clisson**
Pl du Minage. *Tel* 02 40 54 02 22.
☐ May–Sep: Wed–Mon; Oct–Apr:
Wed–Mon pm only. 🎫 📷

Château de Goulaine ⓫

Road map B3. 🚶 Nantes, then
taxi (15km/8 miles). 🚌 Bas
Goulaine. *Tel* 02 40 54 91 42.
☐ opening times change every
year; call for details. 🎫 📷 ♿ grd
fl. chât & butterfly park.
www.chateau.goulaine.online.fr

Only a short distance southeast of Nantes, this is the most

The machicolated entrance tower at the Château de Goulaine

westerly of all the limestone-and-slate Loire châteaux. The same family has made wine here for 1,000 years; the building dates from the 15th century with 17th-century wings. One tower survives from the 14th century. Towers rise from the central building: on one, there is a sculpture of Yolande de Goulaine, who is said to have spurred on her besieging soldiers to repulse the besieging English by threatening to stab herself.

The château survived the Revolution because the family sold it to a Dutchman, only to recover it 70 years later. The present marquis, Robert de Goulaine, has restored the château and also opened a butterfly park where exotic species flutter about a large glasshouse. Butterflies also embellish the label of one of his *sur lie* Muscadets. The multicoloured fireplace in the grand salon is typical of the château's rich decorations.

CINÉSCÉNIE

Puy-du-Fou's late-night show is on a grand scale, with more than 1,100 performers and 14,000 seated spectators. It was conceived as a theatre of Vendée history using the full resources of contemporary open-air multimedia techniques. Laser lighting, music, water-jets and fireworks are all carefully orchestrated by computer.

Against the backdrop of the ruined château and its lake, hundreds of locally-recruited actors form living tableaux to dance or grieve, joust or slaughter each other. Horses thunder about, fountains and fireworks soar, bells ring and the château bursts into "flames".

Although the spectacle can be enjoyed for itself, translations of the commentary are available in English, German, Italian, Spanish and Dutch to 150 of the seats on the huge stand. Warm clothing and advanced booking are advised.

A fire-eater in the Cinéscénie at Puy-du-Fou

Nantes ⑭

The ancient port of Nantes was the ducal capital of Brittany for 600 years, but is now considered to be part of the Pays de la Loire. Many of its fine 18th- and 19th-century buildings and houses were built on profits from maritime trade, especially in slaves, sugar, cotton and ship's supplies. The port has been extended downstream towards St-Nazaire, where a modern bridge, the longest in France, crosses the estuary *(see p34)*. This has become an industrial zone attracting trade and breathing new life into the area. Nantes itself remains a vigorous modern city, with good museums, wide open spaces and chic restaurants, bars and shops.

The Neo-Classical theatre in the place Graslin

Exploring Nantes

The most fashionable area of town is the **quartier Graslin**. Constructed between 1780 and 1900, the district's centrepiece is the place Graslin, with its Neo-Classical theatre approached by a steep flight of monumental steps. The architect, Mathurin Crucy, designed the place Graslin as a rectangle within a semicircle with eight streets radiating from it. The theatre is fronted by eight Corinthian columns, and statues of eight Muses look down on the square. The wall behind the columns is made of glass, allowing light to stream into the foyer during the day.

Crucy's elegant architecture is seen again in the nearby cours Cambronne, a pedestrianized avenue with fine matching houses built in the early 1800s, and in the place Royale with its splendid fountain celebrating ocean and river spirits.

On the **Ile Feydeau**, the former island where Jules Verne *(see p193)* was born, 18th-century town planning combined with middle-class trading wealth helped to produce beautiful Neo-Classical façades along streets such as allée Turenne, allée Duguay-Trouin and especially rue Kervégan where 18th-century architect Pierre Rousseau occupied No. 30. Wrought-iron balconies rise in pyramidal sequence supported by luxuriant carvings.

Just north of the Ile Feydeau is the place du Commerce and the ancient Bourse, an elegant 18th-century building, now the tourist office.

🏛 La Cigale

4 pl Graslin. *Tel* 02 51 84 94 94. ⬜ daily. ♿ See **Restaurants** *p219.*

Facing the theatre, and in dazzling counterpoint to it, stands the famous brasserie-restaurant La Cigale, opened on 1 April 1895. This *fin-de-siècle* fantasy was conceived and largely executed by Emile Libaudière. The building is crammed with Art Nouveau motifs including the cicada from which it takes its name. The rich blues of its Italian tiling, its sinuous wrought-iron, bevelled windows and mirrors, sculptures and painted panels and ceilings have made this restaurant a favourite venue for aesthetes and food-lovers for a century.

🏛 Passage Pommeraye

⬜ daily.

To the east of place Graslin, rue Crébillon is the most elegant shopping street in Nantes. It is linked with the

The dining room of Nantes' Art Nouveau brasserie, La Cigale

The interior of the elegant passage Pommeraye

rue de la Fosse by a remarkable covered shopping arcade, the passage Pommeraye. Named after the lawyer who financed its construction, it opened in 1843 and must have astonished the bourgeoisie visiting its 66 shops.

The arcade's three galleries are on different levels, each linked by a handsome wooden staircase, lined with statues and lamps. The decoration is highly ornate. Charming sculpted figures look down on the galleries, lined with shops and rich with busts, bas-reliefs and other details in stone and metal, all beneath the original glass roof.

🏛 Musée Dobrée
18 rue Voltaire. **Tel** 02 40 71 03 50.
⭕ *Tue–Fri, Sat & Sun pm.* ⚫ *public hols.* 🎫 *(except Sun).*

Thomas Dobrée (1810–95), son of a rich shipowner and industrialist, spent most of his life building this collection of paintings, drawings, sculpture, tapestries, furniture, porcelain, armour, religious

Part of the carved alabaster altarpiece in the Musée Dobrée

works of art, stamps, letters and manuscripts. The impressive and palatial museum he built for them is based on a plan by the Gothic Revival architect

VISITORS' CHECKLIST

Road map B3. 🏘 *291,000.* ✈ *12 km (8 miles) Nantes-Atlantique.* 🚆 *bd Stalingrad.* 🚌 *allée Baco.* ℹ *pl St-Pierre (08 92 46 40 44).* 🛒 *Tue–Sun.* 🎭 *La Folle Journée (music, Jan); Printemps des Arts (Baroque music, painting exhibitions, May–Jun); Les Rendez-vous de l'Erdre (jazz, late Aug–early Sep); Festival des Trois Continents (cinema, Nov).* **www**.nantes-tourisme.com

Eugène-Emmanuel Viollet-le-Duc. One of the reliquaries stands out – it is a gold casket, surmounted by a crown, which contains the heart of Anne of Brittany, who asked for it to be buried in her parents' tomb in Nantes cathedral *(see p55).* A complete 15th-century altarpiece carved in alabaster statues from Nottingham, England, is another treasure.

In a second part of the complex, a modern museum houses an archaeological collection, with Egyptian, Greek and some locally found Gallo-Roman artifacts.

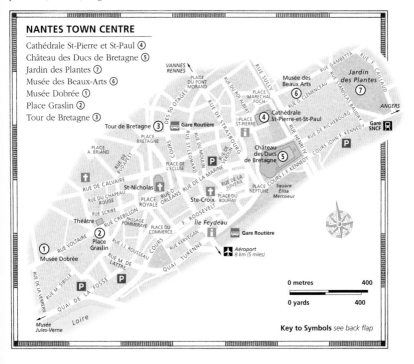

NANTES TOWN CENTRE

Cathédrale St-Pierre et St-Paul ④
Château des Ducs de Bretagne ⑤
Jardin des Plantes ⑦
Musée des Beaux-Arts ⑥
Musée Dobrée ①
Place Graslin ②
Tour de Bretagne ③

0 metres   400
0 yards   400

Key to Symbols *see back flap*

Around the Château

The Tour de Bretagne, the skyscraper built in 1976 that towers above Nantes, is a landmark dividing the city centre around place du Commerce and place Graslin to the west from the older district around the château and cathedral to the east. From the tower the cours des Cinquante Otages sweeps through the centre where the Erdre canal once flowed. This busy avenue has a memorial at the top, in place du Pont Morand, to the 50 hostages after which it is named. Their execution by the Nazis in reprisal for the assassination of the city's military commandant in 1941 turned many Nantais against the Vichy government.

The façade of the Cathédrale St-Pierre et St-Paul

♜ Château des Ducs de Bretagne

4 pl Marc Elder. *Tel 02 51 17 49 00.* ◯ *Jul–Aug: daily; Sep–Jun: Tue–Sun.* ● *1 Jan, 1 May, 1 Nov, 25 Dec.* ▨ *château.* 🎫 &

The château, surrounded by a landscaped moat and strong curtain walls with round bastions, in the style of the Château d'Angers *(see pp74–5)*, has recently reopened after 15 years of restoration. This was the birthplace of Anne of Brittany, who became duchess at 11 and then was coerced into marrying Charles VIII of France in 1491 at the age of 14. Charles died at Amboise in 1498 and, the following year, Anne married his successor, Louis XII, in the château chapel.

Anne's influence can be seen in the dormer windows and loggias of the **Grand Logis** to the right of the entrance, a graceful blend of Flamboyant and Renaissance styles. It was begun by her father, Duc François II, who built most of the château. A smaller royal lodging lies to the west of it. It was here that Henri IV signed the 1598 Edict of Nantes, granting all Protestants permission to worship. The château now hosts a high-tech museum charting the history of Nantes from Gallo-Roman times to the present day.

✠ Cathédrale St-Pierre et St-Paul

Place St-Pierre. ◯ *daily.*

Nantes has the most accident-prone cathedral on the Loire. The story of its construction and destruction over centuries is vividly told in the crypt. Most recently, on 28 January 1972, a workman's match caused an explosion that blew off the roof. Following the resulting fire, a major restoration programme was undertaken. The cathedral has been left with an unusual lightness and unity.

A notable feature of this spacious Flamboyant Gothic building is the splendid black-and-white marble tomb of François II, father of Anne of Brittany, and his two wives, sculpted by Michel Colombe *(see pp116–17)*. Situated in the southern transept, it was created between 1500 and 1507 and is among the earliest examples of the Renaissance style in France.

�🏛 Musée des Beaux-Arts

10 rue Georges Clemenceau. *Tel 02 51 17 45 00.* ◯ *Wed–Mon.* ● *public hols.* ▨ *except 1st Sun of month.* &

The grandeur of this museum and its collections is a good measure of Nantes' civic pride and wealth in the early 19th century. The galleries are on two levels and surround a huge, arched patio, whose clean lines are an appropriate setting for contemporary exhibitions. Although the museum has some sculptures, it is known mainly for its large collection of paintings,

Gustave Courbet's *The Corn Sifters* (1854) in the Musée des Beaux-Arts

Nantes' lovely botanical garden, the Jardin des Plantes

especially those representing key movements from the 15th to the 20th centuries.

Notable Italian works from the 14th century include a *Madonna and Saints* (c.1340) by Bernardo Daddi. This came from the collection of the Cacault brothers who restored Clisson *(see p189)*. So did an elegant altarpiece section by Perugino, *Saints Sebastian and Anthony* (c.1475).

Tranquil Dutch and Flemish landscapes and still lifes are offset by a typically robust Rubens, *The Triumph of Judas Maccabaeus* (1635). The master of light, Georges de la Tour, dominates a section of fine, French 17th-century paintings with some of his best work – *The Hurdy-Gurdy Player, The Dream of St Joseph* and *The Denial of St Peter*, all dating from the 1620s.

Other highlights of the museum are in the 19th- and early 20th-century sections, beginning with a luxuriant portrait by Jean-Auguste-Dominique Ingres, *Madame de Senonnes* (1814). Talented local painters, including James Tissot of Nantes and Paul Baudry of La Roche-sur-Yon, are represented, as well as the great innovators Eugène Delacroix, Gustave Courbet, Claude Monet and Vasili Kandinsky. Perhaps the most famous picture in the museum is Courbet's memorable scene, *The Corn Sifters* (1854).

♣ Musée Jules Verne
3 rue de l'Hermitage. *Tel 02 40 69 72 52.* ◯ *Wed–Sat & Sun pm–Mon.* ● *public hols.* 🖼 🚻 📷
A remarkably comprehensive display representing the life and work of Jules Verne (1828–1905) starts with a room of furnishings from the house in Amiens in which he wrote most of his books. The museum is packed with mementos, splendidly bound books, cartoons, maps, magic lanterns and models.

♣ Jardin des Plantes
Place Charles Leroux. *Tel 02 40 41 90 09.* ◯ *daily.* 🖼 *greenhouse.* 🚻 📷
The plants that make up this extensive botanical garden

began as an 18th-century collection of medicinal and exotic plants. The original specimens were brought to Nantes by homecoming ships when a royal decree obliged sea captains to bring exotic plants and seeds back to their travels.

In the mid-19th century, the director, Dr Ecorchard, made changes to the gardens after a visit to London's Kew Gardens. He introduced the English style of landscaping, with ponds and winding paths, transforming the entire area into a delightful park. Here visitors can see Europe's oldest magnolia tree as well as several outstanding displays of camellias.

THE WORLD OF JULES VERNE
Just past the Pont Anne de Bretagne is a disused section of cobbled quay which, in 1839, was lined with boats. It was here that the 11-year-old Jules Verne slipped aboard a ship to see the world. He got as far as Paimbœuf, a short trip down river, before his father caught up with him. Later, while studying law, Verne started to publish plays and librettos. His science-fiction novels, including *A Journey to the Centre of the Earth* (1864), *Twenty Thousand Leagues Under the Sea* (1870) and *Around the World in Eighty Days* (1873), have been hugely successful, and he is among the most widely read and translated authors in the world.

Bust of Jules Verne (1906) by Albert Roze

TRAVELLERS' NEEDS

WHERE TO STAY 196–207

WHERE TO EAT 208–219

SHOPS AND MARKETS 220–223

SPORTS AND ACTIVITIES 224–227

WHERE TO STAY

Loire Valley hotels are as charming as their surroundings. Family-style inns predominate, with dining rooms that are also popular among locals and comfortable, usually old-fashioned, bedrooms. The region also boasts some prestigious *Relais et Châteaux* establishments, often mansions or châteaux converted into luxury hotels with elegant rooms, superb cuisine – and prices to match. A fascinating alternative is staying in a private château or manor

A hotel doorman

house *(see pp200–201)*, which allows you access to privately-owned, often historic buildings as a (paying) guest of the owners. The hotel listings on pages 202–7 give details of establishments throughout the region, in every price category and style. *Gîtes*, the self-catering accommodation for which France is rightly famous, are also widely available in the Loire Valley, allowing you to take advantage of the marvellous range of fresh ingredients on offer in the local markets.

THE CITY HOTEL

The main towns and cities along the banks of the Loire have at least one long-established *grand hôtel* in the centre. These large hotels typically have spacious entrance halls and public rooms, but some of the once large bedrooms may well have been carved up to allow for en suite bathrooms. Rooms are liable to vary considerably in quality, so it is advisable to ask to see the room offered if you have not made a booking in advance. When you make a reservation, be sure to specify a room away from a main

road or busy square (most of these city hotels have some much quieter rooms, which overlook a courtyard). Bars are likely to be frequented by members of the local business community, who also entertain clients in the hotel restaurant, where you can expect classic French cuisine rather than regional dishes.

THE CHÂTEAU HOTEL

A number of châteaux and manor houses in the Loire Valley have been converted into expensive hotels. Often set in well-kept grounds and offering outstanding cuisine, they

range from Renaissance manor houses to huge, turreted 19th-century piles. The **Relais et Châteaux** association, of which many are members, publishes an annual brochure.

Rooms are usually spacious and elegant, with some suites available. Some château hotels also offer more modest accommodation, in outbuildings or even in bungalows in the grounds, enabling you to acquire a taste for *la vie de château* and enjoy the restaurant's cuisine without breaking the bank. If you prefer to be in the main building, specify this when booking – advance reservations are essential.

THE CLASSIC FAMILY HOTEL

These typically French small hotels, generally run by the same family for several generations, are to be found throughout the Loire Valley. The bar and dining room are likely to be widely used by locals, especially for Sunday lunch in country districts. The atmosphere is usually friendly, with helpful staff able to provide leaflets and other information about local sightseeing and shopping.

Most of these hotels have only a small number of rooms, often reasonably spacious and pleasantly furnished with well-worn antiques and flowery wallpaper. Plumbing may be erratic, although many hotels of this type have made efforts to spruce up their bathrooms. Few family hotels in the rural

The elegant Domaine des Hauts-de-Loire hotel in Onzain *(see p204)*

◁ **Lively Place Plumerau in Tours**

The grand staircase of the Hôtel de l'Univers in Tours *(see p204)*

areas have single rooms, but these are more common in the region's towns.

Many family hotels belong to the **Logis de France** association, which publishes an annual booklet listing more than 3,000 family-run hotels in France. *Logis* hotels are proud of their restaurants, which tend to specialize in regional cuisine. Most are basic roadside inns, with only a few listed in the main towns, but off the beaten track you can find charming farmhouses and inexpensive hotels.

Many family-run hotels are shut in the afternoon and do not like visitors to arrive then, although hotel guests have keys. Their restaurants are also shut at least one day a week (except possibly in the tourist season).

Logo of the Logis de France association

THE MODERN CHAIN HOTEL

France has an increasing number of modern chain hotels, on the edges of towns or close to motorways.

The cheapest are the one-star, very basic **Formule 1** motels. Two-star chains, which are widely used by French families on a low budget, include **Ibis, Campanile** and **Inter Hôtel**. More comfortable, but lacking in atmosphere or regional charm, are the **Kyriad Novotel** and **Mercure** three-star chains. All the chain hotels offer some family rooms, and in some

children can sleep in their parents' room without charge. Most have restaurants where the food is adequate.

THE RESTAURANT-WITH-ROOMS

A few of the well-known and expensive restaurants in the Loire Valley region also have rooms available for overnight guests. The rooms may be as chic as the restaurant. However, they might be modest bedrooms left over from the days before the restaurant was a gourmet's magnet and will therefore allow you to spend an inexpensive night to make up for a budget-busting meal. In rural areas, it may be practical to spend the night at the restaurant, rather than return to a remote hotel. Check in the listings on pages 214–19 for restaurants-with-rooms.

MEALS AND FACILITIES

Because most visitors to the Loire Valley choose to tour around, few hotels offer full-board rates to those who settle in for holidays. However, for more than three nights in one place, it may be possible to obtain *pension* (full-board) or *demi-pension* (half-board). But half-board may apply only to lunch, which makes sightseeing difficult, and the meals for full-board guests are likely to be less interesting than the fixed-price menus. Always

check whether the room rate includes breakfast. If not, you may prefer to have your breakfast in a nearby café.

Traditionally, family hotel rooms offer double beds, but twin beds are more likely to be found in city and chain hotels. Prices are usually fixed per room, but single travellers may be allowed a small reduction. Bathrooms with a shower rather than a bath make the room less expensive. Those with only a *cabinet de toilette* (an alcove containing basin and bidet) are the cheapest.

It is perfectly acceptable to ask to view the room before making a decision.

GRADINGS AND PRICES

French hotels are officially graded into one, two, three and four stars, plus four-star deluxe. These categories take account of facilities such as telephones, televisions and ensuite bathrooms, but do not necessarily indicate the quality of the decor or service. A few very modest hotels do not rate a star ranking.

Prices rise as the number of stars increases. Rooms may vary in quality within an establishment, so it is not easy to classify hotels solely by price. Rates for a double room start at around €60 per night without breakfast, although they may start at €150 in château hotels. Check whether a local tax *(taxe de séjour)* will be added to your bill, but service will already be included. It is usual to leave a small tip for the chambermaid.

Typical Loire Valley manor house hotel

The Domaine des Hautes Roches at Rochecorbon *(see p204)*

BOOKING

Reserve well in advance for hotels in popular tourist areas during July and August. If booking by telephone it may be necessary to give a credit card number or send a fax confirmation. You may need to speak French to make a telephone booking for some hotels, but letters in English are normally acceptable. Local tourist offices can supply listings of hotels and provide a reservation service (for up to a week in advance).

BED AND BREAKFAST

French bed-and-breakfast accommodation, called *chambres d'hôte,* can vary widely from modest rooms above a hayloft to an elegant room in a manor house. Local tourist offices keep lists of those families willing to take in guests. Some hosts will cook dinner if given advance warning. Many such rooms are registered and inspected by the **Gîtes de France** organization – look out for their green and yellow logo.

SELF-CATERING

Gîtes de France and Clévacances are the best-known organizations monitoring and booking self-catering accommodation. Run by the French government, Gîtes de France offers predominantly rural accommodation, ranging from a cottage to an entire wing of a château. Brochures are available from the departmental offices of Gîtes de France, from the Paris head office or via the Internet *(see Directory).* Booking is essential.

Local tourist offices also have lists of properties for rent within the surrounding area, but it is important to book early.

The lower-priced *gîtes* have only very basic facilities. For more luxury properties, the best way forward is to scour the major US and European newspapers, specialist magazines and the Internet, or use a letting agency. Whatever the price, a holiday in a *gîte* is a great way to experience Loire Valley life.

DIRECTORY

HOTELS

Campanile, Kyriad
Tel *08 25 02 80 38.*
www.louvrehotels.com

Formule 1
Tel *08 92 68 56 85.*
www.hotelformule1.com

Ibis, Novotel, Mercure, Sofitel
Tel *08 25 01 20 11.*
www.accorhotels.com

Inter Hôtel
Tel *08 26 10 39 09.*
www.inter-hotel.fr

Logis de France
83 av d'Italie, 75013 Paris. **Tel** *01 45 84 83 84.*
www.logis-de-france.fr

Relais et Châteaux
Tel *(0800) 2000 0002 UK.*
Tel *(800) 735 2478 US.*
www.relaischateaux.com

BED & BREAKFAST/ SELF-CATERING

Clévacances
54 boulevard de l'Embouchure, 31022

Toulouse.
Tel *05 61 13 55 66.*
www.clevacances.com

Maison des Gîtes de France
59 rue St. Lazare, 75009 Paris. **Tel** *01 49 70 75 75.*
www.gites-de-france.fr

CAMPING

Les Castels
Manoir de Terre Rouge, 35270 Bonnemain.
Tel *02 23 16 03 20.*
www.les-castels.com

CAMPING CARNETS

The Camping and Caravanning Club (UK)
Tel *(0845) 130 7631.*
www.campingand caravanning.co.uk

Family Campers & RVers (US)
Tel *(800) 245-9755.*
www.fcrv.org

HOSTELS

CNOUS
69 quai d'Orsay, 75007 Paris.
Tel *01 44 18 53 00.*
www.cnous.fr

Fédération Unie des Auberges de Jeunesse
27 rue Pajol, 75018 Paris.
Tel *01 44 89 87 27.*
www.fuaj.org

YHA (UK)
Tel *01629 592 700*
www.yha.org.uk

AYH (US)
Tel *301 495 1240.*
www.hiusa.org

DISABLED TRAVELLERS

Association des Paralysés de France
17 bd Auguste Blanqui 75013 Paris.
Tel *01 40 78 69 00.*
www.apf.asso.fr

Mobility International USA
132 E.Broadway, Suite 343, Eugene OR 7440.
Tel *(541) 343 1284.*
www.miusa.org

Tourism for All
c/o Vitalise Holidays, Shap Road, Kendal, Cumbria LA9 6NZ.
Tel *(0845) 124 9971.*
www.tourismforall.org.uk

TOURIST OFFICES

French Govt Tourist Office (UK)
Maison de la France, Lincoln House, 300 High Holborn, London WC1V 7JH. **Tel** *09068 244 123.*
www.uk.franceguide. com

French Govt Tourist Office (US)
825 Third Ave, 29th floor, New York, NY 10022.
Tel *(514) 288 1904.*
www.franceguide.com

CAMPING

Camping is a cheap and fun way of seeing the Loire Valley. Information on camp sites can be obtained from departmental tourist offices. Some of these do not accept visitors without a special camping *carnet* (available from the AA and RAC and from the addresses listed in the Directory). French camp sites are graded into four starred categories, but even one-star sites have lavatories, public telephones and running water (although this may be only cold). The top-ranked sites are remarkably well equipped. Always book ahead where possible.

The **Gîtes de France** organization has a guide to unpretentious sites on farm land (ask for *camping à la ferme*), and *camping sauvage* (camping outside official sites) is occasionally possible if you come to an agreement with the landowner. **Les Castels** is an up-market association of sites within the grounds of châteaux and manor houses.

HOSTELS

Hostels provide budget accommodation, but for two or more people sharing a room, an inexpensive hotel will probably cost the same. To stay in a youth hostel, you need to purchase a membership card from the **Youth Hostel Association** in your own country, or buy a *carte d'adhésion* card from FUAJ. Prices include breakfast and linen hire. The website of the **Fédération Unie des Auberges de Jeunesse (FUAJ)**, the national youth hostel organization, provides useful information on becoming a member, booking and prices as well as listing addresses and contact information for hostels all over France. **CNOUS**, the Centre National des Oeuvres Universitaires, provides details of university rooms available during the summer vacation. **Gîtes de France** is once again a valuable source of information: ask for the *Gîtes d'étape* guide to dormitory accommodation in farmhouses for those on walking, riding or cycling holidays.

Youth hostel in the centre of Tours old town

Gîtes de France logo

DISABLED TRAVELLERS

In the UK, **Tourism for All** publishes lists of accessible accommodation and sights in France and provides information on transportation and financial help available for taking holidays. In the US, **Mobility International** publishes several general guides to foreign exchange and travelling abroad with disabilities.

In France, information about accommodation with facilities for disabled travellers is available from the **Association des Paralysés de France**, which has also teamed up with Gîtes de France and Logis de France to recommend country *gîtes*, guest houses and other places to stay that are suitable for people with physical disabilities. These places are listed on a national register that is available free of charge from its website or from the head office of Gîtes de France, and they also appear in listings for each département. The Association des Paralysés de France also has branches in each département.

SOURCES OF INFORMATION

The invaluable guide *The Traveller in France,* listing hotel chains, booking agencies and tour operators specializing in travel to and in France, is published by the **French Government Tourist Office**. The tourist office is also able to supply brochures and booklets for **Logis de France** hotels, **Gîtes de France** and other types of accommodation. **Regional Tourist Committees** will send lists of hotels, hostels, camp sites and private self-catering accommodation. The regional **Loisirs Accueil** centre and Departmental Tourist Committees (in the major city of each department) are also useful sources of information. When you are in the Loire Valley, contact local tourist offices *(see p231)* for hotel lists and details of local families taking in guests.

Camping in a forest in the Loire Valley

Staying in a Château

The establishments featured here have been
selected from our listings of recommended
places to stay on pages 202–7. They offer a
unique opportunity to experience the style of
life in a private Loire Valley château, spending a
night within walls steeped in history, but often
with all the comforts of a modern hotel. You
will be greeted like a house guest, and efforts
are made to make you feel part of the owner's
family, who may have lived in the château for
many generations. They may also create the
atmosphere of a private party at dinner, which
can be booked and paid for in advance.

Château de Monhoudou
*The Monhoudou family have been
living in this lakeside château for 19
generations. Peacocks and swans
walk the grounds. (See p207.)*

Château des Briottières
*This 18th-century château,
furnished in period and
lived in by the same
family for six gener-
ations, has attractive
grounds and a heated
pool. (See p202.)*

0 kilometres   50

0 miles   50

Château de la Millière
*Close to Les Sables d'Olonne, this
19th-century château is set in
extensive grounds, complete with
an outdoor pool. (See p207.)*

Château de Rochecotte
*An elegant hotel since the late 1980s, this
château set in woodland near Langeais was
the residence of Prince Talleyrand. (See p204.)*

The Suite Marin de Vanssay in the Château de la Barre is decorated with 17th- and 18th-century antiques and luxurious fabrics.

Château de la Verrerie
The "Stuarts' château" (see p154), magically reflected in a lake and surrounded by dense woodland, has spacious, comfortable rooms and an attractive cottage-style restaurant on the grounds. (See p205.)

Château de la Barre
Twenty generations of the Counts of Vanssay have resided in this 15th-century château, set in peaceful grounds. (See p206.)

Château de Jallanges
An energetic couple have turned this brick-and-stone Renaissance dwelling, with a period garden and pretty chapel, into a charming home. (See p204.)

Château de la Bourdaisière
A princely greeting (from one of the Princes de Broglie) awaits you in this beautifully modernized château, the birthplace of Gabrielle d'Estrées. (See p203.)

Château du Boisrenault-Indre
With a choice of rooms, suites and apartments, this 19th-century Renaissance-style château is a good base for exploring either Berry or Touraine. (See p205.)

Choosing a Hotel

Hotels have been selected across a wide price range on the basis of their facilities, good value and location. All rooms have private bath or shower. Hotels in the Loire Valley are generally not air-conditioned unless stated here. Check ahead also for disabled facilities. For map references *see inside back cover*.

PRICE CATEGORIES
The following price ranges are for a standard double room and taxes per night during the high season. Breakfast is not included, unless specified:
€ Under €60
€€ €60–€90
€€€ €90–€120
€€€€ €120–€160
€€€€€ over €160

ANJOU

ANGERS Hôtel Mail
P €€
8 Rue des Ursules, 49100 **Tel** *02 41 25 05 25* **Fax** *02 41 86 91 20* **Rooms** *26*   **Map** *C3*

A charming hotel in a quiet corner of the city centre, this 17th-century building with tastefully decorated bedrooms was once part of a convent. A particularly good breakfast is served in the dining room, and there is also a shaded parking area. Friendly owners. **www.hotel-du-mail.com**

ANGERS Hôtel d'Anjou
€€€€
1 Blvd de Maréchal Foch, 49100 **Tel** *02 41 21 12 11* **Fax** *02 41 87 22 21* **Rooms** *53*   **Map** *C3*

The interior of this city-centre hotel is eclectically decorated with Art Deco mosaics, 17th- and 18th-century fixtures, ornate ceilings and stained-glass windows. The rooms are spacious and elegantly furnished. The on-site Le Salamandre restaurant is recommended. Parking available. **www.hoteldanjou.fr**

CHAMPIGNÉ Château des Briottières
€€€€€
Route Marigné, 49330 **Tel** *02 41 42 00 02* **Fax** *02 41 42 01 55* **Rooms** *16*   **Map** *C3*

A family-run 18th-century château set in a vast English-style park. The rooms (ten in the château and six in a charming cottage) all feature luxurious furnishings, with canopied beds and rich fabrics. Romantic dinners are on offer, as well as cooking classes. Reservations required. **www.briottieres.com**

CHÊNEHUTTE-LES-TUFFEAUX Le Prieuré
€€€€
49350 **Tel** *02 41 67 90 14* **Fax** *02 41 67 92 24* **Rooms** *36*   **Map** *C3*

This former priory, dating from the 12th century, has magnificent views over the River Loire. The bedrooms have a romantic, refined decor; two also have cosy fireplaces. The elegant restaurant serves gourmet cuisine prepared with the best regional produce, like pike poached in a Chinon wine sauce. **www.prieure.com**

FONTEVRAUD-L'ABBAYE Le Prieuré St-Lazare
€€€
49590 **Tel** *02 41 51 73 16* **Fax** *02 41 51 75 50* **Rooms** *52*   **Map** *C3*

The surroundings of this hotel, housed in the former St-Lazare priory, within the famous royal abbey complex, are stunning. The rooms are elegantly decorated in a modern, contemporary style. The restaurant, located in the ancient cloister, is a gourmet's delight. **www.hotelfp-fontevraud.com**

GENNES Aux Naulets d'Anjou
€
18 Rue Croix de Mission, 49350 **Tel** *02 41 51 81 88* **Fax** *02 41 38 00 78* **Rooms** *19*   **Map** *C3*

At the edge of the village, in private grounds, is this quiet and comfortable hotel. The genuinely warm welcome compensates for the lack of architectural interest. The rooms are simple and bright, and there are also a reading room and a lounge. The restaurant serves traditional cuisine with no frills. **www.hotel-lesnauletsdanjou.com**

MONTREUIL-BELLAY Relais du Bellay
€€
96 Rue Nationale, 49260 **Tel** *02 41 53 10 10* **Fax** *02 41 38 70 61* **Rooms** *43*   **Map** *C4*

The 17th-century main building and stylishly furnished annexe house the guest rooms. All are calm and quiet. Facilities include a swimming pool, sauna and a Turkish bath. A Jacuzzi and gym are also available. There are two rooms with disabled access. **www.hotelrelaisdubellay.fr**

SAUMUR La Croix de la Voulte
€€
Route de Boumois, 49400 **Tel** *02 41 38 46 66* **Fax** *02 41 38 46 66* **Rooms** *4*   **Map** *C3*

This manor house outside Saumur dates from the 15th century. Built at a crossroads (*croix*), it was the turning point for the royal huntsmen. The bedrooms are all different, with classic furnishings; two also have original Louis XIV fireplaces. In fine weather, breakfast is served at the side of the pool. **www.lacroixdelavoulte.com**

SAUMUR Hôtel Anne d'Anjou
€€€€
32–33 Quai Mayaud, 49400 **Tel** *02 41 67 30 30* **Fax** *02 41 67 51 00* **Rooms** *45*   **Map** *C3*

The decor in this elegant mansion, sitting between the River Loire and the château, is sophisticated and romantic. The fine building features an impressive façade, grand staircase and painted ceiling; it also has guest rooms decorated in Empire or contemporary style. Breakfast is served in the courtyard. **www.hotel-anneanjou.com**

Key to Symbols *see back cover flap*

TOURAINE

AMBOISE Le Choiseul

36 Quai Charles-Guinot, 37400 **Tel** *02 47 30 45 45* **Fax** *02 47 30 46 10* **Rooms** *32*   **Map** *D3*

An ivy-covered 18th-century manor house set in elegant grounds, with views of the River Loire. The comfortably sized guest rooms are tastefully decorated. The airy restaurant serves sophisticated cuisine, and there are pretty flower-filled walks. **www.le-choiseul.com**

AZAY LE RIDEAU La Petite Loge

15 Route de Tours, 37190 **Tel** *02 47 45 26 05* **Rooms** *5*   **Map** *D3*

La Petite Loge is a *chambres d'hôte* on a small side street. There are five rooms, each with its own entrance and bathroom. Breakfast is included in the price and served in the dining room, and guests also have use of a kitchen and outdoor barbecue area. **http://lapetiteloge.free.fr**

AZAY LE RIDEAU Manoir de la Rémonière

La Chapelle Ste-Blaise, 37190 **Tel** *02 47 45 24 88* **Fax** *02 47 45 45 69* **Rooms** *7*   **Map** *D3*

This 15th-century manor house in romantic grounds faces the château at Azay le Rideau. Some of the spacious guest rooms are furnished in a traditional style, others are more modern. The interior has been beautifully restored. Outdoor activities include hot-air ballooning, archery and fishing. Perfect for children. **www.chateaux-france.com**

CHENONCEAUX Hôtel du Bon Laboureur

6 Rue du Dr Bretonneau, 37150 **Tel** *02 47 23 90 02* **Fax** *02 47 23 82 01* **Rooms** *25*   **Map** *D3*

Near the famous château, this inn is set in its own park. The bedrooms are located in a series of 18th-century stone dwellings. They are small but well equipped, and they all have designer bathrooms. Some are suitable for disabled guests. The oak-beamed restaurant serves good food. **www.bonlaboureur.com**

CHINON Hostellerie Gargantua

73 Rue Voltaire, 37500 **Tel** *02 47 93 04 71* **Fax** *02 47 93 08 02* **Rooms** *7*   **Map** *D4*

This hotel, located in the ancient Palais du Bailliage, with its pointed roof and turret, is a local landmark. The guest rooms are comfortable, if somewhat cramped. Each has a theme, from Jeanne d'Arc to the Empire period. Pleasant dining room and terrace. Modern and classic cuisine is served in the restaurant. **www.hotel-gargantua.com**

CHINON Château de Marçay

37500 **Tel** *02 47 93 03 47* **Fax** *02 47 93 45 33* **Rooms** *33*   **Map** *D4*

This elegant hotel is housed in a restored 15th-century fortified château. From the well-appointed bedrooms, guests can enjoy the lovely views over the surrounding parkland and vineyards. Refined and aristocratic atmosphere, impeccable service and cuisine. **www.chateaudemarcay.com**

COUR-CHEVERNY Hôtels des Trois Marchands

Place de l'Eglise, 41700 **Tel** *02 54 79 96 44* **Fax** *02 54 79 25 60* **Rooms** *24*   **Map** *E3*

Just a kilometre (0.6 mile) from the château, this ancient coaching inn with a garden has been in the same family since 1865. The bedrooms are comfortably furnished in a rustic style. Take breakfast in one of the three Louis XIII dining rooms. There is also an excellent restaurant. Parking available. **www.hoteldes3marchands.com**

LOCHES Hôtel de France

6 Rue Picois, 37600 **Tel** *02 47 59 00 32* **Fax** *02 47 59 28 66* **Rooms** *17*   **Map** *D4*

In an elegant former staging post built of local tufa stone with a traditional slate roof, this hotel is situated near the historic medieval gate. The rooms are simply furnished, comfortable and well maintained. The restaurant serves good regional dishes, such as home-smoked salmon. **www.hoteldefranceloches.com**

LUYNES Domaine de Beauvois

Route de Cléré-les-Pins, 37230 **Tel** *02 47 55 50 11* **Fax** *02 47 55 59 62* **Rooms** *34*   **Map** *D4*

This Renaissance manor house built around a 15th-century tower overlooks its own lake. The park is so vast that the pathways have to be signposted. Rooms are large and comfortable, with luxurious marble bathrooms. Guests can enjoy a romantic candlelit dinner in the acclaimed restaurant. **www.beauvois.com**

MONTBAZON Château d'Artigny

Route de Monts, 37250 **Tel** *02 47 34 30 30* **Fax** *02 47 34 30 39* **Rooms** *55*   **Map** *D3*

The grounds of this 20th-century château overlook the River Indre. The grandiose classical exterior is matched by a formal Empire-style interior, and the Baroque-style guest rooms are sumptuous. The splendid restaurant serves gourmet regional specialities, as well as presenting a superb wine list. **www.artigny.com**

MONTLOUIS-SUR-LOIRE Château de la Bourdaisière

25 Rue de la Bourdaisière, 37270 **Tel** *02 47 45 16 31* **Fax** *02 47 45 09 11* **Rooms** *17*   **Map** *D3*

This château was the favourite residence of Gabrielle d'Estrées, mistress of Henri IV. Now refurbished as luxury accommodation, the hotel has elegant, luxurious guest rooms, some of which feature period furniture. The pavilion in the grounds houses six bedrooms. The gardens are open to the public. **www.labourdaisiere.com**

ONZAIN Domaine des Hauts de Loire

Route d'Herbault, 41150 **Tel** *02 54 20 72 57* **Fax** *02 54 20 77 32* **Rooms** *32*   **Map** *D3*

This former hunting lodge with large grounds retains its grandeur, with richly furnished, bright and comfortable guest rooms. This is an unashamedly expensive place to relax. The Michelin-starred restaurant offers cutting-edge and classic food, and a superb selection of local wines. There is also a tennis court. **www.domainehautsloire.com**

ROCHECORBON Domaine des Hautes Roches

86 Quai de la Loire, 37210 **Tel** *02 47 52 88 88* **Fax** *02 47 52 81 30* **Rooms** *15*   **Map** *D3*

Surrounded by Vouvray vineyards, near Tours, this hotel was once a monks' residence. Fully restored, it boasts all modern comforts. The underground rooms, hewn into the tufa chalk, are spacious and characterful. The restaurant has one Michelin star, and you can dine in the château or alfresco, on the terrace. **www.leshautesroches.com**

ST-PATRICE Château de Rochecotte

St-Patrice, Langeais, 37130 **Tel** *02 47 96 16 16* **Fax** *02 47 96 90 59* **Rooms** *35*   **Map** *D3*

Situated a short way from Langeais, Prince Talleyrand's château was completely renovated, and it opened as an elegant hotel in 1986. It is set in a charming, tranquil park with woodland. The interior is decorated sumptuously; the guest rooms are large, and each has a view. **www.chateau-de-rochecotte.fr**

SALBRIS Le Parc

8 Avenue d'Orléans, 41300 **Tel** *02 54 97 18 53* **Fax** *02 54 97 24 34* **Rooms** *23*   **Map** *E3*

A large beautiful house set in its own park with 100-year-old trees. Classic or modern, the bedrooms are comfortable and calm. Features include high ceilings, fireplaces and period furniture. Some rooms have private balconies that overlook the magnificent grounds. **www.leparcsalbris.com**

TOURS Hôtel de l'Univers

5 Boulevard Heurteloup, 37000 **Tel** *02 47 05 37 12* **Fax** *02 47 61 51 80* **Rooms** *85*   **Map** *D3*

Statesmen and royals have stayed at this luxurious hotel; a picture gallery depicts the most famous guests since 1846. The elegant architecture continues in the large, prettily furnished bedrooms, some of which are accessible to the disabled. The restaurant serves classic gourmet cuisine, and there is a private garage. **www.hotel-univers.fr**

VOUVRAY Château de Jallanges

37210 **Tel** *02 47 52 06 66* **Fax** *02 47 52 11 18* **Rooms** *7*   **Map** *D3*

This imposing Renaissance brick château, now a family home, offers comfortable rooms furnished with style. Guests are taken on a guided tour from the private chapel to the top of the turrets, from where there is a superb view. The *table d'hôte* caters for guests on reservation only. A good base for exploring Touraine. **www.jallanges.com**

BLESOIS AND ORLEANAIS

BEAUGENCY Hôtel de la Sologne

6 Place St-Firmin, 45190 **Tel** *02 38 44 50 27* **Fax** *02 38 44 90 19* **Rooms** *16*   **Map** *E3*

This typical Sologne stone building on the main square overlooks the ruined castle keep of St-Firmin. The bedrooms are small, but cosy and bright, and simply furnished. There is a pretty flower-decked patio where breakfast can be taken. Private parking is also available. **www.hoteldelasologne.com**

BLOIS Le Monarque

61 Rue Porte Chartraine, 41000 **Tel** *02 54 78 02 35* **Fax** *02 54 74 37 79* **Rooms** *27*   **Map** *E3*

Located near the Tour Beauvoir, the château and main shopping area, Le Monarque has an exceptionally convivial atmosphere. The rooms are comfortably furnished, smartly decorated and well equipped, with Internet access. Two family rooms also available. The restaurant serves traditional French cuisine. **http://annedebretagne.free.fr**

BUZANCAIS Château Boisrenault

Buzançais 36500 **Tel** *02 54 84 03 01* **Fax** *02 54 84 10 57* **Rooms** *7*   **Map** *F2*

This 19th-century Renaissance-style château, outside a little town between Chateauroux and Tours, is a handy base for the Brenne nature reserve. As well as the spacious bedooms – four of which are suites – there are two self-catering apartments. Entertainment includes a piano, library and games. **www.chateaux-du-boisrenault.com**

CHAMBORD Du Grand St-Michel

Place St-Louis, 41250 **Tel** *02 54 20 31 31* **Fax** *02 54 20 36 40* **Rooms** *40*   **Map** *E3*

Across the lawn from the château, this country house has simple but comfortable rooms, some with views. The vast restaurant is decorated with trophies, photographs and pictures, all related to hunting. There is also a lovely terrace from where guests can enjoy views of the château. Closed for a few weeks in winter. **www.saintmichel-chambord.com**

CHEVERNY Château du Breuil

Route de Fougères, 41700 **Tel** *02 54 44 20 20* **Fax** *02 54 44 30 40* **Rooms** *18*   **Map** *E3*

This 18th-century château is set in extensive grounds. The owners have refurbished the interior, and the spacious, luxurious bedrooms are equipped with Internet access. Magnificent antiques furnish both the guest rooms and the salons. The restaurant is open for residents only. Closed Jan–mid-Mar. **www.chateau-du-breuil.fr**

Key to Price Guide *see p202* **Key to Symbols** *see back cover flap*

GIEN La Poularde

13 Quai de Nice, 45500 **Tel** *02 38 67 36 05* **Fax** *02 38 38 18 78* **Rooms** *9* €€ Map F3

On the banks of the River Loire, just steps away from the Musée de la Faïencerie, is this functional hotel. Although somewhat lacking in charm, the 19th-century bourgeois house offers pleasant rooms simply furnished with Louis-Philippe furniture. The restaurant serves excellent food. **www.lapoularde.fr**

LA FERTÉ-ST-AUBIN L'Orée des Chênes

Route de Marcilly, 45240 **Tel** *02 38 64 84 00* **Fax** *02 39 64 84 20* **Rooms** *26* €€€ Map E3

This hotel-restaurant complex lies in the heart of the Sologne countryside and reflects local architecture. Located in its own parkland, it is an ideal base for fishing and walking. The comfortable rooms are furnished with style and have Internet access. The restaurant serves regional dishes. Sauna available. **www.loreedeschenes.fr**

MUIDES SUR LOIRE Château de Colliers

41500 **Tel** *02 54 87 50 75* **Fax** *02 54 87 03 64* **Rooms** *5* €€€€ Map E3

This château, in the woods a short drive east of Blois, is both rustic and grand. In the 18th century, it belonged to a governor of Louisiana. There is a delightfully romantic tour, at the top of the building, with Empire-period furniture and a roof terrace. Breakfast is included in the price. **www.chateaux-colliers.com**

ORLÉANS Jackotel

18 Cloître St-Aignan, 45000 **Tel** *02 38 54 48 48* **Fax** *02 38 77 17 59* **Rooms** *61* € Map E2

This hotel stands in the medieval centre of Orléans, near the cathedral, surrounded by a good selection of restaurants. A former cloister, it features a charming inner courtyard that leads you to the Place St-Aignan, just in front of the church. Very comfortable rooms. Parking is also available. **www.jackotel.com**

ROMORANTIN-LANTHENAY Grand Hôtel du Lion d'Or

69 Rue G Clémenceau, 41200 **Tel** *02 54 94 15 15* **Fax** *02 54 88 24 87* **Rooms** *16* €€€€€ Map E3

This former Renaissance mansion house is now a gastronomic must in this historic town. From the outside, the building is unimpressive, but the interior has instant charm. The luxury bedrooms lead off from a cobbled courtyard, and the decor is authentic Napoleon III. Formal gardens. **www.hotel-liondor.fr**

ST-LAURENT NOUAN Hôtel Le Verger

14 Rue du Port-Pichard, 41220 **Tel** *02 54 87 22 22* **Fax** *02 54 87 22 82* **Rooms** *14* €€ Map E3

Ideally placed for visiting the famous Loire châteaux, and only 8 kilometres (5 miles) from Chambord, this 19th-century bourgeois house has a pretty interior courtyard and fountain. The rooms are well maintained and spacious. The wooded park around it ensures a peaceful stay. Breakfast is included in the price. **www.hotel-le-verger.com**

SOUVIGNY-EN-SOLOGNE Ferme des Foucault

Ménestreau-en-Villette, 45240 **Tel/Fax** *02 38 76 94 41* **Rooms** *3* €€ Map F4

Deep in the forest in the Sologne countryside is this attractive redbrick-and-timber farmhouse. The immense bedrooms are cosy, with superb bathrooms; one even has a wood-burning stove. The other rooms are decorated with paintings by the owner's daughter. Friendly, relaxed atmosphere. **www.ferme-des-foucault.com**

VENDÔME Capricorne

8 Boulevard de Trémault, 41100 **Tel** *02 54 80 27 00* **Fax** *02 54 77 30 63* **Rooms** *31* € Map D3

A standard hotel near the train station. The rooms are brightly decorated; although not spacious, they are well equipped, and many overlook a pretty interior courtyard. There is also a good choice of restaurants: one serves traditional cuisine, while the other offers a buffet menu. Closed Christmas to early Jan. **www.hotelcapricorne.com**

BERRY

ARGENTON-SUR-CREUSE Manoir de Boisvillers

11 Rue du Moulins de Bord, 36200 **Tel** *02 54 24 13 88* **Fax** *02 54 24 27 83* **Rooms** *16* €€ Map E4

A surprising find in the heart of the Old Town, this an 18th-century manor house with an ivy-clad façade and a cosy atmosphere. Its tree-lined garden centres around the outdoor pool. The rooms are spacious and charming, with tasteful furnishings. Most of them have a view of the Creuse Valley. Closed Jan. **www.manoir-de-boisvillers.com**

AUBIGNY-SUR-NÈRE Château de la Verrerie

Oizon, 18700 **Tel** *02 48 81 51 60* **Fax** *02 48 58 21 25* **Rooms** *12* €€€€ Map F3

This early Renaissance château is owned by the charming de Vogüé family. As well as spacious rooms, all with views of the park or lake, the hotel has a restaurant located in an 18th-century half-timbered house. Tennis, boating, archery, fishing and hot-air ballooning are all available. Closed mid-Dec–Feb. **www.chateaudelaverrerie.com**

BOURGES Le Berry

3 Place du Général Leclerc, 18000 **Tel** *02 48 65 99 30* **Fax** *02 48 24 29 17* **Rooms** *64* €€ Map F4

Opposite the train station, this impersonal, austere grand building has a completely refurbished interior. Rooms are modern, with bright fabrics, contemporary furniture and African paintings. The restaurant also has an exotic decor, and the cuisine takes you on a world tour of flavours. Wi-Fi equipped. **www.le-berry.com**

BRINON-SUR-SAULDRE La Solognote €€

34 Grande Rue, 18410 **Tel** *02 48 58 50 29* **Fax** *02 48 58 56 00* **Rooms** *13*   **Map** *F3*

A charming family-run inn made up of three buildings housing comfortable, tastefully decorated rooms. All overlook the pretty courtyard garden, where breakfast can be taken. The restaurant is airy and bright, with exposed oak beams and antique furniture, and it serves excellent regional cuisine. Closed 3 weeks Mar. **www.lasolognote.com**

ISSOUDUN La Cognette €€€

26 Rue des Minimes, 36100 **Tel** *02 54 03 59 59* **Fax** *02 54 03 13 03* **Rooms** *20*   **Map** *E4*

Each room in this attractive hotel with flower-laden window boxes is individually decorated: there's an immaculate white decor for the Blanche de Castille room and flamboyant red for the Balzac and Madame Anska. Most open out on to a pretty terrace garden, where breakfast can be enjoyed in summer. Wi-Fi equipped. **www.la-cognette.com**

IVOY-LE-PRE Château d'Ivoy €€€€

Château d'Ivoy, 18380 **Tel** *02 48 58 85 01* **Fax** *02 48 58 85 02* **Rooms** *6*   **Map** *F3*

Located northeast of Bourges and on the edge of the Foret d'Ivoy this château, dating from the 16th–17th centuries, is surrounded by an extensive park. The elegant rooms are furnished with antiques and four-poster beds. Public spaces include a billiards room and a library. Activities include croquet, fishing and cycling. **www.chateaudeivoy.com**

LE BLANC Domaine de l'Etape €€

Route de Bélâbre, 36300 **Tel** *02 54 37 18 02* **Fax** *02 54 37 75 59* **Rooms** *25*   **Map** *D4*

This small, peaceful 18th-century château is set in an immense area of parkland. The rooms are decorated in different styles, some with antique furnishings. All are equipped with modern facilities. Guests can use the lake for angling, boating and swimming, and bikes are also available. Closed Oct–Mar. **www.domaineetape.com**

MAISONNAIS Prieure Notre-Dame d'Orsan €€€€

Thaumiers, 18210 **Tel** *02 48 61 81 62* **Fax** *02 48 61 81 82* **Rooms** *10*   **Map** *F4*

The de Bonneval family welcome you to this 18th-century fortress set in a vast park. Some rooms are decorated with elegant furnishings, others with old-fashioned floral fabrics and wall coverings. Tennis courts, Internet access and babysitting on site. Breakfast is included; *table d'hôte* by reservation. Closed Oct–Easter. **www.chateauxhotels.com**

ST-CHARTIER Château de la Vallée Bleue €€€€

Route de Verneuil, 36400 **Tel** *02 54 31 01 91* **Fax** *02 54 31 04 48* **Rooms** *15*   **Map** *E4*

This 19th-century château is now a luxury hotel with two pools (one for children) and a putting green. The best rooms are on the first floor of the main building, but there is also a suite in the ancient dove tower. Dine on the terrace in summer or at the fireside in winter. Closed mid-Nov–mid-Mar. **www.chateauvalleebleue.com**

SANCERRE Château de Beaujeu €€€€

Sens-Beaujeu, 18300 **Tel** *02 48 79 07 95* **Fax** *02 48 79 05 07* **Rooms** *14*   **Map** *F3*

Ideally located for visiting the Sancerre wine cellars, this château features beautiful grounds that extend down to the River Sauldre. The decor is old-fashioned, but the rooms are spacious, with superb views. Breakfast is served in the banquet hall; *table d'hôte* dinner can be reserved. Closed mid-Nov–Mar. **www.chateau-de-beaujeu.com**

VALENÇAY Relais du Moulin €€

44 Rue Nationale, 36600 **Tel** *02 54 00 38 00* **Fax** *02 54 00 38 79* **Rooms** *54*   **Map** *E4*

The guest rooms at this hotel complex beside an ancient mill are functional, with simple modern furnishings, soundproofing and Internet access. The dining room has an attractive terrace overlooking the garden, and the restaurant serves traditional cuisine. Closed mid-Nov–Mar. **www.hotel-lerelaisdumoulin.com**

NORTH OF THE LOIRE

CONFLANS SUR ANILLE Château de la Barre €€€€€

Château de la Barre, 72120 **Tel** *02 37 18 15 15* **Fax** *02 37 36 34 18* **Rooms** *5*   **Map** *D2*

Stay as a guest of the Count and Countess de Vanssay, the 20th generation of the family who live in this 15th-century château in the wooded hills of the Perche, between Chartres and Tours. Breakfast and afternoon tea are served daily; candlelit dinners are available by reservation. Apartments are available for longer rents. **www.chateaudelabarre.com**

DREUX Le Beffroi €€

12 Place Métézeau, 28100 **Tel** *02 37 50 02 03* **Fax** *02 37 42 07 69* **Rooms** *16*   **Map** *E1*

The rooms in this charming hotel on a pedestrianized street have a view of either the River Blaise or the church of St-Pierre. The decor is contemporary, and the owner, an ex-journalist, gives everybody a warm welcome. Internet access is available, and there is a car park nearby. Closed first 2 weeks Aug. **hotel.beffroi@club-internet.fr**

LA CHARTRE-SUR-LE-LOIR Hôtel de France €

20 Place de la République, 72340 **Tel** *02 43 44 40 16* **Fax** *02 43 79 62 20* **Rooms** *24*   **Map** *D3*

This ivy-clad hotel in the city centre has a delightful garden bordering the river. The good-value standard-sized bedrooms are simply furnished but comfortable. The bar and the brasserie are also basic, but the dining room is pleasant and serves generous portions of good food. Pretty garden terrace. **hoteldefrance@worldonline.fr**

Key to Price Guide *see p202* **Key to Symbols** *see back cover flap*

LE MANS Ibis Le Mans Centre
 €€

Quai Ledru-Rollin, 72000 **Tel** *02 43 23 18 23* **Fax** *02 43 24 00 72* **Rooms** *85*   **Map** *C2*

This standard Ibis hotel is pleasantly situated overlooking the River Sarthe and the Old Quarter. This is the best budget hotel in Le Mans, with simple, well-equipped rooms (two with disabled access) and a good buffet breakfast. Wi-Fi Internet is also available. The café-brasserie is open only for dinner. **www.ibishotel.com**

LE MANS Domaine de Chatenay
€€€€

St-Saturnin, 72650 **Tel** *02 43 25 44 60* **Fax** *02 43 25 21 00* **Rooms** *8*   **Map** *C2*

Situated in the countryside outside Le Mans, this elegant 18th-century manor house surrounded by parkland is the ideal place to relax. The spacious rooms are stylishly furnished with period furniture. Breakfast is taken in the First Empire dining room, and candlelit dinners can be booked in advance. Internet access. **www.domainedechatenay.com**

LOUÉ Hôtel Ricordeau
 €€€

13 Rue de la Libération, 72540 **Tel** *02 43 88 40 03* **Fax** *02 43 88 62 08* **Rooms** *13*   **Map** *C2*

A former coaching inn, this lovely stone building has comfortable rooms, each decorated in a different style; all are well equipped and have Internet access. The superb garden leads down to the River Vègre. Breakfast is copious, with cold meats, cheeses, fruit and home-made jams. **www.hotel-ricordeau.fr**

MONHOUDOU Château de Monhoudou
€€€€

72260 **Tel** *02 43 97 40 05* **Fax** *02 43 33 11 58* **Rooms** *5*   **Map** *D2*

The 19th generation of the de Monhoudou family still owns and runs this delightful 18th-century château. Guests can stroll in the gardens among horses, sheep, swans and peacocks. The vast rooms, all with views of the park, are furnished with antiques, and some bathrooms have spa baths. **www.monhoudou.com**

ST-JULIEN-LE-PAUVRE Château de la Renaudière
€€€

72240 **Tel** *02 43 20 71 09* **Rooms** *3*   **Map** *C2*

This gracious château owned by the Marquis de Mascureau is set among rolling meadows between Le Mans and Laval. All the rooms have private bathrooms and are tastefully furnished with period furniture. The charming owners enjoy introducing visitors to the region. Breakfast is included. Closed Nov–Apr. **www.bienvenue-au-chateau.com**

LOIRE-ATLANTIQUE AND THE VENDEE

LE CROISIC Fort de l'Océan
€€€€€

Pointe du Croisic, 44490 **Tel** *02 40 15 77 77* **Fax** *02 40 15 77 80* **Rooms** *9*   **Map** *A3*

Seventeenth-century ramparts enclose this former fortress facing the sea, but nothing remains of the harsh military lifestyle. Comfort is key, and the guest rooms are stylish and plush; one is equipped for disabled visitors. The restaurant serves wonderful seafood. **www.hotelfortocean.com**

LES SABLES D'OLONNE Château de la Millière
 €€€

St-Mathurin, 85150 **Tel** *02 51 22 73 29* **Fax** *02 51 22 73 29* **Rooms** *5*   **Map** *A4*

This elegant 19th-century château with a vast area of parkland is situated close to both the Atlantic coast and the town centre. The rooms are beautifully furnished with hangings and antiques. The library/billiard room is available to guests, and there is also on-site fishing in the private lake. Closed Oct–May. **www.chateau-la-milliere.com**

MISSILAC La Bretesche
 €€€€

Domaine de la Bretesche, 44780 **Tel** *02 51 76 86 96* **Fax** *02 40 66 99 47* **Rooms** *32*   **Map** *A3*

One of the most beautiful hotel-restaurants in the area. The rooms are located in the converted outbuildings that form a square around an inner courtyard, beside the majestic castle. Attractive decor and rich furnishings create a truly sumptuous ambience. Parkland, lake, tennis courts and golf course. Closed Feb. **www.bretesche.com**

NANTES Hôtel La Pérouse
 €€€

3 Allée Duquesne, 44000 **Tel** *02 40 89 75 00* **Fax** *02 40 89 76 00* **Rooms** *46*   **Map** *B3*

This chic hotel has a wonderful Zen atmosphere. The rooms have glossy wooden flooring and crisp contemporary furniture; they are reasonably quiet. The breakfast buffet is good, and there is free Wi-Fi Internet connection and free access to a nearby gym for guests. Municipal parking is available nearby. **www.hotel-laperouse.fr**

NANTES All Seasons
 €€€€

3 Rue de Couëdic, 44000 **Tel** *02 40 35 74 50* **Fax** *02 40 20 09 35* **Rooms** *65*   **Map** *B3*

This modern hotel stands in a busy pedestrianized square in the city centre, well placed to visit the sights. The reasonably sized comfortable rooms come equipped with satellite TV and Wi-Fi Internet access; some have disabled access, too. Good buffet breakfast. Underground municipal parking is available nearby. **www.accorhotels.com**

NOIRMOUTIER-EN-L'ISLE Hotel Fleur de Sel
 €€€€

Rue des Saulniers, 85330 **Tel** *02 51 39 09 07* **Fax** *02 51 39 09 76* **Rooms** *35*   **Map** *A4*

This hotel stands in a vast landscaped Mediterranean-style garden with a swimming pool. Some guest rooms are decorated with English-style pine and face the pool; others have a marine theme and a private terrace. Tennis courts, practice golf and bikes are available. The chef serves some of the best cuisine in the Vendée. **www.fleurdesel.fr**

WHERE TO EAT

A café sign in Berry

In this generally prosperous region, with its excellent local produce, eating out is popular, and interest in cuisine is high even by the standards of this food-loving country. Lunch remains the main meal of the day: even in larger towns such as Tours, Orléans or Nantes, most office workers return home during their two-hour lunch break. Restaurants serve lunch from about noon, and it can be hard to find one willing to serve a meal if you arrive after 1pm, although cafés and brasseries in the towns are more flexible. Dinner is served from about 8pm onwards (sometimes earlier in the main tourist areas). Beware of last orders, which may be as early as 9pm, especially in country districts. The restaurants on pages 214–19 have been carefully selected for their excellence of food, decor and ambience, and cover all price ranges.

An outdoor café in the historic heart of Richelieu

TYPES OF RESTAURANT

In country districts and small towns, the most pleasant restaurants are often to be found in hotels, especially if they belong to the **Logis de France** association, which puts particular emphasis on good (and good value for money) regional cooking. Larger towns offer a broad range of places to eat, from basic pizzerias and crêperies to chic, gourmet establishments via cafés and brasseries. Cafés are handy for a snack, coffee or aperitif, or as places from which to watch the world go by, and brasseries are good for quick meals. Unlike restaurants, brasseries and cafés generally serve a limited range of dishes outside regular mealtimes.

The Loire also has an ever-widening choice of restaurants specializing in foreign cuisines (most commonly Vietnamese and North African).

VEGETARIAN FOOD

True vegetarians do not fare well in France. It can be more convenient to head for a Vietnamese restaurant or a pizzeria, although in some of the university towns, the occasional vegetarian restaurant may be found. A few large cafés or brasseries in the tourist districts of major towns sometimes offer a small number of vegetarian dishes, and omelettes and other egg-based dishes are usually available. Alternatively, ask the chef for the meat or fish to be left out of a salad. In full-scale restaurants, it is essential to enquire in advance whether it is possible to have a vegetarian dish specially prepared. Non-meat-eaters need have no fears: Loire Valley restaurants serve excellent fish dishes, and cafés and brasseries usually offer at least one fish dish on the menu.

READING THE MENU

The vast majority of Loire Valley restaurants offer at least one *menu*, or fixed-price menu. You will often find a range of *menus*, culminating in an expensive *menu gastronomique* (gourmet meal), which may be available only if all members of your party choose it. Look out for a *menu régional* or *menu du terroir*, which will feature a selection of regional specialities.

The less expensive menus often feature starters such as local *charcuterie* (pork specialities), a salad or *crudités* (raw vegetables), whereas gourmet menus offer more complex dishes. Vegetables are often served separately.

Cheese is considered a separate course, served between the main course and dessert – local goats' cheeses are likely to predominate.

A typical Loire Valley restaurant terrace

Many restaurants, especially in country districts, do not have a *carte* from which individual dishes may be selected. If they do, eating *à la carte* almost always works out to be more expensive than choosing from a fixed-price menu, since it is not considered acceptable to skip the starter and order only a main dish (skipping dessert is more acceptable).

Cafés and brasseries offer a *plat du jour* (dish of the day), often with a regional flavour, along with standard French fare such as steak or fish with fried potatoes, complemented by a range of salads or vegetables.

The rustic Auberge de la Petite Fadette in Nohant *(see p218)*

Auberge du Moulin de Chaméron at Bannegon in Berry *(see p217)*

MAKING RESERVATIONS

It is always advisable to book tables in advance at restaurants near the well-known châteaux, especially during the main tourist season (Easter to late September). If you enjoy eating alongside the residents at local restaurants in towns, which rarely take reservations over the telephone, make sure you arrive early. Restaurants in country districts are often closed on Sunday evenings as well as for at least one whole day during the week.

DRESS CODE

Most French people take considerable trouble with their appearance but, with the exception of a few very chic and expensive places, formal dress is rarely a necessity, and ties are rarely a necessity even in the top restaurants, providing you are neatly turned out.

HOW MUCH TO PAY

It is difficult to classify restaurants by price, as most offer a range of fixed-price meals. Prices can be as low as €12 or as high as €75, but good, copious meals can be had everywhere for between €25 and €30.

A service charge of 12.5–15 per cent is usually included in the prices on menus, which are posted up outside for you to study before venturing in. It is usual to leave an extra euro or two as an additional tip. In more expensive restaurants, cloakroom attendants are given about €1 and lavatory attendants expect a small tip of about 30 cents.

Visa credit cards are widely accepted. Check first with the restaurant to find out whether American Express, MasterCard or Diners Club cards can be used.

CHILDREN AND PETS

Children are well received everywhere in the region, but they should be discouraged from leaving their seats and wandering about during the meal. High chairs are sometimes available. Some restaurants offer special low-priced children's menus *(repas d'enfant)*.

Since the French are great dog lovers, well-behaved small dogs are usually accepted at all but the most elegant restaurants (but are often banned from food shops). Do not be surprised to see your neighbour's lapdog sitting on the next door *banquette*.

WHEELCHAIR ACCESS

Because few restaurants make special provision for wheelchairs, it is wise when booking to mention that you or one of your party need space for a *fauteuil roulant*. This will ensure you get a conveniently located table and assistance, if needed, when you arrive. A list on page 198 gives names and addresses of various organizations that offer advice to disabled travellers to the Loire Valley region.

SMOKING

Since 2008, French law has banned smoking in all public places including, somewhat controversially, *lieux de convivialité*, such as bars, cafés and restaurants. Smoking is permitted at outside tables and a few establishments have special enclosed indoor spaces for smokers, which are heavily ventilated in accordance with health regulations.

The elegance of the Michelin-starred Château de Noirieux *(see p214)*

The Flavours of the Loire Valley

This huge area can take pride in a truly diverse range of top quality produce. The seafood from its Atlantic coastline, the freshwater fish from its many rivers, the game birds from its royal hunting forests, the bounty of fresh vegetables and the tiny white mushrooms that flourish in the darkness of its caves, all have helped to create a cuisine fit for kings. Many of the Loire's typical fish and meat dishes have become classics, now found all over France. Others remain very much local treats, using the region's finest and freshest produce, to be sought out and savoured in its many fine restaurants.

Young carrots

The main charcuterie is *rillettes* (shredded and potted slow-cooked pork), a speciality of Tours and the Sarthe. *Rillons* (large chunks of crunchy fried salted belly pork) are also popular. The Vendée produces some excellent cured ham. The Sologne is noted for its terrines, Chartres for its excellent game pies and Berrichon for a pâté that comes baked in pastry with slices of hard-boiled egg.

FISH

The ports of the Loire-Atlantique and the Vendée offer up a variety of fish and shellfish. La Turballe is the main sardine port on the Atlantic coast. The Ile de Noirmoutier is known for line-caught fish, lobster and oysters, as well as farmed turbot. But best of all is the region's freshwater fish, including pike-perch, shad, tench, eels and lampreys.

Fresh hake for sale, direct from the port, in the Loire-Atlantique

MEAT AND CHARCUTERIE

Free-range chickens are raised in the Sarthe, Touraine and Orléanais, and duck in the Vendée. Anjou and Mayenne are home to grass-fed cattle, and the Berry to hardy sheep. The forests and lakes of the Sologne are the domain of deer, hare, wild boar, pheasant and partridge.

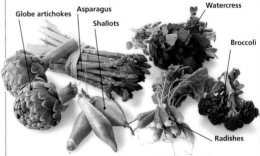

Globe artichokes · **Asparagus** · **Shallots** · **Watercress** · **Broccoli** · **Radishes**

A selection of the superb vegetables grown in the Loire Valley

LOCAL DISHES AND SPECIALITIES

Meals often start with a terrine or pâté, spread thickly on crusty bread. Creamy vegetable soups, such as asparagus or pumpkin, are also popular, as are grilled sardines and shellfish along the coast. Main courses include fish baked in a salt crust or simply poached and served with a creamy *beurre blanc* sauce. Superb poultry may also be on offer, roasted or prepared as a fricassée with cream and butter. The region produces excellent beef and lamb: tender *gigot de sept heures* is a menu favourite. Game dominates the winter table in the Sologne, commonly served with the wild mushrooms that flourish in the area. Many desserts are based on fruit, often baked in a tart or poached in wine.

Ste-Maure cheese

Gigot de Sept Heures *A leg of lamb is cooked slowly until tender with carrots, bacon, garlic, herbs and wine.*

A cheese stall in the market at Loches in the Touraine

along the banks of the Loire, tiny button mushrooms are cultivated. Samphire is gathered from the salt marshes near Nantes, and the Ile de Noirmoutier is famous for its new potatoes. The Sologne produces fine asparagus and lentils are grown in the Berry.

Orchards north of Tours and in the Sarthe are noted for their apples and pears; Comice pears originated near Angers. Other quality fruit includes the succulent plums of the Touraine and sweet strawberries from Saumur.

CHEESE

The Touraine and Berry produce some of France's finest goats' cheeses. The creamy, ash-covered Ste-Maure de Touraine is available both freshly made or matured in damp cellars. Selles-sur-Cher is a mild, flat, rounded, cindered cheese. Valençay, shaped into an ash-covered pyramid, is firmer with a stronger taste, and Pouligny-St-Pierre, a narrower pyramid, is mottled and blueish outside and white within. Most strongly flavoured are the small round Crottin de Chavignol cheeses.

Cows' milk cheeses of note include Feuille de Dreux, a flat, soft cheese with a chestnut leaf on the top, ash-covered Olivet and the washed-rinded Port-Salut.

FRUIT AND VEGETABLES

Thanks to the mild climate, winter vegetables thrive in the Nantes area. Much of France's salad vegetables are grown here, as well as, peas, radishes, turnips, early leeks and carrots. In damp caves

A busy vegetable stall in the daily market at Saumur

ON THE MENU

Alose à l'oseille Shad in a sorrel hollandaise sauce

Canard nantais Roast duck with Muscadet wine sauce

Civet de marcassin Hearty casserole of wild boar.

Géline à la lochoise Géline hen in a cream sauce

Porc aux pruneaux Pork fillets cooked with prunes in a wine and cream sauce

Potage d'asperges Creamy puréed asparagus soup

Prunes au Vouvray Plums stewed in Vouvray wine

Ragoût d'anguilles et cuisses de grenouille A stew of eel and frogs' legs

Tarte aux rillettes Open savoury tart with a filling of potted pork, eggs and cream

Lapin Chasseur *Rabbit is simmered with tomato and mushrooms to make this traditional hunters' stew.*

Sandre au beurre blanc *A poached pike-perch is served with a beurre blanc sauce of butter, cream and shallots.*

Tarte Tatin *This upside-down tart of caramelized apples on a puff pastry base may be offered plain or with cream.*

What to Drink in the Loire

The Loire Valley is a wine region *(see pp30–31)*, so naturally the traditional tipple in cafés and bars is *un petit coup de rouge* or *un petit coup de blanc* (a small glass of red or white wine). The light rosés, such as Rosé d'Anjou or Rosé de Touraine, are drunk chilled, either in the afternoon with a slice of cake or as an apéritif. In November, bars and cafés serve *bernache*, the greenish, fermented juice left after the grapes have been pressed for winemaking. There is also a wide variety of other alcoholic drinks, including *eaux de vie* made with local fruits and light, lager-style beers, as well as non-alcoholic drinks such as coffees, teas and juices.

A waiter in a Loire Valley bar

Vin de Table, *Vin de Pays*, *Vin Délimité de Qualité Supérieure* (VDQS) and finally *Appellation d'Origine Contrôlée* (AOC). *Vin de Table* wines are rarely found in good restaurants. If in doubt, order the house wine *(la réserve)*. Very few restaurants will risk their reputation on an inferior house wine, and they often provide good value for money.

APÉRITIFS AND DIGESTIFS

A glass of locally-produced sparkling wine can be an excellent apéritif or a pleasant accompaniment to the dessert course. Slightly sparkling Vouvray *pétillant* is popular, and further west in Anjou you will find Saumur *champenoise*, made by the *méthode champenoise*. Keep an eye open, too, for Crémant de Loire, another local sparkling wine.

A *kir* – white wine with a touch of *crème de cassis*, a blackcurrant liqueur – is a

White Sancerre   **Red Bourgueil**   **Sparkling wine**

WINE

Wine usually accompanies meals in the Loire, as it does throughout France. Local wine is often served in carafes. Ordering a *demi* (50 cl, approximately ½ pint) or *quart* (25 cl) is an inexpensive way to try out a wide variety of the wines of the region before buying any to take home *(see pp30–31)*.

French law divides domestic wines into four classes, in ascending order of quality:

HOW TO READ A WINE LABEL

Even the simplest label will provide a key to the wine's flavour and quality. It will bear the name of the wine and its producer, its vintage if there is one, and whether it comes from a strictly defined area *(appellation contrôlée* or VDQS) or is a more general *vin de pays* or *vin de table*. It may also have a regional grading. The shape and colour of the bottle is also a guide. Most good-quality wine is bottled in green glass, which helps to protect it from light. The label's design may be appealing, but does not indicate quality.

The property or producer

Estate-bottled, rather than a blend from a merchant or growers' co-operative

Pictures may be accurate or fanciful

Capacity of the bottle

CLOS DU BOURG
SEC
VOUVRAY
APPELLATION VOUVRAY CONTROLEE
S.A. HUET VITICULTEUR "LE HAUT-LIEU" VOUVRAY (I&L) France
750 ml

The address of the vineyard

The wine's *appellation contrôlée*

popular Burgundian apéritif, and an appealing variation, often served as the house apéritif, combines sparkling wine with raspberry or peach liqueur. Bars, cafés and restaurants also stock the usual range of French apéritifs as well as international gins, sherries, ports and whiskies.

After dinner, a little glass of clear fruit brandy made from local raspberries, pears or plums *(eaux de vie de framboise, de poire, de prune)* is a delicious aid to digestion. Other traditional French *digestifs*, such as cognac or calvados, are also drunk after meals in the region.

BEER

The locals drink mostly lager-style draught beer in cafés – ask for *un demi*. A range of bottled beers can also be found, both French (which is considerably cheaper) and imported.

Café crème, often served at breakfast with a fresh croissant

COFFEE AND TEA

Cafes, still the main focus of community life, serve good strong *express* (a tiny cup of black coffee). White coffees are prepared with hot milk and come in two sizes: small *(petit crème)* and large *(grand crème)*. Together with fresh croissants, they make a good breakfast.

Tea served in cafés is often of the teabag variety (with a slice of lemon, it is *un thé citron*). Tearooms in towns, however, are more likely to use tea leaves. Many cafés also offer a range of exotic fruit and herb teas, which are caffeine-free. In restaurants an infusion of limeflower leaves *(tilleul)*, mint *(menthe)* or camomile *(camomille)* is often drunk after dinner as an aid to digestion.

OTHER DRINKS

Children enjoy the colourful drinks served in tall glasses known as *menthe à l'eau* (green, minty syrup with tap water) and *grenadine* (a red fruit syrup), but these may be too sweet for adult tastes. Served with Vittel mineral water, for example, they become *Vittel menthe*, *Vittel grenadine*, and so on. *Vittel citron amer* (with bottled, still bitter lemon) is more refreshing than *Vittel citron* (with lemon syrup). Best of all for quenching the thirst – but also more expensive – is a *citron pressé*: freshly-squeezed lemon juice served with a carafe of water and packets of sugar to mix to taste. *Orange pressée* is orange juice served in the same way. Bottled fruit juices *(jus de fruits)* are also available everywhere.

Tap water is safe to drink, but many people prefer mineral water *(eau minérale)*, either sparkling *(gazeuse)* or still *(non-gazeuse)*.

Locally-made apple juice

WHERE TO DRINK

Cafes are the traditional place to pop in for a coffee or beer, to meet a friend or watch the world go by. City centres have bustling cafés on every corner, and many squares are crowded with outdoor tables when the weather is fine. However, the traditional café, with its long bar counter lined by regulars, is gradually being superseded, at least in towns, by more elaborate places.

Bars and *bars à vin* (old-style wine bars) are often the haunts of more hardened drinkers and of late-night revellers, although hotel bars can attract a more eclectic clientele. In larger towns,

A wood-panelled hotel bar in Touraine

many new-style wine bars, often with high-tech decor, serve wine by the glass, with light meals, plates of *charcuterie* or cheeses with crusty bread. Traditional *salons de thé* (tea-rooms), which serve coffee, tea and hot chocolate, are mainly frequented by women. They also serve *pâtisseries* and chocolates, which can be bought to take away. The newer version offers light lunches and less sophisticated sweets, cakes and tarts to a younger, mixed clientele.

People enjoying a break in a stylish café in Orléans

Choosing a Restaurant

The restaurants in this section have been selected across a wide price range for their excellent food, good value and interesting location. Most restaurants in the Loire Valley offer set menus which may work out cheaper than the price category. For *Flavours of The Loire Valley* see pp210–11. For map references *see inside back cover.*

PRICE CATEGORIES
The following price ranges are for a three course meal for one, including a half-bottle of house wine, tax and service:

ⓔ Under €30
ⓔⓔ €30–€45
ⓔⓔⓔ €45–€65
ⓔⓔⓔⓔ €65–€80
ⓔⓔⓔⓔⓔ Over €80

ANJOU

ANGERS La Ferme
ⓔ
2 Place Freppel, 49000 **Tel** *02 41 87 09 90* — **Map** *C3*

This hectic restaurant near the cathedral spills out on to the shady terrace in summer. Souvenirs of bygone farming days hang on the walls of the rustic dining room, where copious portions of traditional, homely dishes like *poulé au pot* (chicken cooked in a pot), *coq au vin* and *cassoulet* are served. For dessert, try the giant profiteroles.

ANGERS Une Ile
ⓔⓔⓔ
9 Rue Max Richard, 49000 **Tel** *02 41 19 14 48* — **Map** *C3*

A highly rated, stylish restaurant run by a chef who describes his cuisine as a combination of what ingredients are in season and his own whims. Great emphasis is placed on presentation, and there is a particularly good seafood menu. The grilled *foie gras* is also an excellent choice. Closed Sat and Sun.

BOUCHEMAINE La Terrasse
ⓔⓔ
La Pointe de Bouchemaine, 49080 **Tel** *02 41 77 14 46* — **Map** *C3*

Located in a hamlet on the confluence of the rivers Loire and Maine, this restaurant has a stunning panoramic view. The menu features freshly caught eels, pikeperch, salmon and other freshwater fish. Classic dishes, such as *sandre au beurre blanc* (pikeperch in butter), are excellently prepared. Ironically, there is no terrace, so no alfresco dining.

BRIOLLAY Château de Noirieux
ⓔⓔⓔⓔⓔ
26 Route du Moulin, 49125 **Tel** *02 41 42 50 05* — **Map** *C3*

This elegant Michelin-starred hotel-restaurant is located in a splendid château set in grounds overlooking the River Loire. The owner-chef prepares flawless classic dishes, such as sole with morel mushrooms and Racan pigeon pot-roasted with local wine. The exclusivity of the setting is worth the expense. The wine list is extensive.

DOUÉ-LA-FONTAINE Auberge de la Bienvenue
ⓔⓔ
104 Route de Cholet, 49700 **Tel** *02 41 59 22 44* — **Map** *C3*

A pretty inn situated in this town of roses. The menu offers elaborate savoury preparations, such as langoustines in saffron sauce, or calf's liver in port and pepper sauce. Other dishes revolve around local products, including pikeperch, crayfish, lamb and wild mushrooms.

FONTEVRAUD-L'ABBAYE La Licorne
ⓔⓔⓔⓔ
Allée Ste-Catherine, 49590 **Tel** *02 41 51 72 49* — **Map** *C3*

Next to the splendid abbey, this popular restaurant has a pretty courtyard terrace and elegant Louis IV dining room. The menu includes creations such as prawns and basil ravioli in morel sauce and, for dessert, warm chocolate soufflé or pears poached in red wine. Good selection of Saumur wines. Book ahead.

GENNES Auberge du Moulin de Sarré
ⓔ
Route de Louerre, 49350 **Tel** *02 41 51 81 32* — **Map** *C3*

After taking a tour of the 16th-century watermill (the only working one in the region), try either the menu of *fouées* (warm bread puffs made from flour ground at the mill) with fillings such as goat's cheese or *rillettes* (duck pâté), or the fresh trout (fished on the spot). Reservations are required.

MONTSOREAU Diane de Méridor
ⓔⓔⓔ
12 Quai Philippe de Commines, 49730 **Tel** *02 41 51 71 76* — **Map** *C3*

While dining at Diane de Méridor, you have a view of the château, which was the setting for the celluloid interpretation of *La Dame de Montsoreau* by Alexandre Dumas. Carved out of tufa rock, this restaurant is classic-modern, with exposed beams and an open fireplace. It specializes in freshwater fish dishes cooked to perfection.

SAUMUR Auberge St Pierre
ⓔⓔ
6 Place St Pierre, 49400 **Tel** *02 41 51 26 25* — **Map** *C3*

On a square near the château, in a former 15th-century monastery, this convivial restaurant serves regional specialities prepared with care. Dishes include pikeperch fillet and chicken cooked in Loire wine. Finish your meal with a plate of regional cheeses accompanied by a glass of fruity red wine, such as St Nicolas de Bourgueil.

Key to Symbols *see back cover flap*

THOUARCÉ Le Relais de Bonnezeaux

€€

Route Angers, 49380 **Tel** *02 41 54 08 33*

Map *C3*

This large, pleasant dining room is located in a converted railway station overlooking the vineyards – this is sweet-wine country. Imaginative cuisine is created with regional produce in dishes such as eels cooked in Coteaux du Layon, and calf sweetbreads braised in Savennières.

TOURAINE

AMBOISE Le Choiseul

€€€€

36 Quai C Guinot, 37400 **Tel** *02 47 30 45 45*

Map *D3*

The Michelin-starred Choiseul is an elegant 18th-century mansion with a pretty garden and views of the Loire from the airy dining room. The sophisticated menu changes seasonally; in spring, a meal might include asparagus; in summer, roast pikeperch with mustard, or *cassoulet* of crayfish. Good Touraine wines and many other regional wines.

BOURGUEIL Le Moulin Bleu

€€

7 Rue du Moulin-Bleu, 37140 **Tel** *02 47 97 73 13*

Map *D3*

The house at the foot of this pretty blue mill has two vaulted dining rooms where traditional dishes are served in a friendly, convivial atmosphere. The cuisine remains faithful to the region, with Touraine-reared veal served with a Vouvray butter sauce. There are several good Bourgueil producers on the wine list.

CHINON Les Années 30

€€

78 Rue Haute St Maurice, 37500 **Tel** *02 47 93 37 18*

Map *D3*

The chef at this elegant little eatery on the way up to the château has brought back a spark to the menu. Stéphane Charles presents dishes such as a *tartare* of oysters with a seaweed tempura, and pikeperch served with leeks and red peppers flavoured with ginger. Good local wines feature on the list.

FONDETTES Auberge de Port Vallières

€€€

Route de Langeais, 37230 **Tel** *02 47 42 24 04*

Map *D3*

On the banks of the River Loire, this former fisherman's pub has heaps of rustic charm. Regional dishes, such as beef cooked in Chinon wine and local freshwater fish, are prepared by chef Bruno Leroux. There is also a good choice of local wines.

MONTBAZON La Chancelière Jeu de Cartes

€€€

1 Place des Marronniers, 37250 **Tel** *02 47 26 00 67*

Map *D3*

Modern, sophisticated cuisine prepared with precision and skill is on offer at La Chancelière. This restaurant proposes savoury but uncomplicated dishes such as oyster ravioli with a champagne sauce, or pan-fried escalope of *foie gras*. The well-selected wine list features good Vouvray and Bourgueil producers.

ONZAIN Domaine des Hauts de Loire

€€€€€

Route de Herbault, 41150 **Tel** *02 54 20 72 57*

Map *D3*

Haute cuisine is served in this former hunting lodge set within its own park, where superb dishes are presented by chef Rémi Giraud. Among the specialities are scallop *carpaccio* (raw, thin slices), beef poached in Montlouis wine with *foie gras* ravioli, and roast mango with passion-fruit jelly. The restaurant has one Michelin star. Classic wine list.

ROCHECORBON Les Hautes Roches

€€€€€

86 Quai de la Loire, 37210 **Tel** *02 47 52 88 88*

Map *D3*

The dining room in this château is decorated in contemporary tones, and the chef serves modern, Michelin-starred cuisine to match, including irresistible dishes, such as a terrine of *lapin*, Racan pigeon with lemon confit, and Grand Marnier soufflé. The cellar has wonderful wines from the best local producers.

SACHÉ Auberge du XII Siècle

€€€€

1 Rue du Château, 37190 **Tel** *02 47 26 88 77*

Map *D3*

In a historic building, a stone's throw from the Balzac Museum, is Auberge du XII Siècle. The main dining room has a rustic atmosphere with exposed beams. There is a good choice of fixed-price menus with classic dishes, such as snail Parmentier, roasted bass with purée of artichokes and *foie gras*, and chocolate tart with cherry coulis.

SALBRIS Domaine de Valaudran

€€€€

Rue de Romorantin, 41300 **Tel** *02 54 97 20 00*

Map *E3*

Salbris is reputed to be the best place in Sologne to hunt. In season, this restaurant in an 18th-century country house benefits from superb game, which finds its way in dishes such as stuffed pigeon breast with apple sauce. Other fine dishes include bass wrapped in cabbage with a citrus sauce, or scorpion fish with mushrooms, shallots and *foie gras*.

ST-OUEN LES VIGNES L'Aubinière

€€€

29 Rue Jules Gautier, 37530 **Tel** *02 47 30 15 29*

Map *D3*

North of Amboise, this small rustic restaurant opens on to a pretty garden that leads down to the river. Enjoy the creations of chef Jacques Arrayet, who serves outstanding dishes including *foie gras* and lobster, a caramel of beetroot with pistachio oil, and steamed bass with herbs and Paimpol beans.

TOURS L'Atelier Gourmand
37 Rue Etienne Marcel, 37000 **Tel** *02 47 38 59 87*   **Map** D3

A charming small restaurant in a 15th-century building in the old part of Tours. Fabrice Bironneau presents a competitively priced, interesting menu. Seasonal dishes include goat's cheese and red pepper flan, veal sautéed with garlic and black olives, and fondant of chocolate. Warm, homely ambience.

TOURS L'Arche de Meslay
14 Rue des Ailes in Parçay Meslay, 37210 **Tel** *02 47 29 00 07*   **Map** D3

Worth the nine-kilometre (six-mile) detour from the city centre, this refined, contemporary restaurant has a kitchen in full view. Watch the chef prepare a delicious lobster salad with chipped vegetables, *bouillabaisse tourangelle* (a regional fish stew) or bass with Indian spices.

TOURS Charles Barrier
10 Avenue de la Tranchee, 37100 **Tel** *02 47 54 20 39*   **Map** D3

This restaurant, on the north bank of the river, has been an institution in Tours for over 50 years. The cuisine is inventive and the menu changes regularly. If you want a cheaper meal try the adjacent annexe, Le Bistrot de la Tranchee. Closed Sat lunch and Sun.

VEIGNÉ Moulin Fleuri
Route de Ripault, 37250 **Tel** *02 47 26 01 12*   **Map** D3

Classic cuisine is beautifully presented by chef Alain Chaplin in an ancient watermill on the banks of the River Indre. The menu focuses on local ingredients such as Racan pigeon, *rillettes de Tours*, *andouillette* (chitterling sausage), goat's cheese and Richelieu truffles. There is also a decent children's menu.

VILLANDRY Domaine de la Giraudière
Route de Druye, 37510 **Tel** *02 47 50 08 60*   **Map** D3

There are three dining rooms with original features in this 17th-century farmhouse near the château. Domaine de la Giraudière is a working farm of mainly goats, a fact that is reflected in the menu – goat's cheese marinated in herbs, kid goat and goat's milk fromage for dessert. Home-produced pâtés, charcuterie and tarts.

VOUVRAY La Cave Martin
66 Vallée Coquette, 37210 **Tel** *02 47 52 62 18*   **Map** D3

In this famous wine village, this restaurant carved into the tufa rock has a rustic menu with *andouillettes* (chitterling sausages), duck breast and confit, and a decent choice of salads. Start with a glass of local fizzy wine, and finish with an unctuous sweet Vouvray to accompany your dessert. Book ahead.

BLESOIS AND ORLEANAIS

BEAUGENCY Le P'tit Bateau
54 Rue du Pont, 45190 **Tel** *02 38 44 56 38*   **Map** E3

Near the château, Le P'tit Bateau is the most appealing restaurant in town. Popular with locals, it offers traditional cuisine in a rustic dining room with exposed beams and open fireplace. Fresh fish, game (in season) and wild mushrooms all feature on the menu. There is a courtyard terrace for alfresco dining on sunny days. Book ahead.

BLOIS L'Orangerie du Château
1 Avenue Jean Laigret, 41000 **Tel** *02 54 78 05 36*   **Map** E3

Housed in the 15th-century château's former winter garden, L'Orangerie has a fine setting, which is matched by the outstanding food and wine. The menu features traditional regional favourites, such as roast pikeperch and white asparagus from the Sologne. The dependable wine list includes good Touraine producers.

BLOIS Au Rendez-Vous des Pêcheurs
27 Rue du Foix, 41000 **Tel** *02 54 74 67 48*   **Map** E3

This restaurant is famed throughout the region for its menu, which focuses on Loire fish and seafood creations, including pike stuffed with chestnuts, and bream with prawns. There is also Sologne game (in season) and a good selection of wines from the Loire Valley. Book ahead.

BRACIEUX Le Relais de Bracieux
1 Ave de Chambord, 41250 **Tel** *02 54 46 41 22*   **Map** E3

After visiting nearby Chambord and the Cheverny vineyards, take a break at this gourmet restaurant in a former coaching inn. Enthusiastic chef Bernard Robin uses the best local products to create excellent dishes, such as terrine of Loire shad and eels with artichoke salad and creamy sorrel sauce.

CONTRES La Botte d'Asperges
52 Rue Henri Mauger, 41700 **Tel** *02 54 79 50 49*   **Map** E3

Locally grown asparagus features prominently on the menu (in season). Behind the rustic atmosphere is an inspirational chef who prepares such delights as sautéed monkfish infused with vanilla, rabbit with buttered gingerbread, and peanut profiteroles with chocolate sauce. Small, well-chosen wine list. You can also take food away.

Key to Price Guide *see p214* **Key to Symbols** *see back cover flap*

GIEN Restaurant la Poularde
13 Quai de Nice, 45500 **Tel** *02 38 67 36 05*
Map *F3*

This classic restaurant on the banks of the Loire serves traditional cuisine in an elegantly furnished dining room, with Gien tableware. The menu includes succulent crispy langoustines, and local pikeperch cooked in Chinon wine with mushrooms. Game also appears on the menu in season.

LAMOTTE-BEUVRON Hôtel Tatin
5 Avenue de Vierzon, 41600 **Tel** *02 54 88 00 03*
Map *E3*

This elegant hotel-restaurant serves traditional fare made with fresh local produce. The menu includes *foie gras*, salad of home-made pâté and warm goat's cheese, pikeperch, pigeon, steak and the famous *tarte tatin* (which must be ordered in advance). There is a good selection of quality Sancerre and Cheverny wines.

ORLÉANS La Chancellerie
27 Place du Martroi, 45000 **Tel** *02 38 53 57 54*
Map *E2*

This lively brasserie-restaurant is located on the town's main square. Built by order of the Duke of Orléans in 1754, the building was originally used to keep the carriages, and later it became the omnibus station. The interior has high ceilings, a marble bar, leather banquettes and brass trimmings. Staple fare is enlivened by good wines.

ORLÉANS Le Lift
Place de la Loire, 45000 **Tel** *02 38 53 63 48*
Map *E2*

Chef Philippe Bardau's restaurant is housed in a modern building set in a garden overlooking the city. The tables on the terrace have magnificent views of the Loire river to the south and of old Orléans to the north. The interior design and cuisine are both contemporary and creative. On Sundays, brunch is served between 11am and 3pm.

ROMORANTIN-LANTHENAY Le Lion d'Or
69 Rue Georges-Clemenceau, 41200 **Tel** *02 54 94 15 15*
Map *E3*

This hotel-restaurant is set in a beautiful Renaissance manor house. Classic cuisine is prepared by a talented chef, and the subtle, elegant dishes use the best local game, vegetables and fish according to what is in season. The service is precise and professional, and there is a good selection of wines from all regions.

ST-BENOÎT-SUR-LOIRE Grand Saint Benoît
7 Place St André, 45730 **Tel** *02 38 35 11 92*
Map *F3*

This is the renowned restaurant of the Hotel du Labrador, which stands on the village square facing the 11th century church (*see p140*). The decor is contemporary, and the cuisine modern with some reasonably priced set menus on offer. Booking is advised. Closed lunch, Sun evening and Mon.

BERRY

BANNEGON Auberge du Moulin de Chaméron
Le Village, 18210 **Tel** *02 48 61 84 48*
Map *F4*

This welcoming hotel-restaurant is located in a rustic, picturesque 18th-century watermill. The chef pays homage to local produce and prepares regional classics and savoury dishes, such as oxtail braised in Menetou wine. The Auberge also houses a small museum dedicated to flour-making and milling. Friendly ambience.

BOURGES Le Piet à Terre
44 Bd Lahitolle, 18000 **Tel** *02 48 67 95 60*
Map *F4*

You can gaze upon a peaceful garden from the tables of this restaurant, located in an old colonial mansion a short way east of the city centre. The rooms are painted in "gourmet colours": caramel, aubergine and cherry red. A creative cuisine based on market produce is served. Closed Sun and Mon.

BOURGES Le Jacques Cœur
3 Place Jacques Cœur, 18000 **Tel** *02 48 26 53 01*
Map *F4*

Facing the Palais Jacques Cœur, in front of the church, this restaurant offers excellent typical Berry cuisine. There are flavourful dishes, such as pikeperch in Sancerre wine, or classic *coq-au-vin*. The small, intimate dining areas are decorated in period style. Municipal parking is available nearby.

CHÂTEAUROUX Le Bistro Gourmand
10 Rue du Marché, 36000 **Tel** *02 54 07 86 98*
Map *D4*

Only a step away from the market place is this busy bistro with a charming patio at the rear. The menus follow the seasons using locally sourced produce. In the convivial atmosphere diners can enjoy the quality of the *foie gras* and rib beef skilfully prepared by the chef. Wines are available by the glass, or you can bring your own bottle.

LE PETIT PRESSIGNY Restaurant Dallais – La Promenade
11 Rue du Savoureux, 37350 **Tel** *02 47 94 93 52*
Map *D4*

Located in the village centre, the Michelin-starred Dallais has a striking contemporary decor in the dining room. The cuisine is exceptional. Delicately prepared savoury dishes include roast morel mushrooms, *foie gras* and local green asparagus. The sommelier gives good advice on the wide selection of wines on offer.

NOHANT Auberge de la Petite Fadette

Place du Château Nohant, 36400 **Tel** *02 54 31 01 48*

€€€€

Map *E4*

Named after the heroine in one of George Sand's novels, this family-run inn has a Renaissance-style dining room with a medieval fireplace. It is rustic and cosy in winter, with a delightful airy terrace in the heat of the summer. Try the speciality of the Berry region, *poulet en barbouille*, a variation on *coq-au-vin*. Good selection of Loire wines.

SANCERRE Auberge la Pomme d'Or

Place de la Mairie, 18300 **Tel** *02 48 54 13 30*

€€

Map *F3*

This small restaurant in a former coaching inn serves classic dishes created with seasonal produce from the region. Enjoy the simplicity of the Chavignol goat's cheese, pikeperch, Sologne pigeon in honey or shredded duck with raspberry vinegar.

VIGNOUX SUR BARANGEON Le Prieuré

2 Rue Jean-Graczyk, 18500 **Tel** *02 48 51 58 80*

€€€€

Map *E3*

Near to Vierzon, this lovely hotel-restaurant was built in 1862 to serve as the village presbytery. High-quality gourmet cuisine is served in the elegant dining room or on the covered terrace by the pool. Expect to find dishes such as roast pikeperch with Berry lentils and *foie gras*.

NORTH OF THE LOIRE

CHARTRES Le Grand Monarque

22 Place des Epars, 28000 **Tel** *02 37 18 15 15*

€€€€

Map *E2*

Within this magnificent 17th-century staging post are both a gourmet Le Georges restaurant and a brasserie serving traditional food. The cuisine is ambitious and flavourful, with dishes such as red mullet and smoked Loire eel in vinaigrette, and sea bass cooked in a clay crust. Excellent desserts and a first-rate wine cellar complete the experience.

CHÂTEAUDUN Aux Trois Pastoureaux

31 Rue André Gillet, 28200 **Tel** *02 37 45 74 40*

€€€

Map *E2*

The dining room of this well-established restaurant has warm tones; the walls are hung with paintings by a local artist. The chef's dishes combine classic produce and contemporary tastes. Try the melon accompanied by duck breast with *foie gras*, braised veal, and the chocolate and raspberry tart. Good choice of wines by the glass.

EVRON Relais du Gué de Selle

Route de Mayenne, 53600 **Tel** *02 43 91 20 00*

€€€

Map *C2*

Located in the heart of the Mayenne countryside, this restaurant, in a typical old farmhouse, serves regional classic dishes that retain a pleasant rusticity. Locally sourced ingredients, such as Ernée *foie gras* served with a gelée flavoured with sweet Layon wine, Loué chicken and Maine rib of beef are some of the specialities.

LAVAL Le Capucin Gourmand

66 Rue Vaufleury, 53000 **Tel** *02 43 66 02 02*

€€€

Map *B2*

This centrally located restaurant has an ivy-clad façade, dining rooms with bright yellow walls and blue wicker furnishings, and a charming patio terrace for summer dining. The menu includes such refined modern dishes as the turbot with an infusion of vanilla pods and the pigeon pan-fried with pine kernels.

LE MANS Le Nez Rouge

107 Grand-Rue, 72000 **Tel** *02 43 24 27 26*

€€

Map *C2*

A charming timbered restaurant in the medieval part of Le Mans. The chef has trained in some of the best restaurants in France, and his dishes are based on the freshest produce, such as lobster and veal sweetbreads. The dining room is cosy and intimate, and there is a terrace across the road. Book ahead.

LE MANS Le Beaulieu

3 Place des Ifs, 72000 **Tel** *02 43 87 78 37*

€€€€

Map *C2*

Gastronomic cuisine is offered in this elegant restaurant in a 15th-century house in the Old Town. Among the appetizing dishes, made with the most noble produce, are veal sweetbreads with truffles, langoustines, lobster and caviar, *foie gras* and potatoes with truffles and beef with truffles. Worth splashing out on for a treat.

MALICORNE-SUR-SARTHE La Petite Auberge

5 Place Duguesclin, 72270 **Tel** *02 43 94 80 52*

€€€

Map *C3*

In summer, you can dine on the riverside terrace and watch the boats go by; in winter, take refuge around the magnificent medieval fireplace. Enjoy classic cuisine with an innovative twist, including delicious gratin of scallops with smoked salmon or perfectly cooked steak with a red Bourgueil wine sauce.

STE-GEMME-MORONVAL L'Escapade

Place du Docteur-Jouve, 28500 **Tel** *02 37 43 72 05*

€€€€€

Map *E1*

This auberge-restaurant in the heart of the Dreux countryside has a welcoming atmosphere and a smartly furnished dining room. On the menu, classic dishes that respect seasonal produce, such as braised veal, asparagus and girolles mushrooms. There is a pleasant terrace for outside dining.

Key to Price Guide *see p214* **Key to Symbols** *see back cover flap*

SANDARVILLE Auberge de Sandarville

€€

Map E2

14 Rue de la Sente-aux-Prêtres, 28120 **Tel** *02 37 25 33 18*

This lovely old farmhouse houses three characterful dining rooms, with exposed beams and open fireplaces. All this creates a friendly, homely atmosphere to enjoy classics such as seafood salad, *sandre* (pikeperch) in Chinon wine, turbot hollandaise and veal with morel mushrooms. Lovely flower-filled terrace for al fresco dining.

LOIRE-ATLANTIQUE AND THE VENDEE

CHALLANS Chez Charles

€€

Map A4

8 Place du Champ de Foire, 85300 **Tel** *02 51 93 36 65*

At this attractive family-run restaurant with a bistro ambience, the chef carefully selects the produce, respecting the seasons. The menu includes regional dishes such as fricassee of eels, hake from Île d'Yeu and Challandais duck, and classics such as beef with Noirmoutier potatoes. Local producers feature on the wine list.

CLISSON La Bonne Auberge

€€€€€

Map B4

1 Rue Olivier de Clisson, 44190 **Tel** *02 40 54 01 90*

This comfortable auberge in the city centre has three attractive dining rooms, including one set in a conservatory with garden views. The specialities include pan-fried *foie gras*, sea bass with truffle-flavoured potatoes, and tart of ceps and scallops. The desserts are delicate, and the Muscadet is good.

LA ROCHE SUR YON Le Rivoli

€€

Map B4

31 Boulevard Aristide-Briand, 85000 **Tel** *02 51 37 43 41*

Located in the heart of the Vendée, this restaurant overflows with originality. The decor is colourful, and the cuisine is refined yet simple. Dishes include a *tartare* of fish with coriander, venison in red wine, and a delicious strawberry crumble. The wine list is simple but well chosen.

LES SABLES D'OLONNE La Pilotine

€€

Map A4

7 Promenade Georges Clemenceau, 85100 **Tel** *02 51 22 25 25*

At this stylish little restaurant facing the town hall, the menu is based around the catch of the day. The chef prepares inventive fish and shellfish dishes, such as casserole of lobster and Noirmoutier potatoes, or salad of langoustines with asparagus and marinated *foie gras* "chips". Be sure to book ahead.

NANTES La Cigale

€€€

Map B3

4 Place Graslin, 44000 **Tel** *02 51 84 94 94*

This ornate Belle Epoque brasserie dates from 1895, when it was frequented by celebrated writers and the Nantes elite. The quality of the cuisine matches the exceptional interior. Oysters, *carpaccio* (thin, quasi-raw slices) of salmon and beef *à la plancha* (cooked on a hot plate) are among the dishes to try. Extensive wine list. Open all day.

NANTES Le Pressoir

€€€

Map B3

11 Quai Turenne, 44000 **Tel** *02 40 35 31 10*

More than a simple bistro, this restaurant is located on the quays. The young chef presents interesting dishes such as *carpaccio de grison* (thin slices of cured beef), roast bass, scallops with pig's feet, *tartare* of tuna and steak with morel mushrooms. The wine list is extensive, with many offerings by the glass. Book ahead.

NANTES Les Temps Changent

€€€

Map B3

1 Place Aristide-Briand, 44000 **Tel** *02 51 72 18 01*

This welcoming venue provides quality French dishes that combine classic produce and inventive cooking. The menu includes roast langoustines with kumquat, Parmesan and basil, and *chaud-froid* of mullet. Interesting wine list and a big terrace.

NANTES L'Atlantide

€€€€€

Map B3

16 Quai Ernest-Renaud, 44100 **Tel** *02 40 73 23 23*

Simply the best place in town to eat, with a dining room on the fourth floor that offers a superb view. Exotic, innovative cuisine is served up by the well-travelled chef, whose menu includes ray with mango and avocado, and red tuna with a bergamot sauce. Remarkable wine list.

PORNIC Entre Vins et Marées

€€

Map A3

70 Quai Leray, 44210 **Tel** *02 40 82 51 25*

This friendly bistro located on the quay of this fishing port serves wonderfully fresh fish and seafood dishes at very reasonable prices. The menu remains faithful to Brittany. Try the warm cockles, the *prat ar coum* (oyster dish), or cod with chitterling sausage. The selections of wines is remarkable, and there are some interesting choices.

ST-JOACHIM La Mare aux Oiseaux

 €€€€€

Map A3

162 Île de Fédrun, 44720 **Tel** *02 40 88 53 01*

Attractive auberge in the centre of the Marais de Brière. The spontaneous and imaginative cuisine uses the best from the marshlands – pigeon, eel, duck, frog and wild mint – and from the nearby sea – sardines, crab and edible seaweed. The specialities include pigeon and frogs' legs in mint sauce.

SHOPS AND MARKETS

Bourges shop sign

Shopping for specialities of the Loire Valley is always a pleasure, and the region's towns and cities also offer many opportunities to purchase the goods that France is famous for – fashion accessories and clothes, kitchenware, porcelain and crystal, and particularly food. Specialist shops are everywhere, and visiting the region's open-air and indoor food markets gives the visitor a wonderful opportunity to buy a vast range of local produce and culinary specialities. This section provides guidelines on shopping in the Loire Valley, and pages 222–3 show some of the best regional foods, wines and other specialist goods available.

Chocolates on display in La Livre Tournois, a *confiserie* in Tours

OPENING HOURS

Small food shops in the Loire region open early – around 7:30 or 8am – and close at around 12:30 for lunch, then reopen at about 3:30 or 4pm until 7 or 8pm. Other small shops are open from roughly 2 to 6:30 or 7pm on Mondays (many remain closed all day), 9am to noon and 2 to 6:30 or 7pm, Tuesday to Saturday. Small supermarkets generally take a long lunch break, but department stores and large supermarkets do not close for lunch. Sales are usually held in late-June and January.

Open-air food markets take place one, two or three mornings a week, often including Sundays, while the large indoor food markets *(les halles)* are usually open from Tuesday to Saturday for the same hours as small food shops. This guide lists the market days for each town featured.

SPECIALIST SHOPS

Despite the mushrooming of supermarkets and large superstores, small specialist shops have continued to thrive in France, and they add enormously to the pleasure of shopping trips. Food shops in particular often specialize in a single theme. *Boulangeries* sell fresh bread, but they may be *boulangeries–pâtisseries*, which means that tempting cakes and pastries will also be on offer. *Traiteurs* sell prepared dishes, while *épiceries* are small grocers. *Crémeries* specialize in dairy products, *fromageries* sell only cheese and *charcuteries* specialize in cooked and cured meats with a few prepared, cold dishes. An *épicerie fine* focuses on high-class groceries and is a good source of gifts to take home, such as local mustards or vinegars in attractive jars or bottles.

An *alimentation générale* (general food store) may have a self-service system. In small villages, this is sometimes the only shop, although fresh bread will always be available either there or from the local café. A travelling van also supplies fresh bread in some regions.

Cleaning products are bought in a *droguerie*, hardware from a *quincaillerie*, books from a *librairie* and stationery (much of which is particularly stylish in France) from a *papeterie*.

The area has some specialist shops that focus on a single product, such as umbrellas or walking sticks, chess sets or stamps, or in a single field such as militaria or natural history books. Their owners are usually extremely knowledgeable about their particular subject, and they enjoy sharing it if you show an interest. Antique shops *(magasins d'antiquités)* tend to be very pricey. Head instead for a *brocante* (bric-à-brac shop), or try hunting for bargains in local flea markets.

TASTING AND BUYING WINE

The Loire Valley is famous for its wines and the region is scattered with producers.

Signs beside the road saying "*dégustation*" mean that a "tasting" is held in the vineyard. It is important to remember that the local *vigneron* will expect a modest purchase of a few bottles after you have drunk several experimental glasses. However, in Saumur it is possible to tour the *chais* (the wine growers' own cellars) with the minimum of sales pressure. Best of all, visit the *Maisons du Vin* in most major towns, where the literature, information and often free tastings are very helpful and interesting.

Sign for a *charcuterie*

HYPERMARKETS AND CHAIN STORES

Superstores and the larger hypermarkets (*hyper-marchés*) are usually situated on the outskirts of towns, often as part of a *centre commercial* (shopping complex) that may also include small boutiques, a DIY outlet and a petrol station. Many of these big stores belong to the Auchan, Carrefour or Super U chains.

The old-style *grand magasin*, or department store, found in the region's towns has generally either been converted into a series of boutiques or taken over and modernized by the up-market Nouvelles Galeries or Printemps national chains. These chic stores are good for clothes, accessories and perfumes. The popular Monoprix stores are worth visiting if you are looking for inexpensive stationery, lingerie and cosmetics. Many of them also have a reasonably priced food department.

A flower-seller and customer at the village market in Luynes

MARKETS

Open-air food markets are one of the delights of the Loire Valley. Their offerings are mouth-watering: mounds of succulent vegetables, *charcuterie* specialities, goats' cheeses and plump poultry and game. Of this excellent fare, most is produced locally, often in small-scale market gardens owned and worked by the stall-holder. Produce that has

Local goats' cheese for sale in Amboise market

Fresh local produce on sale in the market in Saumur's place St-Pierre

been grown locally is labelled *pays*. Look out for unusual specialities, such as the strangely-shaped squashes and pumpkins that appear in autumn, wild mushrooms and flavoured honeys. Honey stalls often sell honey-flavoured confectionery and honey soap, too. Spice and herb stalls are also interesting, providing a wealth of gift ideas. Some markets have stalls selling clothes or shoes and leather goods. Look out also for local craft work.

Flea markets (*marchés aux puces*) are regular events in many towns and are often held in small towns and villages in countryside districts during the summer holiday season.

VAT REBATES

Since the advent of the Single European Market, rebates of value-added tax (*taxe à la valeur ajoutée* or *TVA*) are only available to those not resident in a European Union country. They apply only to purchases totalling at least €175 in a single shop, on the same day, and taken out of the EU within three months. The export sales form you receive on purchase must be handed to the customs officer as you leave the EU. Reimbursements usually go directly to your bank. Not all articles qualify for rebates. In stores frequented by foreign tourists, staff are familiar with the process.

DIRECTORY

REGIONAL SPECIALITIES

Angers
Pâtisserie La Petite Marquise
22 rue des Lices.
Tel 02 41 87 43 01.
www.chocolat-lapetitemarquise.com
Quernons d'Ardoise and sweets.

Bourges
La Maison des Forestines
3 pl Cujas.
Tel 02 48 24 00 24.
Forestines.

Guérande
La Maison du Sel
Pradel.
Tel 02 40 62 08 80.
Guérande salt.

Nantes
La Friande
12 rue Paul Bellamy.
Tel 02 40 20 14 68.
Nantaise biscuits.

Orléans
Chocolaterie La Duchesse Anne
38 rue du Faubourg Banier.
Tel 02 38 53 02 77.

Tours
La Livre Tournois
6 rue Nationale.
Tel 02 47 66 99 99.
Pruneaux Fourrés and chocolates.

ARTS AND CRAFTS

Chartres
La Galerie du Vitrail
17 rue du Cloître Notre-Dame.
Tel 02 37 36 10 03. *Stained glass panels and associated items.*

Gien
Faïencerie de Gien
78 Pl de la Victoire.
Tel 02 38 05 21 06.
www.gien.com
Porcelain.

Malicorne
Faïenceries d'Art du Bourg-Joly
16 rue Carnot.
Tel 02 43 94 80 10.

Villaines-les-Rochers
Coopérative de Vannerie de Villaines
1 rue de la Cheneillère.
Tel 02 47 45 43 03.
www.vannerie.com
Wickerwork studio and shop.

What to Buy in the Loire Valley

The best buys in the Loire tempt the eye as well as the stomach. A gourmet's paradise, the food shops and open-air markets of the region attract visitors with their delicious scents and sights. Local producers are justifiably proud of their goods and pack them with respect, in attractive crates or pottery jars. But gourmet treats are not the only local goods worth looking for. The region has long been famous for its china from Gien and for the fabric and lace of the Touraine, evocative of the remarkable history of the Loire.

A beautifully wrapped package of sweets

CONFECTIONERY

Local confectionery specialities make good gifts to take home, especially when they are so prettily packaged. The region is well-known for its wide range of sweets, which are available from tearooms and specialist confectioners, and many towns also have their own mouth-watering treats.

Forestines from Bourges

Macaroon biscuits from Cormery

Pruneaux fourrés, prunes stuffed with marzipan

Chocolates resembling traditional slate tiles

Fruit-flavoured sweets

SOUVENIRS

The châteaux and museums of the Loire Valley have well-stocked shops that sell an array of appealing souvenirs. In addition to the usual booklets and posters, many sell gifts with an historical theme, such as replica playing cards or tapestries. Wine bought direct from a local vineyard is another special souvenir (see pp30–31).

Playing cards with historical figures

Wine made at Chenonceau

THE FLAVOURS OF THE LOIRE

It is impossible to visit the Loire without being amazed by the abundance of delicious food. Much comes perfectly packaged for travelling. Near the game-filled forests of the Berry, you can buy jars and tins of pâtés and terrines. Goats' cheeses are moulded into a variety of shapes, and the firmer varieties travel successfully. Heather honey from Berry's heathland and wine vinegars from Orléans are also specialities of the region.

Confiture de vin, jelly made from wine

Poulain chocolate made in Blois

Pickled samphire

Goats' cheese

Cotignac, quince jelly from Orléans

Sea salt from Guérande

Crémant de Loire, sparkling wine

LOCAL CRAFTS

Traditional crafts survive throughout the Loire Valley, and you can often visit craftsmen and women at work in their studios. Many towns in the region have long been renowned for their craft specialities, such as Malicorne for its lattice-work faïence, Villaines-les-Rochers for its baskets or Gien for its china.

Pottery from La Borne in Berry

Gien china side plate

Wicker basket from Villaines

Dinner plate from Gien

ACTIVITIES IN THE LOIRE VALLEY

Aholiday in the Loire Valley can combine the cultural highlights of visits to the spectacular châteaux with enjoyment of the region's wealth of natural environments. The gentle terrain and beautiful forests are perfect for exploration on foot, horseback or mountain bike, and the clear waters of the lakes and rivers – not to mention the spectacular Atlantic coastline – are enticing spots for swimming or boating. Here is a selection of just a few of the activities on offer in the region. For more information contact the departmental Loisirs–Accueil offices *(see p227)*, which focus on leisure activities, or the local tourist offices in towns and villages.

WALKING

The Loire Valley is renowned for its many accessible and scenic walks, which are called *Randonnées (see pp28–9)*. Although these routes are generally clearly signposted, it is a good idea to carry a large-scale map or a Topo-Guide. These are only available in French but do contain maps, a description of the itinerary, details of sites of architectural or natural interest to be found along the route, an estimate of the time it will take you to complete the walk and the addresses of local hotels, restaurants, hostels and camp sites. Most Topo–Guides cost around €15. A complete list is available from the **Fédération Française de la Randonnée Pédestre**.

You will never be more than a day's walk away from a town or village where you will be able to find food and accommodation, so it is not necessary to carry a large amount of equipment, but, as always, you should wear good, strong walking shoes. Remember that some paths can be damp and muddy during the spring and autumn.

CYCLING

The generally flat landscape of the Loire Valley makes it perfect for cyclists. Because many of the châteaux are so near to each other, it is easy to visit several by bicycle in only a few days. Mountain bike enthusiasts will enjoy riding the clearly signposted paths through the region's forests and nature reserves.

Motorways and some major roads are forbidden to cyclists; the sign has a white background with a red border and a cyclist in the middle. Cycle lanes, when they exist, are compulsory. Bicycles must have two working brakes, a bell, a red rear reflector and yellow reflectors on the pedals, as well as a white front light and a red rear light after dark. It is also advisable to wear a helmet and to carry essential spare parts in case of break-down. While bicycle shops are common, foreign spare parts may not be available.

It is possible to hire touring bicycles and mountain bikes throughout the region. Local tourist offices will be able to provide you with a list of cycle hire centres.

Transporting your bicycle on local trains is free in most cases, although on major train routes the SNCF requires you to register your bicycle and will levy a small charge. The booklet *Train et Vélo*, available at most train stations, gives more information on carrying bikes on trains, and you can also visit www.velo.sncf.com.

Among a number of organized itineraries for cyclists, the most ambitious is *Loire à Vélo*, a 150-km (93-mile) trail tracking the River Loire from Angers to Tours. There are eight bike hire outlets along the route, with the possibility of one-way rentals. Hotels, camp sites and *chambres d'hôte* marked with the *Accueil Vélo* sign welcome cyclists and will forward luggage to the next stop if required. A handbook with maps and accommodation listings is available from local tourist offices or the Comité Régional du Tourisme Centre. The *Pays des Châteaux à Vélo* leaflet describes 11 circuits around Blois and Chambord The website www.chateauavelo. com has information on routes, accommodation and bike hire.

The **Fédération Française de Cyclisme** is the umbrella organization for more than 2,800 cycling clubs in France. They provide advice and cycling itineraries if you write to them well in advance.

Cycling, one of the most pleasant ways to see the Loire Valley

A riverside pony trek in the beautiful Vendée region

HORSE RIDING AND PONY TREKKING

Horse lovers will enjoy a visit to the National Riding School in the important equestrian town of Saumur, where the world-famous Cadre Noir riding team perform in regular displays (*see p83*).

The forests of the Loire Valley, with their well-maintained networks of trails and well-marked bridle paths, are ideal for riding. Topo-Guides are as useful for riders as they are for walkers.

Experienced riders can hire horses by the hour, half-day or day from numerous stables in the region. A sign reading *Loueur d'Equidés* means that horses are for hire without an instructor. If you prefer to be accompanied when riding, you should search out an *Ecole d'Equitation* or a *Centre Equestre* (riding school).

Many stables also offer longer treks on horseback, called *randonnées*, which last between a weekend and a week. Small groups are accompanied on the trek by an experienced guide, and accommodation is usually in quite basic hotels or hostels, although some luxury tours are also available.

The rental of old-fashioned horse-drawn caravans is becoming increasingly popular in the Loire Valley. Travellers sleep in the carriage overnight and journey at a slow, leisurely pace during the day. Generally caravans come

in two sizes: the smaller one carries four adults or two adults and three children; the other carries six to eight people. There are also larger, open wagons, driven by a guide, that are used for group excursions of up to 15.

FISHING

The rivers of the Loire Valley are teeming with fresh-water fish, including bream, bullhead, carp, grey mullet, perch, pike, roach, shad and zander. There are also trout in some of the faster-running tributaries of the Loire.

Freshwater fish

To fish in private waters, you must make arrangements with the owner. To fish in state–controlled waters, you must buy a permit, which is available from many tackle shops. Applicants must provide proof that they are a member of an angling association at home and pay a fishing tax.

There are two kinds of fishing tax: the basic tax covers fishing with worms in rivers that do not have trout runs; the special tax covers spinning, fly-fishing, and fish-bait fishing

in all rivers, including those with trout. You cannot fish more than half an hour before sunrise or after sunset. There are set seasons for certain fish and limits on their size.

The **Fédération Nationale pour la Pêche en France**, which represents more than 4,000 local fishing associations, provides information on the regulations regarding fresh-water fishing and the starting dates of the different fishing seasons in France. Ocean fishing is free from any tax as long as you do not use nets, although there are restrictions on the equipment a boat can carry.

Fly–fishing on the tranquil River Loir

GOLF

Evidence of the growing popularity of golf in France can be seen throughout the Loire Valley, which has many beautiful and challenging courses. Some of the region's golf courses, such as the Golf du Val de l'Indre, located near Châteauroux in Berry, and La Bretesche in Missillac in the Loire-Atlantique, are set in the grounds of châteaux.

In the Loiret, seven courses around Orléans have joined up to provide a golf pass that combines greens fees for the different courses and the added option of accommodation in nearby two- or three-star hotels. For more information, contact the *Loiret Loisirs Accueil* office in Orléans, or the respective golf courses.

A similar deal is available in the Western Loire, where a pass offers reductions at two golf courses near Nantes: Golf Nantes Erdre (tel 02 40 59 21 21) and Golf Nantes Carquefou (tel 02 40 52 73 74). Contact the Nantes tourist office *(see p231)* or the participating golf courses for more information.

BOATING AND WATER SPORTS

Because the Loire Valley is criss-crossed with beautiful rivers, most visitors cannot resist the temptation to take at least one boat trip. A wide variety of short excursions

are available from riverside *ports de plaisance* (marinas) throughout the Loire region, and in general they do not require advance reservations.

The marshes of the Marais Poitevin *(see pp182–5)* are best viewed from its canal network in a *barque* (the traditional, flat-bottomed boat).

One option is to base your entire visit on the water by renting a house-boat or a cruiser for a period of a few days or for one or two weeks. Boats of different sizes and styles are available, from old-fashioned canal boats to sophisticated modern cruisers. Most prices are for round trips and include bedding, kitchen equipment and full training, and it may also be possible to rent bicycles or canoes, or to make a one-way *(simple)* trip. Further information is available from the main tourist offices.

If you are looking for a more adventurous way of enjoying the region's rivers, try canoeing or kayaking. It is best to take a guided tour from one of the clubs based along the river. Although the river may look calm, there can be dangerous undercurrents and obstacles.

Kayaking on the River Mayenne

There are good activity centres beside many of the rivers and lakes in the Loire Valley, and there may also be facilities for renting pedaloes, canoes and yachts – some centres even offer water-skiing. A good number of the Atlantic coastal resorts also have facilities for renting windsurfers – Les Sables d'Olonne *(see p181)* was host to the world wind-surfing championships in 1988.

Swimmers should stay in the approved areas. While the sand banks may look inviting, there are risks from strong currents and shifting sands. Further information on water safety is given on pages 234–5.

Windsurfing at La Tranche-sur-Mer on the Atlantic Coast

THE LOIRE FROM THE AIR

One of the most luxurious ways to see the Loire Valley is from a hot-air balloon (*montgolfière* in French). There are daily flights in the summer, weather permitting, from Tours, Nantes and Amboise. **France Montgolfières** will put together custom-made excursions.

You can also take a tour in a helicopter or light aircraft. In addition to major airports at Tours and Nantes, there are many other airfields throughout the region. The tourist offices provide complete information. Flying lessons are also available at some of these centres. Learning to fly in France can be much cheaper than elsewhere. Details can be obtained from the **Fédération Française Aéronautique**. Visitors interested in gliding or hang-gliding should contact the **Fédération Française de Vol Libre**.

Ballooning over Le Plessis-Bourré in Anjou

DIRECTORY

SERVICES LOISIRS ACCUEIL

Cher
5 rue de Séraucourt, 18014 Bourges.
Tel 02 48 48 00 18.

Eure-et-Loir
10 rue Docteur Maunoury, 28000 Chartres.
Tel 02 37 84 01 01.

Indre
Centre Colbert, place Eugène Rolland Bat 1, 36003 Châteauroux.
Tel 02 54 27 70 49.

Indre-et-Loire
Val de Loire Tourisme, 75 av de la République, 37714 Chambray-les-Tours. *Tel 02 47 27 27 31.*

Loire-Atlantique
11 rue du Château de l'Erauclière, 44306 Nantes.
Tel 02 51 72 95 31.

Loiret
8 rue d'Escures, 45000 Orléans.
Tel 02 38 62 04 88.

Mayenne
84 av Robert Buron, 53003 Laval.
Tel 08 20 15 30 53.

Sarthe
31 rue Edgar Brandt, 72000 Le Mans.
Tel 02 43 40 22 60.

WALKING

Fédération Française de la Randonnée Pédestre
64 rue du Dessous des Berges, 75013 Paris.
Tel 01 44 89 93 93.
 www.ffrandonnee.fr

CYCLING

Comité Régional du Tourisme Centre
37 av de Paris, 45000 Orléans. *Tel 02 38 79 95 28.* www.loire-a-velo.fr

Fédération Française de Cyclisme
Batîment Jean Monnet, 5 rue de Rome, 93561 Rosny-sous-Bois Cedex.
Tel 01 49 35 69 00.
www.ffc.fr

FISHING

Fédération Nationale pour la Pêche en France
17 rue Bergère, 75009 Paris. *Tel 01 48 24 96 00.*
www.unpf.fr

GOLF

Fédération Française de Golf
68 rue Anatole France, 92300 Levallois Perret.
Tel 01 41 49 77 00.
www.ffgolf.org

HORSE RIDING

Fédération Française d'Equitation
81–83 av Edouard Vaillant, 92517 Boulogne Billancourt
Tel 01 58 17 58 17.
www.ffe.com

SAILING/SURFING

Fédération Française de Voile
17 rue Henri-Bocquillon, 75015 Paris.
Tel 01 40 60 37 00.
www.ffvoile.org

CANOEING AND KAYAKING

Fédération Française de Canoë-Kayak
87 quai de la Marne, 94344 Joinville le Pont Cedex.
Tel 01 45 11 08 50.
www.ffcanoe.asso.fr

THE LOIRE FROM THE AIR

Fédération Française de Vol Libre
4 rue de Suisse, 06000 Nice. *Tel 04 97 03 82 82*
www.ffvl.fr.

Fédération Français Aéronautique (FFA)
155 av de Wagram, 75017 Paris. *Tel 01 44 29 92 00.* www.ff.aero.fr

France Montgolfières
24 rue Nationale, 41400 Montrichard.
Tel 02 54 32 20 48.
www.france-montgolfieres.com

SURVIVAL
GUIDE

PRACTICAL INFORMATION

In the Loire Valley, as elsewhere in France, the peak holiday period is from mid-June to the end of August. The area is very well prepared to meet the practical needs of its many visitors, however, providing accommodation ranging from top hotels and private châteaux to small camp sites, as well as a selection of excellent restaurants.

Because of the profusion of places of great historical, aesthetic or natural interest, ranging from stunning châteaux and cathedrals to windswept Atlantic beaches and wild marshlands, it is a

FNOTSI

National logo for tourist information

good idea to draw up a list of priority visits before you travel. You should also check that the places you plan to visit are not closed for seasonal breaks or for restoration work. Before you leave home, the French Government Tourist Offices are invaluable sources of information. The local tourist information offices in most towns in the region offer advice on the spot.

With a wide variety of activities available, the Loire Valley has something to offer all its visitors. The following tips and suggestions will help you make the most of your visit.

Tourist information office in Fontenay-le-Comte

TOURIST INFORMATION

Most large towns have a tourist information office, known either as the *Syndicat d'Initiative* or the *Office de Tourisme*. This guide provides the address and telephone number of the tourist office in each town featured in its pages. In smaller towns the town hall *(hôtel de ville)* will offer information. Tourist offices supply free maps, advice on accommodation (which can include booking hotels) and information on regional recreational and cultural activities, such as festivals. The main branches are listed opposite. You can also obtain details in advance from French Government Tourist Offices before leaving your own country.

OPENING TIMES

Most shops and banks open from 8 or 9am until noon, and from 2 or 3pm until 4:30pm (banks) or 6:30 or 7:30pm (shops), Tuesday to Saturday *(see pp220–21 and pp236–7)*. Opening hours vary with the size of town. Many shops and banks are closed on Mondays and also close for lunch daily, although big department stores, super-markets, tourist offices and some sights may remain open all day. Restaurants may close for one day a week, so do check before setting off *(see pp208–19)*.

Off season, some seaside resorts, as well as many châteaux and smaller museums, close down for

tourisme.fr

Logo for official tourism website

several months, so it is best to telephone to check details.

SIGHTSEEING

In France, it is common for many museums to close for lunch – normal opening hours are between 9am and noon and from 2pm to 5:30pm. National museums and sights normally close on Tuesdays, with a few exceptions that close on Mondays. Opening times can also vary considerably by season, especially for country châteaux, estates and gardens. Many are open daily in the peak May to September holiday season and then close from November to March. Most sights are closed on Christmas day and New Year's day.

Tables outside a café in Les Sables d'Olonne

◁ **Château de Noirmoutier viewed from the quayside**

Entertainment at a festival in Luçon

Museum admission charges range from around €2 to €7. Passes for more than one museum or monument are rare. Normally, you will need to buy separate tickets for each sight within a town.

There are usually some discounts available for students who have valid International Student Identity Cards (ISIC) *(see p233)*. Anyone aged under 18 or over 65 can also be eligible for a price reduction. Some museums and monuments are free for one day a month, usually the first Sunday; some may also offer reductions on certain days. Call ahead or check the website for details beforehand. Churches and cathedrals open every day but may shut during lunch. There is sometimes a small charge to visit cloisters, bell-towers and crypts.

National logo for the disabled

DISABLED ACCESS

Although in some of the Loire Valley's medieval villages, narrow streets can make it difficult for disabled travellers to get around, wheel-chair access in the area is generally good. Many châteaux and museums offer special services and facilities for disabled visitors, which staff are happy to explain; however, it is advisable to telephone and check about access before your visit. Access to hotels and restaurants has been improved in many cases to accommodate disabled customers. Information specific to the area is available from town halls or from regional tourist offices. Parking spaces reserved for vehicles that have disabled permits are marked with a special sign. For more information about special facilities for the disabled before departure, contact the International Relations Department of the **Association des Paralysés de France (APF)**.

Two websites (www.handiweb.fr and www.handitec.com) offer detailed information about the legal provision in France for disabled travellers, as well as useful information and relevant addresses.

ENTERTAINMENT INFORMATION

There are several sources of entertainment information in the Loire Valley. Magazines and brochures listing forth-coming events are available at tourist information offices as well as in many hotels and camp sites. Both newsagents *(maisons de la presse)* and some tobacconists' shops *(tabacs)* sell newspapers and magazines. Local papers can also provide details of festivals and sporting events as well as the weather forecast.

Sign for a tobacconist

DIRECTORY

FRENCH GOVERNMENT TOURIST OFFICES ABROAD

Australia
Level 13, 25 Bligh St, Sydney, NSW 2000. **Tel** *(02) 9231 5244.*
http://au.franceguide.com

Canada
1918 Ave McGill College, Suite 1010, Montréal, Quebec H3A 3J6. **Tel** *(514) 288 2026.*
http://ca-en.franceguide.com

United Kingdom
Lincoln House, 300 High Holborn, London WC1V 7JH.
Tel *09068 244 123.*
http://uk.franceguide.com

United States
825 Third Ave, 29th floor, New York, NY 10022. **Tel** *(514) 288 1904.* http://us.franceguide.com

TOURIST OFFICES IN THE LOIRE VALLEY

Angers
7 pl Kennedy. **Tel** *02 41 23 50 00.*
www.angersloiretourisme.com

Blois
23 pl du Château.
Tel *02 54 90 41 41.*
www.loiredeschateaux.com

Bourges
21 rue Victor–Hugo.
Tel *02 48 23 02 60.*
www.bourges-tourisme.com

Chartres
Pl de la Cathédrale.
Tel *02 37 18 26 26.*
www.chartres-tourisme.com

Le Mans
Rue de l'Etoile. **Tel** *02 43 28 17 22.* www.lemanstourisme.com

Nantes
2 pl St Pierre. **Tel** *08 92 46 40 44.*
www.nantes-tourisme.com

Orléans
2 pl de l'Etape. **Tel** *02 38 24 05 05.* www.tourisme-orleans.com

Tours
78 rue Bernard Palissy. **Tel** *02 47 70 37 37.* www.ligeris.com

DISABLED TRAVELLERS

Association des Paralysés de France (APF)
31A bd Albert Einstein, 44323 Nantes Cedex 3.
Tel *02 51 80 68 00.*
www.apf.asso.fr

VISAS

There are no visa requirements for citizens of the European Union. Tourists from the United States, Canada, Australia and New Zealand who are staying in France for less than 90 days need not apply for a visa. After 90 days, a *visa de long séjour* is required. Visitors from other countries should request visa information from the French authorities in their own country before departure.

TAX-FREE GOODS

If you are resident outside the European Union, you can reclaim the TVA (VAT or sales tax) on certain French goods if you spend more than €175 (including tax) in the same shop in one day, obtain *un bordereau de vente à l'exportation* (an export sales form) and take the goods out of the EU within three months. Ask for this form when making your purchases. It consists of two sheets that must be signed by the retailer and yourself. Present both form and goods at customs when leaving the EU. On returning home, send the pink sheet back to the retailer (who must receive it within six months of the sale), and the refund will be sent on to you, usually via your bank.

The main exceptions for *détaxe* rebate are food and drink, medicines, tobacco, cars and motorbikes.

DUTY-FREE LIMITS

For travel within the EU duty free was abolished in June 1999. For non-EU nationals arriving in the EU, the following may be imported: up to 2 litres of wine, and a litre of spirits or 2 litres of drink less than 22° proof; 50g of perfume; 500g of coffee; 100g of tea; and up to 200 cigarettes. Visitors under 17 may not import or export duty-free tobacco or alcohol, even as gifts.

French perfumes, available tax-free

DUTY-PAID LIMITS

There are no longer any restrictions on the quantities of duty-paid and VAT-paid goods you are allowed to take from one European Union country to another, as long as the goods are for your own use and are not intended for resale. Customs officers may ask you to prove that the goods are for your personal use if they exceed the suggested amounts: 10 litres of spirits, 90 litres of wine, 110 litres of beer and 800 cigarettes.

IMPORTING OTHER GOODS

In general, personal goods (such as a car or a bicycle) may be imported to France duty-free and without any paperwork as long as they are obviously for personal use and not for resale. *Voyagez en toute liberté*, a brochure

available from the **Info Douane Service**, clarifies this. At the border, customs officers are also able to give advice and information, although this is likely to be in French.

Special rules apply, both within and without the EU, for the import and export of endangered plant and animal species, works of art and national treasures, human medicines, weapons and ammunition. Consult your own, or French, customs.

An ISIC international student card

STUDENT INFORMATION

Students who hold a valid International Student Identification Card (ISIC card) can benefit from discounts of 50 per cent or more when they produce the card at museums, theatres, cinemas and at many public monuments. Students are also entitled to the same discounts available to everyone in France aged 25 or under. The region's principal universities are in Nantes and Tours. Other large universities are located in the towns of Le Mans, Angers, Laval, Orléans and La Roche-sur-Yon.

In Orléans, the **Centre Régional d'Information Jeunesse** offers a great deal of useful information about student life in the area and can also provide a list of inexpensive accommodation for young people.

ANIMALS

There is no bar to bringing pets to France, so long as the animal is at least three months old, has microchip identification and a certificate of vaccination against rabies, issued by a registered vet.

ETIQUETTE

It is important to respect the French rituals of politeness,

Friends greeting each other with two or three kisses

which apply in the Loire Valley just as much as they do elsewhere in the country. When you are introduced to someone, it is correct to shake hands with them. In shops, you should be prepared to say *bonjour* to the assistant before asking for what you want, and then *merci* when you receive your change and finally *au revoir*, *bonne journée* (good-bye, have a nice day) when you depart. The usual greeting among friends of either sex is generally two or three kisses on the cheek.

Throughout the Loire Valley region, and particularly in the smaller communities, all efforts by English speakers to make enthusiastic use of their French, however limited, and to show a real interest in the area will be met with encouragement by the local people.

LOIRE VALLEY TIME

The Loire Valley is one hour ahead of Greenwich Mean Time (GMT). France is in the same time zone as Germany, Italy, Spain and other western European countries.

Standard time differences between the Loire Valley and some major cities of the world are as follows: London: minus 1 hour; New York: minus 6 hours; Dallas: minus 7 hours; Los Angeles: minus 9 hours; Perth: plus 7 hours; Sydney: plus 9 hours; Auckland: plus 11 hours; and Tokyo: plus 8 hours. These can vary according to local summer alterations to the time.

The French use the 24-hour clock (they do not use the am and pm system): after midday, just continue counting 13, 14 and so on to provide the 24-hour clock time. For example, 1pm = 13:00.

CONVERSION CHART

Imperial to metric
1 inch = 2.54 centimetres
1 foot = 30 centimetres
1 mile = 1.6 kilometres
1 ounce = 28 grams
1 pound = 454 grams
1 pint = 0.6 litre
1 gallon = 4.6 litres

Metric to imperial
1 millimetre = 0.04 inch
1 centimetre = 0.4 inch
1 metre = 3 feet 3 inches
1 kilometre = 0.6 mile
1 gram = 0.04 ounce
1 kilogram = 2.2 pounds
1 litre = 1.8 pints

French two-pin electrical plug

ELECTRICAL ADAPTORS

The Voltage in France is 220 volts. The plugs on French electrical appliances have two small round pins; the heavier-duty appliances have two large round pins. Some up-market hotels offer built-in adaptors for shavers only.

Multi-adaptors, which are useful because they have both large and small pins, can be bought at most airports before departure. Standard adaptors can be purchased from most department stores.

RELIGIOUS SERVICES

Although the major religion in the region is Catholicism, the Loire Valley also has many Protestant churches, and some Jewish synagogues and Islamic mosques, particularly in the larger towns. These reflect the religious diversity of modern French society.

DIRECTORY

Personal Security and Health

On the whole, the Loire Valley is a safe place for visitors: take normal precautions, such as keeping an eye on your possessions at all times, and avoid isolated and unlit urban areas at night. If you fall ill during your stay, pharmacies are an excellent source of advice. Consular offices can offer help and advice in an emergency. In the case of a serious medical problem, call the emergency services.

French police officers

POLICE

Violent crime is not a major problem in the Loire Valley, but as in any destination it is advisable to be on your guard against petty theft, especially in cities. If you are robbed, lose any property or are the victim of any other type of crime, report the incident as soon as possible at the nearest *commissariat de police* (police station). In an emergency, dialling 17 will also connect you to the police, but you will still have to go to a station to make a statement. In small towns and villages, crime is reported to the *gendarmerie*, the force mainly responsible for rural policing. The *mairie* (town hall) is also a good place to go for help but this will only be open during office hours.

At all police stations you will be required to make a statement, called a *PV* or *procès verbal*, listing any lost or stolen items. You will need your passport, and, if relevant, your vehicle papers. It is important to keep a copy of your police statement for your insurance claim.

IN AN EMERGENCY

The phone number for all emergency services is 112, but in practice it is often quicker to call the relevant authority direct on their traditional two-digit numbers. In a medical emergency call the **Service d'Aide Médicale Urgence** (SAMU), who will send an ambulance. However, it can sometimes be faster to call the **Sapeurs Pompiers** (fire service) who also offer first aid and can take you to the nearest hospital. This is particularly true in rural areas, where the fire station is likely to be much closer than the ambulance service based in town. If you do call out an ambulance the paramedics are called *secouristes*.

Police car

Fire engine

Ambulance

LOST AND STOLEN PROPERTY

In big cities, try not to carry conspicuous valuables with you and only take as much cash as you think you will need. Traveller's cheques are the safest method of carrying large sums of money.

In major towns, most multi-storey car parks are kept under surveillance by video cameras. Parking there will reduce the threat of car crime and avoid the greater risk of parking in an illegal space and being towed away to a police pound.

For lost or stolen property, it may be worth returning to the station where you reported the incident to check if the police have retrieved some of the items. In addition, all French town halls have a *Bureau d'Objets Trouvés* (lost property office), although they are often inefficient and finding items can take time. Lost property offices can also be found at larger train stations, which will be open during office hours.

If your passport is lost or stolen, notify your consulate immediately *(see p671)*. The loss of credit or debit cards should also be reported as soon as possible to your bank to avoid fraudulent use.

PERSONAL SAFETY

Violent crime is rare in the Loire Valley. If travelling late at night, it is a good idea, especially for women, to remain within busy, well-lit areas and to be careful about talking to, or accompanying, strangers. If you are involved in a dispute or car accident, avoid confrontation, try to stay calm and speak French if you can to diffuse the situation.

TRAVEL INSURANCE

All travellers in France should have a comprehensive travel insurance policy providing adequate cover for any eventuality, including potential medical and legal expenses, theft, lost luggage and other personal property, accidents, travel delays and the option of immediate repatriation by air in the event of a major medical emergency. Adventure sports are not covered by standard travel policies so if you are planning to undertake any extreme sports in the Loire Valley you will need to pay an additional premium to ensure you are protected. All insurance policies should come with a 24-hour emergency number in case of need.

A green flag shows the sea is safe for bathers

HOSPITALS AND PHARMACIES

All European Union nationals holding a European Health Insurance Card (EHIC) are entitled to use the French national health service. However, under the French system patients must pay for all treatments and then reclaim most of the cost from their health authorities. Therefore, non-French EU nationals who use health services in France will need to ensure they keep the statement of costs (*fiche*) that is provided by the doctor or hospital. The statement should include stickers for any prescription drugs, which must be stuck onto the statement by the pharmacist once you have made your purchase. Around 80 per cent of the cost can be claimed back by following the instructions provided with your EHIC card. This can be a time-consuming process and it can often be simpler to use private travel insurance. Non-EU nationals must have full private medical insurance while in France and pay for services in the same way, claiming their costs back in full from their insurance company.

Well-equipped public hospitals can be found throughout France. In all towns and cities there are hospitals with general casualty/emergency departments (called *urgences*

or *service des urgences*) that can deal with immediate medical problems. If your hotel cannot direct you to one, call the SAMU or fire service. Should you require an English-speaking doctor, your consulate should be able to recommend one in the area, and in some cities in France, there are both American and British private hospitals.

Pharmacies, identified by an illuminated green cross sign, are plentiful and easy to find. French pharmacists are highly trained and can diagnose minor health problems and suggest appropriate treatments. When one is closed, a card in the window will give details of the nearest *pharmacie de garde* that is open on Sundays or during the night.

BEACH AND RIVER SAFETY

Most of the beaches on the Atlantic coast are guarded in the summer by life-guards (*sauveteurs*). There are a number of good family beaches, where bathing is not generally dangerous. However, look for the system of coloured flags, which tells bathers whether it is safe to swim. Green flags mean that bathing is permitted and is safe. Orange flags warn that bathing may be dangerous and usually only part of the beach is guarded. The guarded area is marked out by flags, beyond which you should not swim. Very dangerous conditions (high waves, shifting sands and strong undercurrents) are denoted by red flags, which mean that any bathing is strictly forbidden. Many of the region's beaches also display the blue flags, which are used throughout the European Union as a sign of cleanliness.

The River Loire and its tributaries also tempt summer bathers, but beware of the treacherous currents and shifting sands. It is safest to stick to established bathing areas.

Banking and Local Currency

In the Loire Valley, as elsewhere in France, the banks usually offer the best rates of exchange. Privately owned *bureaux de change* are common in tourist areas, especially around the châteaux, but tend to have more variable rates. Take care to check the commission and minimum charges before you complete a transaction. Traveller's cheques are still the safest form of money, but using credit or debit cards to withdraw cash from automated teller machines (ATMs) beats bank queues any day, although you will undoubtedly be charged by the card issuer for this service.

BANKING HOURS

Generally speaking, banks in larger French towns are open from 9am to noon and from 2 to 4:30pm, Tuesday to Saturday. Most are often closed on Mondays. Over public holiday weekends, banks may be shut from noon Friday until Tuesday morning. Be aware that opening hours can be more limited in smaller towns.

OBTAINING MONEY

There is no limit to the amount of money visitors may bring into or take out of France. If you are carrying cash or traveller's cheques worth more than €7,600, however, you should declare it to French customs.

French banks offer foreign currency exchange services only to their existing clients, unless they have a dedicated foreign exchange counter. As a result, the simplest and most convenient way to get cash in France is to use one of the many ATMs found at airports, banks and shopping malls, among other places. Most ATMs take major credit and debit cards, with Visa and MasterCard the most widely accepted. To with-draw money, you need to enter a four-digit PIN (Personal Identification Number, or *code confidentiel*). ATM instructions are usually given in several languages, including English.

Keypad to check your PIN

Another alternative is changing money in main post offices in larger towns or at an independent *bureau de change*; however, the latter may offer less attractive exchange rates.

In some banks, it is also possible to withdraw cash on Visa or MasterCard at the counter. You will need your passport or some form of ID to make the transaction.

TRAVELLER'S CHEQUES AND CREDIT CARDS

Traveller's cheques can be obtained from American Express, Thomas Cook or your bank, building society or some post offices. American Express cheques are widely accepted in France, and Amex offices exchange them without charging commission.

In France, Visa/ Carte Bleue and Eurocard/MasterCard are the most common credit cards, while American Express cards are not always accepted.

French credit and debit cards are now smart cards *(cartes à puce)*. Retailers are equipped with machines that read smart cards and older magnetic strips. If your card cannot be read in the smart card slot, you will be told you have a *puce morte*.

Ask the cashier to put the card through the *bande magnétique* (magnetic reader). You may also have to tap in your PIN and press the green key *(validez)* on a small keypad.

DIRECTORY

BUREAUX DE CHANGE

Angers
Office de Tourisme,
7 pl Président
Kennedy.
Tel 02 41 23 50 00.

Blois
La Poste, 2 rue Gallois.
Tel 02 54 57 17 17.

Bourges
La Poste Principale,
29 rue Moyenne.
Tel 02 48 68 82 82.

Chartres
Place de la Cathédrale
Tel 02 37 36 42 33.

Le Mans
La Poste,
13 pl de la République.

Nantes
Le Change Graslin,
17 rue Jean-Jacques
Rousseau.
Tel 02 40 69 24 64.

Orléans
La Poste,
pl de Gaulle.
Tel 02 38 77 35 35.

Tours
La Gare (train station),
pl du Maréchal Leclerc.
Tel 02 47 66 78 89.

LOST CARDS AND TRAVELLER'S CHEQUES

Visa
Tel 0800 90 11 79.

American Express Paris
Tel 01 47 77 72 00.

MasterCard
Tel 0800 90 13 87.

THE EURO

The Euro (€) is the common currency of the European Union. It went into general circulation on 1 January 2002, initially for twelve participating countries. France was one of those countries, and the franc was phased out by March 2002. EU members using the Euro as sole official currency are known as the Eurozone. Several EU members have opted out of joining.

Euro notes are identical thoughout the Eurozone countries, each one including designs of fictional architectural structures and monuments. The coins, however, have one side identical (the value side) and one side with an image unique to each country. Both notes and coins are exchangeable in each of the participating countries.

Bank Notes

Euro bank notes have seven denominations. The €5 note (grey in colour) is the smallest, followed by the €10 note (pink), €20 note (blue), €50 note (orange), €100 note (green), €200 note (yellow) and €500 note (purple). All notes show the 12 stars of the European Union.

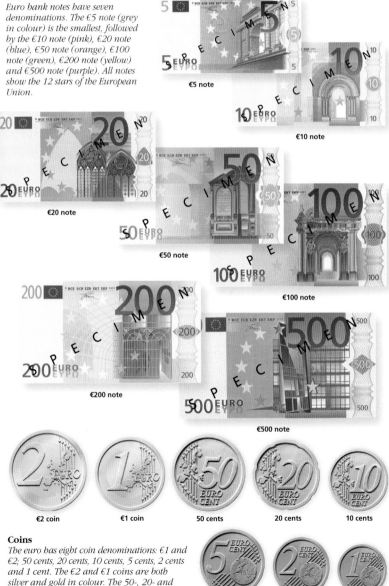

€5 note

€10 note

€20 note

€50 note

€100 note

€200 note

€500 note

€2 coin

€1 coin

50 cents

20 cents

10 cents

Coins

The euro has eight coin denominations: €1 and €2; 50 cents, 20 cents, 10 cents, 5 cents, 2 cents and 1 cent. The €2 and €1 coins are both silver and gold in colour. The 50-, 20- and 10-cent coins are gold. The 5-, 2- and 1-cent coins are bronze.

5 cents

2 cents

1 cent

Communications and Media

Sign for public telephone

French telecommunications are among the most advanced in the world. The national agency is France Télécom, while postal services are run by La Poste. Public telephones are well distributed throughout the Loire Valley. They take a telephone card *(télécarte)*, which can be purchased at local shops. Post offices, or *bureaux de postes*, are identified by the blue-on-yellow La Poste sign. Road signs may still say PTT, as La Poste was formerly known. Foreign newspapers are available in most large towns, and some TV channels broadcast English-language programmes.

Mail boxes throughout France are a distinctive yellow

TELEPHONING IN FRANCE

All French public phone boxes now take phone cards *(télécartes)* and most take credit cards. The last few coin telephones vanished with the advent of the euro. Phone cards are sold in units of either 50 or 120, and are easy to use. They can be purchased at post offices, tobacconists *(tabacs)* and some newsagents.

To call a number in France, simply dial the ten-digit number. Numbers beginning 06 are mobile phones and more expensive to call, 08 indicates a special rate number and all 0800 numbers are free to call. To call abroad, you can either dial direct or make a reverse-charge call *(PCV)* via the international operator. A cheaper option is to buy a pre-paid phone card *(carte à codes)* from a tobacconist or newsagent. Each card has a unique code that you dial to access a line. Alternatively, arrange a phone charge card

through your phone company before you travel to France. You will be issued with a personal identification number (PIN), which you can use to dial from any phone; the costs are billed to your home account or to a credit card.

Avoid making international calls from hotels, since they tend to add a hefty surcharge.

Cheap rates operate from 7pm to 8am Monday to Friday, as well as all day Saturday and Sunday and public holidays.

Some large train stations and post offices have staffed telephone booths *(cabines)* where you pay after you have made your call. This can be a cheaper option when making long-distance calls.

To call France from abroad, dial 00 33 and omit the initial zero from the 10-digit French number. You cannot call French 08 numbers from outside the country.

MOBILE PHONES

French mobiles use the European-standard 900 and 1900 MHz frequencies, so most European mobile phones will work if they have a roaming facility enabled. North American mobile phones will only operate in France if they are tri- or quad-band. Always check roaming charges with your service provider before travelling, as making and receiving calls can be very expensive. Some companies offer "packages" for foreign calls which can work out cheaper.

If you expect to use your phone frequently it can be more economical to get a

France Télécom public telephones are found throughout the region

cheap pay-as-you-go French mobile from one of the main local providers such as Orange France (www.orange.fr) or Bouygues Télécom (www. bouyguestelecom.fr). Both companies have shops in most towns. You can also insert a local SIM card into your own phone, but this will only work if your phone has not been blocked by your service provider.

INTERNET ACCESS

France is rapidly expanding its network of Wi-Fi Internet hotspots (usually known by the English name but sometimes called *point Wi-Fi* or *borne Wi-Fi*). Inevitably, they are concentrated in the cities rather than the countryside, and most are located in hotels for the use of guests. Other hotspots can be found in airports, train stations, conference centres, motorway service areas and libraries. Internet cafés are on the decline and are being replaced by conventional bars and cafés offering wireless Internet access. Hotspots are usually clearly signed but if you need to find one there are several directories online including www.linternaute.com.

French Wi-Fi servers often use different frequencies to those common in the UK and North America, so you may need to manually search for the network. For more information on how to do this see the Orange WiFi website (www.orange-wifi. com). If you need to use a cable connection, note that the French modem socket is incompatible with US and UK plugs. Adaptors are available, but it is often cheaper and easier to buy a French modem lead.

SENDING A LETTER

The postal system in France is fast and usually reliable. There are post offices in most towns, and there are large main offices in all cities. Postage stamps *(timbres)* are sold at La Poste singly or in *carnets* of ten. They are also sold at tobacconists. There are three different price zones for international mail.

Post office hours vary. The minimum hours are around 9am to 5pm from Monday to Friday with a two-hour lunch break from noon to 2pm. On Saturdays they are open from 9am until noon. In larger towns, the main post office may remain open on weekdays from 8am until 7pm. Try to avoid post offices when they first open, as this is when they are at their busiest.

Letters and parcels can be sent worldwide. Letters are dropped into yellow mail boxes, which often have three lots – one for the town you are in; one for the surrounding *département* (the Loire Valley is divided into eleven *départements*, each with its own postcode); and one for other destinations *(autres destinations)*. There are eight different price zones for international mail.

For a small collection fee, you can also receive or send mail care of post offices in France *(poste restante)*. The sender should write the recipient's name in block letters, followed by "Poste Restante", then the postcode and the name of the town to which the letter is to be sent.

To collect anything, you will need to show your passport.

Information on all mail services is available on the La Poste website (www. laposte.com).

OTHER SERVICES

At post offices you can consult telephone directories *(annuaires)*, send or receive money orders *(mandats)* and make use of fax and telex. Most main post offices also have Internet terminals. To use them, buy a rechargeable pre-paid card at the counter.

TELEVISION AND RADIO

The major nationwide TV channels in France are TF1 and France 2. *Canal Plus* (or *Canal+*) is a popular subscription only channel that offers a broad mix of programmes, including live sports and a good range of films in English with French subtitles. A film shown in its original language is listed as *VO (Version Originale)*; a film dubbed into French is indicated as *VF (Version Française)*. Most hotels subscribe to *Canal+*.

BBC World, CNN, Sky, MTV and other major satellite channels are available in many hotels. The Franco-German channel ARTE broadcasts programmes and films from all over the world, often in the original language with French subtitles.

It is easy to pick up UK radio stations in France, including *Radio 4* (198 long wave). Details for the BBC World Service can be found at www.bbc.co.uk/worldservice. *Voice of America* can be found at 90.5, 98.8 and 102.4 FM. *Radio France International* (738 AM) usually gives daily news in English from 3–4pm.

NEWSPAPERS AND MAGAZINES

Newspapers and magazines can be bought at newsagents

A range of the newspapers available in the Loire Valley

(maison de la presse) or news-stands *(kiosques)*. Regional newspapers tend to be more popular than Paris-based national papers such as the conservative *Le Figaro*, weighty *Le Monde* or leftist *Libération*. In most main towns, English-language newspapers such as the *International Herald Tribune*, the *Guardian* and the *Financial Times* are often available for sale on the day of issue. Most other English newspapers as well as Swiss, Italian, German and Spanish titles are sold on the day of publication during the summer months and a day later out of season.

Les Inrockuptibles magazine has information on current music, film and other arts from all over France. Many smaller cities have their own listings magazines, usually in French and often free. They can often be found at tourist offices.

USEFUL DIALLING CODES

- To **call France**, dial: from the UK and US: 00 33; from Australia: 00 11 33. Omit the first 0 of the French area code.
- For **operator service**, dial 118 218 or visit www.118218.fr.
- For **international directory enquiries**, dial: 118 008.
- To make direct **international calls**, dial 00 first.
- The **country codes** are:
  Australia, 61;
  Canada and US, 1;
  Eire, 353;
  New Zealand, 64;
  UK, 44.
- In the event of an **emergency**, dial 122.
- For low-cost **international phone calls** see www.telerabais.fr.

TRAVEL INFORMATION

Forming a broad band about 110 km (70 miles) south of Paris and stretching from the centre of France in the east to the Atlantic coast in the west, the Loire Valley is relatively well served by international motorway and rail links. The city of Nantes has an international

Road sign to Nantes airport

airport with flights to many major European cities; while discount airlines from Britain and Ireland now serve Tours and Angers. For travelling across the region, the TGV *(see pp242–4)* is a swift option; and the motorways are excellent, if a little crowded in summer.

ARRIVING BY AIR

The Loire has three airports of its own but Paris can be just as convenient an arrival point, particularly if you are going to start your visit in the east of the region. From Charles de Gaulle or Orly airports you can get to the Loire by public transport, hire car or even by connecting domestic flight. If you are hiring a car, however, Orly is a better option as you won't need to go in or around the city.

The region's main gateway is Nantes-Atlantique Airport, which has flights from many European cities, and Canada. Coming from Britain and Ireland, you can now also fly to Angers and Tours. Nantes-Atlantique and Angers airports have information desks where staff will make hotel reservations, if necessary. Nantes also has a bank with a bureau de change; when it is closed, you can get euros at the information desk. There is no currency exchange facility at Angers or Tours, though Angers does have an ATM machine.

From Nantes and Angers airports, there are shuttle buses to and from the town centres timed to coincide with most flight arrivals and departures. At Tours, the shuttle bus meets Ryanair flights only. A taxi to central Nantes will cost about €35, to Angers €40 and to Tours €30. The main car rental companies also have outlets at the airports.

AIRLINE DETAILS

British Airways flies from London Heathrow to Paris. Budget carrier Ryanair operates from Dublin to

Nantes and from Shannon in Ireland to Nantes. Ryanair also flies to Tours from Stansted several times a week (Apr–Oct). Flybe links London Gatwick to Paris while Aer Arann operates from Cork to Nantes (May–mid-Sep). From Canada, Air Canada and Air France fly direct to Paris; while Air Transat operates a flight from Montreal direct to Nantes (May–Oct). Several airlines offer direct flights to Paris from the US, while from Australia and New Zealand you will have to travel via London or another European hub. Air France operates at least four daily flights from Paris to Nantes.

FARES AND DEALS

Ryanair, Flybe and Aer Arann offer the cheapest flights, especially if you book well in advance. Low-season promotional fares can cost next to nothing. Fares on full-service airlines, such as BA and Air France, are at their highest over the Easter period and in July and August. Other airlines may have different peak periods, so check to find out which fares will apply when you travel.

For flights only, Advance Purchase Excursion fares (APEX) are relatively inexpensive but they have to be booked well in advance. They cannot be changed or

The interior of Nantes-Atlantique Airport

cancelled without a penalty
and contain minimum and
maximum stay clauses. The
price of a standard fare ticket
is often cheaper if your visit
includes at least one Saturday
overnight stay.

These days there are some
very attractive deals on offer,
both for charter and regular
scheduled flights, so look
around for the best option.

If you book a cheap deal
with a discount agent, check
that the agent belongs to a
recognized regulatory body.
This may guarantee that you
will get a refund if the agent
should cease trading. Do not
part with the full fare until you
have seen the ticket. Check
with the relevant airline to
ensure that your seat has been
confirmed, and reconfirm
your return journey.

FLY-DRIVE AND FLY-RAIL

Air France and the French
railways offer combined fares
for flight and train. You fly
into Paris and then catch a
train. Good deals are available
to Angers, Nantes and Tours.
Other companies offer tailor-
made package holidays in the
Loire Valley with flight, car
hire and accommodation
all included in the cost.

A Boeing 737 jet belonging to the national airline, Air France

FLIGHT TIMES

On long-haul flights you
will need to change
planes in Paris or London.
Approximate flight times to
the region from major cities
are as follows:

London: 1 hour, 25 mins.
Paris: 1 hour.
New York: 10 hours.

SAFETY IN THE AIR

Passengers should make sure
that their baggage is securely
fastened and tagged and not
left unattended at the airport.
Never look after or check in
baggage for somebody else.
You are likely to be asked

whether you are carrying any
electrical goods; it is advisable
to keep these to a minimum.

If you are travelling with
very young children, advise
the airline as soon as
possible in order to reserve
a "skycot".

Pregnant women should
check in advance with the
airline to ensure they will be
allowed to fly: most airlines
have a cut-off date of 36
weeks. Between 28 and 36
weeks it is necessary to have
a letter from your doctor
stating that you are healthy
enough to travel, and giving
your estimated delivery date.

You should inform the
airline in advance if you have
any specific dietary needs.

DIRECTORY

AIRPORT INFORMATION

Angers Airport
Tel 02 41 33 50 20.
www.angersloire
aeroport.fr

Nantes-Atlantique Airport
Tel 02 40 84 80 00.
www.nantes-aeroport.fr

Tours Airport
Tel 02 47 49 37 00.
www.tours.aeroport.fr

AIRLINE TELEPHONE NUMBERS

Aer Arann
UK *Tel 0870 876 7676.*
Ireland *Tel 0818 210 210.*
www.aerarann.com

Air Canada
UK *Tel 0871 220 1111.*
France *Tel 0825 880 881.*
www.aircanada.ca

Air France
UK *Tel 0871 663 3777.*
France *Tel 0820 830 820.*
www.airfrance.com

Air Transat
France *Tel 0825 120 248.*
www.airtransat.com

British Airways
UK *Tel 0844 493 787.*
France *Tel 0825 82 54 00.*
www.britishairways.com

Delta
UK *Tel 0845 600 0950.*
France *Tel 0811 640 005.*
www.delta.com

Flybe
UK *Tel 0871 700 2000.*
www.flybecom

Qantas Airways
UK *Tel 0845 774 7767.*
France *Tel 0811 980
002.* www.qantas.com

Ryanair
UK *Tel 0871 246 0000.*
France *Tel 0892 232 375.*
www.ryanair.com

DISCOUNT TRAVEL AGENCIES

Loire Valley

Nouvelles Frontières
Angers, Bourges, Nantes,
Orléans and Tours
Tel 08 25 00 08 25.
Le Mans *Tel 02 43 24 32 43.*
www.nouvelles-
frontieres.fr

UK

Trailfinders
Tel 0845 058 5858.
www.trailfinders.co.uk

Travelbag
Tel 0871 703 4700.
www.travelbag.co.uk

TAILOR-MADE PACKAGE HOLIDAYS

Allez France
Tel 0845 268 1400.
www.allezfrance.com

Can Be Done Ltd
(for disabled travellers)
Tel (020) 8907 2400.
www.canbedone.co.uk

Cresta Holidays
Tel 0844 800 7020.
www.crestaholidays.
co.uk.

Getting Around by Train

Travelling to the Loire Valley by train is fast and efficient. The French state railway, the Société Nationale des Chemins de Fer Français (SNCF), is one of Europe's best equipped and most punctual. The train journey from Paris to Nantes or to Tours is very quick – the TGV *(Train à Grande Vitesse)* takes only 2 hours and 10 minutes to Nantes, and 75 minutes to Tours. With the Eurostar high-speed service running through the Channel Tunnel, travel from London to the Loire Valley takes around 5–6 hours.

Automatic ticket machine

MAIN ROUTES

The main train routes to the Loire Valley from Northern Europe pass through Paris. The TGV network links the port of Calais with Paris Gare du Nord station. From there, passengers must transfer to Gare Montparnasse, before continuing their journey on the TGV Atlantique to the main towns in the Loire region. Corail express trains to Nantes also leave from Gare Montparnasse, while Corail express trains to all other Loire Valley destinations leave from Gare d'Austerlitz.

SNCF logo

Tickets from London to all the Loire Valley towns, travelling via the Eurostar, hovercraft or ferry, are available from Rail Europe and SNCF offices. From southern Europe, trains run to Nantes from Madrid in Spain (with a journey time of around 16 hours) and Milan in Italy (with a journey time of around 11 hours).

Within the Loire Valley, the route along the River Loire via Nantes, Angers and Orléans is popular, so it is best to reserve tickets in advance on this and other *Grandes Lignes*.

BOOKING IN THE UK

French railways have UK postal and telephone contacts. Reservations made in the UK may be difficult to change in France, due to different computer booking systems. If you need to alter your return date you may have to pay for another reservation or, with Motorail, you will have to buy another ticket and then claim a refund on your return.

BOOKING IN FRANCE

Ticket counters at all the stations are computerized. There are also automatic ticket and reservation machines (with English instructions) on the concourse of main stations. You can also check timetables and purchase tickets online. For travel by TGV, a ticket reservation is necessary, but this can be made as little as five minutes before the train leaves. Ticket prices for all trains rise considerably at peak times, and reservations are compulsory during public holidays. The SNCF's international ticket and reservation system is connected by computer to most European travel agents and stations, allowing direct booking on services throughout Europe.

FARES AND BOOKING

TGVs have two price levels for 2nd class, normal and peak, and a single level for 1st class. The cost of the obligatory seat reservation is included in the ticket price.

Tickets for other trains have just one price level for both first and second class. Seat reservations, where available, are included. Be aware that some trains, including the TGV, also charge additional supplements, which are usually included in the price.

If you intend to take several journeys while you are in France you will be better off buying a discount travel card or a rail pass. SNCF rail cards *(cartes)* give up to 50 per cent discount on fares for qualifying passengers. The *Carte Enfant+* is for children up to the age of 12. The *Carte 12–25* is for children and young people between 12 and 25 years of age and the *Carte Senior* for anyone over 60.

Railpasses give unlimited travel within a specified period of time for a one-off fee but they must be purchased in your own country before you come to France. They come in two varieties: "global" passes which cover several European countries and "one country" passes which are

The ticket office at Chartres railway station

just for travel in, in this case, France. For European residents these passes are called Interrail and to non-European residents Eurail. Rail Europe is the best source of advice on all rail passes.

TIMES AND PENALTIES

Timetables change twice a year, and leaflets for main routes are free at stations. Trains in France are almost always on schedule. When reading French train time-tables, pay particular attention to any footnotes which may be indicated by a number or letter at the top of the column. *Circule* means to run or operate, so *circule tous des jours* means a train runs every day. *Sauf* means except, as in *sauf les dimanche et jours fériés*: not on Sundays or public holidays. Whatever

the timetable says, it's worth double-checking the train time when you arrive at the station; very occasionally there may be some delay with the service. The status of the train will be displayed in a panel over the entrance to the platforms.

Yellow *composteur* machines are located in station halls and at the head of each platform. Insert tickets and reservations separately, printed side up. The *composteur* will punch your ticket and print the time and date on the back. A penalty may be imposed by the inspector on the train if you fail to do this.

BICYCLES

On main rail routes and on TER trains, bicycles are carried free. On TGVs, they must be dismantled, placed in

a carrying bag and stored in luggage spaces. On trains other than TGVs, they can be carried in the guard's van or other designated places and do not need to be dismantled. When purchasing a rail ticket – whether in France or abroad – it is also possible to pre-book a bike *(Train + Vélo)* to await you at your destination.

DISABLED TRAVELLERS

People with disabilities can call the freephone number for the **SNCF Accessibilité Service** *(see p244)* for practical help and information. It is best to make any arrangements at least 24 hours in advance. **Les Compagnons du Voyage** *(see p244)* is an association that provides a suitable companion to travel with you on any train journey outside the Paris area.

TGV RAIL SERVICE

Trains à Grande Vitesse, or high-speed trains, travel at up to 300 km/h (185 mph). Their speed and comfort make them relatively expensive. You must always reserve a seat in advance, the cost of which depends on your destination and on the time and date of your journey.

KEY

- Nord
- Atlantique
- Sud-Est
- Est

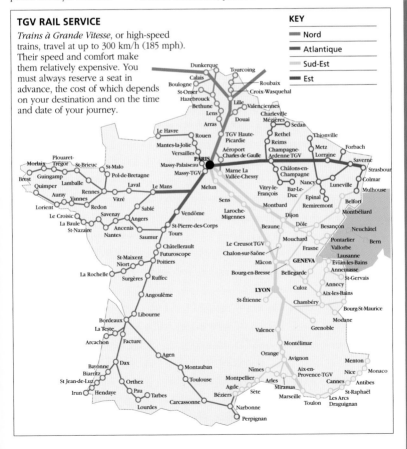

A high-speed TGV

MAIN LINE STATIONS

Nantes has two station exits, the Sortie Sud, which brings you out in the new Cité des Congrès district, and the Sortie Nord, in the Jardin des Plantes district. Both are within walking distance of each other.

In Tours, most trains arrive at the suburban station of St-Pierre-des-Corps, from which a shuttle train *(navette)* takes passengers on to the town centre station in ten minutes.

A similar shuttle service operates in Orléans, where many main line trains arrive at Les Aubrais station, 3 km (2 miles) outside the town centre. In both cases, the price of the shuttle is included in the cost of the ticket, and shuttles are timed so that they coincide with main line services. When leaving, check whether the departure time given on your ticket is for the shuttle or the main line train.

EUROSTAR

Eurostar's striking yellow-and-white trains currently run about 15 services per day between London's Waterloo International Station and the Gare du Nord in Paris. Each train has first- and second-class compartments, with the option of a waiter-service meal in first class. You can also buy refreshments in the buffet car. The journey takes 3 hours. You must book tickets in advance and check in at least 20 minutes before the departure time. To book, contact the **Rail Europe** office in London, ring the **Eurostar** bookings line or visit their website.

EUROTUNNEL

The Eurotunnel shuttle-service carries cars and coaches and their passengers through the Channel Tunnel in 35 minutes. Tickets can be bought in advance from travel agents, by calling the **Eurotunnel** Customer Service Centre or online, but it is also possible to purchase a ticket for the next train when you arrive at the terminals in Folkestone or Calais. There are up to four trains an hour during peak times in the summer, and roughly one every two hours at night. The terminals at each end have a range of restaurants and shops. Before boarding you go through passport and customs controls for both countries. This means you drive straight onto the motorway when you arrive at the other side.

The station forecourt in Tours

Getting Around by Road

France is a motorist's paradise, and the main route to the Loire Valley is via an excellent, if expensive, *autoroute* (motorway) network. There are many beautiful roads in the Loire region, particularly those running along the banks of the rivers. Popular routes, especially the Atlantic coastal roads and the roads leading between the châteaux, can be busy in high season, but are clearer at other times of year. The minimum age for driving in France is 18.

WHAT TO TAKE

If you are taking your own car, it is advisable to obtain a green card (a free extension of an existing policy from some insurers). Without it you only have third-party coverage in France, regardless of whether you have comprehensive cover in your own country. Drivers' organizations and most large insurance companies also offer special policies. It is compulsory to take the original registration document for your car, a current insurance certificate and a valid driving licence. You should also carry a passport or identification card. If your car is not fitted with number plates showing the country of registration, a sticker indicating this must be displayed on the rear of the vehicle. The headlights of right-hand drive cars must be adjusted – kits for this are available at most ports. You must also carry a red warning triangle. Other recommended accessories include spare headlight bulbs, a first-aid kit, a fire extinguisher and a reflective jacket.

GETTING TO THE LOIRE VALLEY

Travellers from the UK arriving at Calais and Boulogne can avoid Paris by taking the A16 motorway south to Abbeville and then the newly opened A28 via Rouen to Le Mans. At Le Mans, you can take the A11 for Chartres, Angers and Nantes, or head across country to Tours, Blois and Orléans. Alternatively, brave Paris and take the A1 south, skirt around the city centre and connect with the A10 for Orléans and Tours, and the A11.

From western Spain, take the A8 from San Sebastian to the border, then the A63 to Bordeaux and the A10 to Tours and Orléans. From the eastern Spanish coast you can reach Orléans on the A9, A62 and A20, passing via Narbonne and Toulouse. From Italy take the A8 and A7 or the A43 to Lyon, which is where the A72 and A71 head north to Bourges and Orléans. From anywhere in Germany, the quickest way to get to the Loire Valley is via Paris.

In high season, the motorways get crowded and, if you have time, it may be worth taking more minor (and more attractive) roads. Try not to travel over the first and last weekends in July and August, when thousands of holidaymakers are on the roads.

USING THE AUTOROUTE TOLL

When you join an autoroute, take a ticket from the machine. This identifies your starting point on the autoroute. You do not pay until you reach an exit tollbooth. Charges are made according to the distance travelled and the type of vehicle.

Motorway Sign
These signs indicate the name and distance to the next tollbooth. They are usually blue and white; some show the various tariff rates for cars, motorbikes, caravans and large trucks.

Tollbooth with Attendant
When you hand in your ticket at a staffed toll-booth, the attendant tells you the cost of your journey on the autoroute and the price will be displayed. You can pay with coins, notes or credit cards. A receipt is issued on request.

Automatic Machine
On reaching the exit tollbooth, insert your ticket into the machine and the price of your journey will be displayed in euros. You can pay either with coins or by credit card. The machine will give change and can issue a receipt.

CAR HIRE

It is worth contacting a number of car-hire firms before you go, as there are often special offers if you pre-pay or book online. Other options include fly-drive packages, and the train and car-hire deals from the SNCF, with collection from main stations.

Requirements for car hire vary, but in general you must be over 21 and have held a driving licence for at least a year. You will need to present your licence, passport and a credit card against a deposit.

Three of the most widely available car-hire firms in the Loire Valley

RULES OF THE ROAD

Remember to drive on the right. The *priorité à droite* rule also applies, which means that you must give way to any vehicle coming out of a side turning on the right, unless signposting indicates otherwise. However, the *priorité à droite* rule no longer applies at roundabouts, so give way to cars already on the roundabout.

Seat belts are compulsory for both front and back seats. Overtaking when there is a single solid centre line is heavily penalized.

Be aware that instant fines are issued for speeding and drink-driving.

No entry for any vehicles   **One-way system**

VOUS N'AVEZ PAS LA PRIORITÉ

Give way at roundabouts   **Right of way ends, give way to right**

One of the motorways in the Loire Valley region

FAST THROUGH ROUTES

There are three main motorways in the Loire Valley: the A11 (*L'Océane*) from Nantes to Chartres via Angers; the A10 (*L'Aquitaine*) from Tours to Orléans via Blois; and the A71 from Orléans to Bourges. There are police stations at motorway exits.

COUNTRY ROUTES

One of the pleasures of touring the Loire Valley is turning off the main routes onto small country roads. The RN and D (*Route Nationale* and *Départementale*) roads are usually marked in yellow or white on maps, and are often a good alternative to motorways. They are generally well sign-posted but it is wise to have a 1:250,000 map with you. It takes longer to meander across country, and you'll have to slow down through villages, but the rewards are worth the extra time and effort. Popular scenic drives include the riverside stretch of the D951 and the D751 from Chambord to Tours.

The *Bison futé* ("crafty bison") signs will indicate alternative routes to avoid heavy traffic, and are particularly helpful during the French holiday periods, which are appropriately known as the *grands départs*. The worst weekends are in mid-July, and at the beginning and end of August when the French holidays start and finish.

SPEED LIMITS

The speed limits in the Loire Valley are as follows:

- **Toll motorways** 130 km/h (80 mph) in dry weather, 110 km/h (68 mph) when it rains;
- **Dual carriageways and non-toll motorways** 110 km/h (68 mph), 100 km/h (60 mph) in the rain; 50 km/h (30 mph) in towns;
- **Other roads** 90 km/h (56 mph), 80 km/h (50 mph) in the rain;
- In **towns** 50 km/h (30 mph).
- In **fog**, 50 km/h (30 mph).

MAPS

The best general maps of the Loire Valley are the orange Michelin regional maps (No. 517 for the Pays de la Loire and No. 518 for Centre). **IGN** (*Institut Géographique National*) also produces two good touring maps covering this area: Central France (R08) and Pays de la Loire (R07).

Town plans are usually provided free by local tourist offices. In large towns you may need a more detailed map, and these are published by Michelin or **Blay-Foldex**. In the UK, **Stanfords** in London is famous for its range of maps.

PETROL (GASOLINE)

Petrol (*essence*) is relatively expensive in France, especially on autoroutes. Large supermarkets and hypermarkets sell petrol at a discount.

Many petrol stations in France tend to be self-service (*libre service*), but if an attendant is on duty, it may be helpful to know that *faire le plein* means "to fill up the tank".

Petrol stations in France sell unleaded petrol (*sans plomb*) and diesel (*gazole* or *gasoil*).

An *horodateur*, or pay-and-display parking meter

Leaded petrol is no longer available, though some stations offer lead-replacement petrol (*Super ARS*) or a lead-substitute additive. LPG gas is also widely available. A list on the French Government Tourist Office website *(see p231)* indicates petrol stations selling LPG gas in the region.

Not all filling stations are open 24 hours, especially away from the big towns. Although most supermarket petrol stations are unstaffed, out of shopping hours you can serve yourself from automatic pumps using a credit card up to a maximum permitted amount. Insert the card in the slot and follow the on-screen instructions.

PARKING REGULATIONS

Parking in the large towns is strictly regulated. If you are illegally parked, you may be towed away instantly to the police pound and face a stiff fine. Loire Valley towns now have pay-and-display machines (*horodateurs*). Many towns offer free parking from noon to 2pm, overnight (usually 7pm–9am), and all day on Sundays and public holidays.

Even if you are legally parked, it is possible that you will find yourself hemmed in when you return: the French usually honk their horns to attract the guilty party.

COACH AND BUS TRAVEL

Eurolines operates coach services on Wednesdays and Fridays from London Victoria coach station to Tours, Angers and Nantes. The journey to Nantes takes around 13 hours and is an expensive option compared to a flight with one of the discount airlines.

Local buses operate from most towns' gare routière, which is often located near the train station (gare SNCF). Although the bus service in the Loire Valley region is relatively good, timetables in many rural areas tend to be geared towards the needs of schoolchildren and people going to work, or around market days. As a result, morning departures tend to be very early and the service may not run on a daily basis.

For more information on bus routes and timetables, contact local town halls or tourist information offices.

TAXIS

Prices for taxis tend to vary from one part of the region to another. The charges, predictably, are highest in the busy tourist areas. The pick-up charge is usually around €4, and €1 or more for every kilometre. An extra charge will be made for any luggage. All taxis must use a meter (*compteur*).

Hailing a taxi is not customary in the Loire Valley – you must go to a taxi rank or book a car over the phone. A good website for finding and ordering a taxi is www.taxis-de-france.com.

HITCHHIKING

Hitchhiking in France is legal except on motorways, though it is possible to hitch from one service station to another. A safer option is to use **Allostop**, an organization that puts you in touch with cars travelling in France and Europe. After paying an initial fee, which is determined by the length of the trip, hitchhikers pay the driver a fixed rate per kilometre, which includes petrol costs and motorway tolls. The organization keeps records of drivers' and hitchhikers' details for security reasons.

DIRECTORY

CAR RENTAL

Avis
UK *Tel* 0870 581 0147.
France *Tel* 0820 050505.
Nantes *Tel* 0820 611 676.
Orléans *Tel* 02 38 62 27 04.
www.avis.fr

Budget
UK *Tel* 0844 544 3407.
France *Tel* 0825 00 35 64.
www.budget.fr

Europcar
UK *Tel* 0870 607 50 00.
France *Tel* 0825 358 358.
Orléans *Tel* 02 38 73 00 40.
Nantes *Tel* 02 40 47 19 38.
www.europcar.com

Hertz
UK *Tel* 08708 44 88 44.
France *Tel* 0825 861 861.
www.hertz.com

National/Citer
UK *Tel* 0870 400 45 81.
France *Tel* 0825 16 12 12.
www.nationalcar.fr

TRAFFIC INFORMATION

Autoroutes
Tel 0892 70 26 34.
www.autoroutes.fr

Bison Futé (other roads)
Tel 0800 100 200 (French only).

MAPS

Espace IGN
107 rue la Boétie,
75008 Paris.
Tel 01 43 98 80 00.
www.ign.fr

Stanfords
12–14 Long Acre,
London WC2E 9LP.
Tel (020) 7836 1321.
www.stanfords.co.uk

COACH TRAVEL

Eurolines
UK *Tel* 0871 81 81 81.
France *Tel* 08 92 899 091.
www.eurolines.com

HITCHHIKING SERVICE

Allostop
Paris *Tel* 01 53 20 42 42.
www.allostop.net

General Index

Acknowledgments

Dorling Kindersley would like to thank the following people whose assistance contributed to the preparation of this book.

Main Contributor
Jack Tresidder has been living and writing in France since 1992. A former newspaper journalist and theatre critic, he has edited and written books on art, cinema and photography as well as travel.

Editorial Consultant
Vivienne Menkes-Ivry.

Contributors and Consultants
Sara Black, Hannah Bolus, Patrick Delaforce, Thierry Guidet, Jane Tresidder.

Additional Photography
Andy Crawford, Tony Gervis, Andrew Holligan, Paul Kenward, Jason Lowe, Ian O'Leary, Clive Streeter.

Additional Illustrators
Robert Ashby, Graham Bell, Stephen Conlin, Toni Hargreaves, The Maltings Partnership, Lee Peters, Kevin Robinson, Tristan Spaargaren, Ed Stuart, Mike Taylor.

Cartography
Lovell Johns Ltd, Oxford.

Technical Cartographic Assistance
David Murphy.

Design and Editorial
Duncan Baird Publishers
MANAGING EDITOR Louise Bostock Lang
MANAGING ART EDITOR David Rowley
PICTURE RESEARCH Jill De Cet, Michèle Faram
RESEARCHER Caroline Mackenzie
DTP DESIGNER Alan McKee

Dorling Kindersley Limited
SENIOR EDITOR Fay Franklin
SENIOR MANAGING ART EDITOR Gillian Allan
DEPUTY EDITORIAL DIRECTOR Douglas Amrine
DEPUTY ART DIRECTOR Gaye Allen
MAP CO-ORDINATORS Michael Ellis, David Pugh
PRODUCTION David Proffit

PROOF READER Sam Merrell
INDEXER Brian Amos

Claire Baranowski, Susana Smith, Sonal Bhatt, Poppy Body, Sophie Boyack, Anna Freiberger, Rhiannon Furbear, John Grain, Richard Hansell, Matt Harris, Nicholas Inman, Gail Jones, Laura Jones, Nancy Jones, Maite Lantaron, Ciaran McIntyre, Rebecca Milner, Emma O'Kelly, Lyn Parry, Pollyanna Poulter, Philippa Richmond, Zoe Ross, Sands Publishing Solutions, Jill Stevens, Alison Verity, Dora Whitaker.

Special Assistance
Mme Barthez, Château d'Angers; M Sylvain Bellenger, Château de Blois; Tiphanie Blot, Loire-Atlantique Tourisme; M Bertrand Bourdin, France Télécom; M Jean-Paul and Mme Caroline Chaslus, Abbaye de Fontevraud; M Joël Clavier, Conseil Général du Loiret; Mme Dominique Féquet, Office de Tourisme, Saumur; Katia Fôret, Nantes Tourisme; M Gaston Huet, Vouvray; Mme Pascale Humbert, Comité Départemental du Tourisme de l'Anjou; M Alain Irlandes and Mme Guylaine Fisher, Atelier Patrimoine, Tours; Mme Sylvie Lacroix and M Paul Lichtenberg, Comité Régional du Tourisme, Nantes; M André Margotin, Comité Départemental du Tourisme du Cher; M Jean Méré, Champigny-sur-Veude, Touraine; Séverine Michau, Comité Régional du Tourisme Centre; Mme Marie-France de Peyronnet, Route Jacques-Cœur, Berry; M R Pinard, L'Ecole des Ponts et Chaussées, Paris; Virginie Priou, Comité Régional du Tourisme des Pays de la Loire; Véronique Richard, Vallée du Loir; Père Rocher, Abbaye de Solesmes; M Loïc Rousseau, Rédacteur, Vallée du Loir; M Pierre Saboureau, Lochois; Bertrand Sachet, Fédération Régionale de Randonnée Pédestre, Indre; M de Sauveboeuf, Le Plessis- Bourré; M Antoine Selosse and M Frank Artiges, Comité Départemental du Tourisme de Touraine; Mme Sabine Sévrin, Comité Régional du Tourisme, Orléans; Mme Tissier de Mallerais, Château de Talcy.

Photography Permissions
Dorling Kindersley would like to thank the following for their assistance and kind permission to photograph at their establishments: M François Bonneau, Conservateur, Château de Valençay; M Nicolas de Brissac, Château de Brissac; Caisse Nationale des Monuments Historiques et des Sites; Conseil Général du Cher; Marquis and Marquise de Contades, Château de Montgeoffroy; M Robert de Goulaine, Château de Goulaine; Mme Jallier, Office de Tourisme, Puy-du-Fou; Château de Montsoreau, Propriété du Département de Maine-et-Loire; Musée Historique et Archéologique de l'Orléanais; M Jean-Pierre Ramboz, Sacristain, Cathédrale de Tours; M Bernard Voisin, Conservateur, Château de Chenonceau and all other churches, museums, hotels, restaurants, shops and sights too numerous to thank individually.

Gabrielle d'Estrées in her Bath French School 17th century 96c; Musée d'Orsay, Paris *Marcel Proust* Jacques-Emile Blanche c.1891–2 24tc; Musée de la Venerie, Senlis *Diane de Poitiers as Diana the Hunter* Fontainebleau School 16th century 55crb; British Museum 54–5; Michael Bussell's Photography: 29tl and br.

Cahiers Ciba: 77crb; Camera Press: 77tr; Cephas: Stuart Boreham 63bl; Hervé Champollion 63cra, 152tr; Mick Rock 29crb; Jean-Loup Charmet, Paris: 45b, 51b, 57cra; Château d'Angers: Centre des Monuments Nationaux / Damien Perdriau 75bl; Château de Chamerolles: 137cbl; Château de la Barre: 201tl; Château de Monhoudou: 200tr; Château de Montgeoffroy: 71cl; Château de Noirieux: 209br; Château de Rochecotte: 200br; Château de Villandry: 94br; Château du Boisrenault: 201br; Christie's Images, London: 53b; Bruce Coleman: NG Blake: 71bc; Denis Green 185cr; Udo Hirsch 185bl; Hans Reinhard 184bl; Uwe Walz 71bl, 71br, 185br; Comité Départemental du Tourisme du Cher: 27cra; Comité Régional du Tourisme, Nantes: 226t and b, JP Guyonneau 227tl, J Lesage 225tr; Comité du Tourisme de L'anjou: 84b, JP Guyonneau 84c; Corbis: Adam Woolfitt 11tr.

Diatotale: Château de Chenonceau 106t.

Editions Gaud: Château de Villandry *Jeune Infante Pantoja de la Cruz* 94tl; C Errath: 26br, 182tr, 183bl; Et Archive: 50bl, 100br; Mary Evans Picture Library: 9inset, 24tl, 53cl, 61inset, 151tl, 195inset, 227inset; Explorer: F Jalain 56cl.

Fédération Nationale de Logis de France: 197c; Fédération Unie des Auberges de Jeunesse: 199tr; FNOTSI: 230c, 230tc; Fontenay-le-Comte Office de Tourisme: 230cl; Fontevraud Abbey: 41b, 87b; Fontgombault Abbey: Frère Eric Chevreau 147C.

Giraudon, Paris: 48tr and bl, 76tr and c, 135c; Archives Nationales, Paris 50tl; Bibliothèque Municipale, Laon 50–51cra; Château de Versailles *Louis XIII – Roi de France et de Navarre* after Vouet 47br, 56bl; Musée Antoine Lécuyer 134bl; Musée Carnavalet, Paris 30tl, *Madame Dupin de Francueil* 109tr; Musée Condé, Chantilly 52br, 108b; Musée d'Histoire et des Guerres de Vendée, Cholet *Henri de la Rochejaquelein au Combat de Cholet le 17 Octobre 1793* Emile Boutigny 69cl; Musée de Tessé, Le Mans 166tr; Musée des Beaux-Arts, Blois 169crb; Musée du Vieux Château, Laval 160b (all rights reserved); Telarci 51cla; Victoria & Albert Museum, London 95tl; Gîtes de France: 199ct; La Goélette: JJ Derennes *The Three Graces* Charles-André Van Loo 106br.

Sonia Halliday Photographs: 53tl; Robert Harding: 37br; Paolo Koba 17br; Sheila Terry 102b; D Hodges: 167b; Kit Houghton: 38c; Hulton-Deutsch Collection: 46tr, 111tc, 134cla.

Image Bank: 34clb; David W Hamilton 32; Image de Marc 16b, 90c, 103b, 117b; Nicolas Inman: 234bl; Inventaire Général: Musée du Grand-Pressigny 48cla, 104c.

Jerrican/berenguier: 13bl.

Lonely Planet Images: John Elk III 10br; Diana Mayfield 10cla.

Mairie de Blois: J-Philippe Thibaut 42b; Mansell Collection: 30b; T Mezerette: 28t, 29tl; Musées d'Angers: 18t, 51clb, 57crb, 77cra; Collection Musée

d'Art Et D'histoire de Cholet: 57b, Studio Golder, Cholet *Jacques Cathelineau* Anne-Louis Girodet-Trioson 1824 187b; Musée d'Arts Décoratifs Et Musée du Cheval, Château de Saumur: 82cr; Musée des Beaux-arts de Rennes: Louis Deschamps *Bal à la Cour des Valois* 109cbr; Musée des Beaux-Arts, Tours: *Vue Panoramique de Tours en 1787* Pierre-Antoine Demachy 8–9; P Boyer *Christ in the Olive Grove* Andrea Mantegna 114b; Musée de Blois: J Parker 126c, 127br; Musées de Bourges: Musée des Arts Décoratifs, Hôtel Lallemant *Concert Champêtre Instrumental* French-Italian School 150t; Musée Dobrée, Nantes: 55clb, 191tl; Collection Musée Estève © ADAGP/DACS: Dubout *Samsâra* Maurice Estève oil on canvas 150b; Courtesy, Museum of Fine Arts Boston: *Valley of the Petite Creuse* Claude Monet 1889 oil on canvas Bequest of David P Kimball in Memory of his Wife, Clara Bertram Kimball (© 1995. All rights reserved) 147br; Musée Historique d'Orléans: 48clb; Musées du Mans: 166c; Musée des Marais Salants, Batz-Loire-Atlantique: G Buron 179cr; Collection du Musée de La Marine de Loire, Châteauneuf-sur-Loire (Loiret): 33bc.

NHPA: Manfred Danegger 185cl; M Garwod: 79b; Helio & Van Ingen 182tl; R Sorensen & JB Olsen 184br; National Motor Museum, Beaulieu: 57tr.

Parc Naturel Régional du Poitevin: 185tr; John Parker: 1c, 20bc, 26bl, 27tl, 35crb, 36crb, 37cla and cl, 38bl, 51cra, 54clb, 55cra, 58tl, 63br, 72tl, 73c, 75bc, 87tc, 95bc, 106cla, 107cb, 110bl, 111br, 115c, 116tr, 117cr, 121br, 126cl, 127bl, 128tl, 130tl and bl, 131tc and bc, 132tl, cl, clb and br, 133tc, cr, bc and br, 144tr, 170br, 171br, 220cl; Photographers' Library: 159b; 199b; By kind permission from Puy du Fou: 43t.

Runion des Musées Nationaux, Paris: Château de Versailles *Château de Chambord* PD Martin © (Photo RMN) 134crb; Rex Features/Sipa Press: Riclafe 59tr, Tall 58bl; Route Historique Jacques Cœur: 18b; David Rowley: 83b.

The Science Museum/Science & Society Picture Library, London: 56br; Science Photo Library/CNES: 11tr; SNCF - Society National des Chemins de Fer: 242c, 244tl; Spectrum Colour Library: 137cr; Tony Stone worldwide: 63tl and tr, Charlie Waite 154t.

Telegraph Colour Library: Jean-Paul Nacivet: 26cla; TRH Pictures: 58tr.

Ville d'Ambroise: Musée de la Poste 33cb; Roger Viollet: 52bl, Bibliothèque Nationale 56clb, 137tr, Musée d'Orléans *Entrée de Jeanne d'Arc à Orléans* Jean-Jacques Sherrer 137br.

J Warminski: 79t; C Watier: 67t, 70b; Wildlife Matters: 94tr, 95c and br; WYSE Travel Confederation: 232cr.

Front endpaper: all commissioned photography.

Jacket: Front - Alamy Images: Andre Jenny main image; DK Images: John Parker clb. Back - DK Images: John Heseltine cla; Kim Sayer clb, bl; Getty Images: Stone / Charlie Waite tl. Spine - Alamy Images: Andre Jenny t; DK Images: Kim Sayer b.

All other images © Dorling Kindersley.

For further information, see: www.dkimages.com

Phrase Book

In Emergency

Help!	**Au secours!**	oh se**koor**
Stop!	**Arrêtez!**	aret-**ay**
Call a doctor!	**Appelez un médecin!**	apuh-**lay** uñ med**sañ**
Call an ambulance!	**Appelez une ambulance!**	apuh-**lay** oon oñboo-**loñs**
Call the police!	**Appelez la police!**	apuh-**lay** lah poh-**lees**
Call the fire brigade!	**Appelez les pompiers!**	apuh-lay leh poñ-**peeyay**
Where is the nearest telephone?	**Où est le téléphone le plus proche?**	oo ay luh tehleh**fon** luh ploo **prosh**
Where is the nearest hospital?	**Où est l'hôpital le plus proche?**	oo ay l'opee**tal** luh ploo **prosh**

Communication Essentials

Yes	**Oui**	wee
No	**Non**	noñ
Please	**S'il vous plaît**	seel voo **play**
Thank you	**Merci**	mer-**see**
Excuse me	**Excusez-moi**	exkoo-**zay** mwah
Hello	**Bonjour**	boñ**zhoor**
Goodbye	**Au revoir**	oh ruh-**vwar**
Good night	**Bonsoir**	boñ-**swar**
Morning	**Le matin**	matañ
Afternoon	**L'après-midi**	l'apreh-**meedee**
Evening	**Le soir**	swar
Yesterday	**Hier**	eeyehr
Today	**Aujourd'hui**	oh-zhoor-**dwee**
Tomorrow	**Demain**	duh**mañ**
Here	**Ici**	ee-**see**
There	**Là**	lah
What?	**Quel, quelle?**	kel, kel
When?	**Quand?**	koñ
Why?	**Pourquoi?**	poor-**kwah**
Where?	**Où?**	oo

Useful Phrases

How are you?	**Comment allez-vous?**	kom-moñ tala**y voo**
Very well, thank you.	**Très bien, merci.**	treh byañ, mer-**see**
Pleased to meet you.	**Enchanté de faire votre connaissance.**	oñshoñ-**tay** duh fehr votr kon-ay-**sans**
See you soon.	**A bientôt.**	Ah byañ-**toh**
That's fine	**C'est parfait**	say par**fay**
Where is/are...?	**Où est/sont...?**	oo ay/soñ
How far is it to...?	**Combien de kilomètres d'ici à...?**	kom-**byañ** duh keelo-**metr** d'ee-**see** ah
Which way to...?	**Quelle est la direction pour...?**	kel ay lah **deer**-ek-**syoñ** poor
Do you speak English?	**Parlez-vous anglais?**	par-**lay** voo oñg-**lay**
I'm sorry.	**Excusez-moi.**	exkoo-**zay** mwah
I don't understand.	**Je ne comprends pas.**	zhuh nuh kom-**proñ** pah

Could you speak slowly please?	**Pouvez-vous parler moins vite s'il vous plaît?**	poo-**vay** voo par-**lay** mwañ veet seel voo play

Useful Words

big	**grand**	groñ
small	**petit**	puh-**tee**
hot	**chaud**	show
cold	**froid**	frwah
good	**bon**	boñ
bad	**mauvais**	moh-**veh**
enough	**assez**	as**say**
well	**bien**	byañ
open	**ouvert**	oo-**ver**
closed	**fermé**	fer-**meh**
left	**gauche**	gohsh
right	**droite**	drwaht
straight on	**tout droit**	too drwah
near	**près**	preh
far	**loin**	lwañ
up	**en haut**	oñ **oh**
down	**en bas**	oñ **bah**
early	**de bonne heure**	duh bon **urr**
late	**en retard**	oñ ruh-**tar**
entrance	**l'entrée**	l'on-**tray**
exit	**la sortie**	sor-**tee**
toilet	**les toilettes, les WC**	twah-let, vay-**see**
free, unoccupied	**libre**	leebr
free, no charge	**gratuit**	grah-**twee**

Making a Telephone Call

I'd like to place a long-distance call.	**Je voudrais faire un appel interurbain.**	zhuh voo-dreh fehruñ apel añter-oorbañ
I'd like to make a reverse charge call.	**Je voudrais faire une communication PCV.**	zhuh voo**dreh** fehr oon **syoñ** komoonikah-peh-seh-veh
I'll try again later.	**Je rappelerai plus tard.**	zhuh rapel-**eray** ploo tar
Can I leave a message?	**Est-ce que je peux laisser un message?**	es-**keh** zhuh puh leh-**say** uñ meh**sazh**
Hold on.	**Ne quittez pas, s'il vous plaît.**	nuh kee-**tay** pah seel voo play
Could you speak up a little please?	**Pouvez-vous parler un peu plus fort?**	poo-**vay** voo par-**lay** uñ puh ploo for
local call	**la communication locale**	komoonikah-**syoñ** low-kal

Shopping

How much does this cost?	**C'est combien s'il vous plaît?**	say kom-**byañ** seel voo play
I would like ...	**je voudrais...**	zhuh voo-**dray**
Do you have?	**Est-ce que vous avez?**	es-**kuh** voo zavay

I'm just looking.	**Je regarde seulement.**	zhuh ruh**gar** suhl**moñ**
Do you take credit cards?	**Est-ce que vous acceptez les cartes de crédit?**	es-**kuh** voo zaksept-**ay** leh kart duh kreh-**dee**
Do you take traveller's cheques?	**Est-ce que vous acceptez les chèques de voyage?**	es-**kuh** voo zaksept-**ay** leh shek duh vwa**yazh**
What time do you open?	**A quelle heure vous êtes ouvert?**	ah kel urr voo zet oo-**ver**
What time do you close?	**A quelle heure vous êtes fermé?**	ah kel urr voo zet fer-**may**
This one.	**Celui-ci.**	suhl-wee-**see**
That one.	**Celui-là.**	suhl-wee-**lah**
expensive	**cher**	shehr
cheap	**pas cher, bon marché**	pah shehr, boñ mar-**shay**
size, clothes	**la taille**	tye
size, shoes	**la pointure**	pwañ-**tur**
white	**blanc**	bloñ
black	**noir**	nwahr
red	**rouge**	roozh
yellow	**jaune**	zhohwn
green	**vert**	vehr
blue	**bleu**	bluh

Types of Shop

antique shop	**le magasin d'antiquités**	maga-**zañ** d'oñteekee-**tay**
bakery	**la boulangerie**	booloñ-**zhuree**
bank	**la banque**	boñk
book shop	**la librairie**	lee-**brehree**
butcher	**la boucherie**	boo-**shehree**
cake shop	**la pâtisserie**	patee-**sree**
cheese shop	**la fromagerie**	fromazh-**ree**
chemist	**la pharmacie**	farmah-**see**
dairy	**la crémerie**	krem-**ree**
department store	**le grand magasin**	groñ maga-**zañ**
delicatessen	**la charcuterie**	sharkoot-**ree**
fishmonger	**la poissonnerie**	pwasson-**ree**
gift shop	**le magasin de cadeaux**	maga-**zañ** duh ka**doh**
greengrocer	**le marchand de légumes**	mar-**shoñ** duh lay-**goom**
grocery	**l'alimentation**	alee-moñta-**syoñ**
hairdresser	**le coiffeur**	kwa**fuhr**
market	**le marché**	marsh-**ay**
newsagent	**le magasin de journaux**	maga-**zañ** duh zhoor-**no**
post office	**la poste, le bureau de poste, le PTT**	pohst, booroh duh pohst, peh-teh-teh
shoe shop	**le magasin de chaussures**	maga-**zañ** duh show-**soor**
supermarket	**le supermarché**	soo pehr-**marshay**
tobacconist	**le tabac**	tabah
travel agent	**l'agence de voyages**	l'azhoñs duh vwayazh

Sightseeing

abbey	**l'abbaye**	l'abay-**ee**
art gallery	**le galerie d'art**	galer-**ree** dart
bus station	**la gare routière**	gahr roo-tee-**yehr**
cathedral	**la cathédrale**	katay-**dral**
church	**l'église**	l'ay**gleez**
garden	**le jardin**	zhar-**dañ**
library	**la bibliothèque**	beeb**leeo**-tek
museum	**le musée**	moo-**zay**
railway station	**la gare (SNCF)**	gahr (es-en-say-ef)
tourist information office	**les renseignements touristiques**	roñsayn-**moñ** too-rees-**teek**, sandee-ka d'eenee-syat**eev**
town hall	**le syndicat d'initiative**	
private mansion	**l'hôtel de ville**	l'ohtel duh veel
	l'hôtel particulier	l'oh**tel** partikoo-**lyay**
closed for public holiday	**fermeture**	fehrmeh-**tur**
	jour férié	zhoor fehree-**ay**

Staying in a Hotel

Do you have a vacant room?	**Est-ce que vous avez une chambre?**	es-kuh voo-zavay oon shambr
double room	**la chambre pour deux personnes**	shambr poor duh pehr-**son**
with double bed	**avec un grand lit**	avek un gronñ lee
twin room	**la chambre à deux lits**	shambr ah duh lee
single room	**la chambre pour une personne**	shambr poor oon pehr-**son**
room with a bath, shower	**la chambre avec salle de bains, une douche**	shambr avek sal duh bañ, oon doosh
porter	**le garçon**	gar-**soñ**
key	**la clef**	klay
I have a reservation.	**J'ai fait une réservation.**	zhay fay oon rayzehrva-**syoñ**

Eating Out

Have you got a table?	**Avez-vous une table libre?**	avay-**voo** oon tahbl leebr
I want to reserve a table.	**Je voudrais réserver une table.**	zhuh voo-**dray** rayzehr-**vay** oon tahbl
The bill please.	**L'addition s'il vous plaît.**	l'adee-**syoñ** seel voo **play**
I am a vegetarian.	**Je suis végétarien.**	zhuh swee vezhay-**tehryañ**
Waitress/ waiter	**Madame, Mademoiselle/ Monsieur**	mah-**dam**, mah-demwah**zel**/ muh-**syuh**
menu	**le menu, la carte**	men-**oo**, kart
fixed-price menu	**le menu à prix fixe**	men-**oo** ah pree feeks
cover charge	**le couvert**	koo-**vehr**
wine list	**la carte des vins**	**kart**-deh vañ
glass	**le verre**	vehr
bottle	**la bouteille**	boo-**tay**
knife	**le couteau**	koo-**toh**
fork	**la fourchette**	for-**shet**

spoon	**la cuillère**	kwee-**yehr**
breakfast	**le petit**	puh-**tee**
	déjeuner	deh-**zhuh-nay**
lunch	**le déjeuner**	deh-**zhuh-nay**
dinner	**le dîner**	dee-**nay**
main course	**le plat principal**	plah prañsee-**pal**
starter, first	**l'entrée, le hors-**	l'oñ-**tray**, or-
course	**d'œuvre**	duhvr
dish of the day	**le plat du jour**	plah doo zhoor
wine bar	**le bar à vin**	bar ah vañ
café	**le café**	ka-**fay**
rare	**saignant**	**say**-noñ
medium	**à point**	ah **pwañ**
well done	**bien cuit**	byañ **kwee**

Menu Decoder

l'agneau	l'anyoh	lamb
l'ail	l'eye	garlic
la banane	banan	banana
le beurre	burr	butter
la bière	bee-**yehr**	beer
la bière	bee-**yehr**	draught beer
pression	pres-**syoñ**	
le bifteck, le steak	beef-**tek**, stek	steak
le bœuf	buhf	beef
bouilli	boo-**yee**	boiled
le café	kah-**fay**	coffee
le canard	kanar	duck
le chocolat	**shoko**-lah	chocolate
le citron	see-**troñ**	lemon
le citron	see-**troñ**	fresh lemon juice
pressé	press-**eh**	
les crevettes	kruh-**vet**	prawns
les crustacés	**kroos**-ta-say	shellfish
cuit au four	kweet oh foor	baked
le dessert	deh-**ser**	dessert
l'eau minérale	l'oh **meeney**-ral	mineral water
les escargots	leh zes-kar-**goh**	snails
les frites	freet	chips
le fromage	from-**azh**	cheese
le fruit frais	frwee freh	fresh fruit
les fruits de mer	frwee duh mer	seafood
le gâteau	gah-**toh**	cake
la glace	glas	ice, ice cream
grillé	gree-**yay**	grilled
le homard	omahr	lobster
l'huile	l'weel	oil
le jambon	zhoñ-**boñ**	ham
le lait	leh	milk
les légumes	lay-**goom**	vegetables
la moutarde	moo-**tard**	mustard
l'œuf	l'uf	egg
les oignons	leh zonyoñ	onions
les olives	leh zoleev	olives
l'orange	l'oroñzh	orange
l'orange	l'oroñzh	fresh orange juice
pressée	press-**eh**	
le pain	pan	bread
le petit pain	puh-**tee** pañ	roll
poché	posh-**ay**	poached
le poisson	pwah-**ssoñ**	fish
le poivre	pwavr	pepper
la pomme	pom	apple
les pommes	pom-duh	potatoes
de terre	tehr	
le porc	por	pork
le potage	poh-**tazh**	soup
le poulet	poo-**lay**	chicken
le riz	ree	rice
rôti	row-**tee**	roast
la sauce	sohs	sauce
la saucisse	sohsees	sausage, fresh
sec	sek	dry
le sel	sel	salt
la soupe	soop	soup
le sucre	sookr	sugar
le thé	tay	tea
le toast	toast	toast
la viande	vee-**yand**	meat
le vin blanc	vañ **bloñ**	white wine
le vin rouge	vañ roozh	red wine
le vinaigre	vee**naygr**	vinegar

Numbers

0	**zéro**	zeh-**roh**
1	**un, une**	uñ, oon
2	**deux**	duh
3	**trois**	trwah
4	**quatre**	katr
5	**cinq**	sañk
6	**six**	sees
7	**sept**	set
8	**huit**	weet
9	**neuf**	nerf
10	**dix**	dees
11	**onze**	oñz
12	**douze**	dooz
13	**treize**	trehz
14	**quatorze**	ka**torz**
15	**quinze**	kañz
16	**seize**	sehz
17	**dix-sept**	dees-**set**
18	**dix-huit**	dees-**weet**
19	**dix-neuf**	dees-**nerf**
20	**vingt**	vañ
30	**trente**	tront
40	**quarante**	karoñt
50	**cinquante**	sañkoñt
60	**soixante**	swasoñt
70	**soixante-dix**	swasoñt-**dees**
80	**quatre-vingts**	katr-**vañ**
90	**quatre-vingts-dix**	katr-vañ-**dees**
100	**cent**	soñ
1,000	**mille**	meel

Time

one minute	**une minute**	oon mee-**noot**
one hour	**une heure**	oon urr
half an hour	**une demi-heure**	oon **duh-mee** urr
Monday	**lundi**	luñ-**dee**
Tuesday	**mardi**	mar-**dee**
Wednesday	**mercredi**	mehrkruh-**dee**
Thursday	**jeudi**	zhuh-**dee**
Friday	**vendredi**	voñdruh-**dee**
Saturday	**samedi**	sam-**dee**
Sunday	**dimanche**	dee-**moñsh**

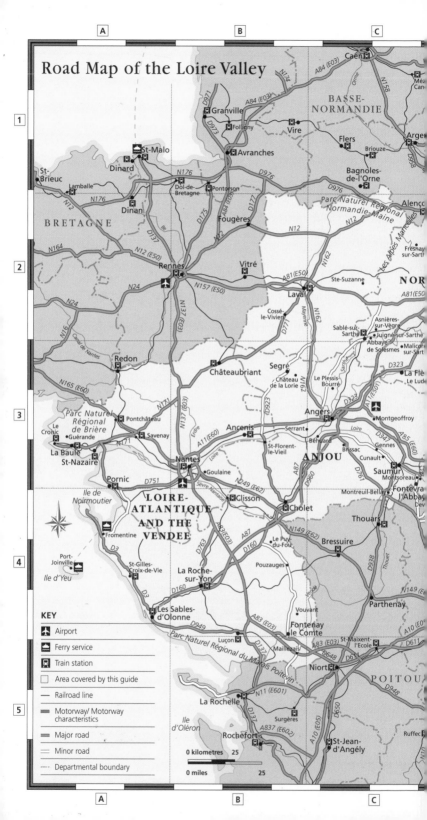